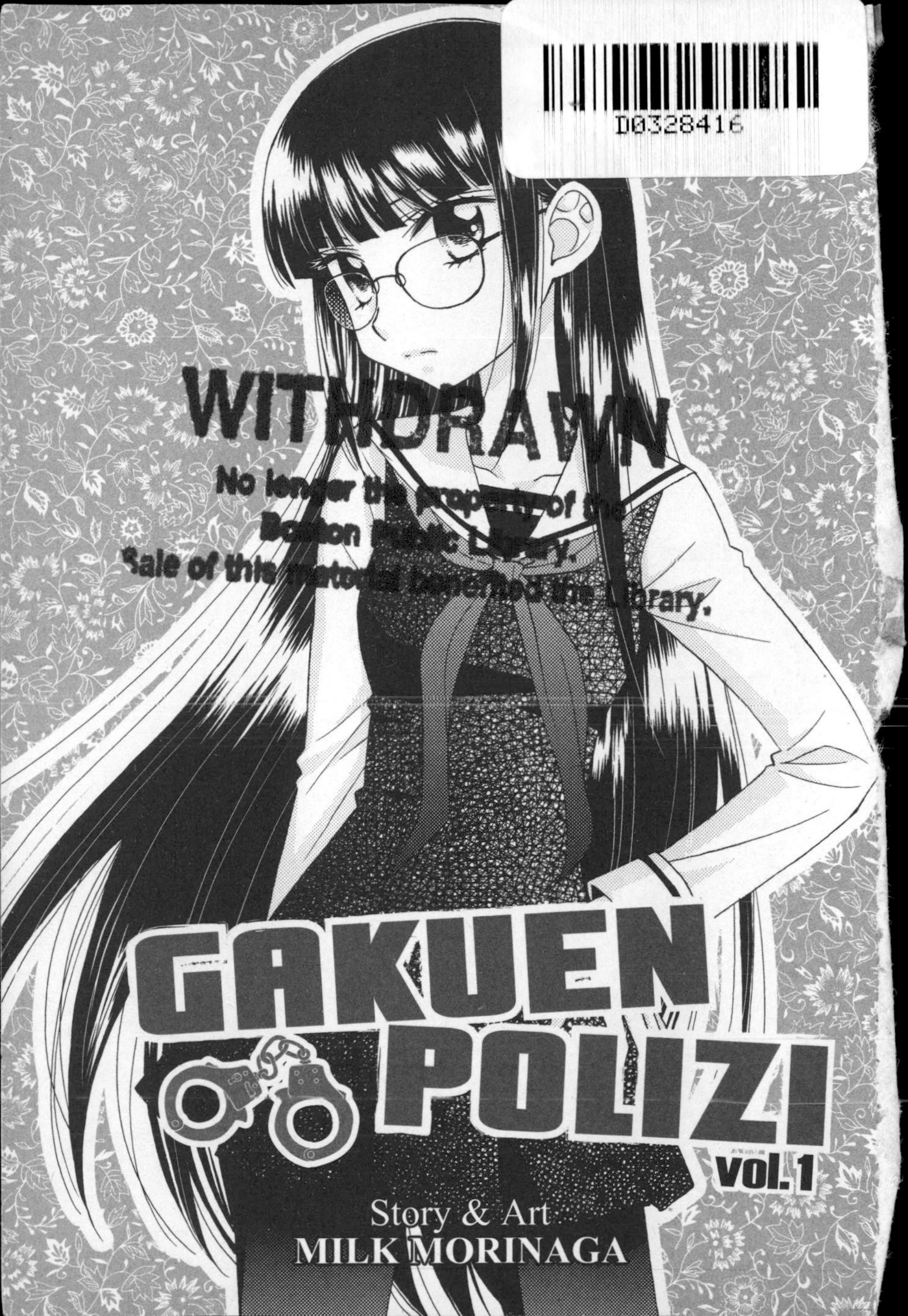
GAKUEN
POLIZI
vol. 1
Story & Art
MILK MORINAGA

SEVEN SEAS ENTERTAINMENT PRESENTS

GAKUEN POLIZI

story and art by MILK MORINAGA

VOLUME 1

TRANSLATION
Nan Rymer

ADAPTATION
Shannon Fay

LETTERING AND LAYOUT
Jennifer Skarupa

LOGO DESIGN
Courtney Williams

COVER DESIGN
Nicky Lim

PROOFREADER
Katherine Bell
Conner Crooks

MANAGING EDITOR
Adam Arnold

PUBLISHER
Jason DeAngelis

GAKUEN POLIZI VOLUME 1

First published in Japan in 2012 by Futabasha Publishers Ltd., Tokyo.
English translation published by Seven Seas Entertainment, LLC.
under license from Futabasha Publishers Ltd.

Seven Seas books may be purchased in bulk for educational, business, or promotional use. For information on bulk purchases, please contact Macmillan Corporate & Premium Sales Department at 1-800-221-7945 (ext 5442) or write specialmarkets@macmillan.com.

ISBN: 978-1-626920-30-9

Printed in Canada

First Printing: June 2014

10 9 8 7 6 5 4 3 2 1

FOLLOW US ONLINE: ***www.gomanga.com***

READING DIRECTIONS

This book reads from ***right to left***, Japanese style. If this is your first time reading manga, you start reading from the top right panel on each page and take it from there. If you get lost, just follow the numbered diagram here. It may seem backwards at first, but you'll get the hang of it! Have fun!!

1
2
3
4
5
6
7
8
9

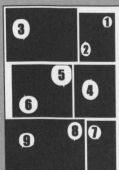

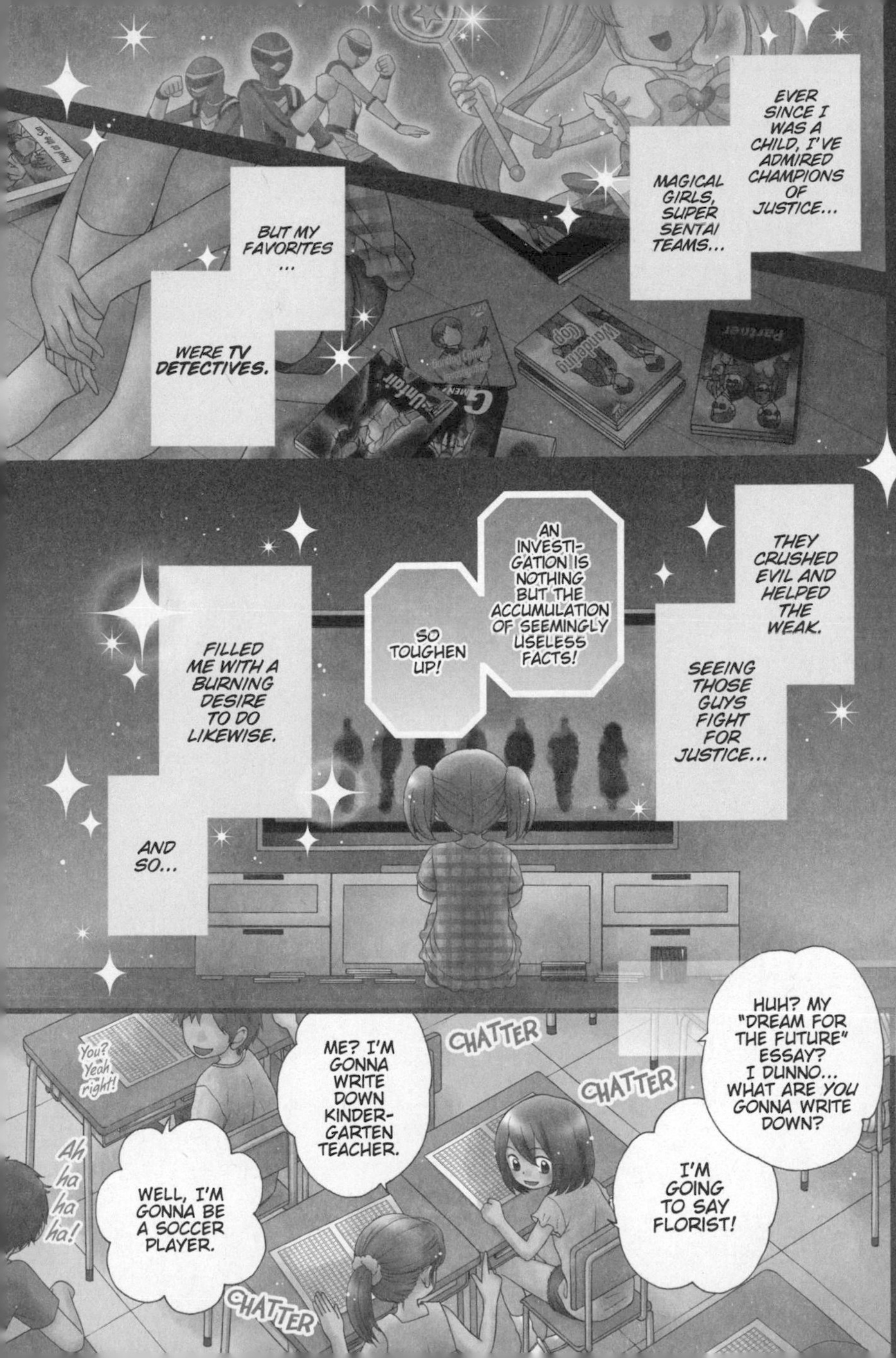
EVER SINCE I WAS A CHILD, I'VE ADMIRED CHAMPIONS OF JUSTICE...
MAGICAL GIRLS, SUPER SENTAI TEAMS...
BUT MY FAVORITES ...
WERE TV DETECTIVES.
Partner
Wandering Cop
Unfair
THEY CRUSHED EVIL AND HELPED THE WEAK.
SEEING THOSE GUYS FIGHT FOR JUSTICE...
AN INVESTIGATION IS NOTHING BUT THE ACCUMULATION OF SEEMINGLY USELESS FACTS!
SO TOUGHEN UP!
FILLED ME WITH A BURNING DESIRE TO DO LIKEWISE.
AND SO...
HUH? MY "DREAM FOR THE FUTURE" ESSAY? I DUNNO... WHAT ARE YOU GONNA WRITE DOWN?
CHATTER
CHATTER
I'M GOING TO SAY FLORIST!
ME? I'M GONNA WRITE DOWN KINDERGARTEN TEACHER.
You? Yeah, right!
WELL, I'M GONNA BE A SOCCER PLAYER.
Ah ha ha ha!
CHATTER

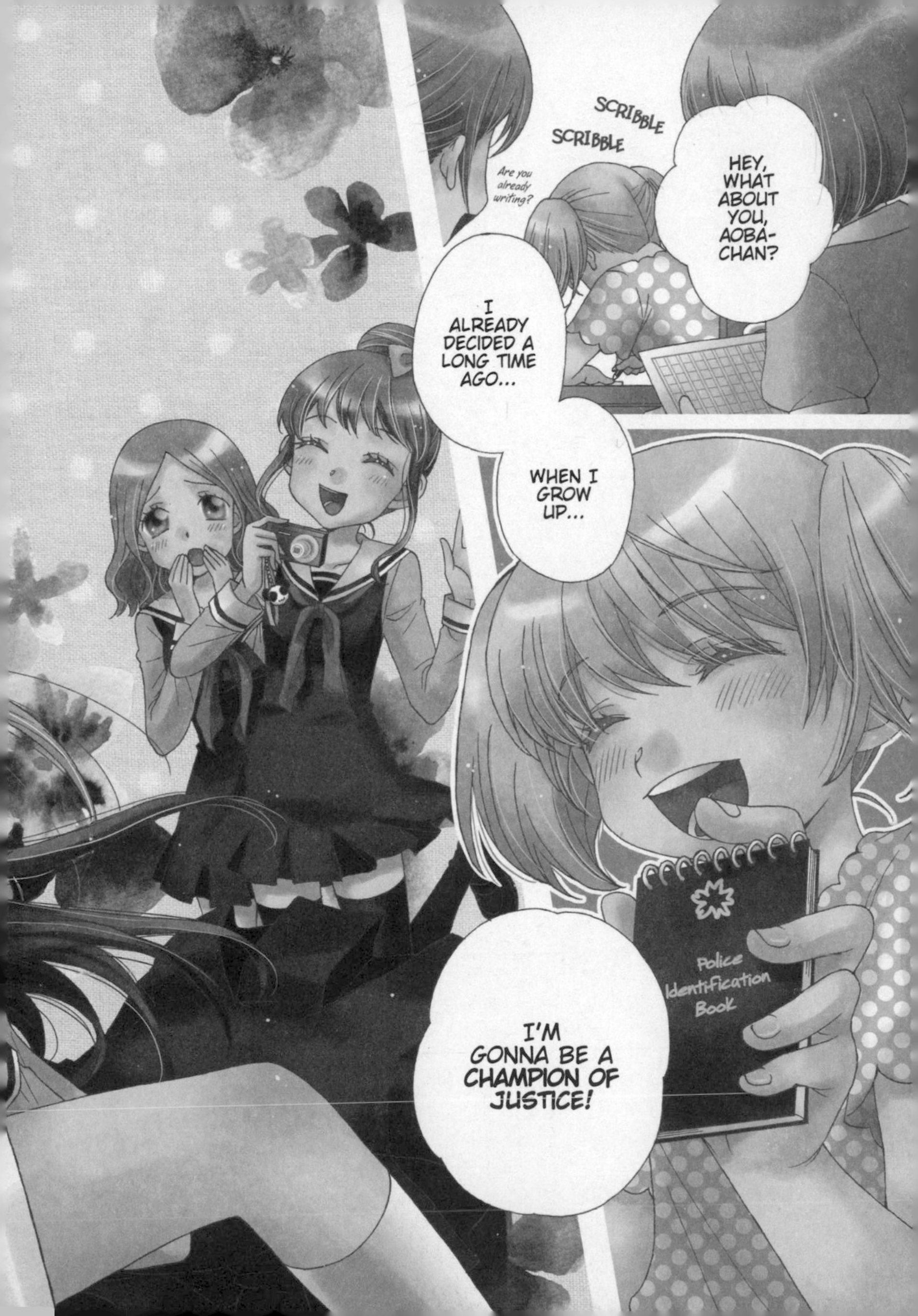
SCRIBBLE
SCRIBBLE
Are you already writing?
HEY, WHAT ABOUT YOU, AOBA-CHAN?
I ALREADY DECIDED A LONG TIME AGO...
WHEN I GROW UP...
Police Identification Book
I'M GONNA BE A CHAMPION OF JUSTICE!

CHAPTER 1

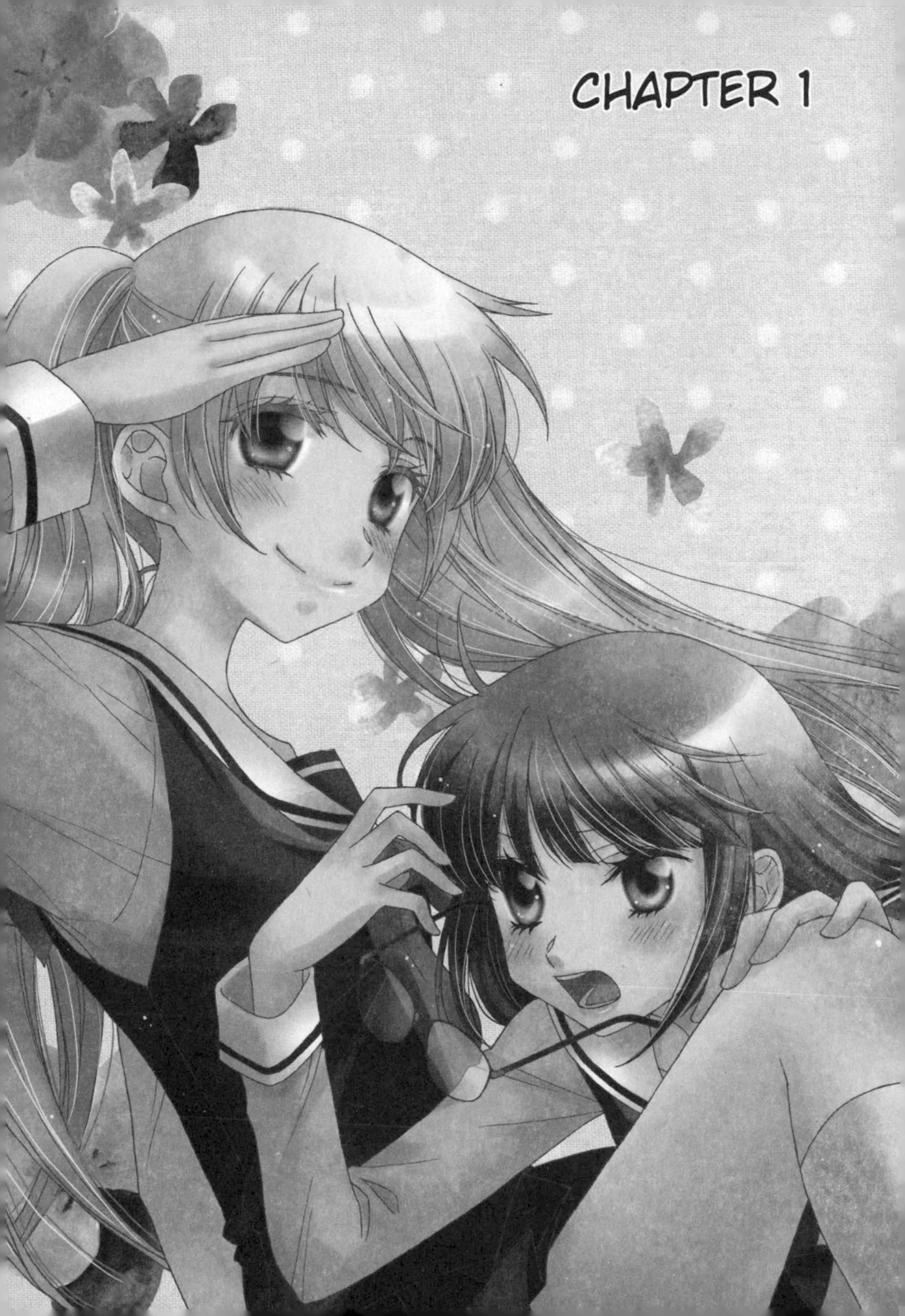

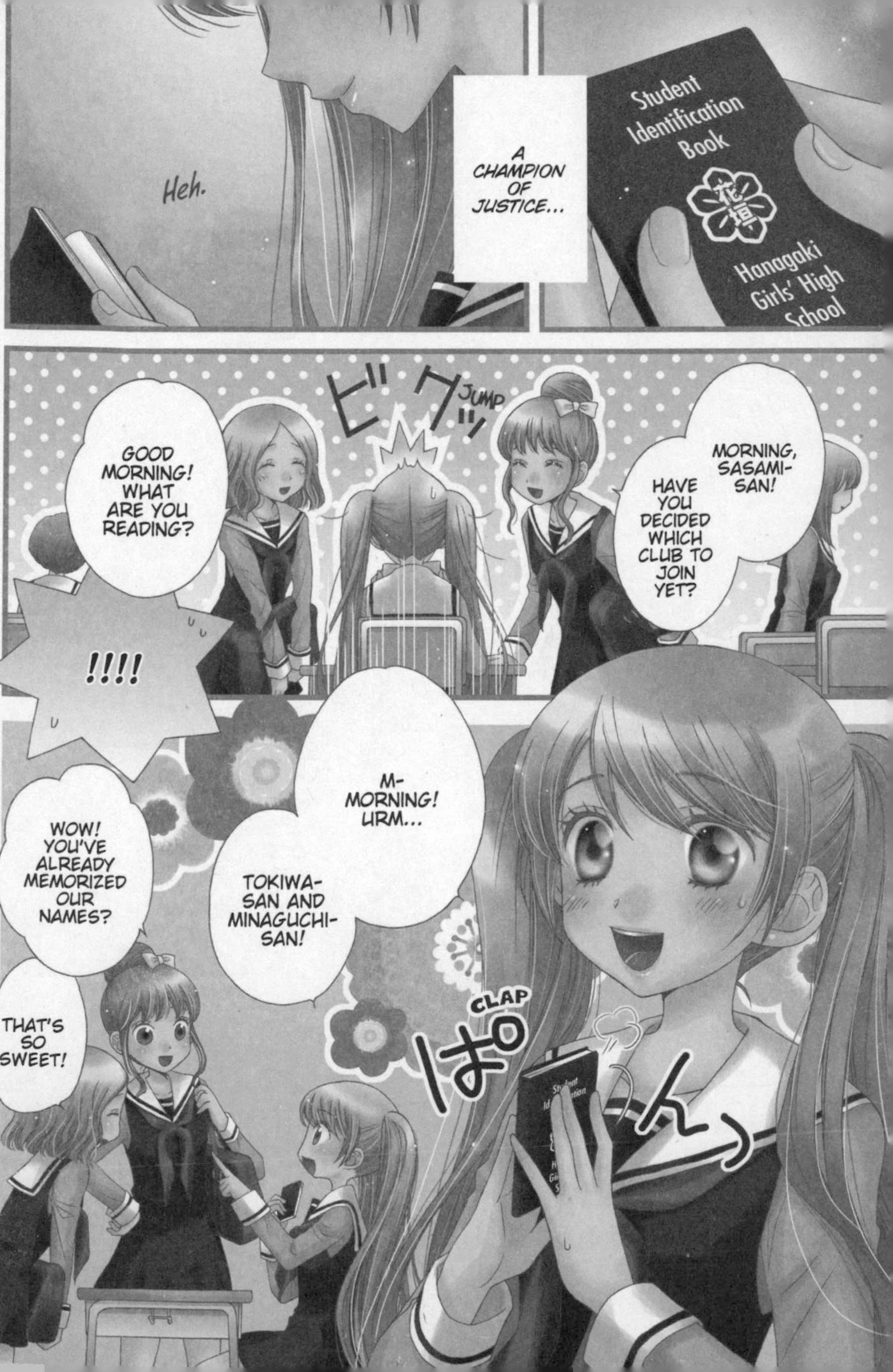
Student Identification Book
Hanagaki Girls' High School
A CHAMPION OF JUSTICE...
Heh.
MORNING, SASAMI-SAN!
HAVE YOU DECIDED WHICH CLUB TO JOIN YET?
JUMP
GOOD MORNING! WHAT ARE YOU READING?
!!!!
M-MORNING! URM...
TOKIWA-SAN AND MINAGUCHI-SAN!
WOW! YOU'VE ALREADY MEMORIZED OUR NAMES?
THAT'S SO SWEET!
CLAP

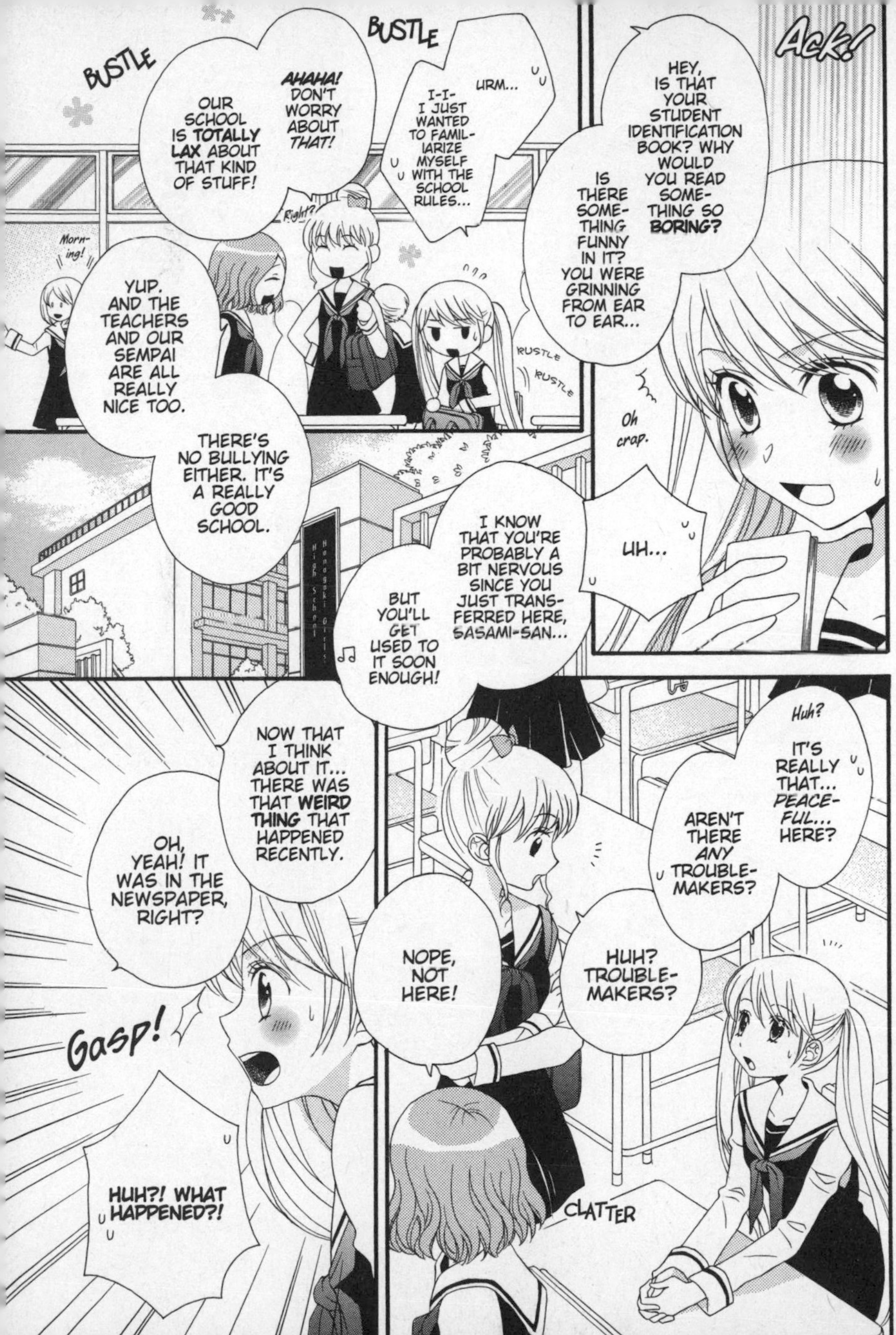
Ack!
HEY, IS THAT YOUR STUDENT IDENTIFICATION BOOK? WHY WOULD YOU READ SOMETHING SO BORING?
IS THERE SOMETHING FUNNY IN IT? YOU WERE GRINNING FROM EAR TO EAR...
RUSTLE RUSTLE
Oh crap.
UH...
BUSTLE
BUSTLE
URM...
I-I- I JUST WANTED TO FAMILIARIZE MYSELF WITH THE SCHOOL RULES...
AHAHA! DON'T WORRY ABOUT THAT!
OUR SCHOOL IS TOTALLY LAX ABOUT THAT KIND OF STUFF!
Right?
Morning!
YUP. AND THE TEACHERS AND OUR SEMPAI ARE ALL REALLY NICE TOO.
THERE'S NO BULLYING EITHER. IT'S A REALLY GOOD SCHOOL.
I KNOW THAT YOU'RE PROBABLY A BIT NERVOUS SINCE YOU JUST TRANSFERRED HERE, SASAMI-SAN...
BUT YOU'LL GET USED TO IT SOON ENOUGH!
Huh?
IT'S REALLY THAT... PEACEFUL... HERE?
AREN'T THERE ANY TROUBLEMAKERS?
HUH? TROUBLEMAKERS?
NOPE, NOT HERE!
CLATTER
NOW THAT I THINK ABOUT IT... THERE WAS THAT WEIRD THING THAT HAPPENED RECENTLY.
OH, YEAH! IT WAS IN THE NEWSPAPER, RIGHT?
Gasp!
HUH?! WHAT HAPPENED?!

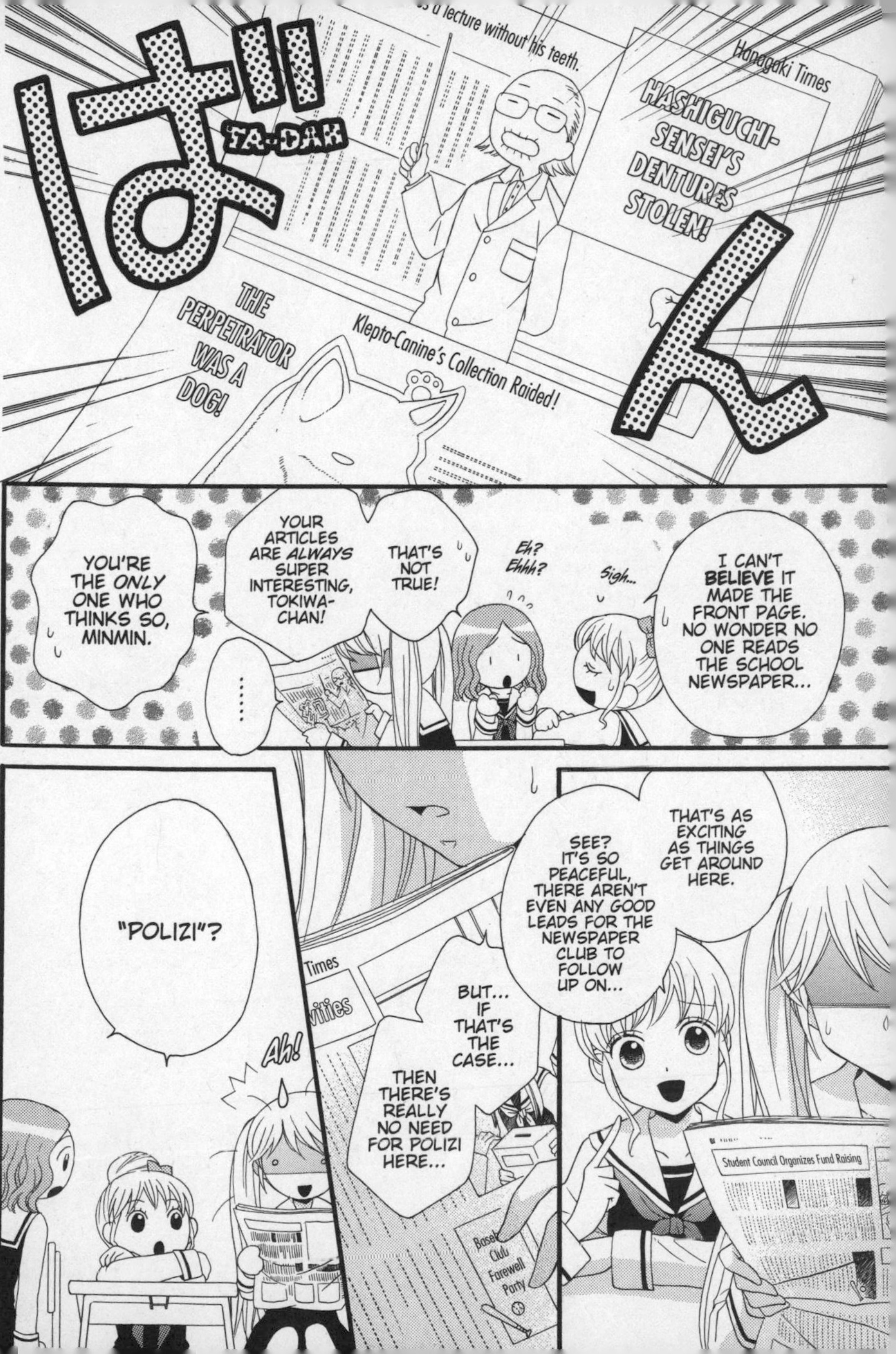

Hanagaki Times
HASHIGUCHI-SENSEI'S DENTURES STOLEN!
...s a lecture without his teeth.
Klepto-Canine's Collection Raided!
THE PERPETRATOR WAS A DOG!
ばん
TA-DAH
I CAN'T **BELIEVE** IT MADE THE FRONT PAGE. NO WONDER NO ONE READS THE SCHOOL NEWSPAPER...
Sigh...
Eh? Ehhh?
THAT'S NOT TRUE!
YOUR ARTICLES ARE *ALWAYS* SUPER INTERESTING, TOKIWA-CHAN!
YOU'RE THE *ONLY* ONE WHO THINKS SO, MINMIN.
......
THAT'S AS EXCITING AS THINGS GET AROUND HERE.
SEE? IT'S SO PEACEFUL, THERE AREN'T EVEN ANY GOOD LEADS FOR THE NEWSPAPER CLUB TO FOLLOW UP ON...
Student Council Organizes Fund Raising
Club Farewell Party
BUT... IF THAT'S THE CASE...
THEN THERE'S REALLY NO NEED FOR POLIZI HERE...
Times
"POLIZI"?
Ah!

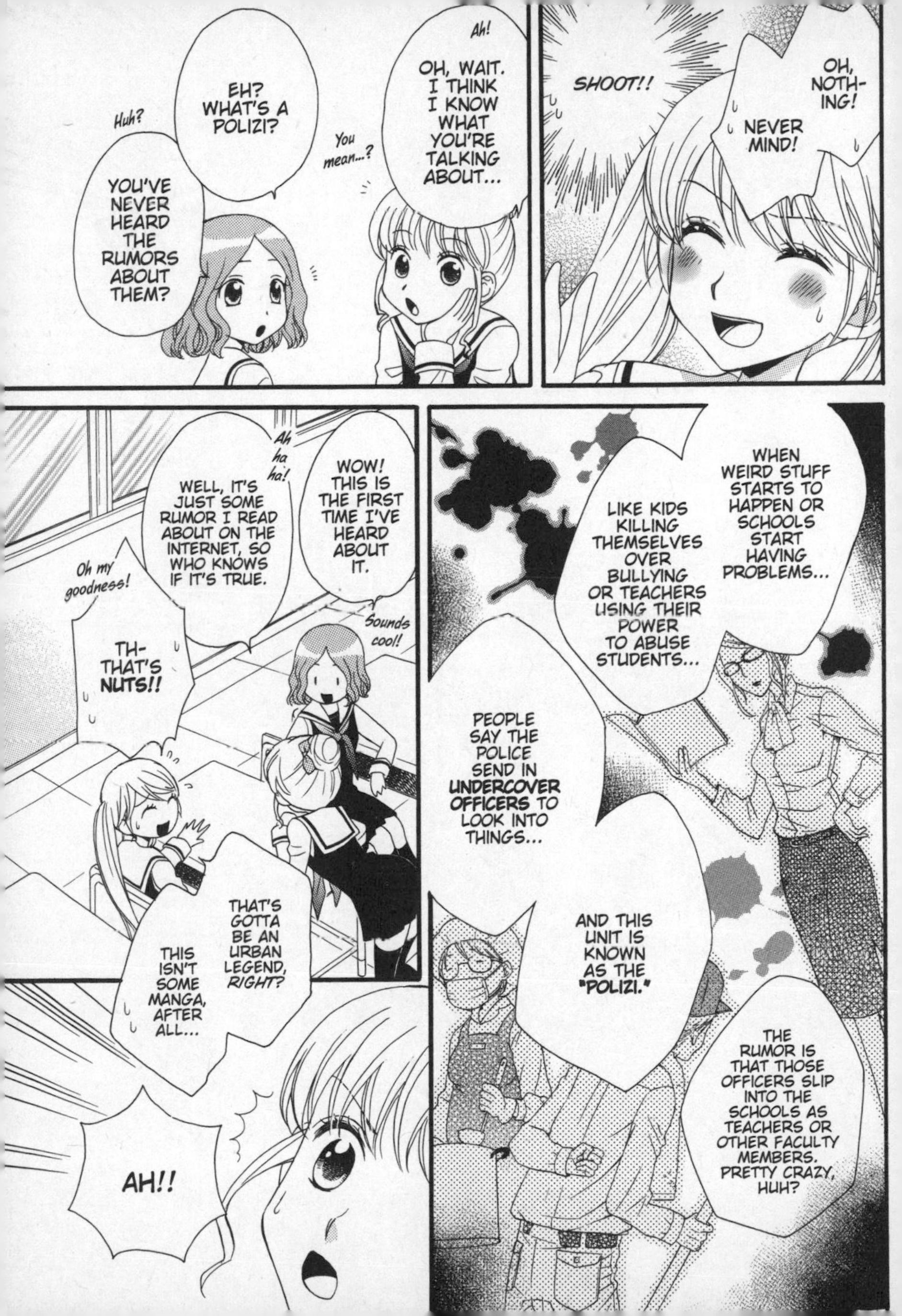
SHOOT!!
OH, NOTHING!
NEVER MIND!
Ah!
OH, WAIT. I THINK I KNOW WHAT YOU'RE TALKING ABOUT...
You mean...?
EH? WHAT'S A POLIZI?
Huh?
YOU'VE NEVER HEARD THE RUMORS ABOUT THEM?
WHEN WEIRD STUFF STARTS TO HAPPEN OR SCHOOLS START HAVING PROBLEMS...
LIKE KIDS KILLING THEMSELVES OVER BULLYING OR TEACHERS USING THEIR POWER TO ABUSE STUDENTS...
PEOPLE SAY THE POLICE SEND IN **UNDERCOVER OFFICERS** TO LOOK INTO THINGS...
AND THIS UNIT IS KNOWN AS THE **"POLIZI."**
THE RUMOR IS THAT THOSE OFFICERS SLIP INTO THE SCHOOLS AS TEACHERS OR OTHER FACULTY MEMBERS. PRETTY CRAZY, HUH?
WOW! THIS IS THE FIRST TIME I'VE HEARD ABOUT IT.
Ah ha ha!
WELL, IT'S JUST SOME RUMOR I READ ABOUT ON THE INTERNET, SO WHO KNOWS IF IT'S TRUE.
Sounds cool!
Oh my goodness!
TH-THAT'S **NUTS!!**
THAT'S GOTTA BE AN URBAN LEGEND, *RIGHT?*
THIS ISN'T SOME MANGA, AFTER ALL...
AH!!

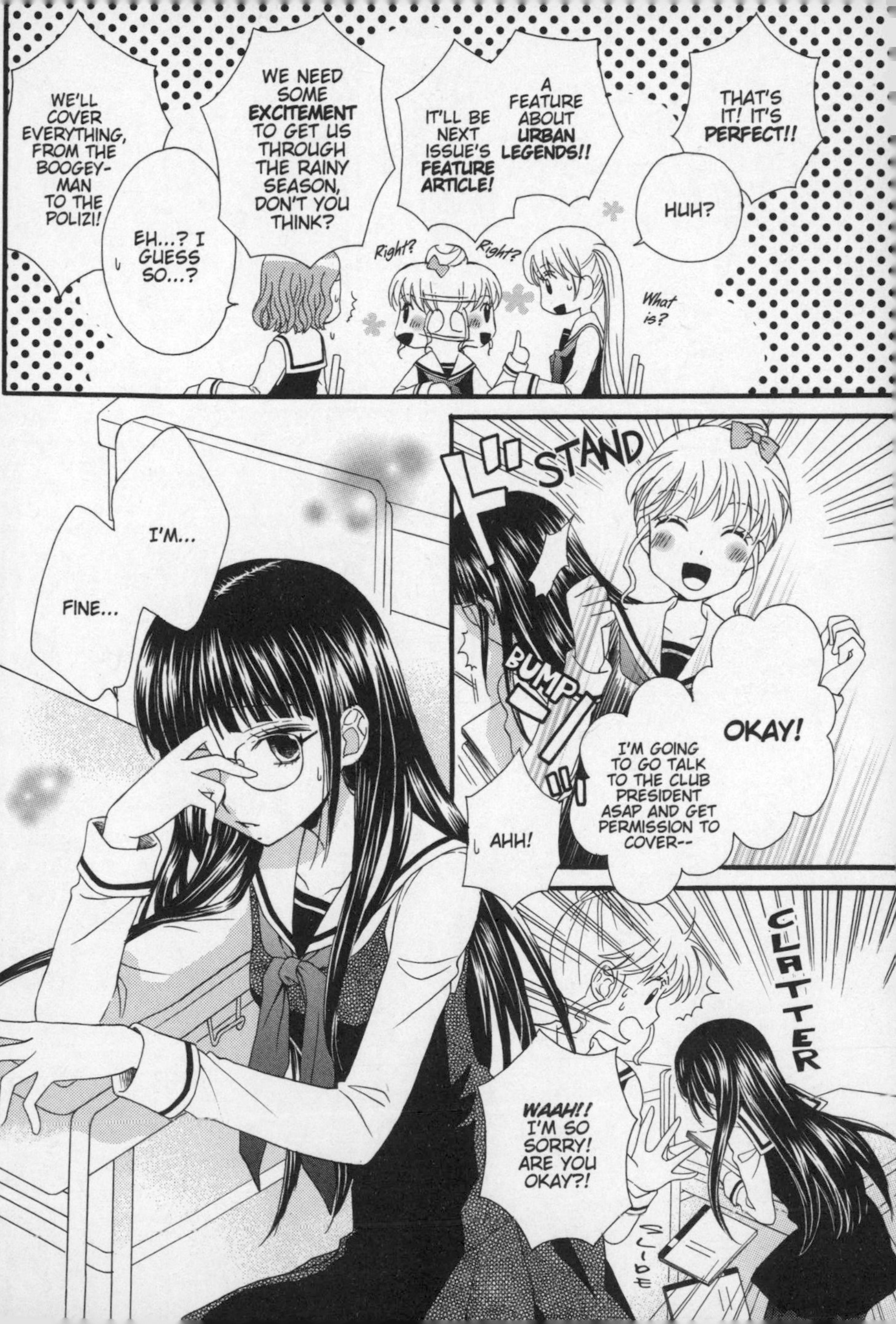
THAT'S IT! IT'S PERFECT!!
HUH?
What is?
A FEATURE ABOUT URBAN LEGENDS!!
IT'LL BE NEXT ISSUE'S FEATURE ARTICLE!
Right?
Right?
WE NEED SOME EXCITEMENT TO GET US THROUGH THE RAINY SEASON, DON'T YOU THINK?
WE'LL COVER EVERYTHING, FROM THE BOOGEY-MAN TO THE POLIZI!
EH...? I GUESS SO...?
STAND
OKAY!
I'M GOING TO GO TALK TO THE CLUB PRESIDENT ASAP AND GET PERMISSION TO COVER--
BUMP
AHH!
CLATTER
WAAH!! I'M SO SORRY! ARE YOU OKAY?!
SLIDE
I'M...
FINE...

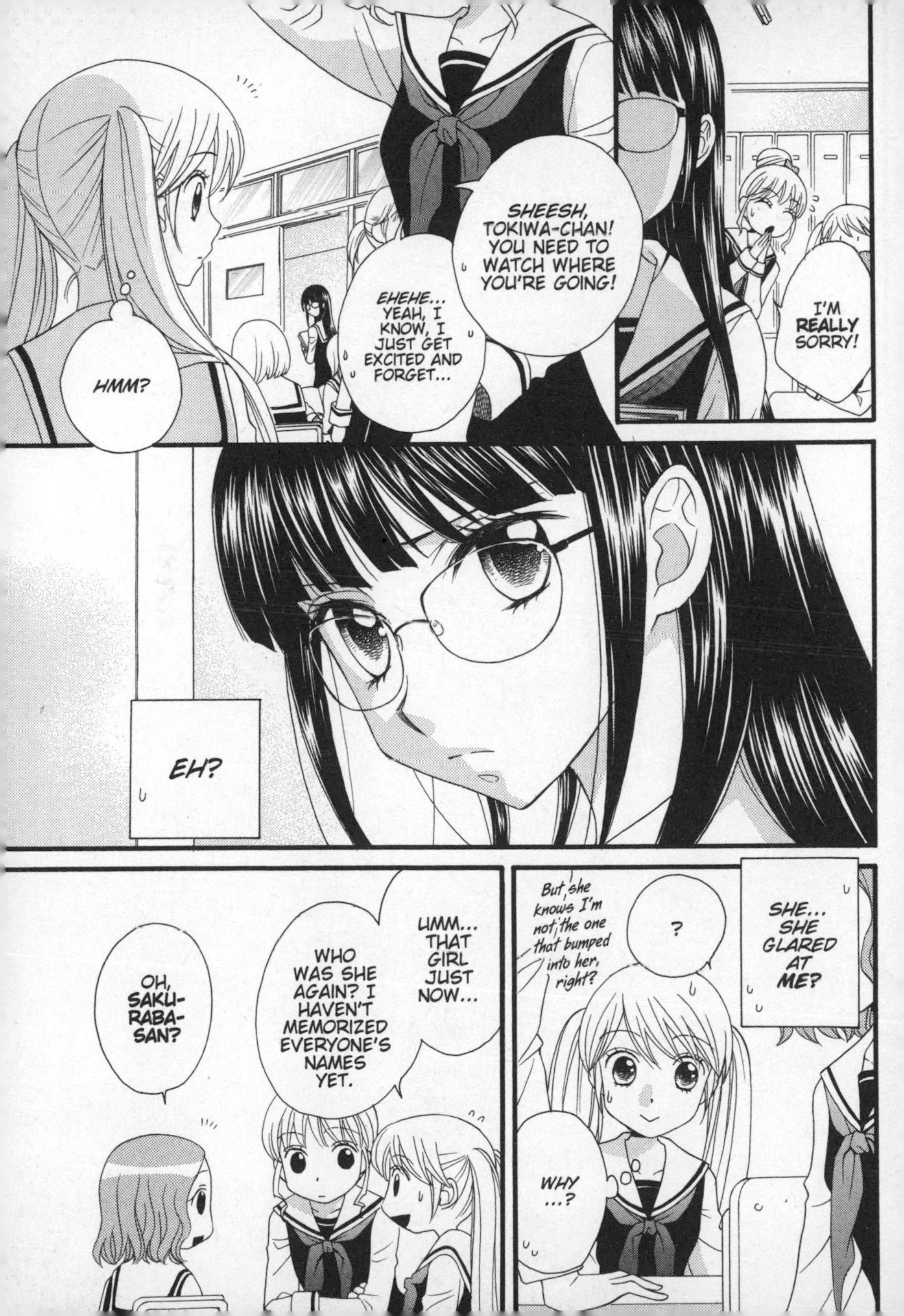
I'M REALLY SORRY!
SHEESH, TOKIWA-CHAN! YOU NEED TO WATCH WHERE YOU'RE GOING!
EHEHE... YEAH, I KNOW, I JUST GET EXCITED AND FORGET...
HMM?
EH?
SHE... SHE GLARED AT ME?
?
But, she knows I'm not the one that bumped into her, right?
WHY ...?
UMM... THAT GIRL JUST NOW...
WHO WAS SHE AGAIN? I HAVEN'T MEMORIZED EVERYONE'S NAMES YET.
OH, SAKURA-BA-SAN?

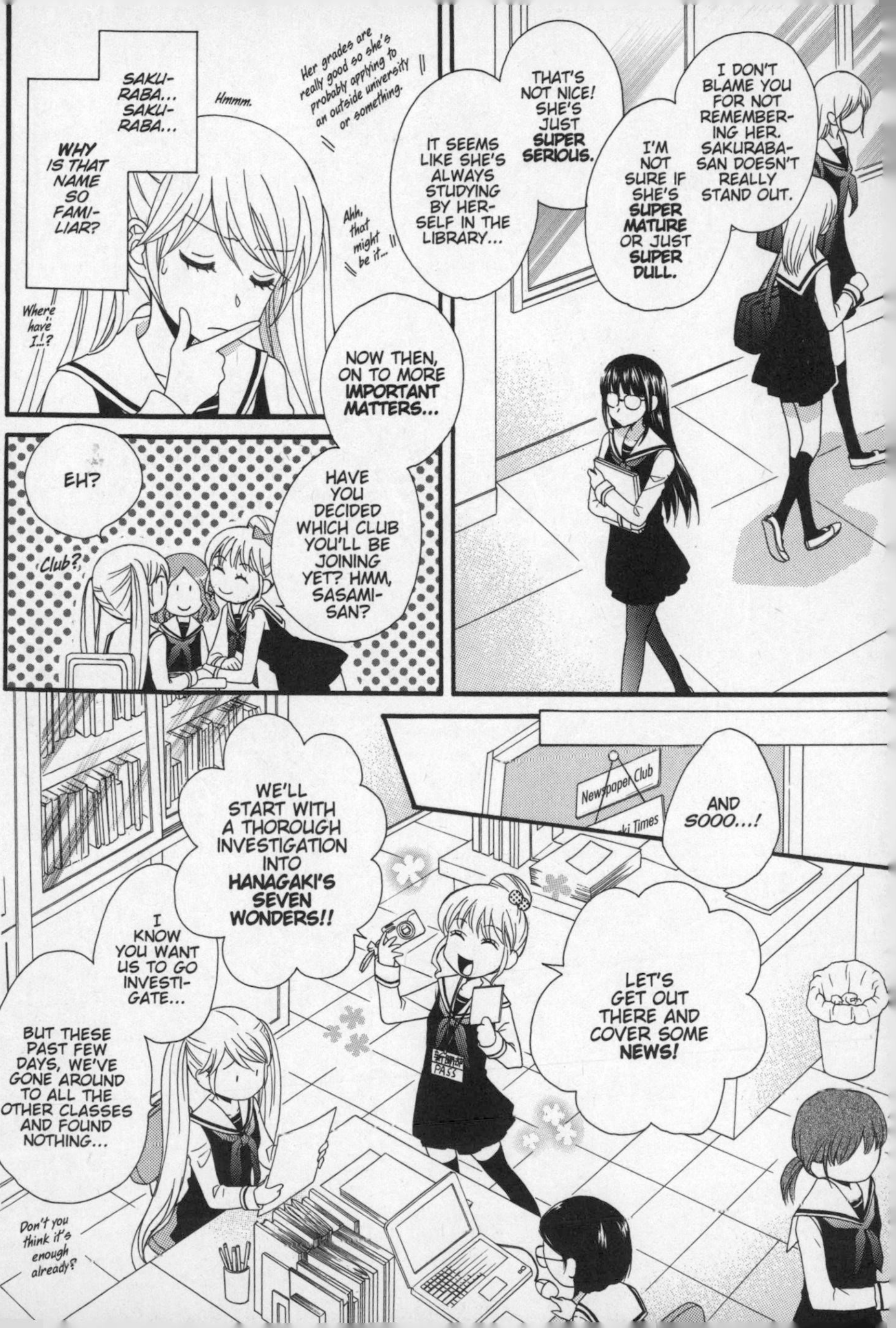
I DON'T BLAME YOU FOR NOT REMEMBERING HER. SAKURABA-SAN DOESN'T REALLY STAND OUT.
I'M NOT SURE IF SHE'S SUPER MATURE OR JUST SUPER DULL.
THAT'S NOT NICE! SHE'S JUST SUPER SERIOUS.
IT SEEMS LIKE SHE'S ALWAYS STUDYING BY HERSELF IN THE LIBRARY...
Her grades are really good so she's probably applying to an outside university or something.
Hmmm.
SAKURABA... SAKURABA...
WHY IS THAT NAME SO FAMILIAR?
Ahh, that might be it...
Where have I...!?
NOW THEN, ON TO MORE IMPORTANT MATTERS...
HAVE YOU DECIDED WHICH CLUB YOU'LL BE JOINING YET? HMM, SASAMI-SAN?
EH?
Club?
Newspaper Club
AND SOOO...!
WE'LL START WITH A THOROUGH INVESTIGATION INTO HANAGAKI'S SEVEN WONDERS!!
LET'S GET OUT THERE AND COVER SOME NEWS!
PASS
I KNOW YOU WANT US TO GO INVESTIGATE...
BUT THESE PAST FEW DAYS, WE'VE GONE AROUND TO ALL THE OTHER CLASSES AND FOUND NOTHING...
Don't you think it's enough already?

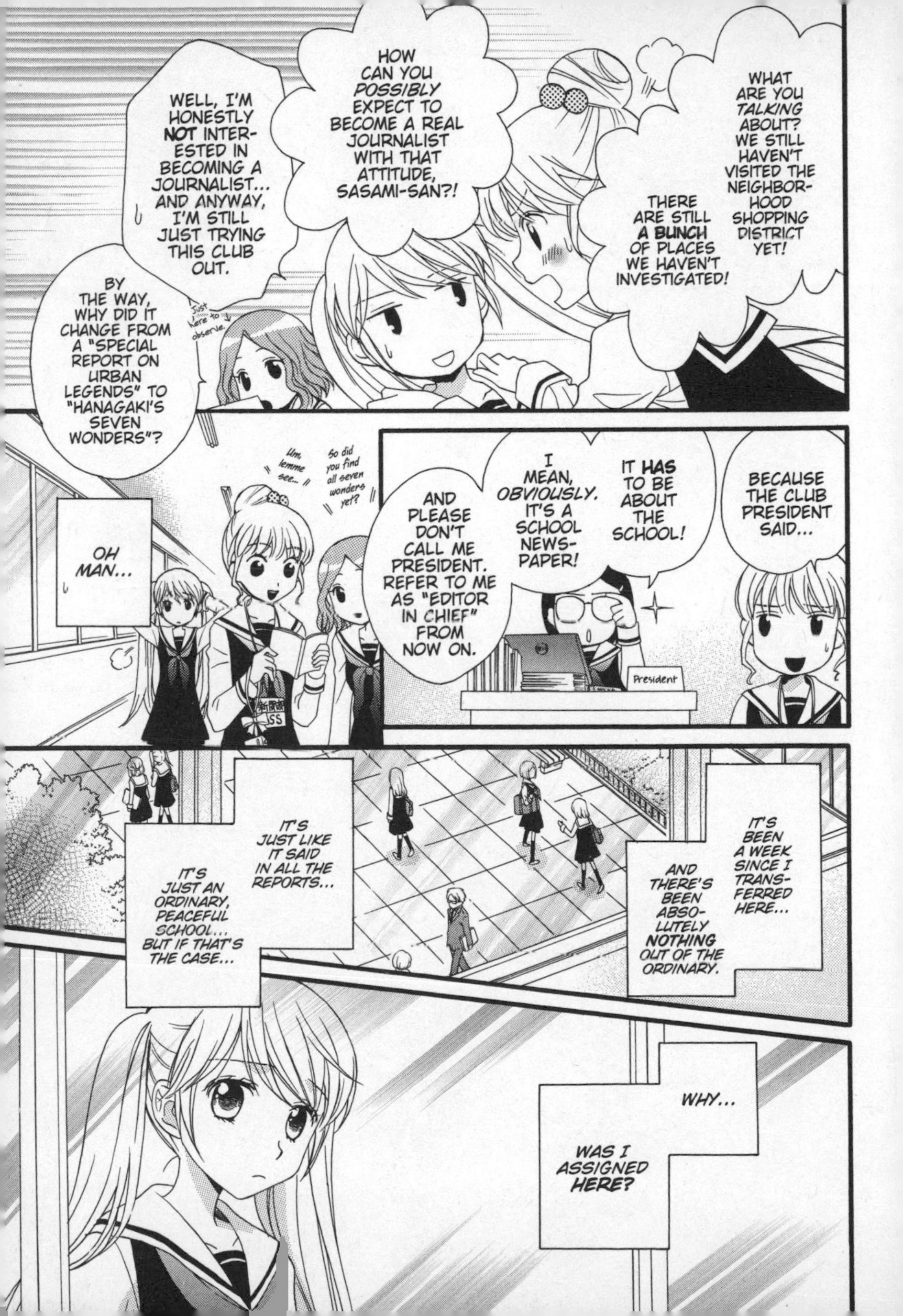
WHAT ARE YOU TALKING ABOUT? WE STILL HAVEN'T VISITED THE NEIGHBOR-HOOD SHOPPING DISTRICT YET!
THERE ARE STILL A BUNCH OF PLACES WE HAVEN'T INVESTIGATED!
HOW CAN YOU POSSIBLY EXPECT TO BECOME A REAL JOURNALIST WITH THAT ATTITUDE, SASAMI-SAN?!
WELL, I'M HONESTLY NOT INTER-ESTED IN BECOMING A JOURNALIST... AND ANYWAY, I'M STILL JUST TRYING THIS CLUB OUT.
Just here to observe.
BY THE WAY, WHY DID IT CHANGE FROM A "SPECIAL REPORT ON URBAN LEGENDS" TO "HANAGAKI'S SEVEN WONDERS"?
BECAUSE THE CLUB PRESIDENT SAID...
IT HAS TO BE ABOUT THE SCHOOL!
I MEAN, OBVIOUSLY. IT'S A SCHOOL NEWS-PAPER!
AND PLEASE DON'T CALL ME PRESIDENT. REFER TO ME AS "EDITOR IN CHIEF" FROM NOW ON.
President
So did you find all seven wonders yet?
Um, lemme see...
OH MAN...
IT'S BEEN A WEEK SINCE I TRANS-FERRED HERE...
AND THERE'S BEEN ABSO-LUTELY NOTHING OUT OF THE ORDINARY.
IT'S JUST LIKE IT SAID IN ALL THE REPORTS...
IT'S JUST AN ORDINARY, PEACEFUL SCHOOL... BUT IF THAT'S THE CASE...
WHY...
WAS I ASSIGNED HERE?

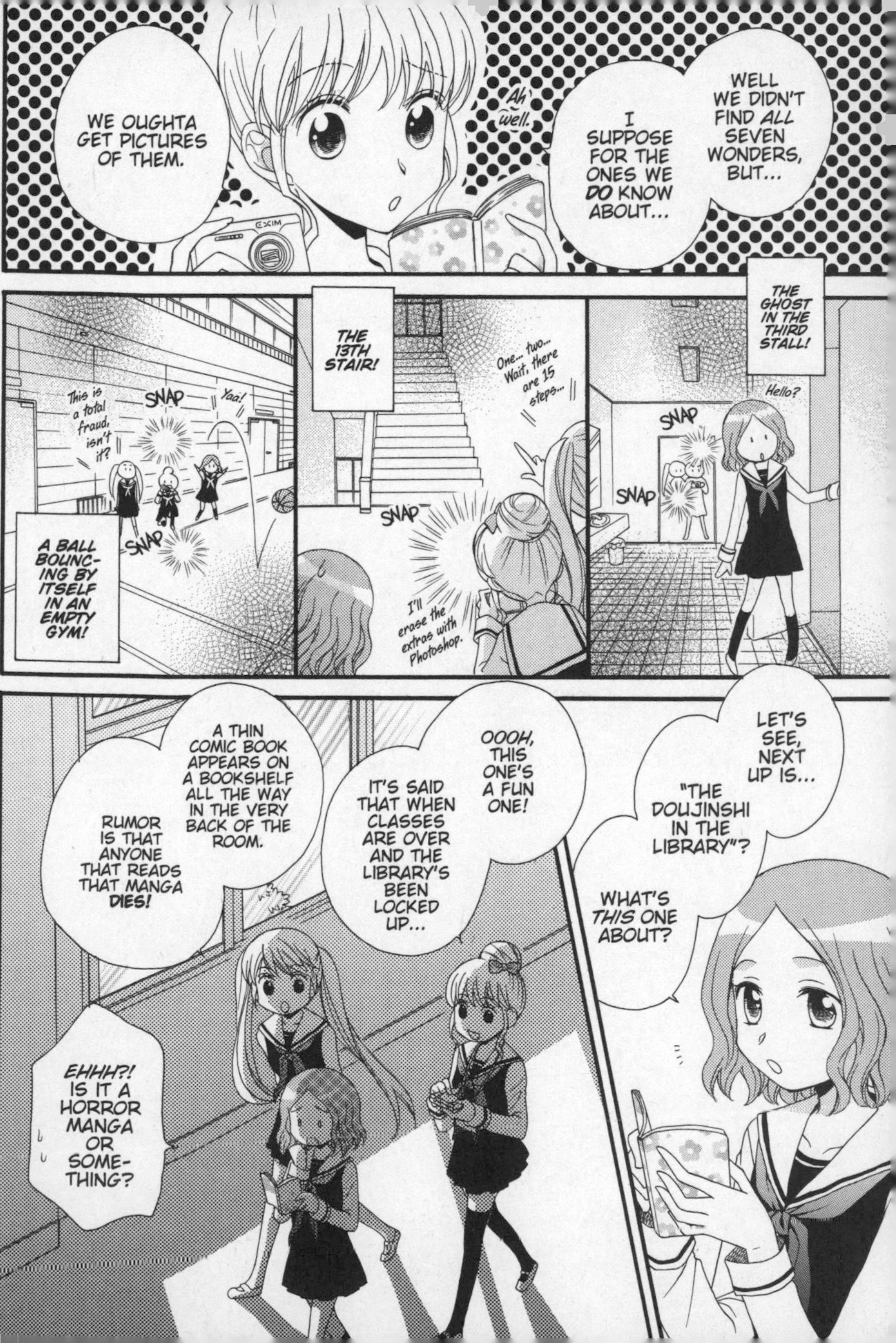
WELL WE DIDN'T FIND ALL SEVEN WONDERS, BUT...
I SUPPOSE FOR THE ONES WE DO KNOW ABOUT...
Ah well.
WE OUGHTA GET PICTURES OF THEM.
THE GHOST IN THE THIRD STALL!
Hello?
SNAP
SNAP
THE 13TH STAIR!
One... two... Wait, there are 15 steps...
SNAP
I'll erase the extras with Photoshop.
Yaa!
SNAP
This is a total fraud, isn't it?
SNAP
A BALL BOUNCING BY ITSELF IN AN EMPTY GYM!
LET'S SEE, NEXT UP IS...
"THE DOUJINSHI IN THE LIBRARY"?
WHAT'S THIS ONE ABOUT?
OOOH, THIS ONE'S A FUN ONE!
IT'S SAID THAT WHEN CLASSES ARE OVER AND THE LIBRARY'S BEEN LOCKED UP...
A THIN COMIC BOOK APPEARS ON A BOOKSHELF ALL THE WAY IN THE VERY BACK OF THE ROOM.
RUMOR IS THAT ANYONE THAT READS THAT MANGA DIES!
EHHH?! IS IT A HORROR MANGA OR SOMETHING?

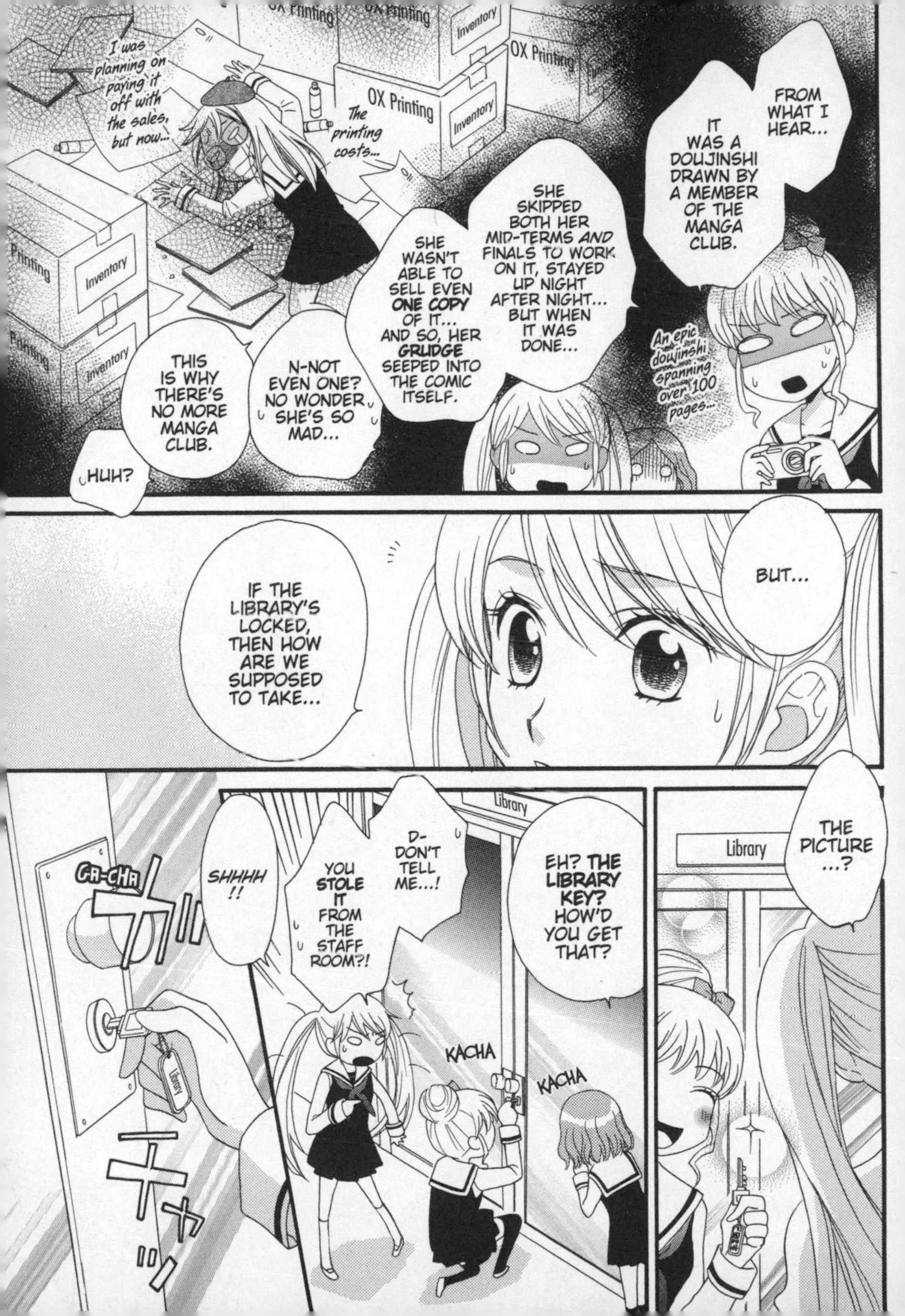
FROM WHAT I HEAR...
IT WAS A DOUJINSHI DRAWN BY A MEMBER OF THE MANGA CLUB.
An epic doujinshi spanning over 100 pages...
SHE SKIPPED BOTH HER MID-TERMS AND FINALS TO WORK ON IT, STAYED UP NIGHT AFTER NIGHT... BUT WHEN IT WAS DONE...
SHE WASN'T ABLE TO SELL EVEN ONE COPY OF IT... AND SO, HER GRUDGE SEEPED INTO THE COMIC ITSELF.
OX Printing
Inventory
The printing costs...
I was planning on paying it off with the sales, but now...
N-NOT EVEN ONE? NO WONDER SHE'S SO MAD...
THIS IS WHY THERE'S NO MORE MANGA CLUB.
HUH?
BUT...
IF THE LIBRARY'S LOCKED, THEN HOW ARE WE SUPPOSED TO TAKE...
Library
THE PICTURE ...?
EH? THE LIBRARY KEY? HOW'D YOU GET THAT?
D-DON'T TELL ME...!
YOU STOLE IT FROM THE STAFF ROOM?!
KACHA
KACHA
SHHHH !!
GA-CHA

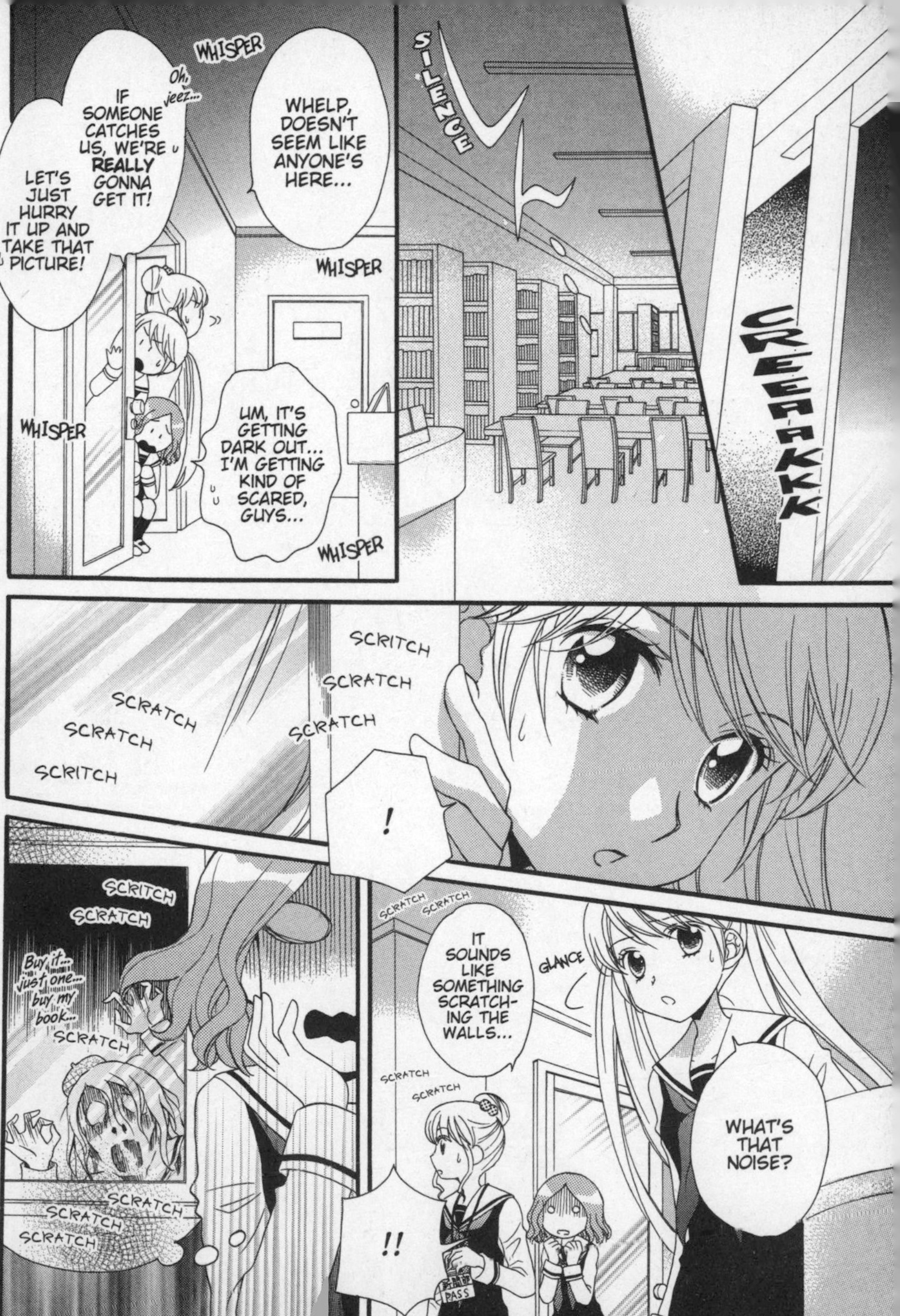
CREEAKKK
SILENCE
WHELP, DOESN'T SEEM LIKE ANYONE'S HERE...
WHISPER
IF SOMEONE CATCHES US, WE'RE **REALLY** GONNA GET IT!
Oh, jeez...
LET'S JUST HURRY IT UP AND TAKE THAT PICTURE!
WHISPER
UM, IT'S GETTING DARK OUT... I'M GETTING KIND OF SCARED, GUYS...
WHISPER
WHISPER
SCRITCH
SCRATCH
SCRATCH
SCRATCH
SCRATCH
SCRITCH
!
WHAT'S THAT NOISE?
GLANCE
IT SOUNDS LIKE SOMETHING SCRATCH-ING THE WALLS...
SCRATCH SCRATCH
SCRATCH
SCRATCH
!!
PASS
SCRITCH
SCRATCH
Buy it... just one... buy my book...
SCRATCH
SCRATCH
SCRATCH
SCRATCH

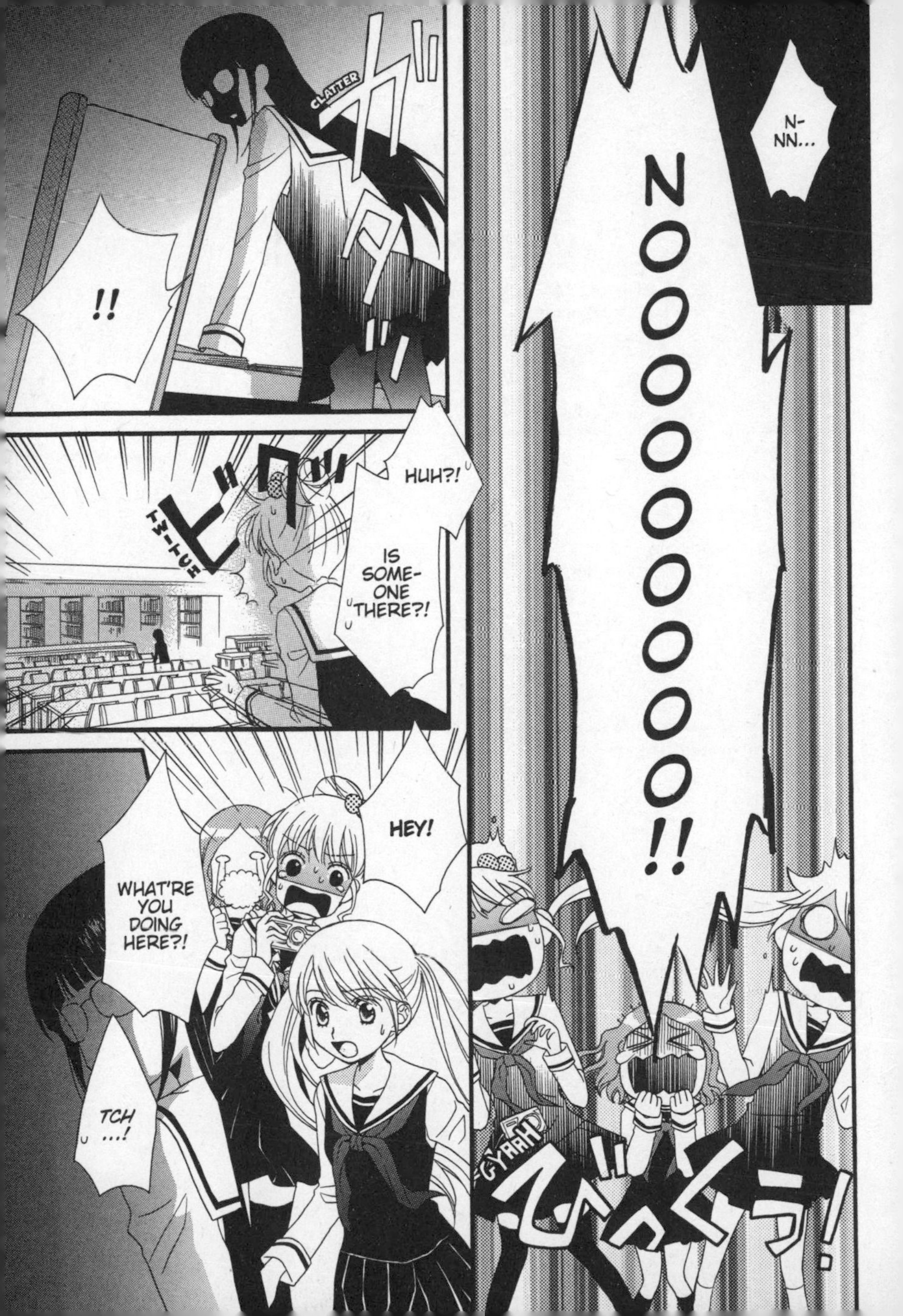
N-
NN...
NOOOOOOOOOOO!!
GYAAH
CLATTER
!!
HUH?!
IS SOMEONE THERE?!
TWITCH
HEY!
WHAT'RE YOU DOING HERE?!
TCH ...!

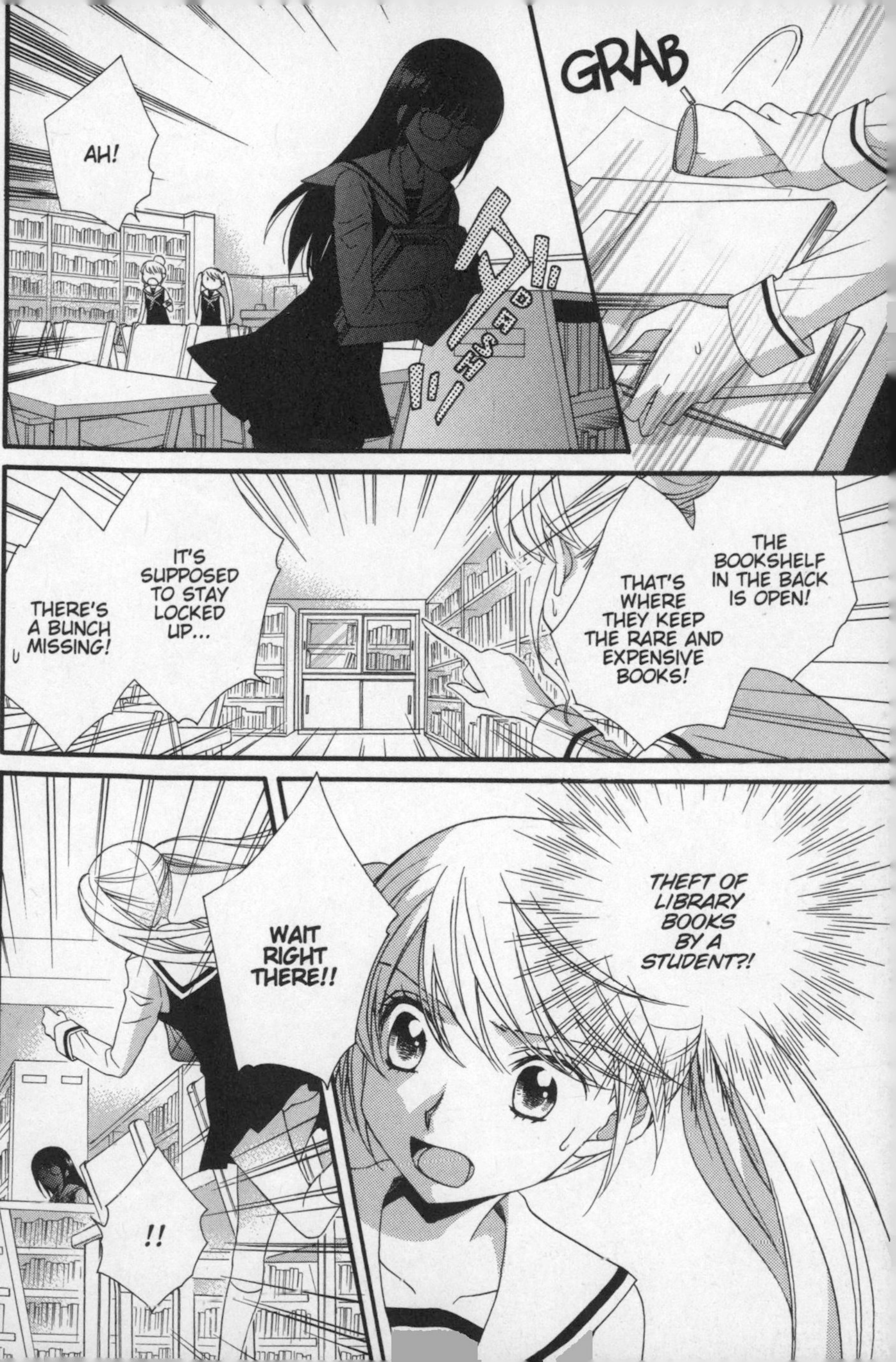
GRAB
AH!
THE BOOKSHELF IN THE BACK IS OPEN!
THAT'S WHERE THEY KEEP THE RARE AND EXPENSIVE BOOKS!
IT'S SUPPOSED TO STAY LOCKED UP...
THERE'S A BUNCH MISSING!
THEFT OF LIBRARY BOOKS BY A STUDENT?!
WAIT RIGHT THERE!!
!!

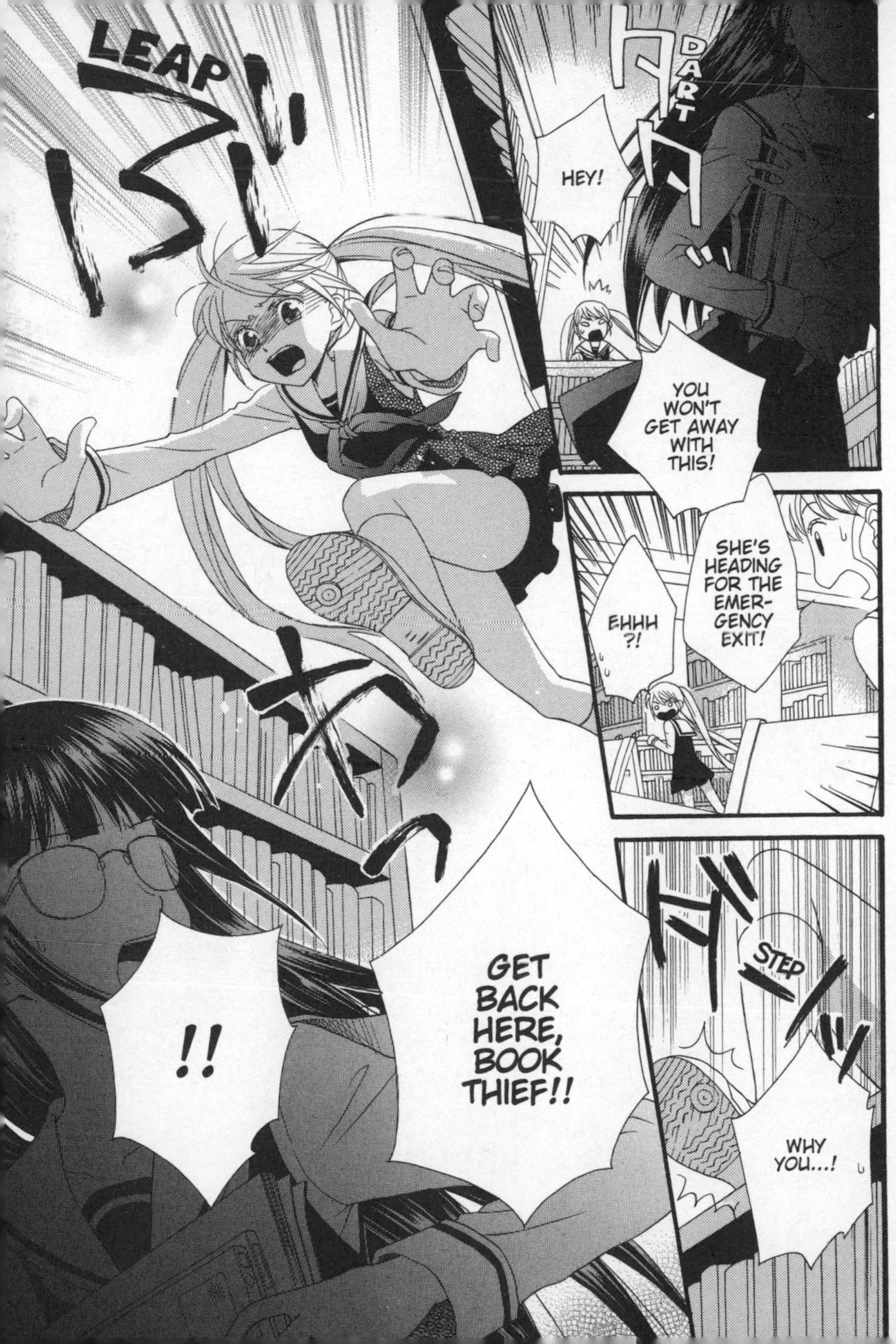
DART
HEY!
YOU WON'T GET AWAY WITH THIS!
SHE'S HEADING FOR THE EMERGENCY EXIT!
EHHH?!
STEP
WHY YOU...!
LEAP
GET BACK HERE, BOOK THIEF!!
!!

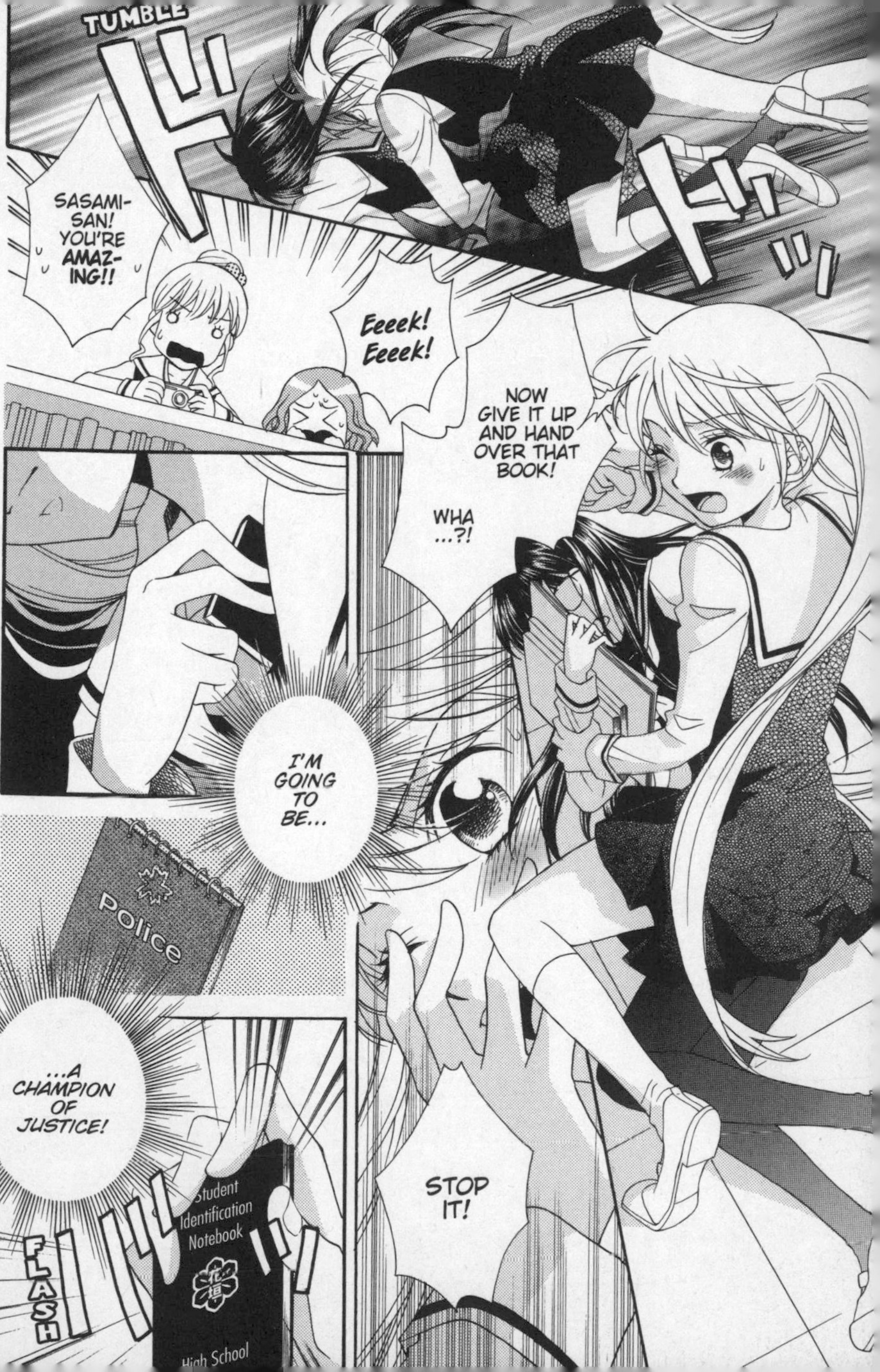
TUMBLE
Eeeek! Eeeek!
SASAMI-SAN! YOU'RE AMAZING!!
NOW GIVE IT UP AND HAND OVER THAT BOOK!
WHA ...?!
STOP IT!
I'M GOING TO BE...
Police
...A CHAMPION OF JUSTICE!
Student Identification Notebook
High School
FLASH

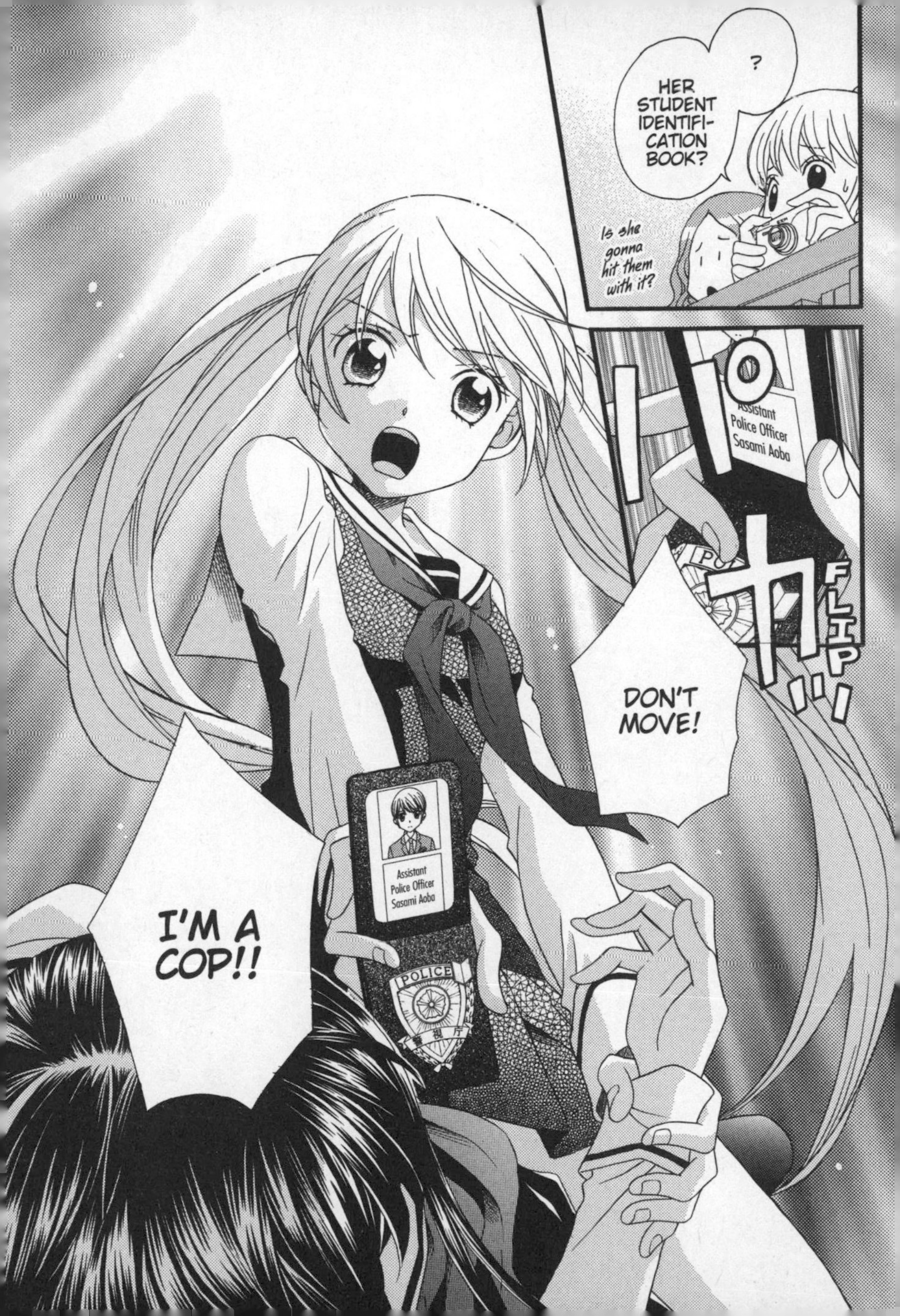
?
HER STUDENT IDENTIFI-CATION BOOK?
Is she gonna hit them with it?
Assistant Police Officer Sasami Aoba
FLIP
DON'T MOVE!
Assistant Police Officer Sasami Aoba
POLICE
I'M A COP!!

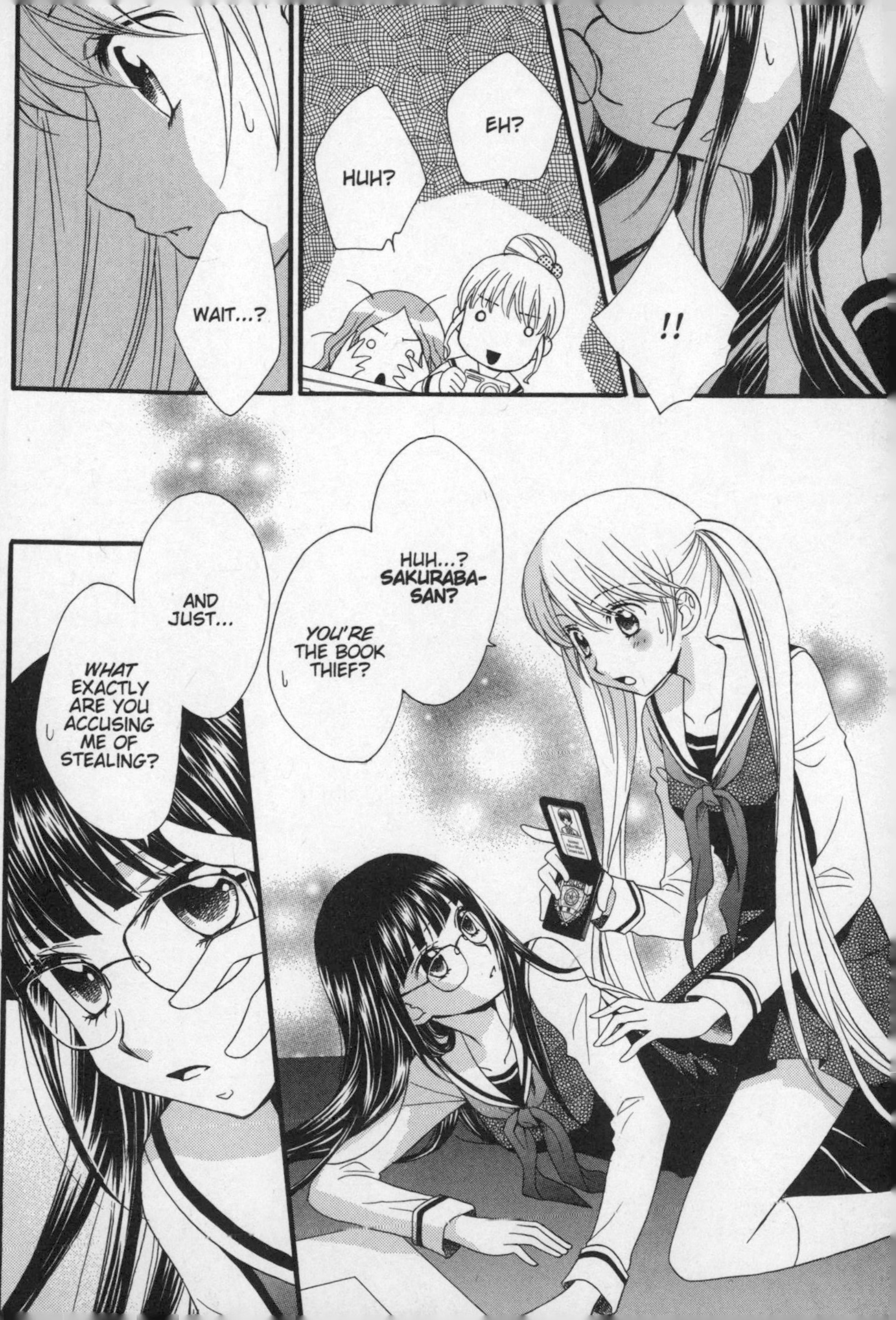
!!
EH?
HUH?
WAIT...?
HUH...? SAKURABA-SAN?
YOU'RE THE BOOK THIEF?
AND JUST...
WHAT EXACTLY ARE YOU ACCUSING ME OF STEALING?

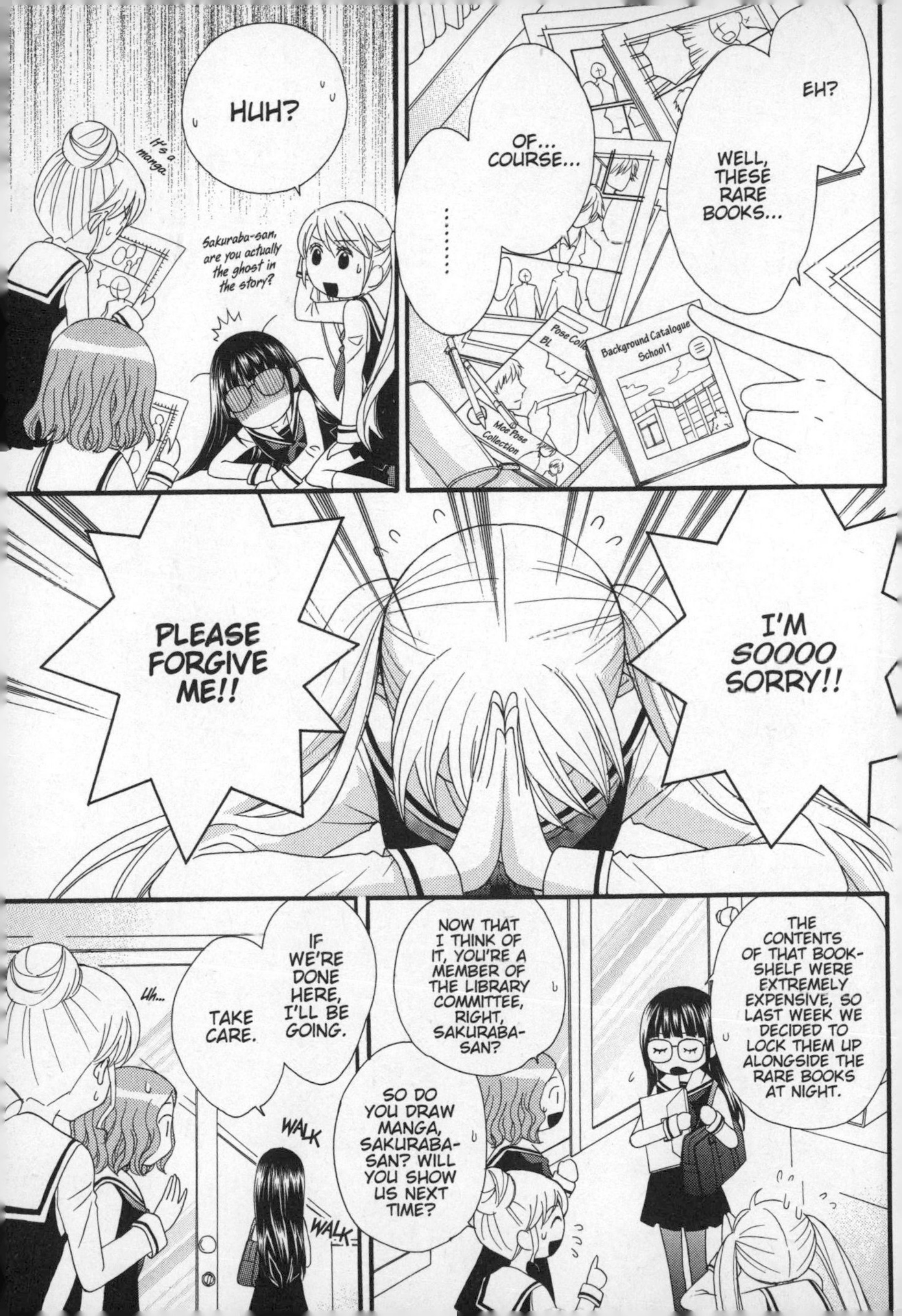
EH?
WELL, THESE RARE BOOKS...
OF... COURSE...
......
Pose Colle
BL
Background Catalogue School 1
Moe Pose Collection
HUH?
It's a manga.
Sakuraba-san, are you actually the ghost in the story?
I'M SOOOO SORRY!!
PLEASE FORGIVE ME!!
THE CONTENTS OF THAT BOOK-SHELF WERE EXTREMELY EXPENSIVE, SO LAST WEEK WE DECIDED TO LOCK THEM UP ALONGSIDE THE RARE BOOKS AT NIGHT.
NOW THAT I THINK OF IT, YOU'RE A MEMBER OF THE LIBRARY COMMITTEE, RIGHT, SAKURABA-SAN?
SO DO YOU DRAW MANGA, SAKURABA-SAN? WILL YOU SHOW US NEXT TIME?
IF WE'RE DONE HERE, I'LL BE GOING.
TAKE CARE.
Uh...
WALK
WALK

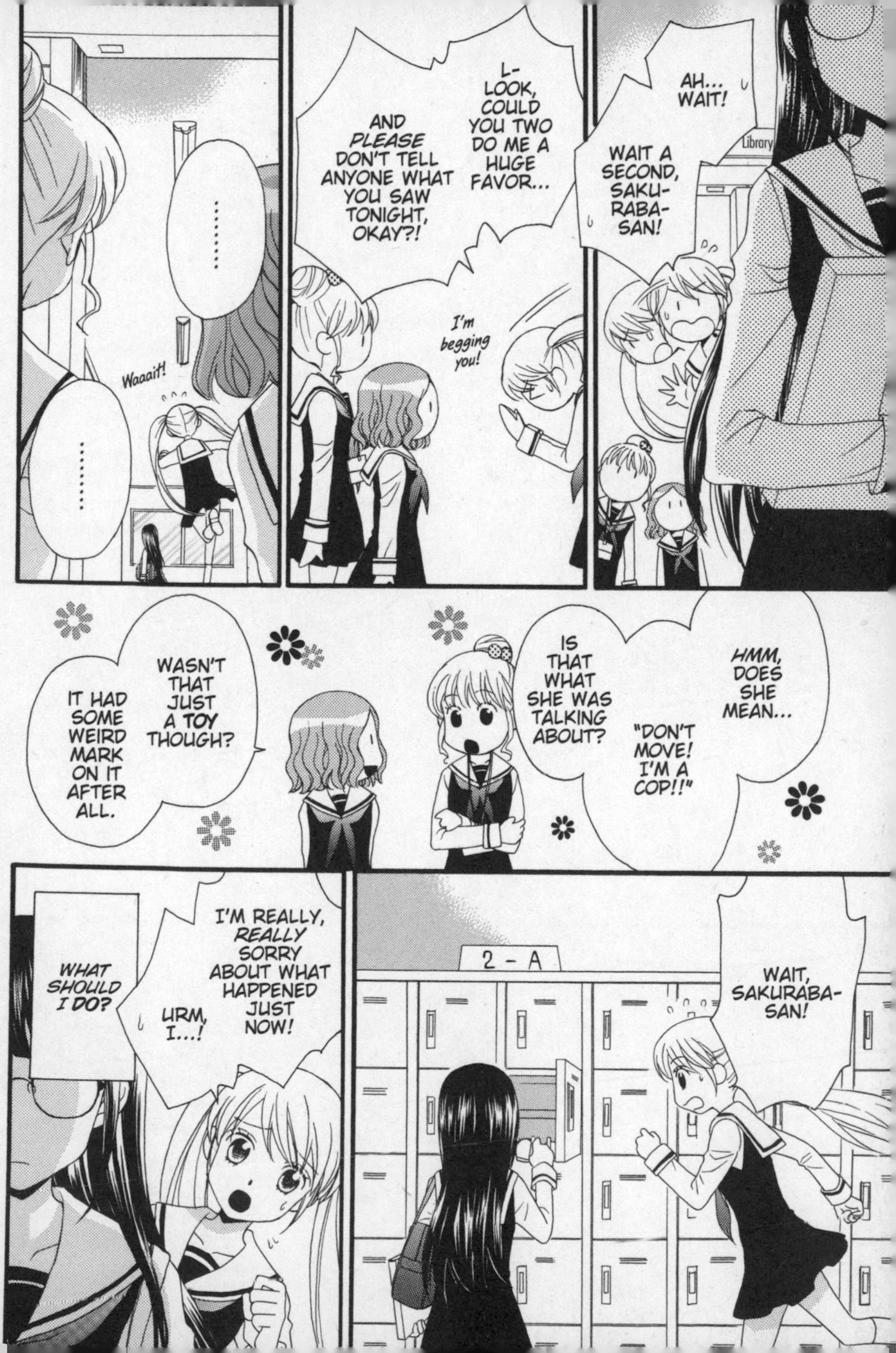
AH... WAIT!
WAIT A SECOND, SAKURABA-SAN!
Library
L-LOOK, COULD YOU TWO DO ME A HUGE FAVOR...
AND *PLEASE* DON'T TELL ANYONE WHAT YOU SAW TONIGHT, OKAY?!
I'm begging you!
......
Waaait!
......
HMM, DOES SHE MEAN...
"DON'T MOVE! I'M A COP!!"
IS THAT WHAT SHE WAS TALKING ABOUT?
WASN'T THAT JUST A **TOY** THOUGH?
IT HAD SOME WEIRD MARK ON IT AFTER ALL.
2-A
WAIT, SAKURABA-SAN!
I'M REALLY, *REALLY* SORRY ABOUT WHAT HAPPENED JUST NOW!
URM, I...!
WHAT SHOULD I DO?

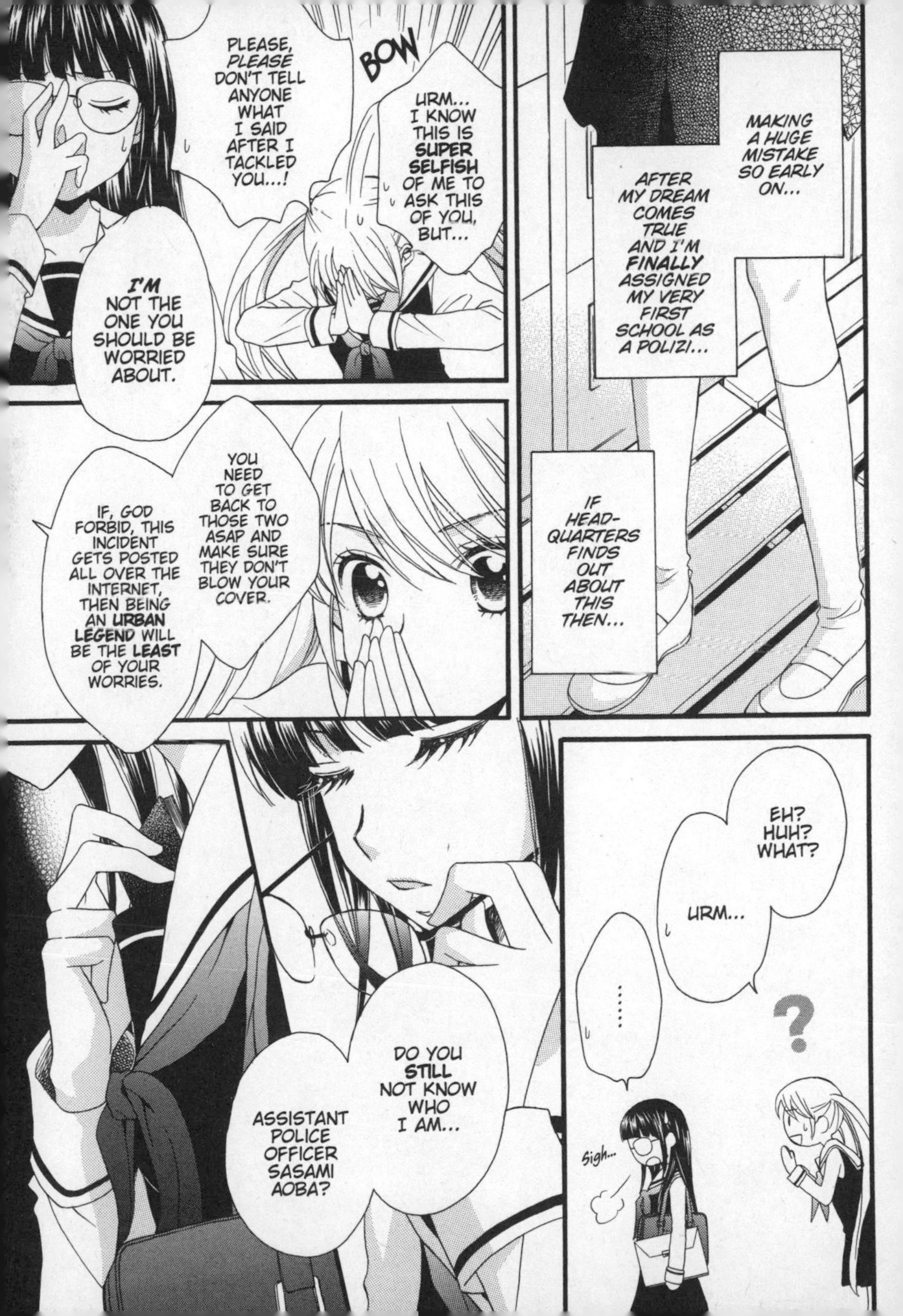
MAKING A HUGE MISTAKE SO EARLY ON...
AFTER MY DREAM COMES TRUE AND I'M FINALLY ASSIGNED MY VERY FIRST SCHOOL AS A POLIZI...
IF HEAD-QUARTERS FINDS OUT ABOUT THIS THEN...
BOW
URM... I KNOW THIS IS SUPER SELFISH OF ME TO ASK THIS OF YOU, BUT...
PLEASE, PLEASE DON'T TELL ANYONE WHAT I SAID AFTER I TACKLED YOU...!
I'M NOT THE ONE YOU SHOULD BE WORRIED ABOUT.
YOU NEED TO GET BACK TO THOSE TWO ASAP AND MAKE SURE THEY DON'T BLOW YOUR COVER.
IF, GOD FORBID, THIS INCIDENT GETS POSTED ALL OVER THE INTERNET, THEN BEING AN URBAN LEGEND WILL BE THE LEAST OF YOUR WORRIES.
EH? HUH? WHAT?
URM...
......
?
Sigh...
DO YOU STILL NOT KNOW WHO I AM...
ASSISTANT POLICE OFFICER SASAMI AOBA?

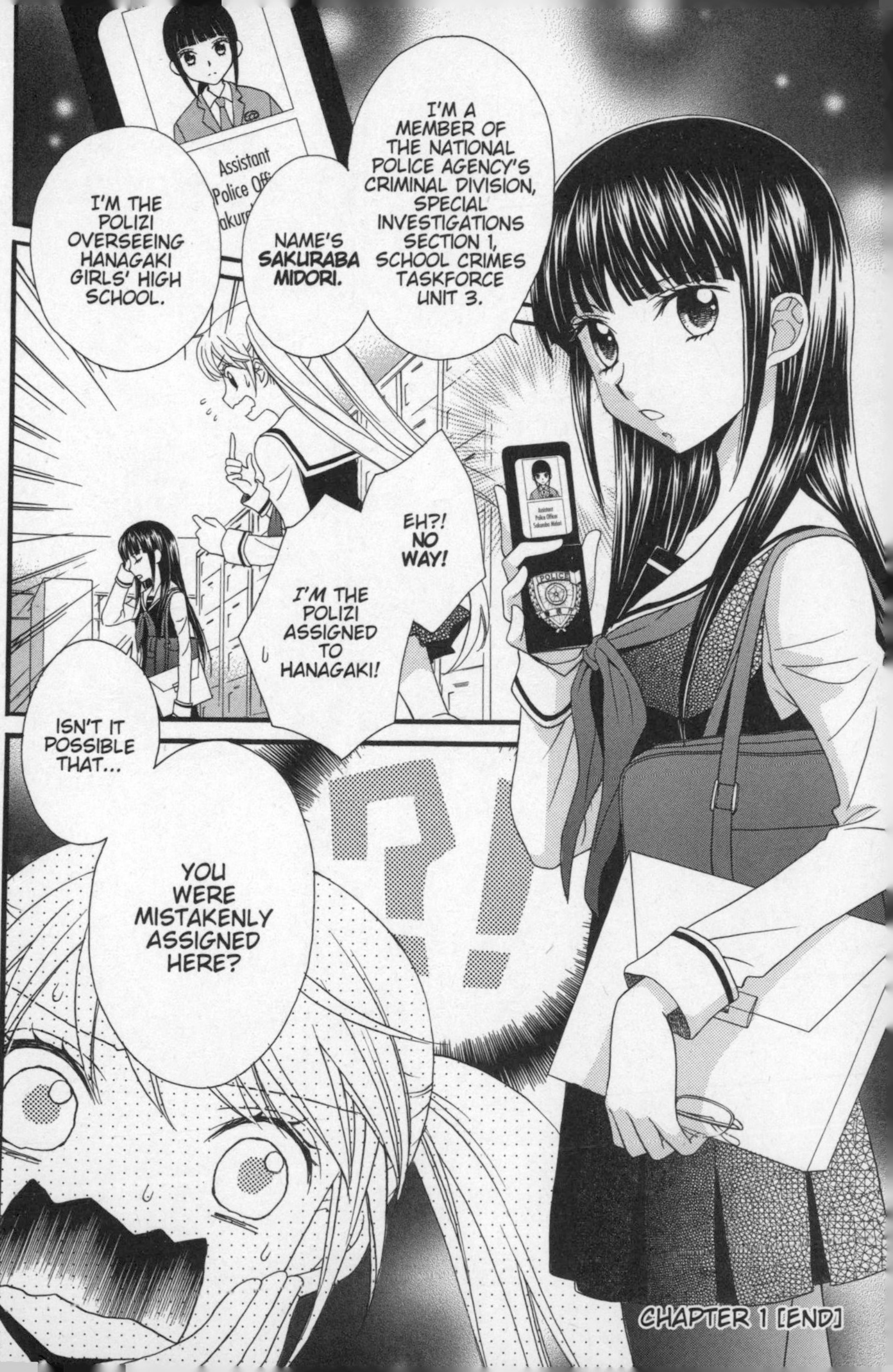
I'M A MEMBER OF THE NATIONAL POLICE AGENCY'S CRIMINAL DIVISION, SPECIAL INVESTIGATIONS SECTION 1, SCHOOL CRIMES TASKFORCE UNIT 3.
NAME'S **SAKURABA MIDORI.**
I'M THE POLIZI OVERSEEING HANAGAKI GIRLS' HIGH SCHOOL.
EH?! NO WAY!
I'M THE POLIZI ASSIGNED TO HANAGAKI!
POLICE
ISN'T IT POSSIBLE THAT...
YOU WERE MISTAKENLY ASSIGNED HERE?
?!
CHAPTER 1 [END]

GAKUEN POLIZI

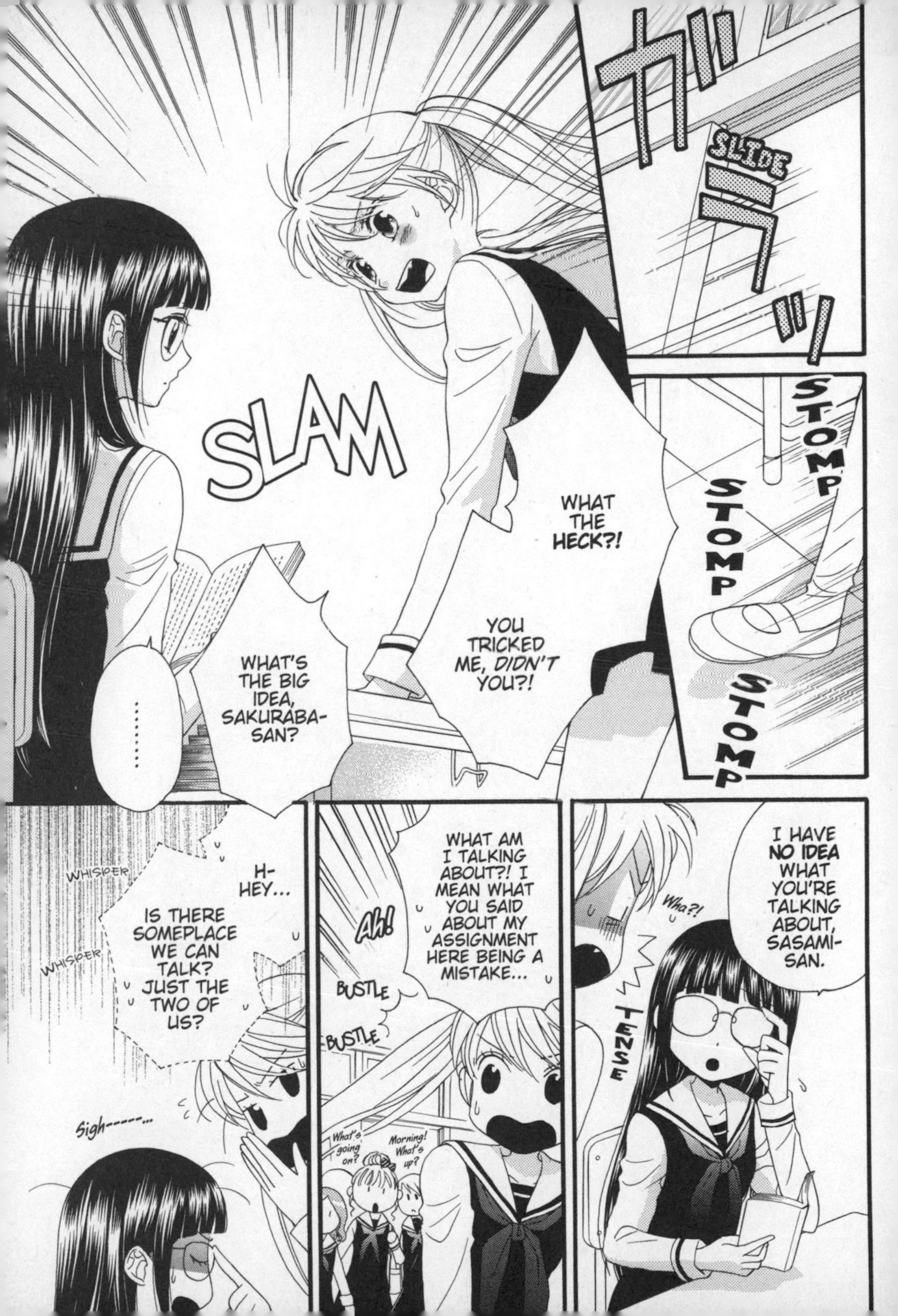
SLIDE
STOMP
STOMP
STOMP
STOMP
SLAM
WHAT THE HECK?!
YOU TRICKED ME, *DIDN'T* YOU?!
WHAT'S THE BIG IDEA, SAKURABA-SAN?
......
I HAVE NO IDEA WHAT YOU'RE TALKING ABOUT, SASAMI-SAN.
Wha?!
TENSE
WHAT AM I TALKING ABOUT?! I MEAN WHAT YOU SAID ABOUT MY ASSIGNMENT HERE BEING A MISTAKE...
Ah!
BUSTLE
BUSTLE
Morning! What's up?
What's going on?
H-HEY...
IS THERE SOMEPLACE WE CAN TALK? JUST THE TWO OF US?
WHISPER
WHISPER
Sigh-----...

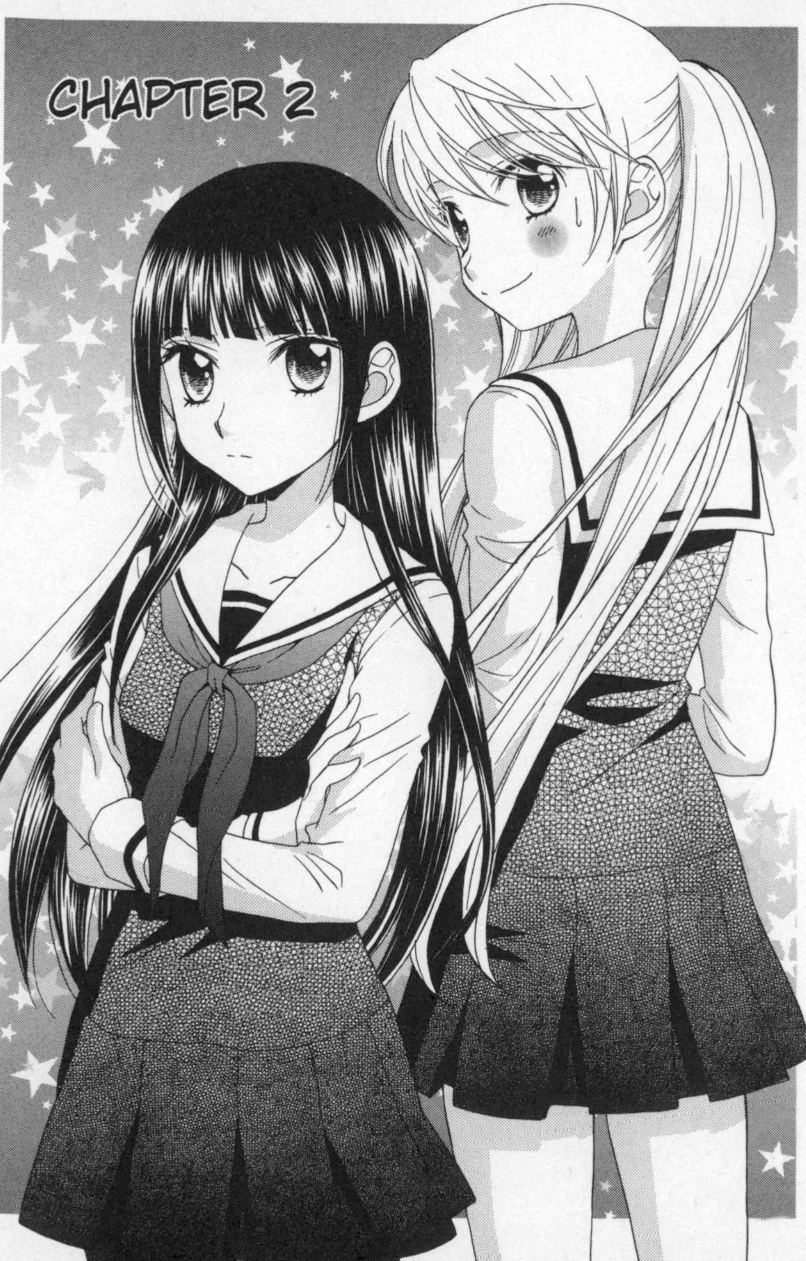
CHAPTER 2

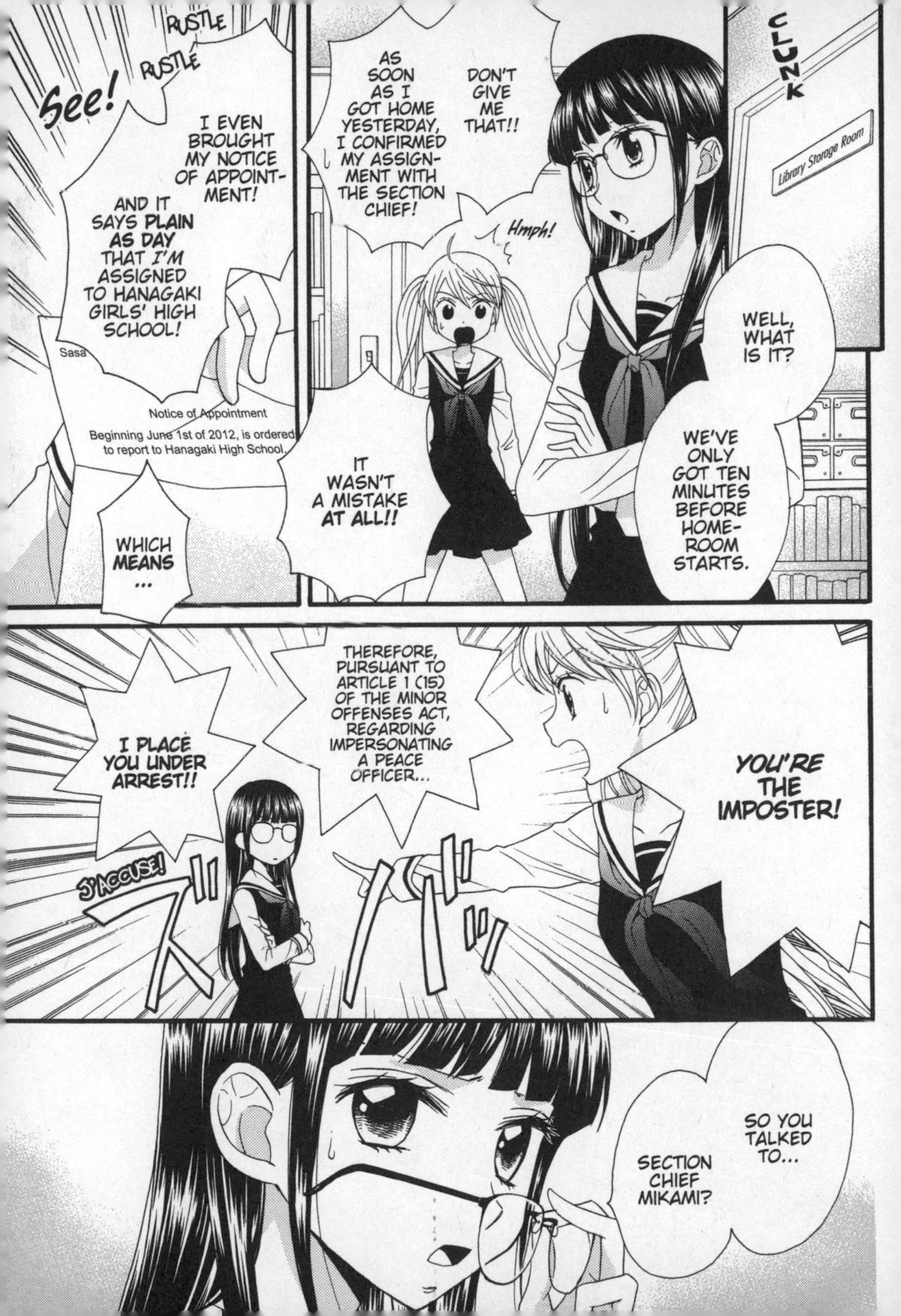
CLUNK
Library Storage Room
WELL, WHAT IS IT?
WE'VE ONLY GOT TEN MINUTES BEFORE HOME-ROOM STARTS.
Hmph!
DON'T GIVE ME THAT!!
AS SOON AS I GOT HOME YESTERDAY, I CONFIRMED MY ASSIGN-MENT WITH THE SECTION CHIEF!
IT WASN'T A MISTAKE AT ALL!!
RUSTLE
RUSTLE
See!
I EVEN BROUGHT MY NOTICE OF APPOINT-MENT!
AND IT SAYS PLAIN AS DAY THAT I'M ASSIGNED TO HANAGAKI GIRLS' HIGH SCHOOL!
Sasa
Notice of Appointment
Beginning June 1st of 2012, is ordered to report to Hanagaki High School.
WHICH MEANS...
YOU'RE THE IMPOSTER!
THEREFORE, PURSUANT TO ARTICLE 1 (15) OF THE MINOR OFFENSES ACT, REGARDING IMPERSONATING A PEACE OFFICER...
I PLACE YOU UNDER ARREST!!
J'ACCUSE!
SO YOU TALKED TO...
SECTION CHIEF MIKAMI?

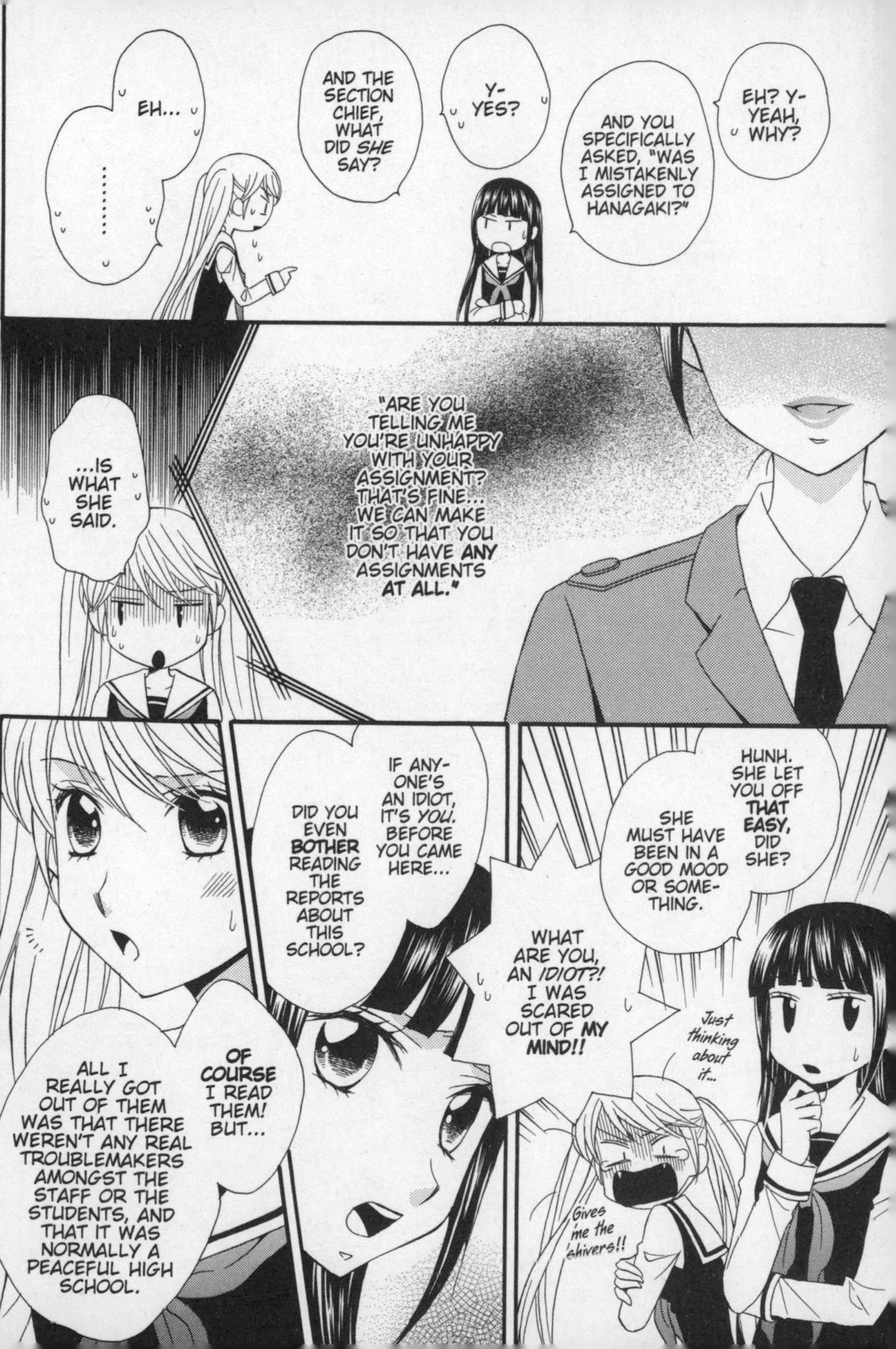
EH? Y-YEAH, WHY?
AND YOU SPECIFICALLY ASKED, "WAS I MISTAKENLY ASSIGNED TO HANAGAKI?"
Y-YES?
AND THE SECTION CHIEF, WHAT DID SHE SAY?
EH... ......
"ARE YOU TELLING ME YOU'RE UNHAPPY WITH YOUR ASSIGNMENT? THAT'S FINE... WE CAN MAKE IT SO THAT YOU DON'T HAVE ANY ASSIGNMENTS AT ALL."
...IS WHAT SHE SAID.
HUNH. SHE LET YOU OFF THAT EASY, DID SHE?
SHE MUST HAVE BEEN IN A GOOD MOOD OR SOME-THING.
WHAT ARE YOU, AN IDIOT?! I WAS SCARED OUT OF MY MIND!!
Just thinking about it...
Gives me the shivers!!
IF ANY-ONE'S AN IDIOT, IT'S YOU. BEFORE YOU CAME HERE...
DID YOU EVEN BOTHER READING THE REPORTS ABOUT THIS SCHOOL?
OF COURSE I READ THEM! BUT...
ALL I REALLY GOT OUT OF THEM WAS THAT THERE WEREN'T ANY REAL TROUBLEMAKERS AMONGST THE STAFF OR THE STUDENTS, AND THAT IT WAS NORMALLY A PEACEFUL HIGH SCHOOL.

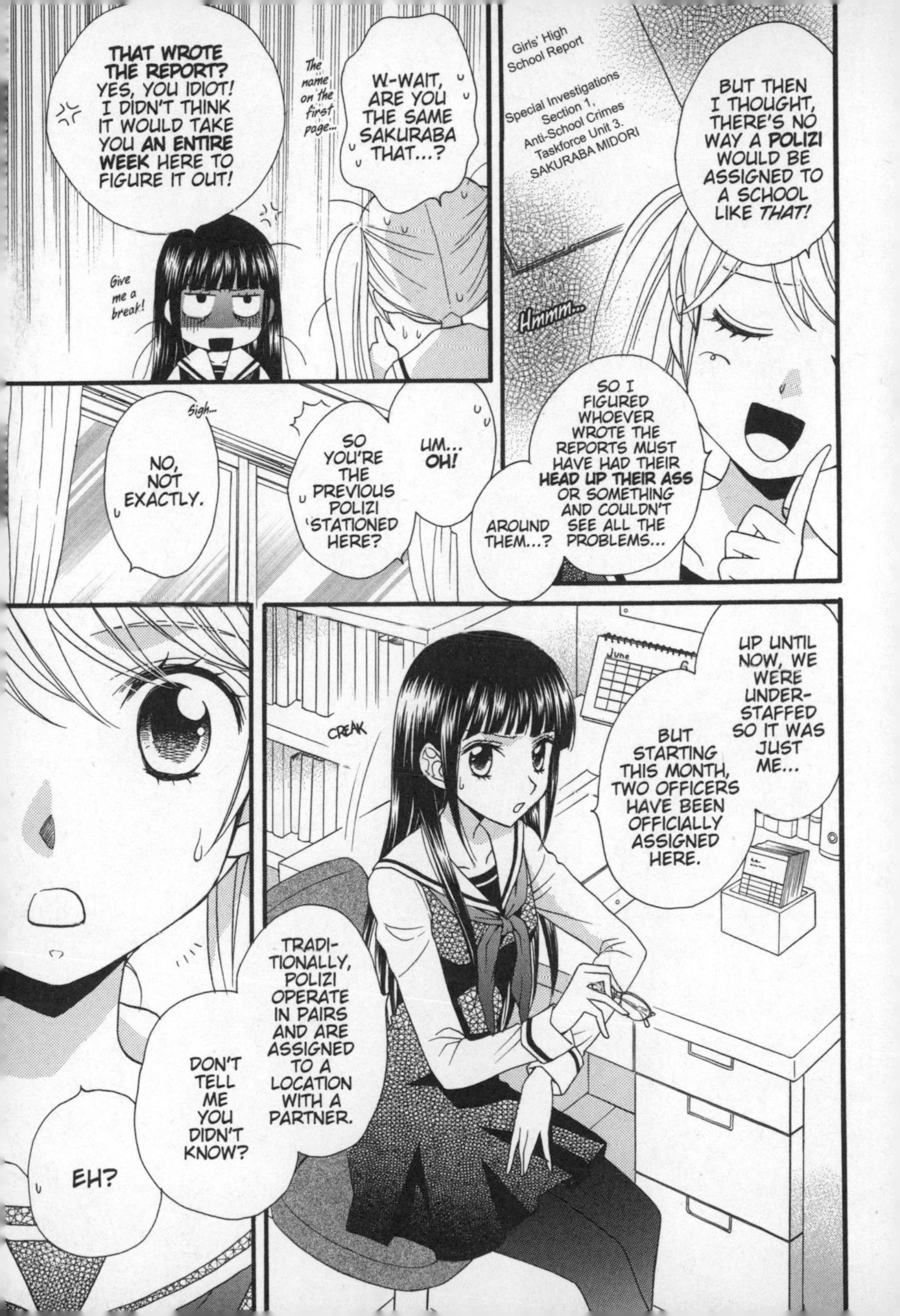
Girls' High School Report
Special Investigations Section 1, Anti-School Crimes Taskforce Unit 3. SAKURABA MIDORI
BUT THEN I THOUGHT, THERE'S NO WAY A **POLIZI** WOULD BE ASSIGNED TO A SCHOOL LIKE *THAT!*
Hmmm...
The name on the first page...
W-WAIT, ARE YOU THE SAME SAKURABA THAT...?
THAT WROTE THE REPORT? YES, YOU IDIOT! I DIDN'T THINK IT WOULD TAKE YOU **AN ENTIRE WEEK** HERE TO FIGURE IT OUT!
Give me a break!
SO I FIGURED WHOEVER WROTE THE REPORTS MUST HAVE HAD THEIR **HEAD UP THEIR ASS** OR SOMETHING AND COULDN'T SEE ALL THE PROBLEMS...
AROUND THEM...?
UM... **OH!**
SO YOU'RE THE PREVIOUS POLIZI STATIONED HERE?
Sigh...
NO, NOT EXACTLY.
UP UNTIL NOW, WE WERE UNDER-STAFFED SO IT WAS JUST ME...
BUT STARTING THIS MONTH, TWO OFFICERS HAVE BEEN OFFICIALLY ASSIGNED HERE.
CREAK
TRADI-TIONALLY, POLIZI OPERATE IN PAIRS AND ARE ASSIGNED TO A LOCATION WITH A PARTNER.
DON'T TELL ME YOU DIDN'T KNOW?
EH?

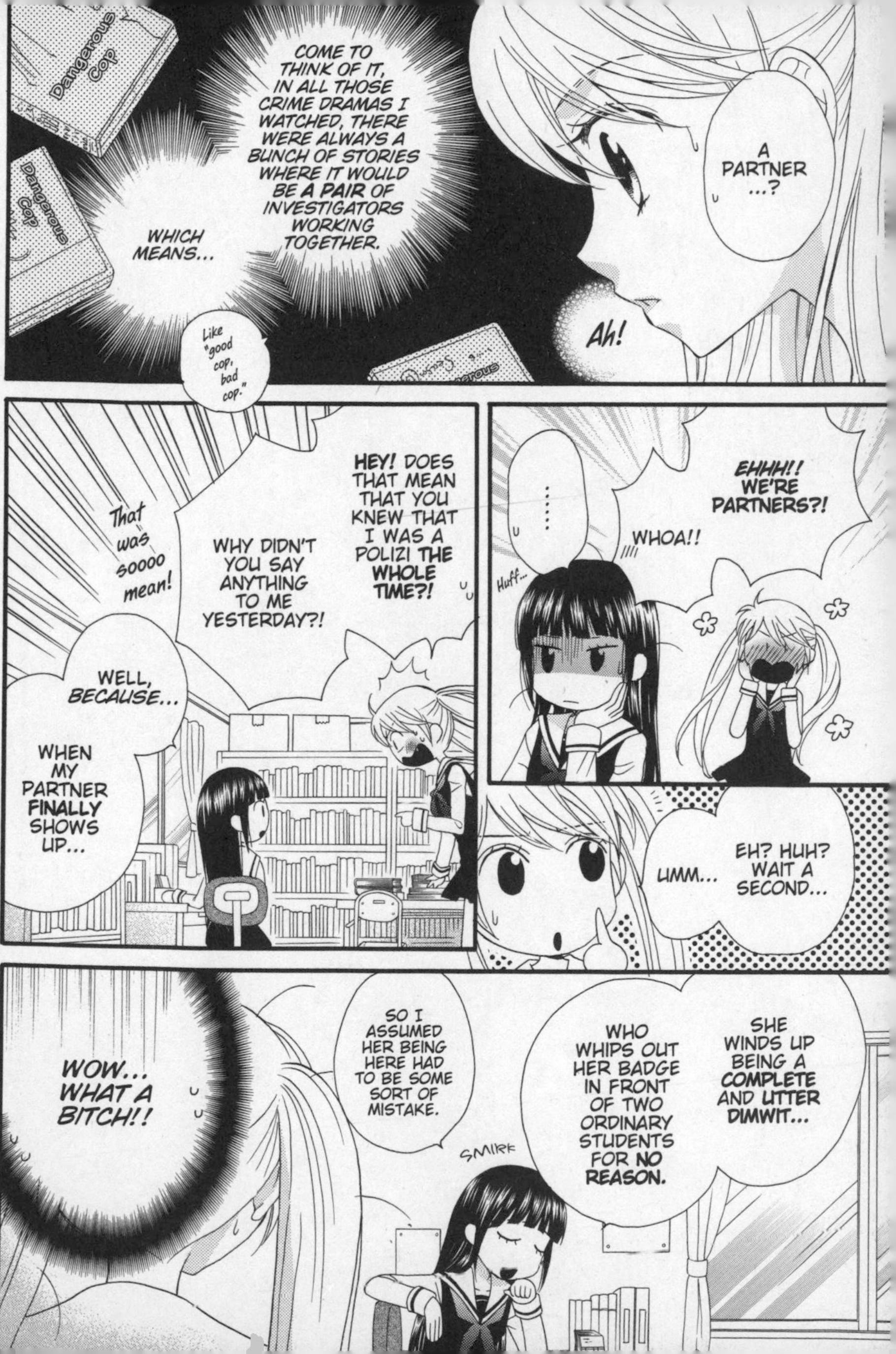
A PARTNER ...?
Ah!
COME TO THINK OF IT, IN ALL THOSE CRIME DRAMAS I WATCHED, THERE WERE ALWAYS A BUNCH OF STORIES WHERE IT WOULD BE A PAIR OF INVESTIGATORS WORKING TOGETHER.
WHICH MEANS...
Like "good cop, bad cop."
Dangerous Cop
Dangerous Cop
EHHH!! WE'RE PARTNERS?!
WHOA!!
......
Huff...
EH? HUH? WAIT A SECOND...
UMM...
HEY! DOES THAT MEAN THAT YOU KNEW THAT I WAS A POLIZI THE WHOLE TIME?!
WHY DIDN'T YOU SAY ANYTHING TO ME YESTERDAY?!
That was soooo mean!
WELL, BECAUSE...
WHEN MY PARTNER FINALLY SHOWS UP...
SHE WINDS UP BEING A COMPLETE AND UTTER DIMWIT...
WHO WHIPS OUT HER BADGE IN FRONT OF TWO ORDINARY STUDENTS FOR NO REASON.
SO I ASSUMED HER BEING HERE HAD TO BE SOME SORT OF MISTAKE.
SMIRK
WOW... WHAT A BITCH!!

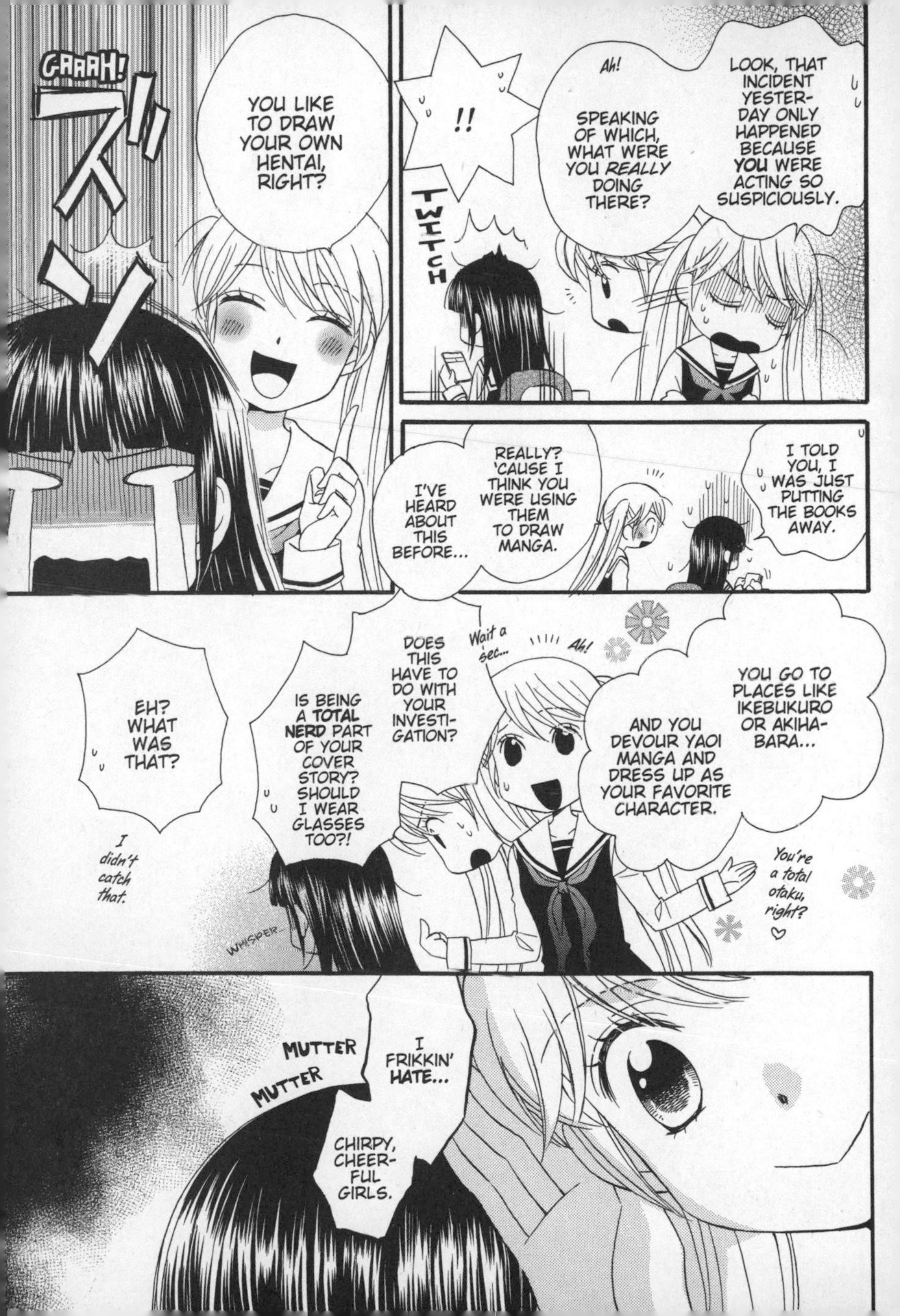
LOOK, THAT INCIDENT YESTER-DAY ONLY HAPPENED BECAUSE YOU WERE ACTING SO SUSPICIOUSLY.
Ah!
SPEAKING OF WHICH, WHAT WERE YOU REALLY DOING THERE?
!!
TWITCH
I TOLD YOU, I WAS JUST PUTTING THE BOOKS AWAY.
REALLY? 'CAUSE I THINK YOU WERE USING THEM TO DRAW MANGA.
I'VE HEARD ABOUT THIS BEFORE...
YOU LIKE TO DRAW YOUR OWN HENTAI, RIGHT?
GRAAAH!
Ah!
YOU GO TO PLACES LIKE IKEBUKURO OR AKIHA-BARA...
AND YOU DEVOUR YAOI MANGA AND DRESS UP AS YOUR FAVORITE CHARACTER.
You're a total otaku, right?
Wait a sec...
DOES THIS HAVE TO DO WITH YOUR INVESTI-GATION?
IS BEING A TOTAL NERD PART OF YOUR COVER STORY? SHOULD I WEAR GLASSES TOO?!
WHISPER...
EH? WHAT WAS THAT?
I didn't catch that.
I FRIKKIN' HATE...
CHIRPY, CHEER-FUL GIRLS.
MUTTER
MUTTER

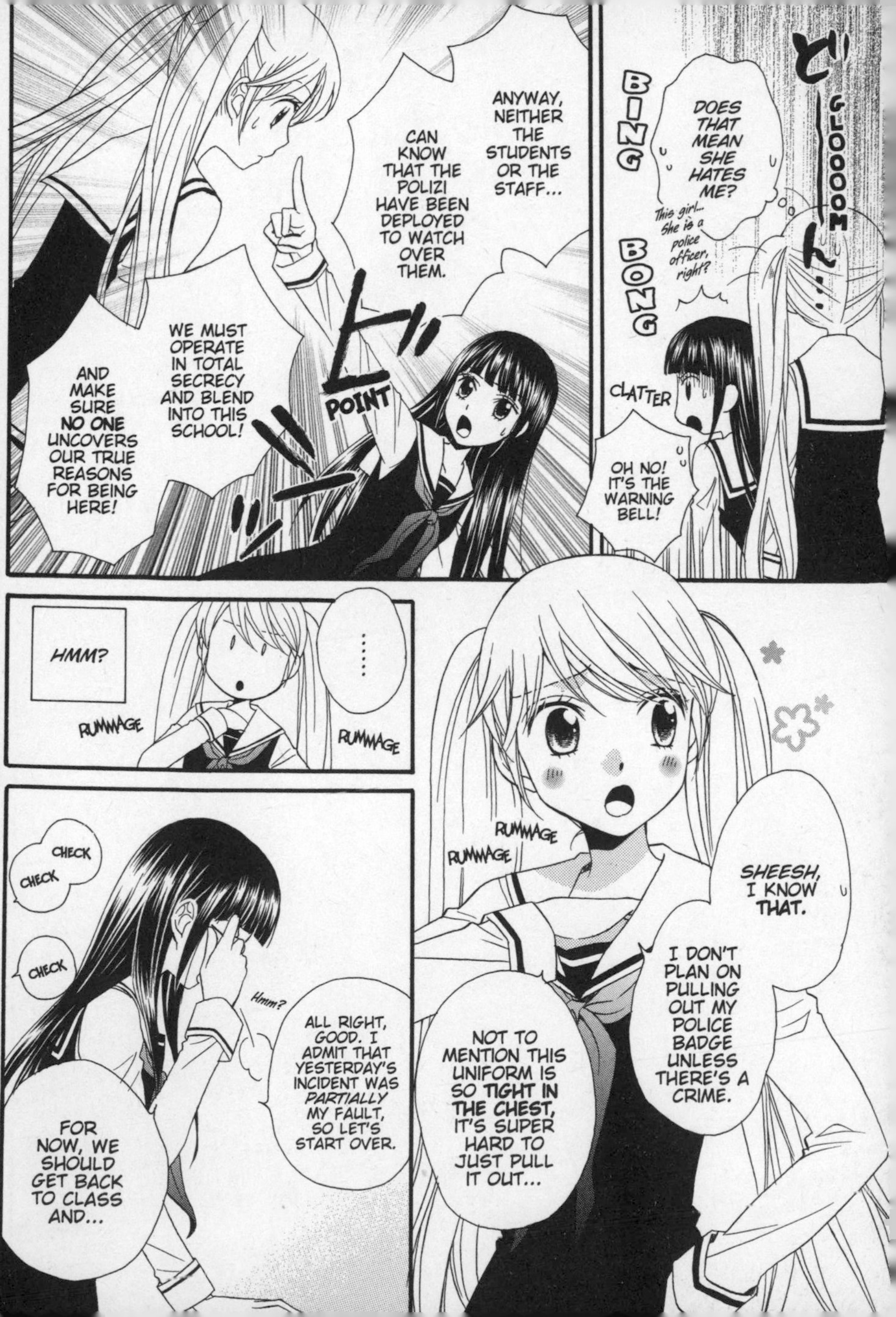
どーん…
GLOOOOOM
DOES THAT MEAN SHE HATES ME?
This girl... She is a police officer, right?
BING BONG
CLATTER
OH NO! IT'S THE WARNING BELL!
ANYWAY, NEITHER THE STUDENTS OR THE STAFF...
CAN KNOW THAT THE POLIZI HAVE BEEN DEPLOYED TO WATCH OVER THEM.
POINT
WE MUST OPERATE IN TOTAL SECRECY AND BLEND INTO THIS SCHOOL!
AND MAKE SURE NO ONE UNCOVERS OUR TRUE REASONS FOR BEING HERE!
SHEESH, I KNOW THAT.
I DON'T PLAN ON PULLING OUT MY POLICE BADGE UNLESS THERE'S A CRIME.
NOT TO MENTION THIS UNIFORM IS SO TIGHT IN THE CHEST, IT'S SUPER HARD TO JUST PULL IT OUT...
RUMMAGE
RUMMAGE
......
HMM?
RUMMAGE
RUMMAGE
ALL RIGHT, GOOD. I ADMIT THAT YESTERDAY'S INCIDENT WAS PARTIALLY MY FAULT, SO LET'S START OVER.
Hmm?
FOR NOW, WE SHOULD GET BACK TO CLASS AND...
CHECK
CHECK
CHECK

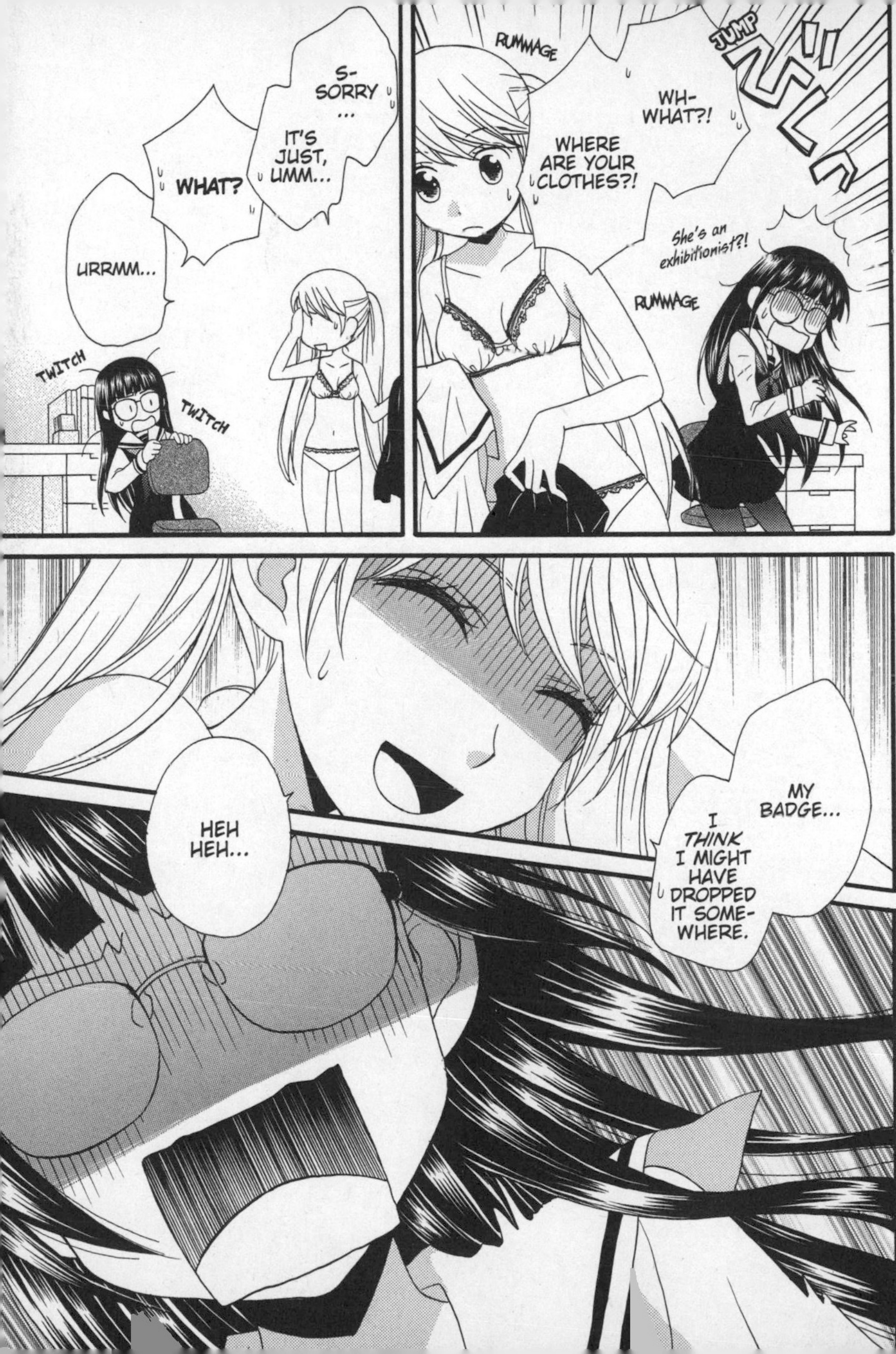
JUMP
WH- WHAT?!
RUMMAGE
WHERE ARE YOUR CLOTHES?!
She's an exhibitionist?!
RUMMAGE
S- SORRY ...
IT'S JUST, UMM...
WHAT?
URRMM...
TWITCH
TWITCH
MY BADGE...
I *THINK* I MIGHT HAVE DROPPED IT SOME-WHERE.
HEH HEH...

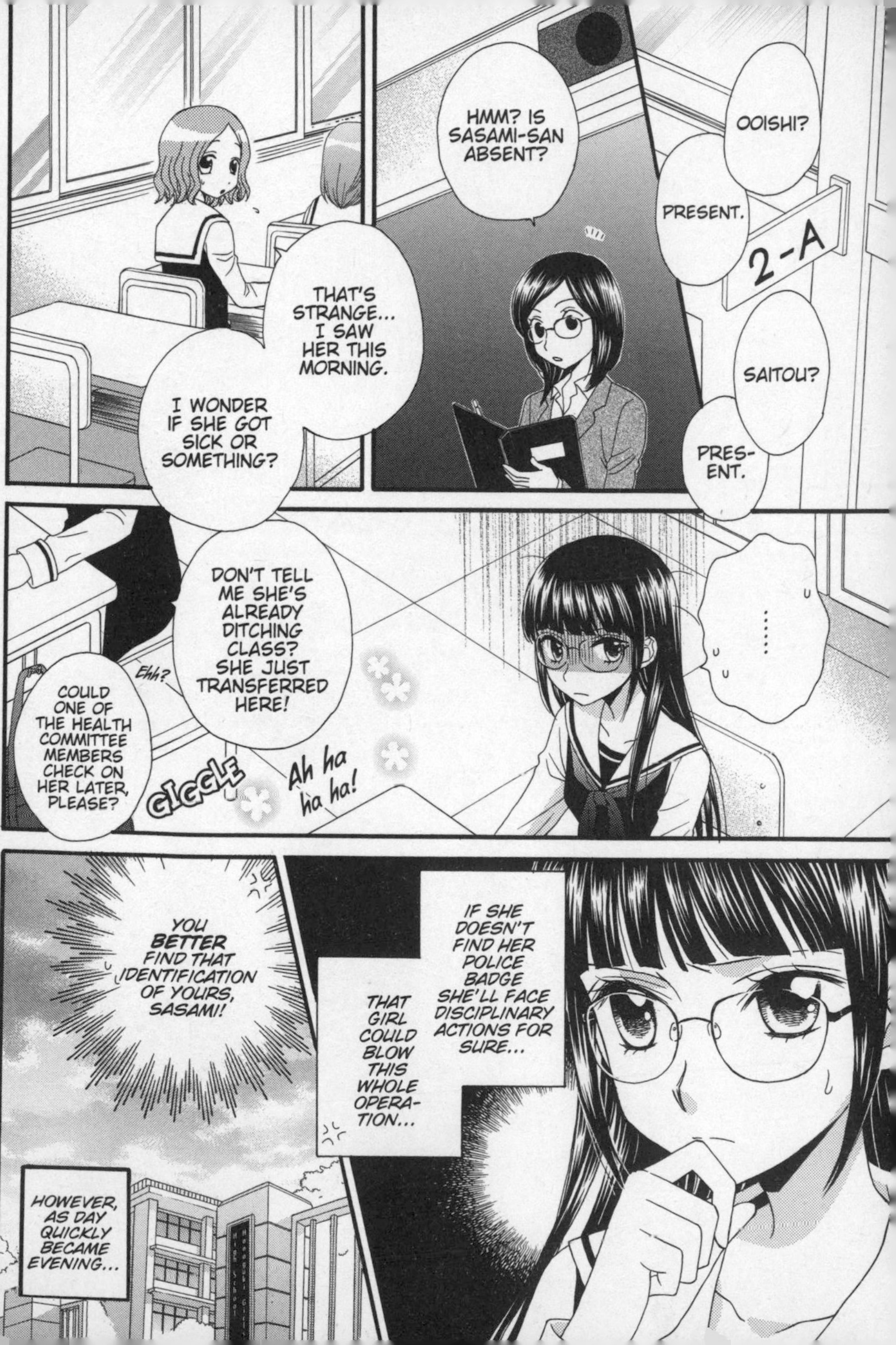
OOISHI?
PRESENT.
2-A
SAITOU?
PRES-ENT.
HMM? IS SASAMI-SAN ABSENT?
THAT'S STRANGE... I SAW HER THIS MORNING.
I WONDER IF SHE GOT SICK OR SOMETHING?
......
DON'T TELL ME SHE'S ALREADY DITCHING CLASS? SHE JUST TRANSFERRED HERE!
Ehh?
COULD ONE OF THE HEALTH COMMITTEE MEMBERS CHECK ON HER LATER, PLEASE?
Ah ha ha ha!
GIGGLE
IF SHE DOESN'T FIND HER POLICE BADGE SHE'LL FACE DISCIPLINARY ACTIONS FOR SURE...
THAT GIRL COULD BLOW THIS WHOLE OPERA-TION...
YOU BETTER FIND THAT IDENTIFICATION OF YOURS, SASAMI!
HOWEVER, AS DAY QUICKLY BECAME EVENING...

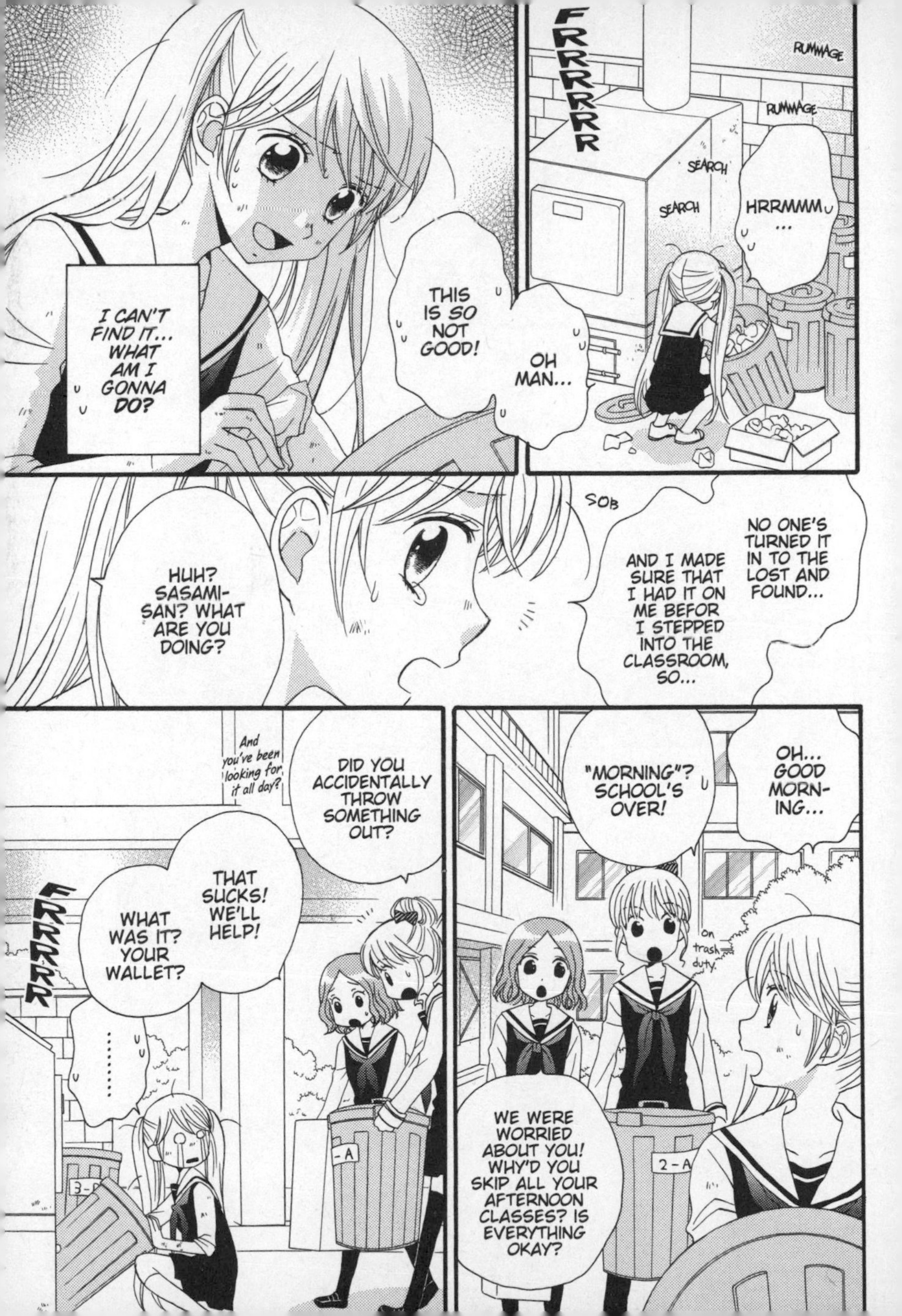
FRRRRRR
RUMMAGE
RUMMAGE
SEARCH
SEARCH
HRRMMM...
THIS IS SO NOT GOOD!
OH MAN...
I CAN'T FIND IT... WHAT AM I GONNA DO?
SOB
NO ONE'S TURNED IT IN TO THE LOST AND FOUND...
AND I MADE SURE THAT I HAD IT ON ME BEFOR I STEPPED INTO THE CLASSROOM, SO...
HUH? SASAMI-SAN? WHAT ARE YOU DOING?
OH... GOOD MORNING...
"MORNING"? SCHOOL'S OVER!
On trash duty.
WE WERE WORRIED ABOUT YOU! WHY'D YOU SKIP ALL YOUR AFTERNOON CLASSES? IS EVERYTHING OKAY?
2-A
DID YOU ACCIDENTALLY THROW SOMETHING OUT?
And you've been looking for it all day?
THAT SUCKS! WE'LL HELP!
WHAT WAS IT? YOUR WALLET?
FRRRRR
......
-A

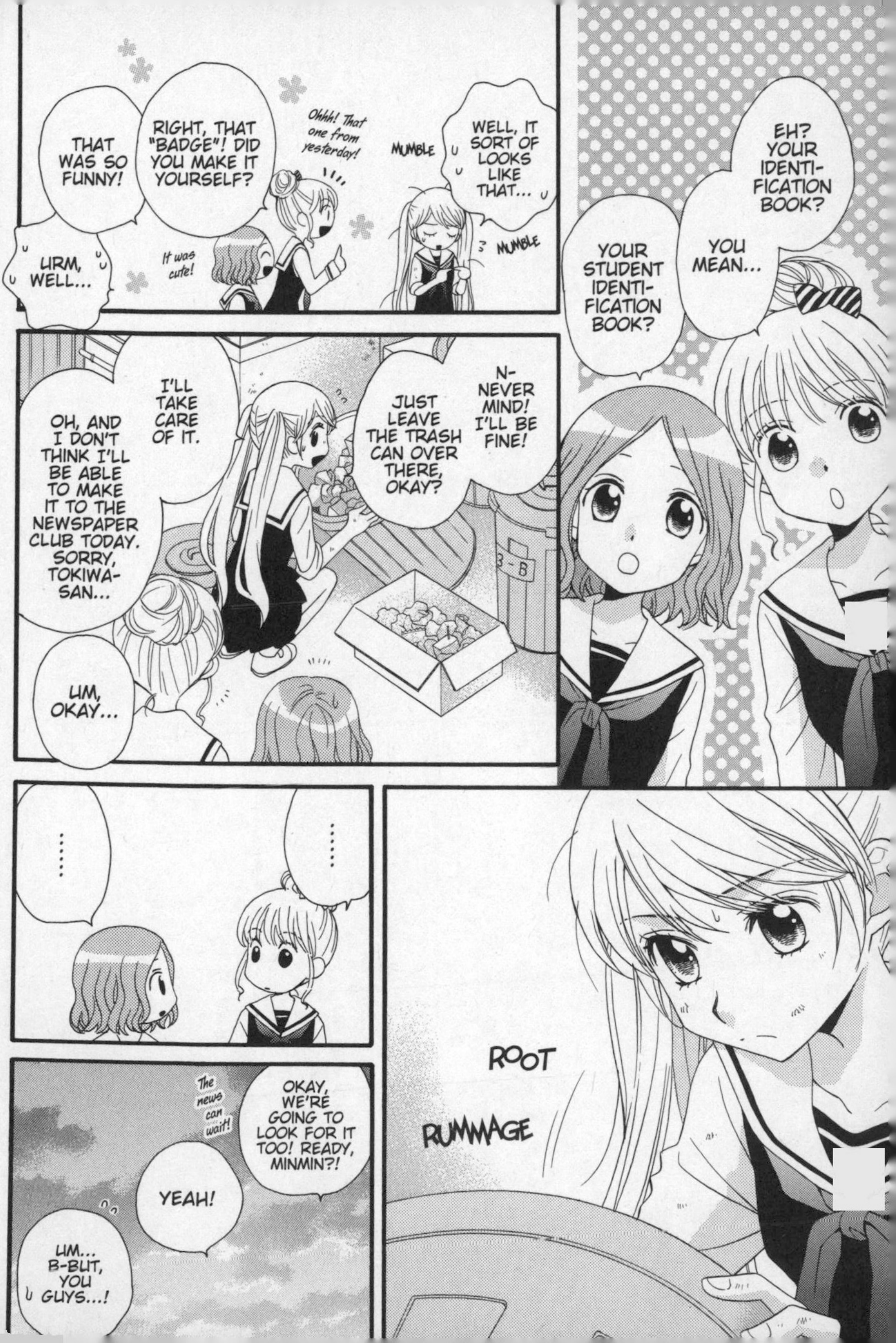
EH? YOUR IDENTIFICATION BOOK?
YOU MEAN...
YOUR STUDENT IDENTIFICATION BOOK?
WELL, IT SORT OF LOOKS LIKE THAT...
MUMBLE
MUMBLE
Ohhh! That one from yesterday!
RIGHT, THAT "BADGE"! DID YOU MAKE IT YOURSELF?
THAT WAS SO FUNNY!
It was cute!
URM, WELL...
N-NEVER MIND! I'LL BE FINE!
JUST LEAVE THE TRASH CAN OVER THERE, OKAY?
I'LL TAKE CARE OF IT.
OH, AND I DON'T THINK I'LL BE ABLE TO MAKE IT TO THE NEWSPAPER CLUB TODAY. SORRY, TOKIWA-SAN...
UM, OKAY...
ROOT
RUMMAGE
......
......
OKAY, WE'RE GOING TO LOOK FOR IT TOO! READY, MINMIN?!
The news can wait!
YEAH!
UM... B-BUT, YOU GUYS...!

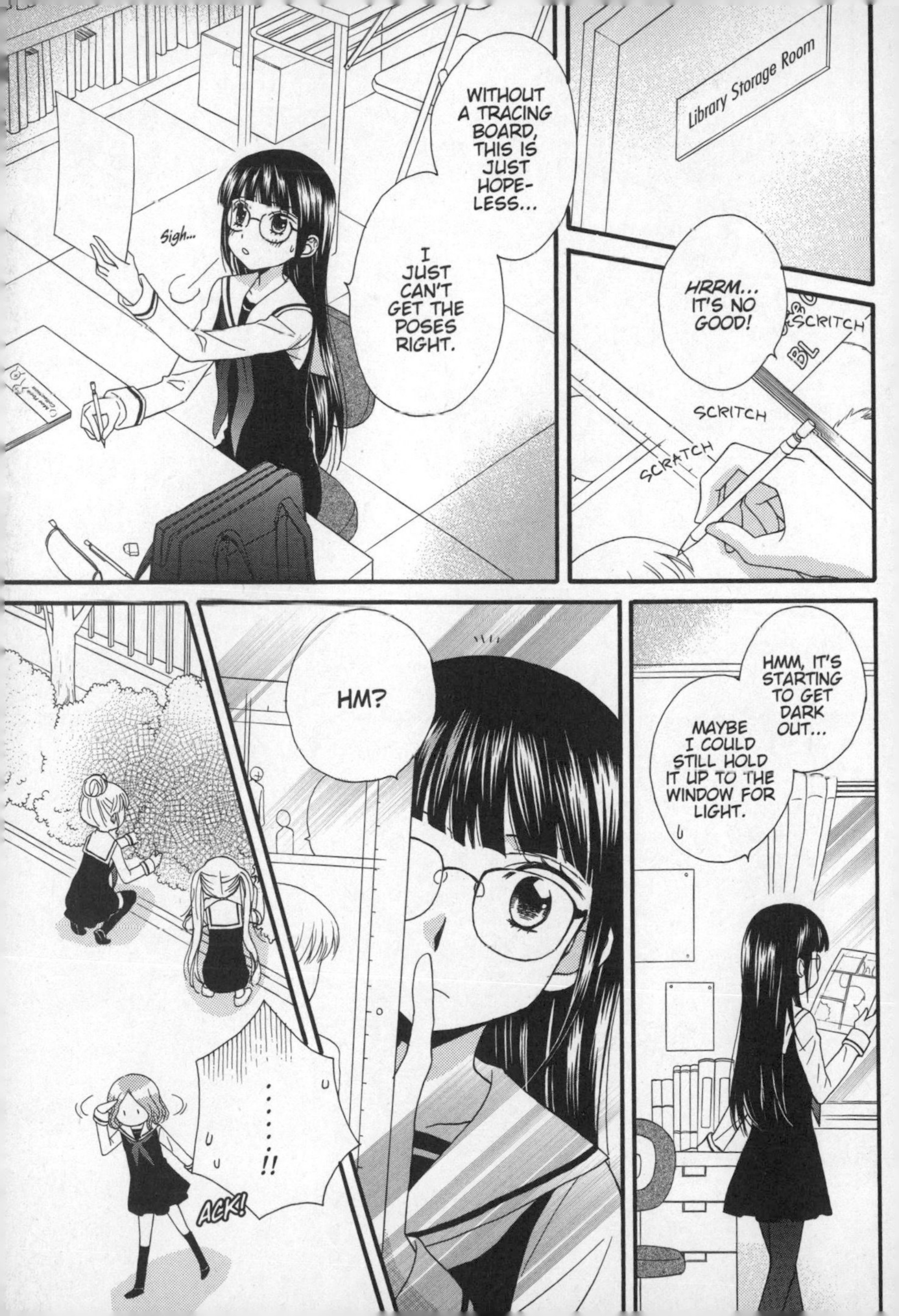
Library Storage Room
HRRM... IT'S NO GOOD!
SCRITCH
BL
SCRITCH
SCRATCH
WITHOUT A TRACING BOARD, THIS IS JUST HOPE-LESS...
I JUST CAN'T GET THE POSES RIGHT.
Sigh...
HMM, IT'S STARTING TO GET DARK OUT...
MAYBE I COULD STILL HOLD IT UP TO THE WINDOW FOR LIGHT.
HM?
......!!
ACK!

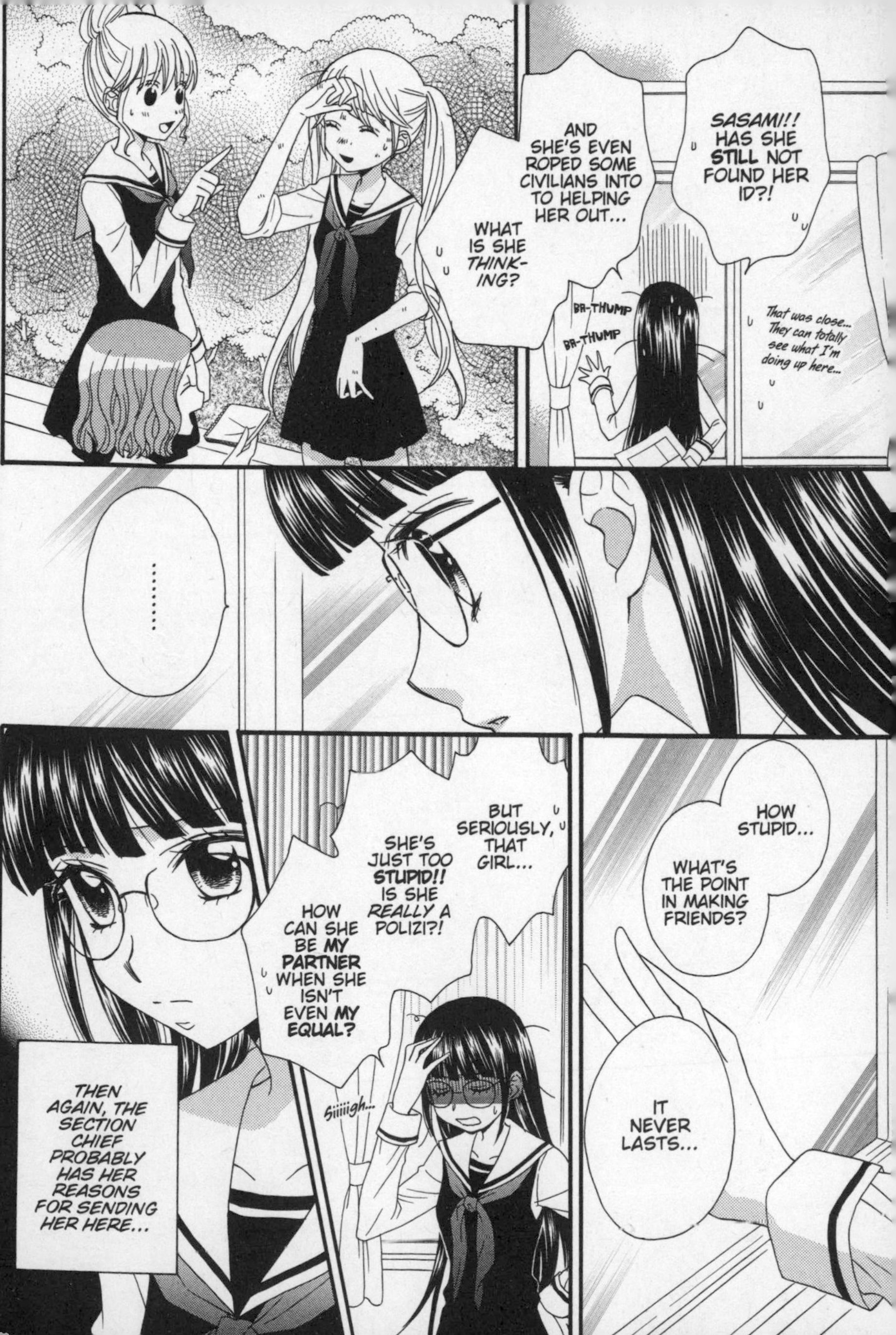
SASAMI!! HAS SHE STILL NOT FOUND HER ID?!
AND SHE'S EVEN ROPED SOME CIVILIANS INTO TO HELPING HER OUT...
WHAT IS SHE THINKING?
BA-THUMP
BA-THUMP
That was close... They can totally see what I'm doing up here...
......
HOW STUPID...
WHAT'S THE POINT IN MAKING FRIENDS?
IT NEVER LASTS...
BUT SERIOUSLY, THAT GIRL...
SHE'S JUST TOO STUPID!! IS SHE REALLY A POLIZI?!
HOW CAN SHE BE MY PARTNER WHEN SHE ISN'T EVEN MY EQUAL?
Siiiiigh...
THEN AGAIN, THE SECTION CHIEF PROBABLY HAS HER REASONS FOR SENDING HER HERE...

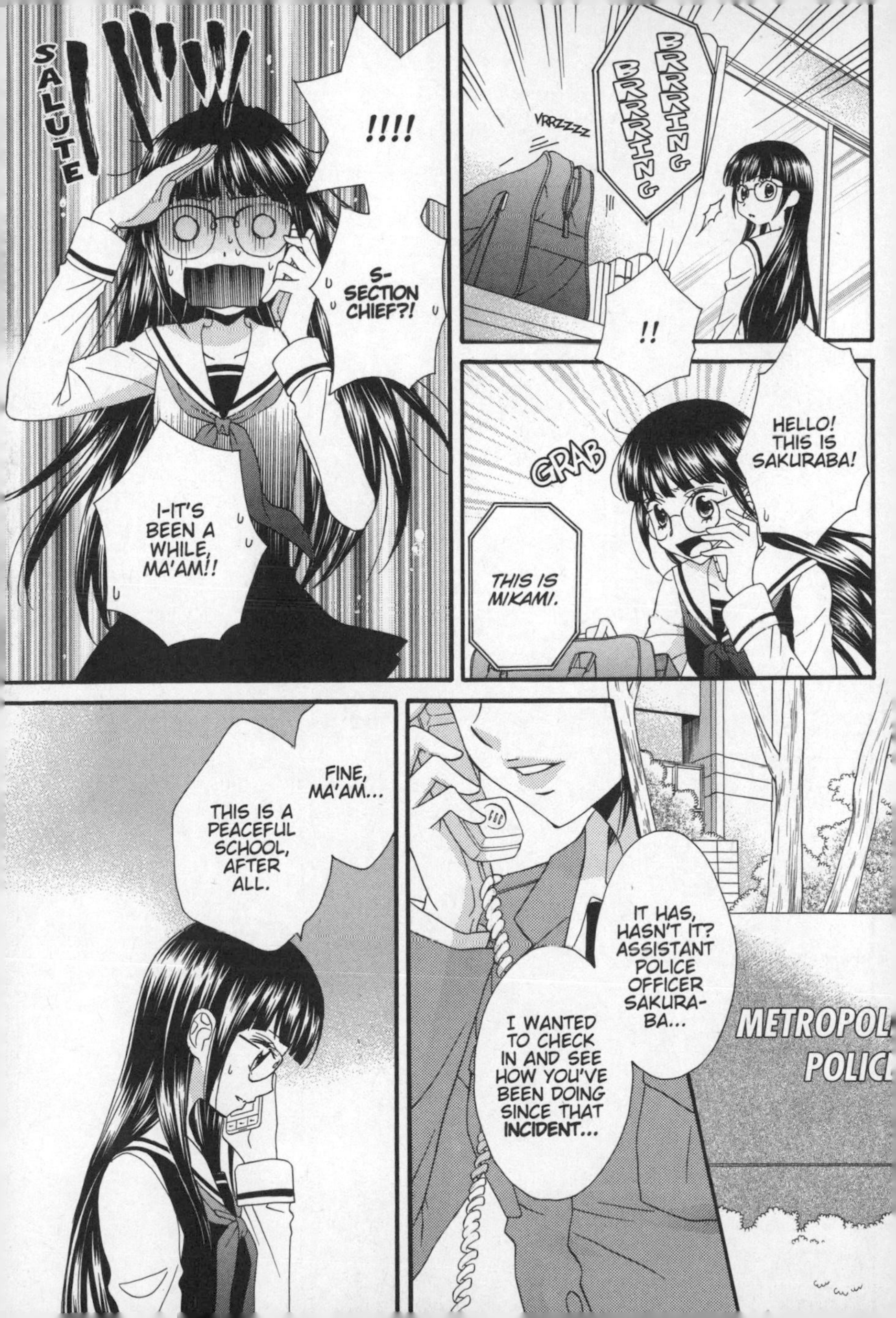
BRRRING
BRRRING
VRRZZZZ
!!
HELLO! THIS IS SAKURABA!
GRAB
THIS IS MIKAMI.
!!!!
SALUTE
S- SECTION CHIEF?!
I-IT'S BEEN A WHILE, MA'AM!!
METROPOL
POLIC
IT HAS, HASN'T IT? ASSISTANT POLICE OFFICER SAKURABA...
I WANTED TO CHECK IN AND SEE HOW YOU'VE BEEN DOING SINCE THAT INCIDENT...
FINE, MA'AM...
THIS IS A PEACEFUL SCHOOL, AFTER ALL.

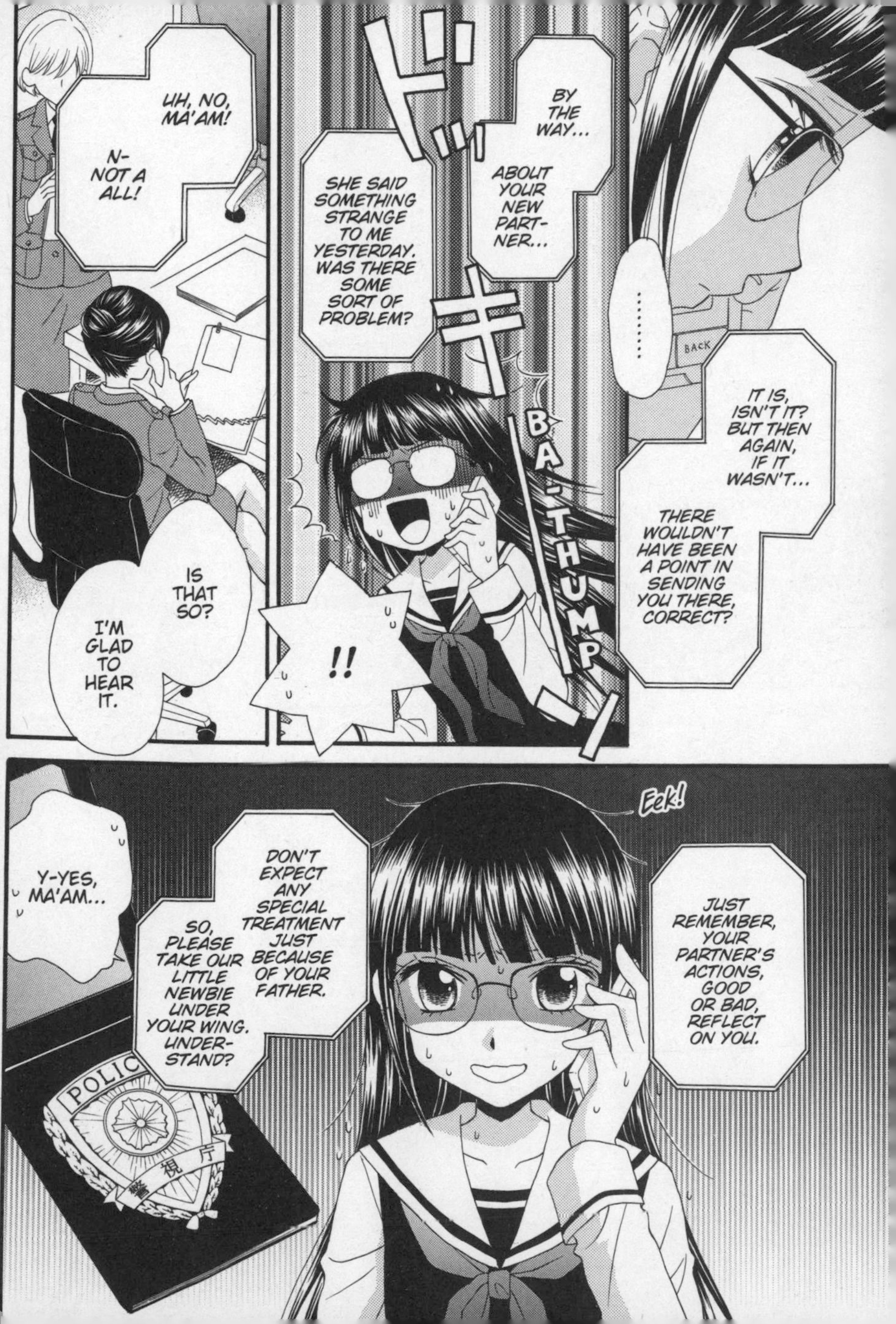
......
IT IS, ISN'T IT? BUT THEN AGAIN, IF IT WASN'T...
THERE WOULDN'T HAVE BEEN A POINT IN SENDING YOU THERE, CORRECT?
BACK
ドッ
BY THE WAY... ABOUT YOUR NEW PARTNER...
SHE SAID SOMETHING STRANGE TO ME YESTERDAY. WAS THERE SOME SORT OF PROBLEM?
キ
BA-THUMP
!!
UH, NO, MA'AM!
N-NOT A ALL!
IS THAT SO?
I'M GLAD TO HEAR IT.
Eek!
JUST REMEMBER, YOUR PARTNER'S ACTIONS, GOOD OR BAD, REFLECT ON YOU.
DON'T EXPECT ANY SPECIAL TREATMENT JUST BECAUSE OF YOUR FATHER.
SO, PLEASE TAKE OUR LITTLE NEWBIE UNDER YOUR WING. UNDER-STAND?
Y-YES, MA'AM...
POLIC
警視庁

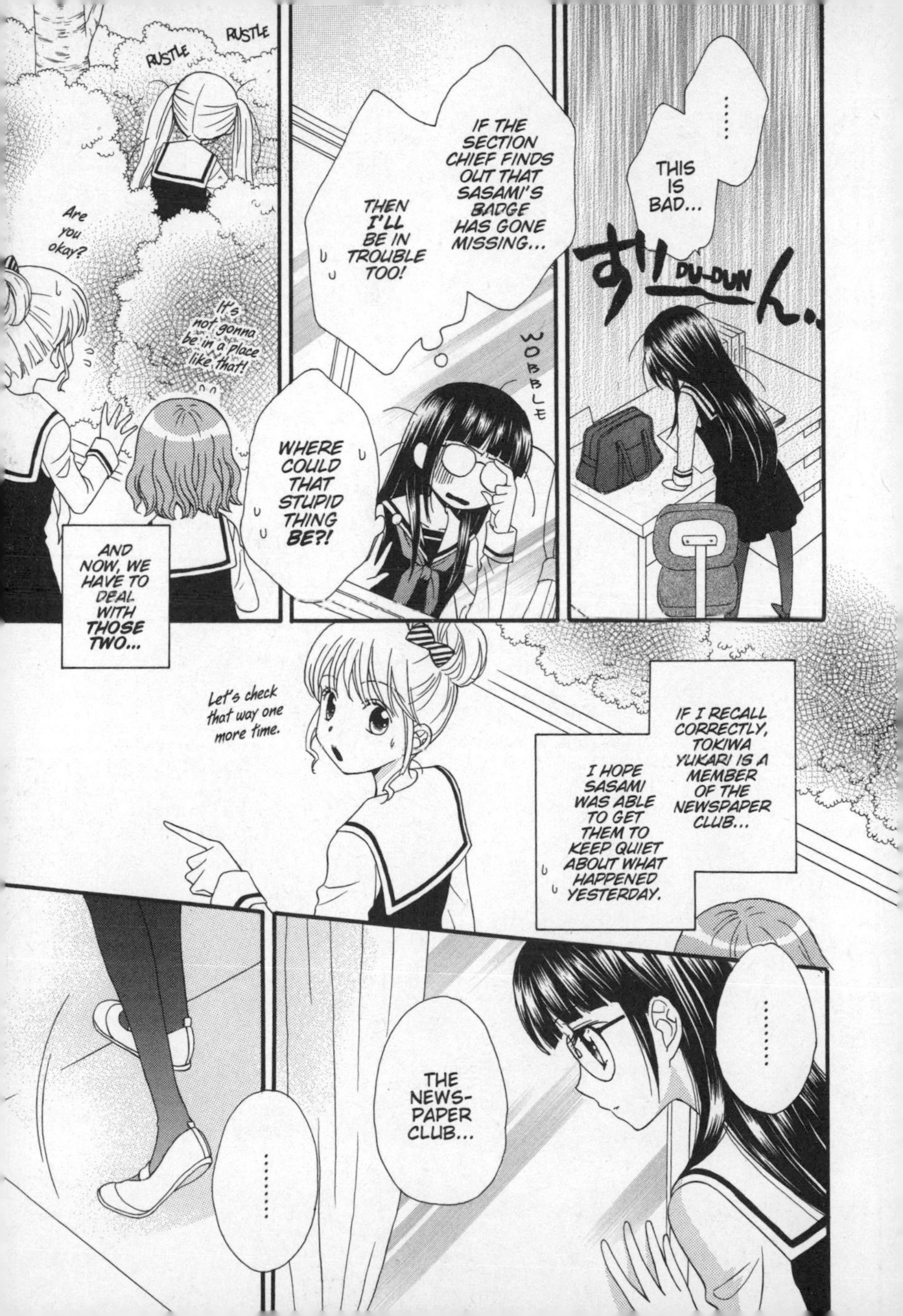
......
THIS IS BAD...
すDU-DUNん..
IF THE SECTION CHIEF FINDS OUT THAT SASAMI'S BADGE HAS GONE MISSING...
THEN I'LL BE IN TROUBLE TOO!
WOBBLE
WHERE COULD THAT STUPID THING BE?!
RUSTLE
RUSTLE
Are you okay?
It's not gonna be in a place like that!
AND NOW, WE HAVE TO DEAL WITH THOSE TWO...
IF I RECALL CORRECTLY, TOKIWA YUKARI IS A MEMBER OF THE NEWSPAPER CLUB...
I HOPE SASAMI WAS ABLE TO GET THEM TO KEEP QUIET ABOUT WHAT HAPPENED YESTERDAY.
Let's check that way one more time.
......
THE NEWS-PAPER CLUB...
......

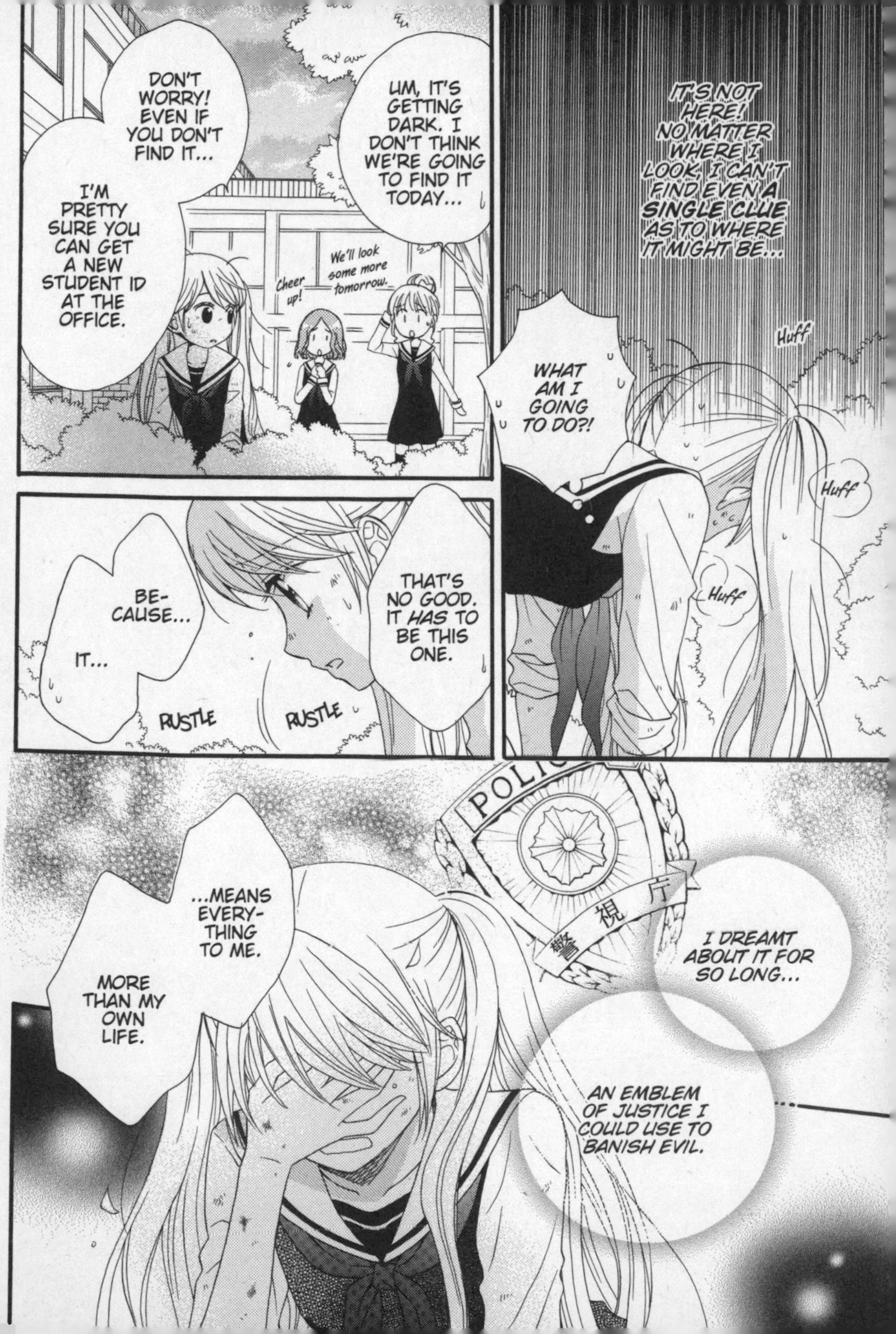
IT'S NOT HERE! NO MATTER WHERE I LOOK, I CAN'T FIND EVEN A SINGLE CLUE AS TO WHERE IT MIGHT BE...
Huff
WHAT AM I GOING TO DO?!
Huff
Huff
UM, IT'S GETTING DARK. I DON'T THINK WE'RE GOING TO FIND IT TODAY...
We'll look some more tomorrow.
Cheer up!
DON'T WORRY! EVEN IF YOU DON'T FIND IT...
I'M PRETTY SURE YOU CAN GET A NEW STUDENT ID AT THE OFFICE.
THAT'S NO GOOD. IT *HAS* TO BE THIS ONE.
BE-CAUSE... IT...
RUSTLE
RUSTLE
警視庁
I DREAMT ABOUT IT FOR SO LONG...
AN EMBLEM OF JUSTICE I COULD USE TO BANISH EVIL.
...MEANS EVERY-THING TO ME.
MORE THAN MY OWN LIFE.

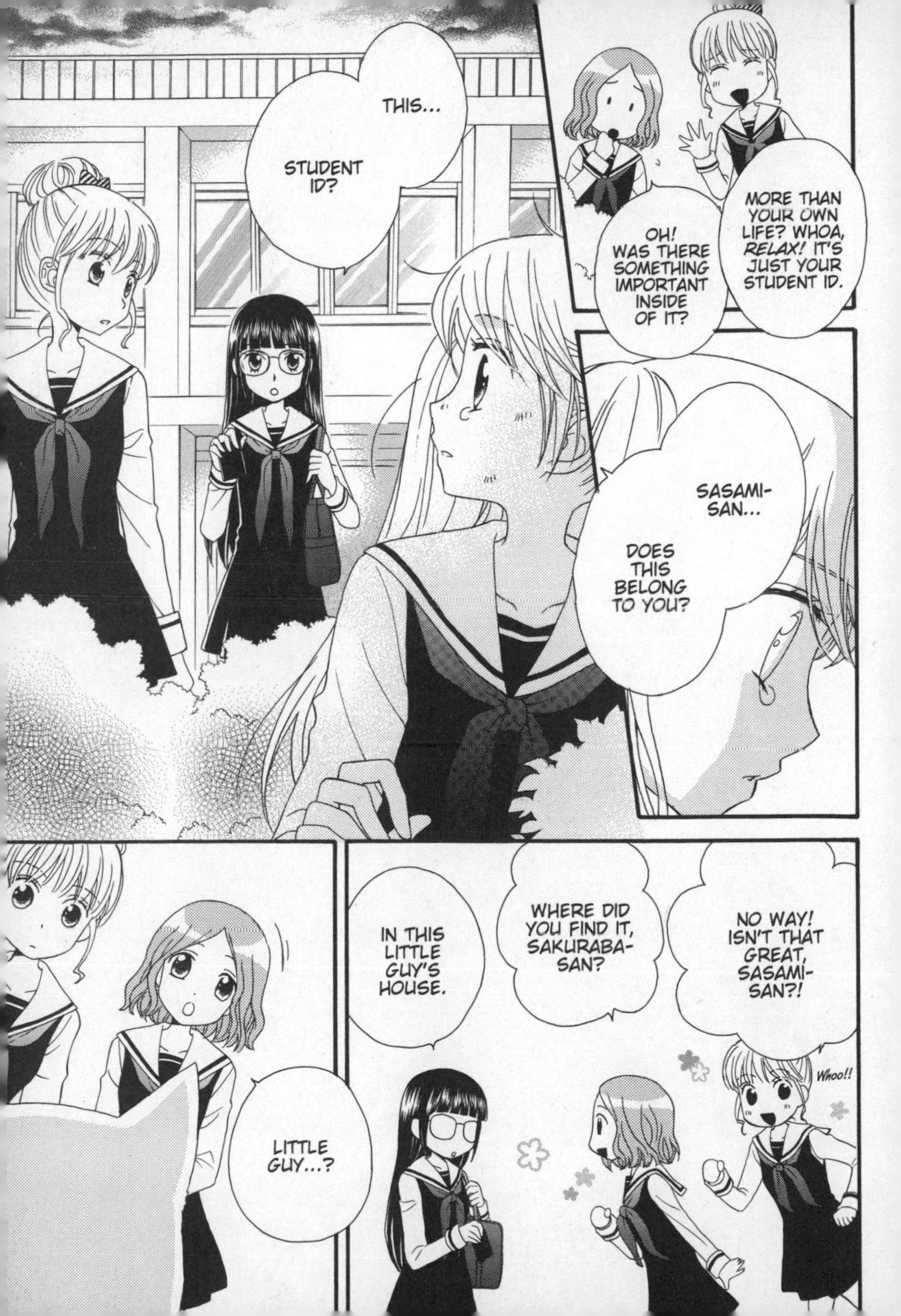
MORE THAN YOUR OWN LIFE? WHOA, *RELAX!* IT'S JUST YOUR STUDENT ID.
OH! WAS THERE SOMETHING IMPORTANT INSIDE OF IT?
SASAMI-SAN...
DOES THIS BELONG TO YOU?
THIS...
STUDENT ID?
NO WAY! ISN'T THAT GREAT, SASAMI-SAN?!
Whoo!!
WHERE DID YOU FIND IT, SAKURABA-SAN?
IN THIS LITTLE GUY'S HOUSE.
LITTLE GUY...?

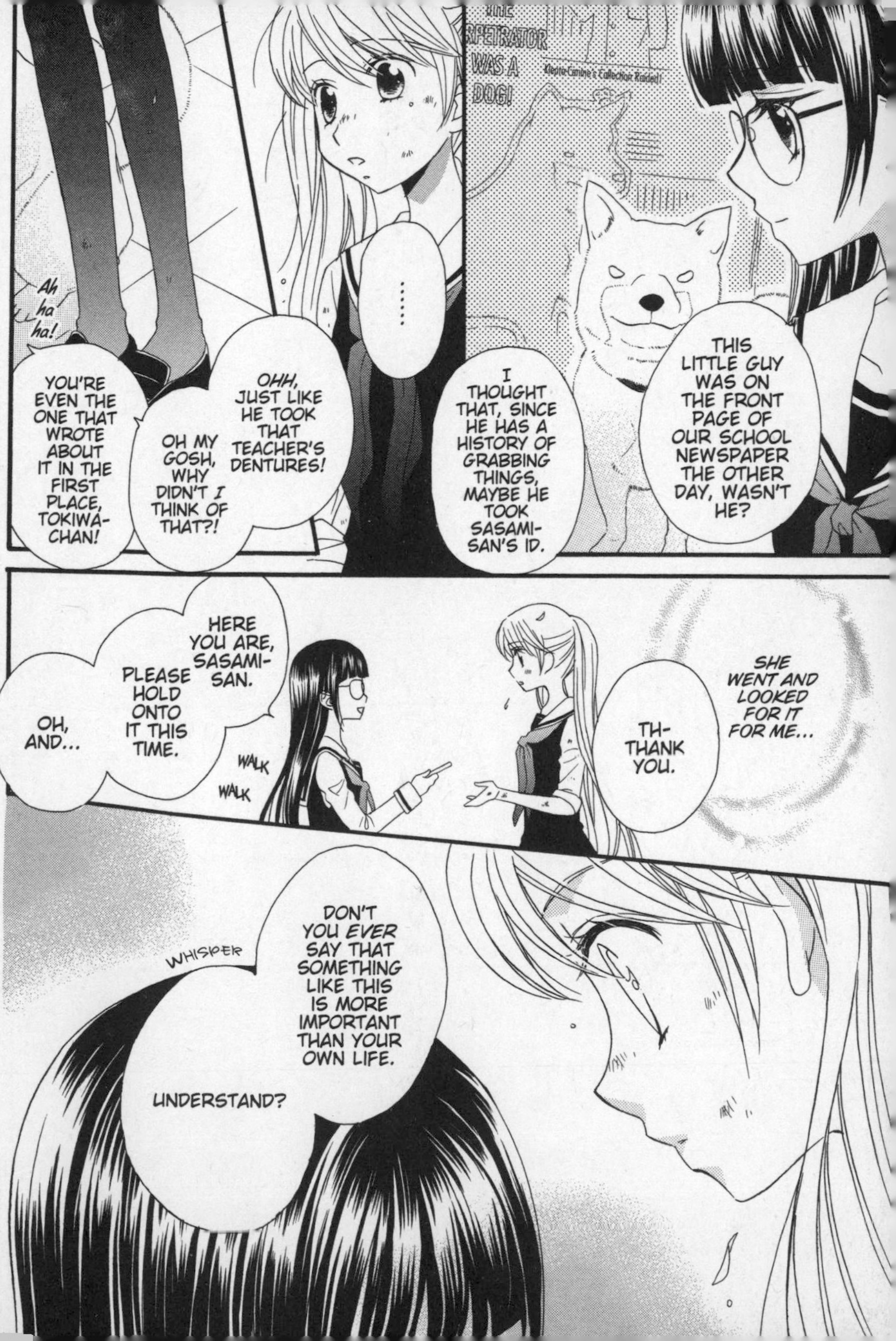
RPETRATOR WAS A DOG!
Klepto-Canine's Collection Raided!
THIS LITTLE GUY WAS ON THE FRONT PAGE OF OUR SCHOOL NEWSPAPER THE OTHER DAY, WASN'T HE?
I THOUGHT THAT, SINCE HE HAS A HISTORY OF GRABBING THINGS, MAYBE HE TOOK SASAMI-SAN'S ID.
......
OHH, JUST LIKE HE TOOK THAT TEACHER'S DENTURES!
OH MY GOSH, WHY DIDN'T *I* THINK OF THAT?!
Ah ha ha!
YOU'RE EVEN THE ONE THAT WROTE ABOUT IT IN THE FIRST PLACE, TOKIWA-CHAN!
SHE WENT AND LOOKED FOR IT FOR ME...
TH-THANK YOU.
HERE YOU ARE, SASAMI-SAN.
PLEASE HOLD ONTO IT THIS TIME.
WALK
WALK
OH, AND...
DON'T YOU *EVER* SAY THAT SOMETHING LIKE THIS IS MORE IMPORTANT THAN YOUR OWN LIFE.
UNDERSTAND?
WHISPER

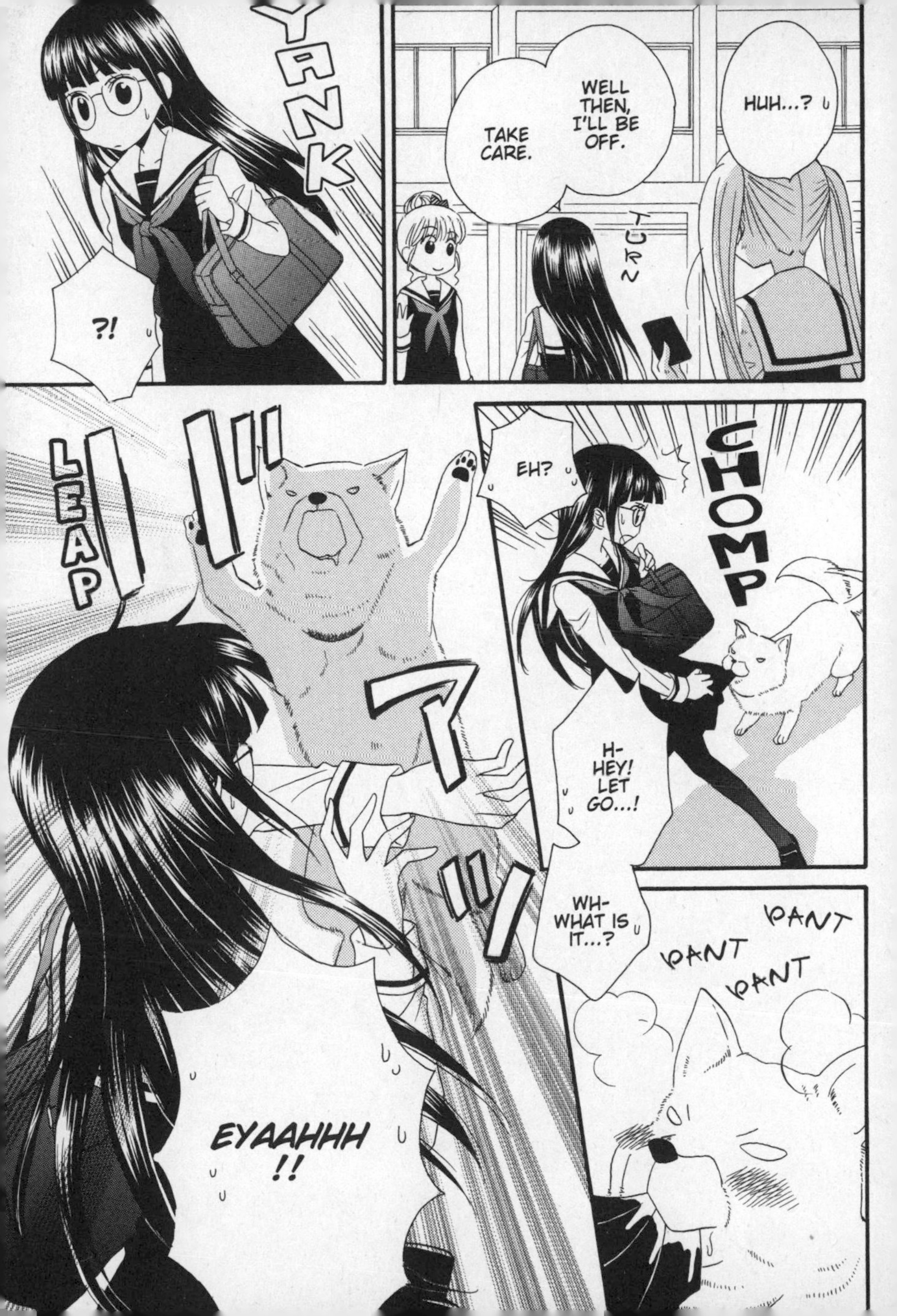
HUH...?
WELL THEN, I'LL BE OFF.
TAKE CARE.
TURN
YANK
?!
CHOMP
EH?
H-HEY! LET GO...!
PANT
PANT
PANT
WH-WHAT IS IT...?
LEAP
EYAAHHH!!

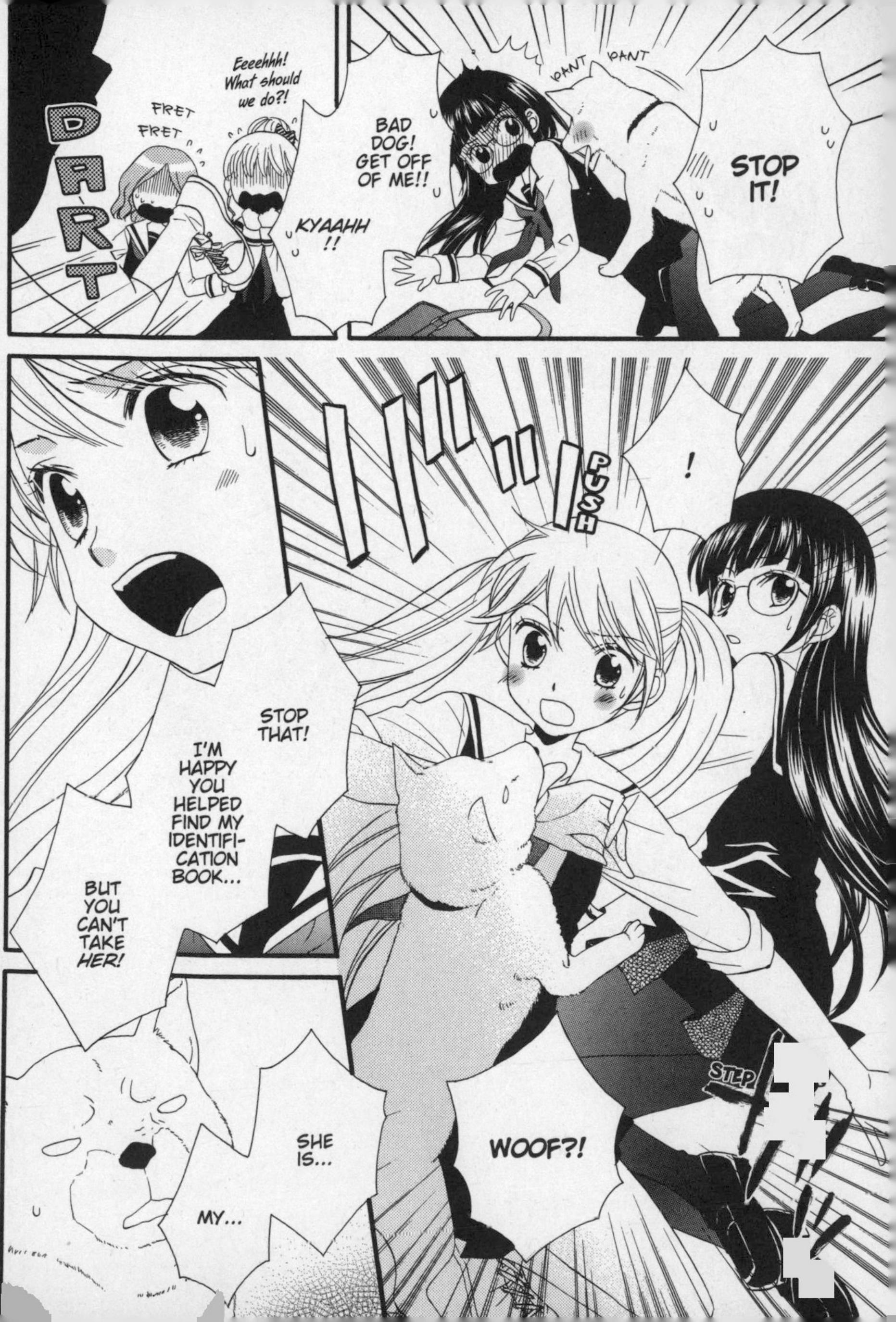
PANT PANT
STOP IT!
BAD DOG! GET OFF OF ME!!
KYAAHH !!
Eeeehhh! What should we do?!
FRET FRET
DART
!
PUSH
STOP THAT!
I'M HAPPY YOU HELPED FIND MY IDENTIFICATION BOOK...
BUT YOU CAN'T TAKE HER!
STEP
WOOF?!
SHE IS...
MY...

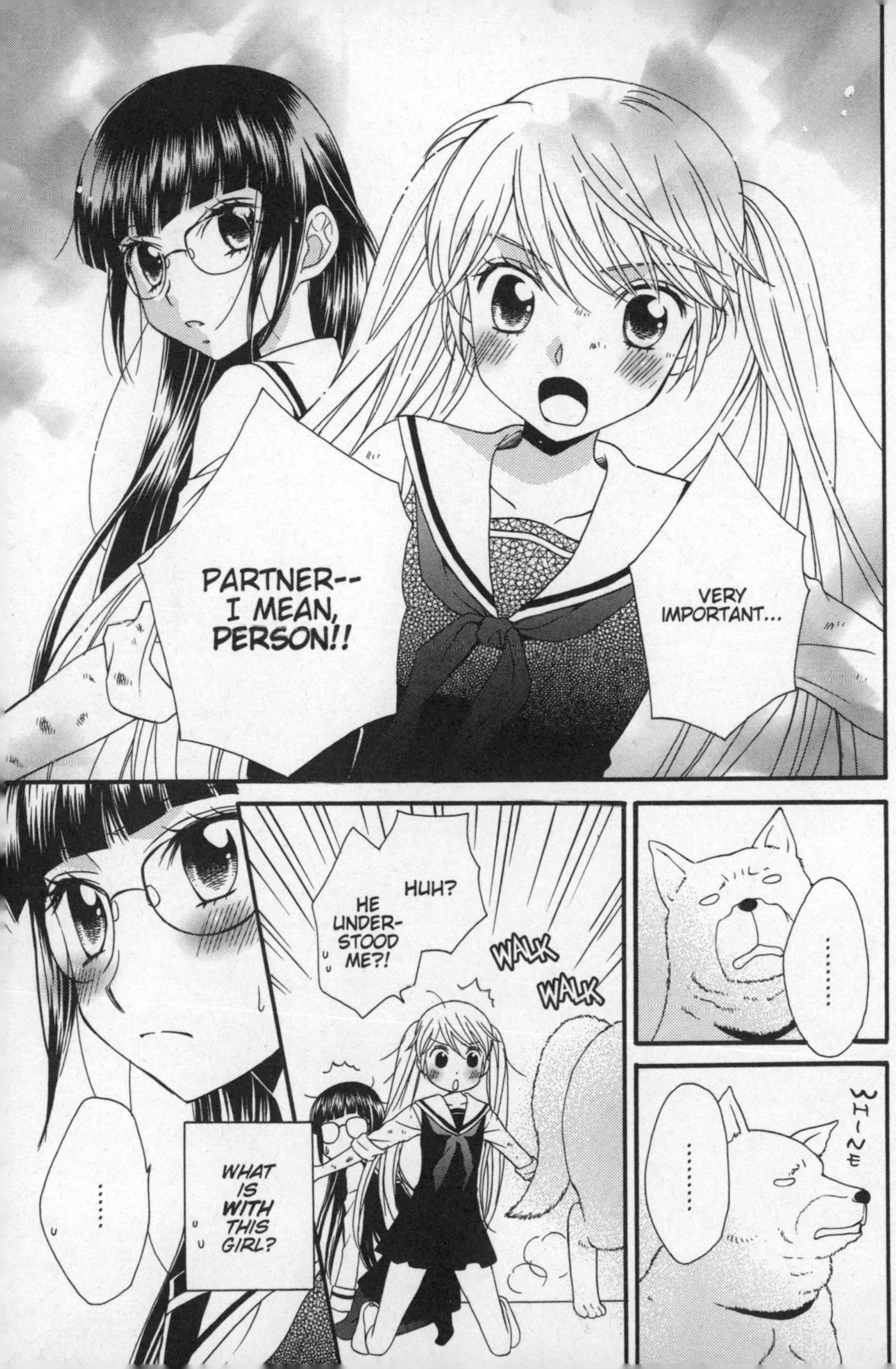
VERY IMPORTANT...
PARTNER-- I MEAN, PERSON!!
......
......
WHINE
HUH?
HE UNDERSTOOD ME?!
WALK
WALK
WHAT IS WITH THIS GIRL?
......

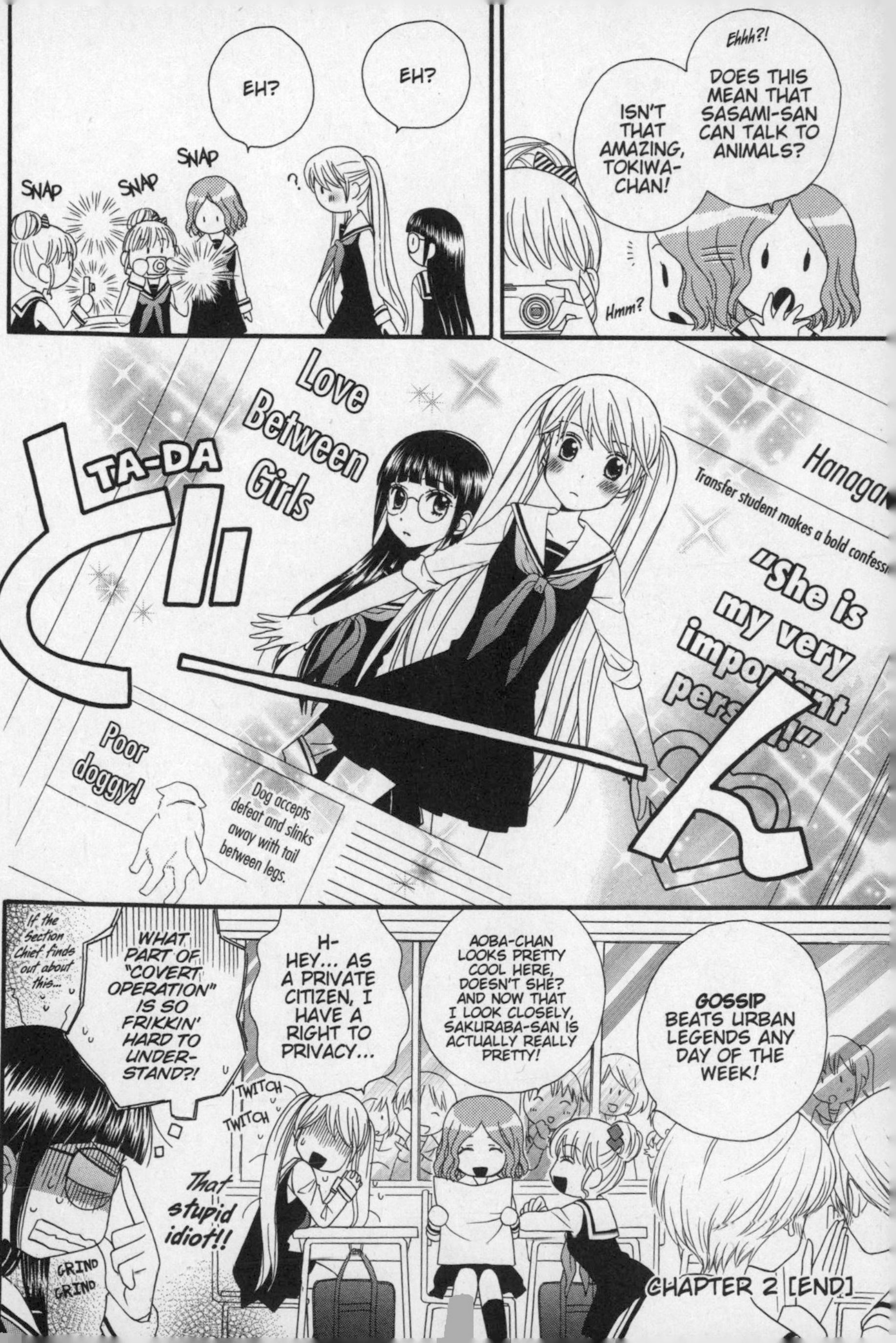
Ehhh?!
DOES THIS MEAN THAT SASAMI-SAN CAN TALK TO ANIMALS?
ISN'T THAT AMAZING, TOKIWA-CHAN!
Hmm?
EH?
EH?
SNAP
SNAP
SNAP
Hanaga
Transfer student makes a bold confess
“She is my very impor
tant
pers
!”
Love Between Girls
TA-DA
Poor doggy!
Dog accepts defeat and slinks away with tail between legs.
GOSSIP BEATS URBAN LEGENDS ANY DAY OF THE WEEK!
AOBA-CHAN LOOKS PRETTY COOL HERE, DOESN'T SHE? AND NOW THAT I LOOK CLOSELY, SAKURABA-SAN IS ACTUALLY REALLY PRETTY!
H- HEY... AS A PRIVATE CITIZEN, I HAVE A RIGHT TO PRIVACY...
WHAT PART OF "COVERT OPERATION" IS SO FRIKKIN' HARD TO UNDER-STAND?!
If the Section Chief finds out about this...
TWITCH
TWITCH
That stupid idiot!!
GRIND
GRIND
CHAPTER 2 [END]

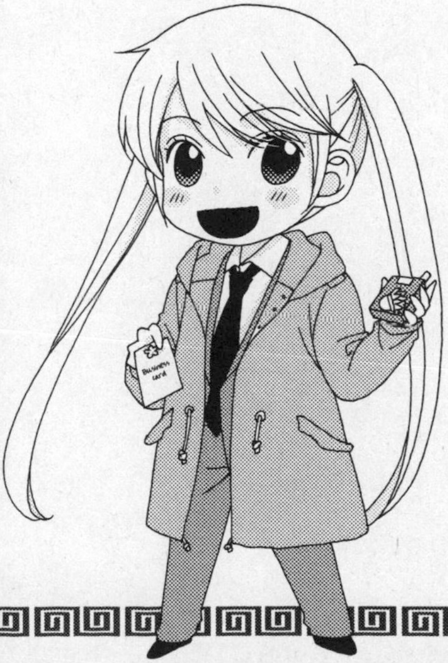
Business card

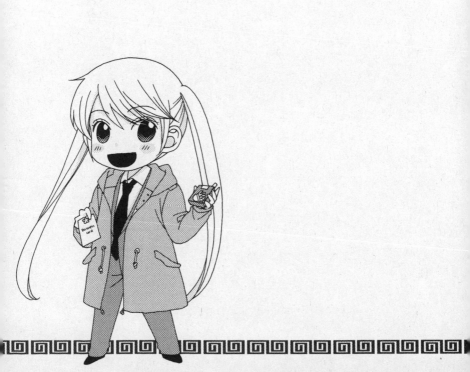

GAKUEN POLIZI

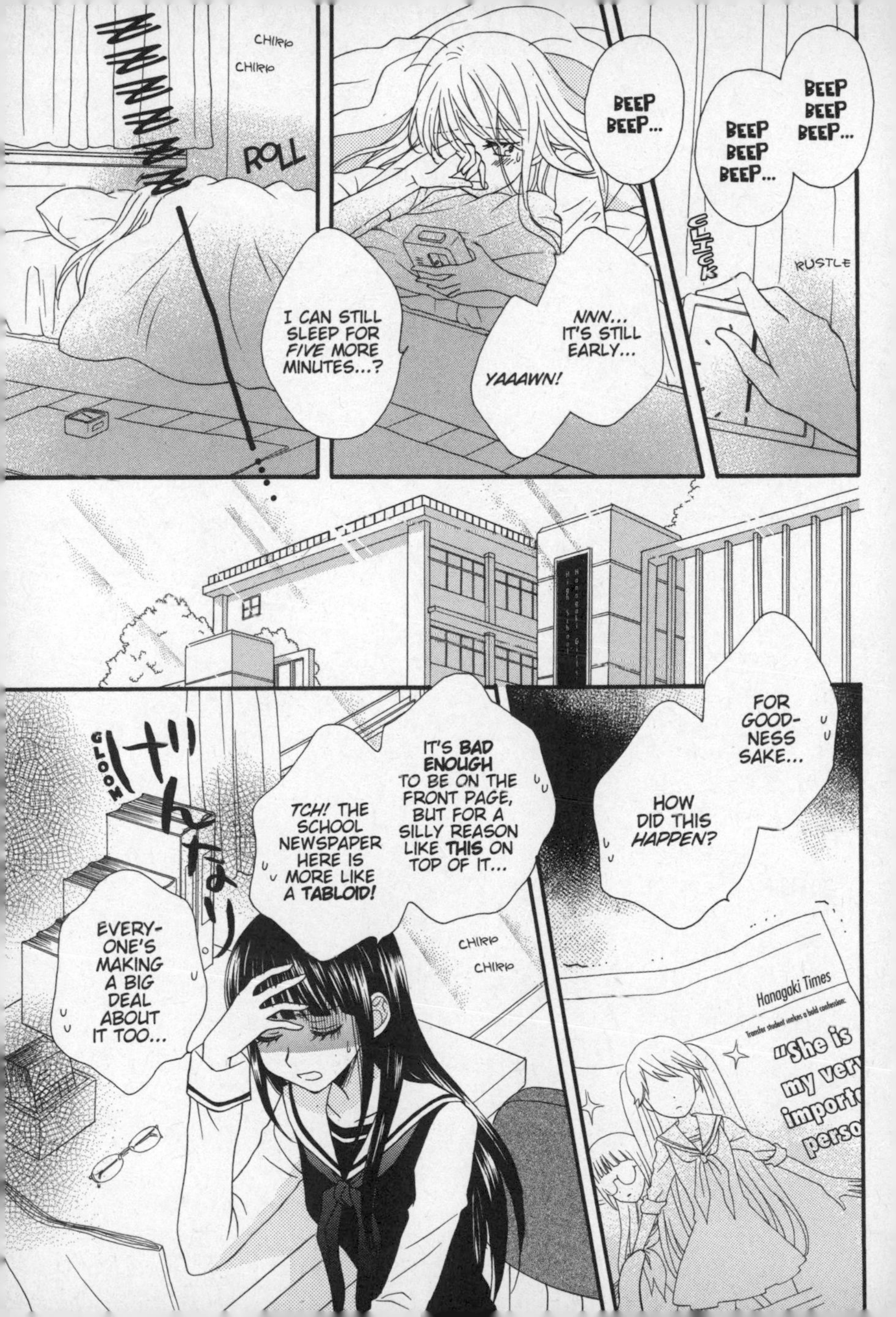
BEEP BEEP...
BEEP BEEP BEEP...
BEEP BEEP BEEP...
CLICK
RUSTLE
NNN... IT'S STILL EARLY...
YAAAWN!
I CAN STILL SLEEP FOR *FIVE* MORE MINUTES...?
CHIRP
CHIRP
ROLL
FOR GOODNESS SAKE...
HOW DID THIS *HAPPEN?*
Hanagaki Times
Transfer student makes a bold confession:
IT'S **BAD ENOUGH** TO BE ON THE FRONT PAGE, BUT FOR A SILLY REASON LIKE **THIS** ON TOP OF IT...
TCH! THE SCHOOL NEWSPAPER HERE IS MORE LIKE A **TABLOID!**
CHIRP
CHIRP
GLOOM
EVERYONE'S MAKING A BIG DEAL ABOUT IT TOO...

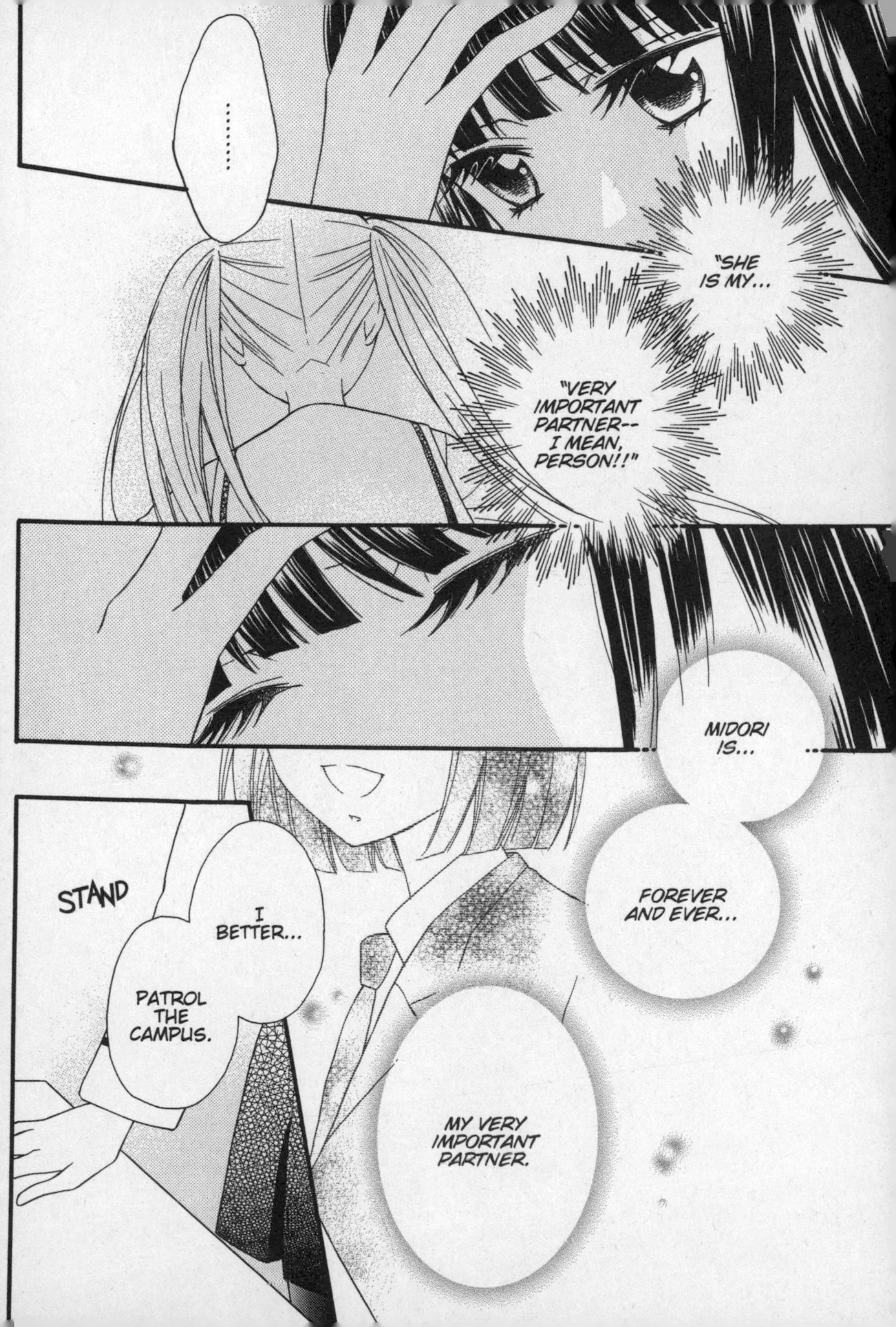
......
"SHE IS MY...
"VERY IMPORTANT PARTNER-- I MEAN, PERSON!!"
MIDORI IS...
FOREVER AND EVER...
MY VERY IMPORTANT PARTNER.
STAND
I BETTER...
PATROL THE CAMPUS.

CHAPTER 3

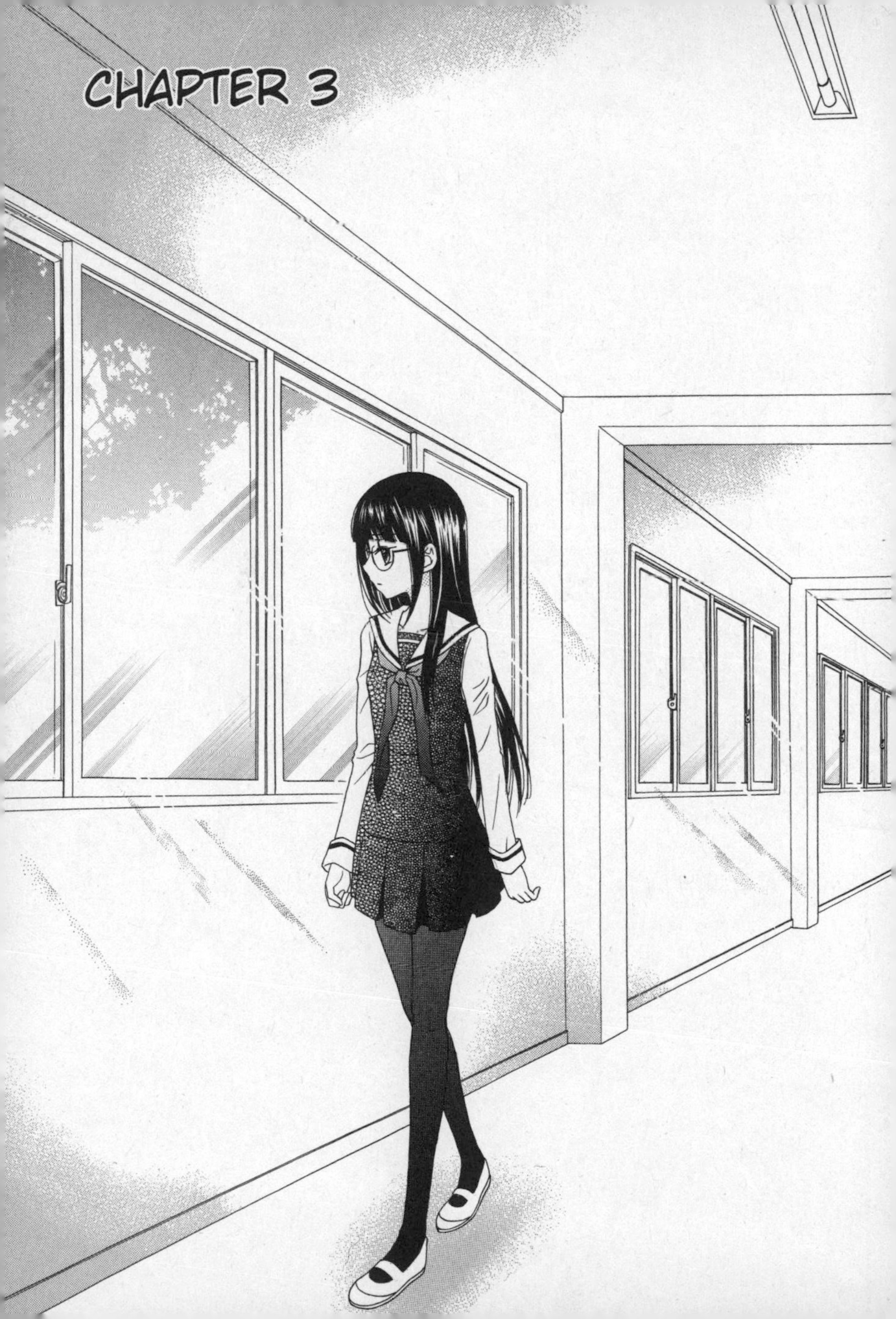

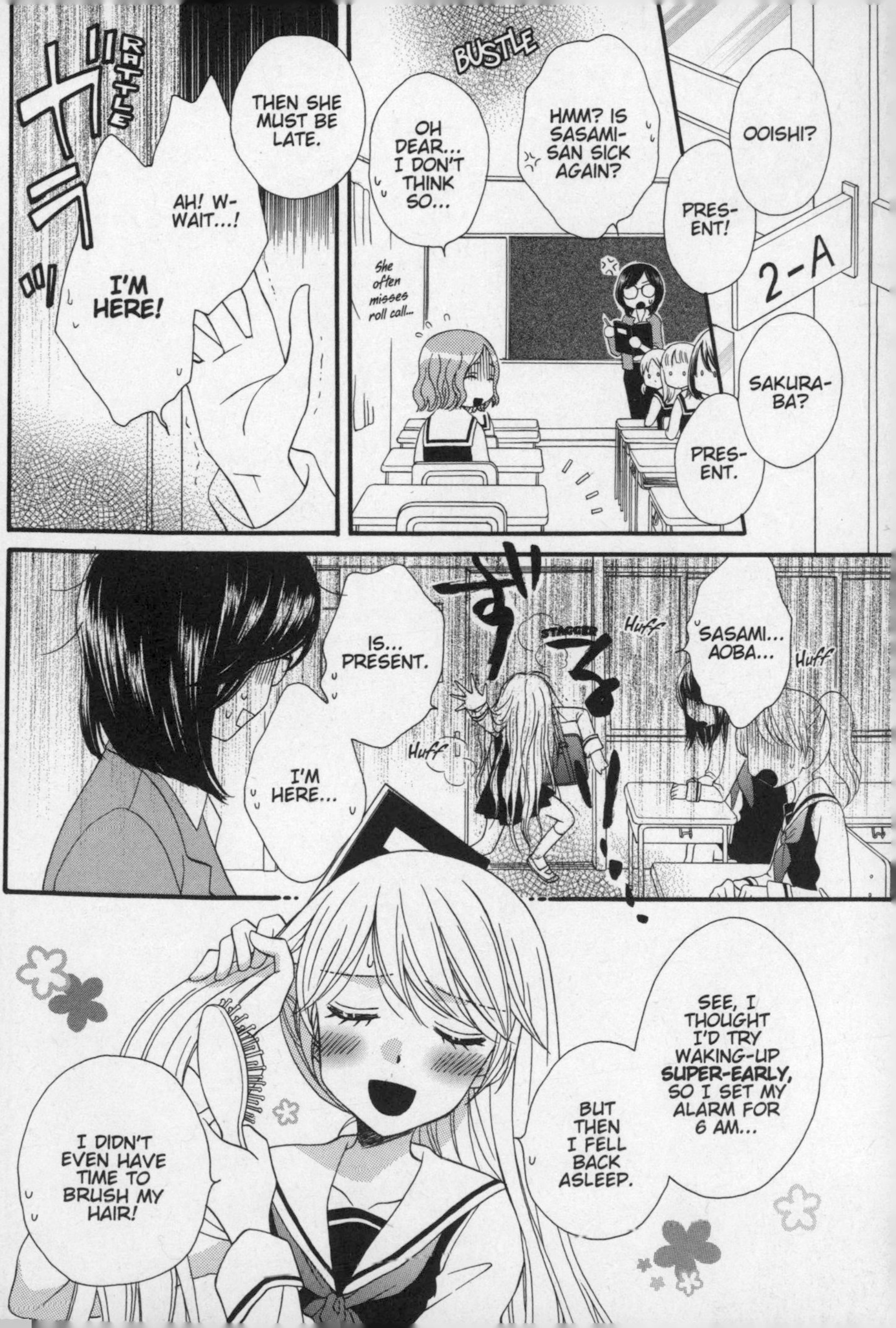

2-A
OOISHI?
PRESENT!
SAKURA-BA?
PRES-ENT.
BUSTLE
HMM? IS SASAMI-SAN SICK AGAIN?
OH DEAR... I DON'T THINK SO...
She often misses roll call...
THEN SHE MUST BE LATE.
RATTLE
AH! W-WAIT...!
I'M HERE!
Huff
SASAMI... AOBA...
Huff
STAGGER
Huff
IS... PRESENT.
I'M HERE...
SEE, I THOUGHT I'D TRY WAKING-UP SUPER-EARLY, SO I SET MY ALARM FOR 6 AM...
BUT THEN I FELL BACK ASLEEP.
I DIDN'T EVEN HAVE TIME TO BRUSH MY HAIR!

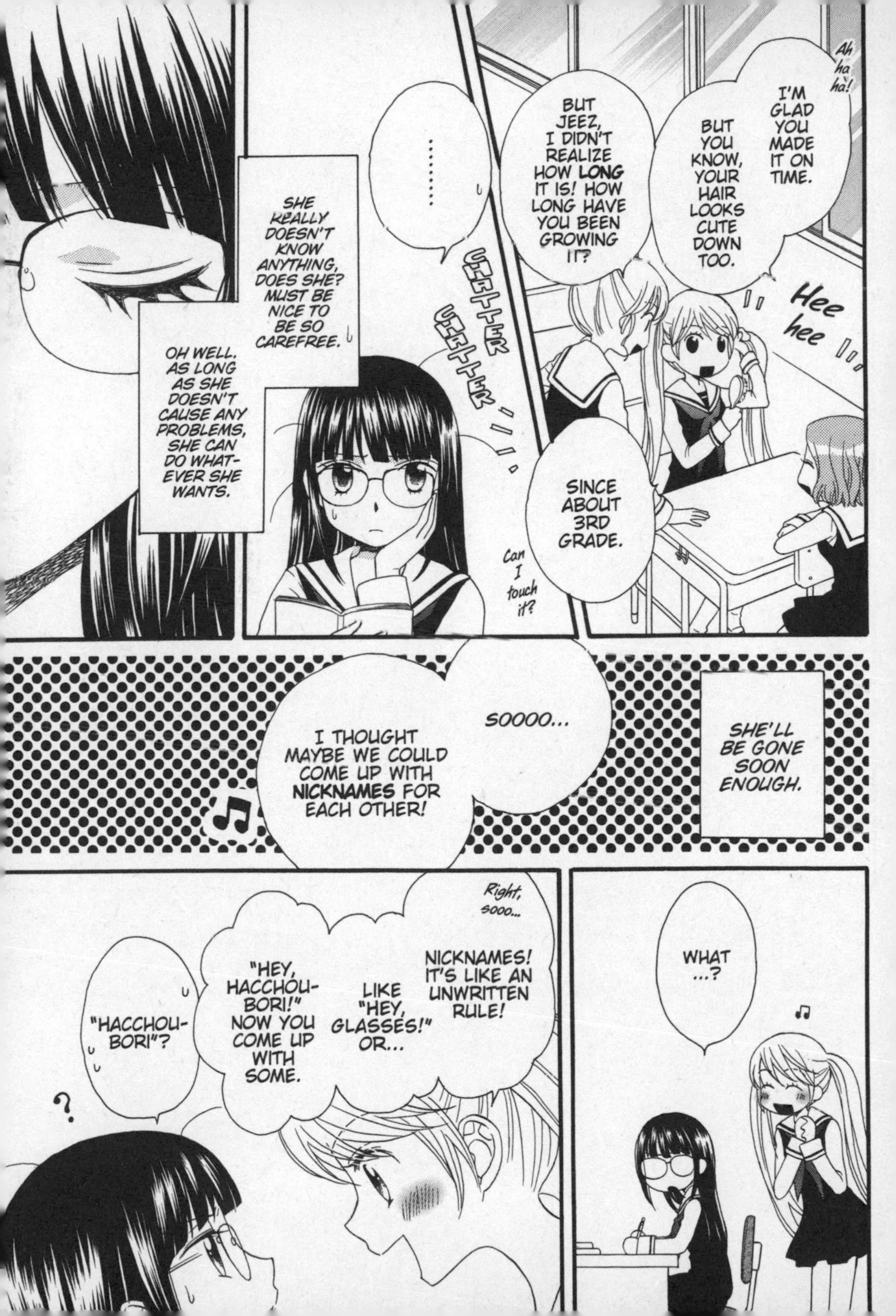
Ah ha ha!
I'M GLAD YOU MADE IT ON TIME.
BUT YOU KNOW, YOUR HAIR LOOKS CUTE DOWN TOO.
BUT JEEZ, I DIDN'T REALIZE HOW LONG IT IS! HOW LONG HAVE YOU BEEN GROWING IT?
Hee hee
SINCE ABOUT 3RD GRADE.
Can I touch it?
......
CHATTER CHATTER
SHE REALLY DOESN'T KNOW ANYTHING, DOES SHE? MUST BE NICE TO BE SO CAREFREE.
OH WELL. AS LONG AS SHE DOESN'T CAUSE ANY PROBLEMS, SHE CAN DO WHAT-EVER SHE WANTS.
SHE'LL BE GONE SOON ENOUGH.
SOOOO...
I THOUGHT MAYBE WE COULD COME UP WITH NICKNAMES FOR EACH OTHER!
WHAT ...?
Right, sooo...
NICKNAMES! IT'S LIKE AN UNWRITTEN RULE!
LIKE "HEY, GLASSES!" OR...
"HEY, HACCHOU-BORI!" NOW YOU COME UP WITH SOME.
"HACCHOU-BORI"?

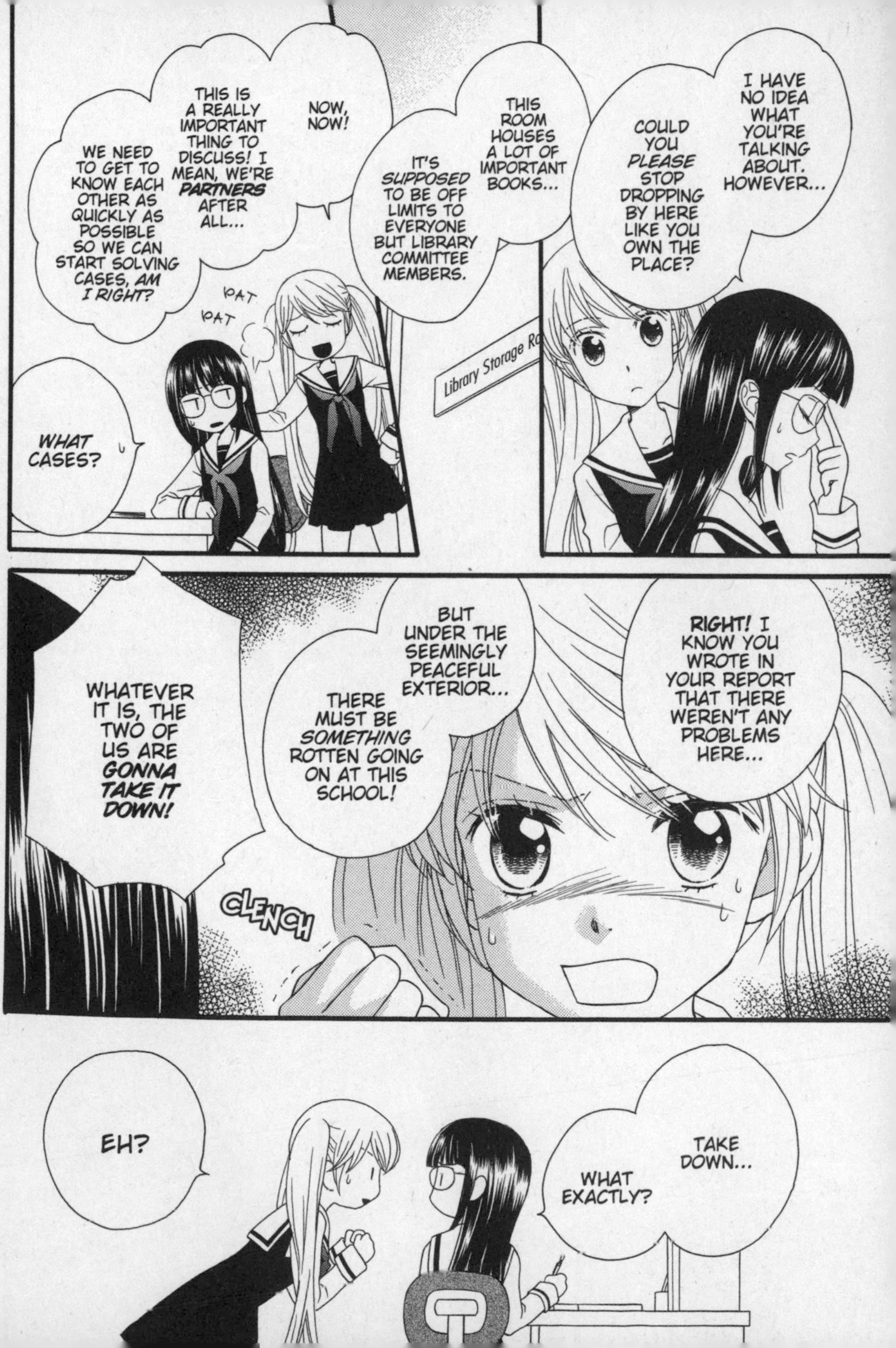
I HAVE NO IDEA WHAT YOU'RE TALKING ABOUT. HOWEVER...
COULD YOU *PLEASE* STOP DROPPING BY HERE LIKE YOU OWN THE PLACE?
THIS ROOM HOUSES A LOT OF IMPORTANT BOOKS...
IT'S *SUPPOSED* TO BE OFF LIMITS TO EVERYONE BUT LIBRARY COMMITTEE MEMBERS.
Library Storage Ro
NOW, NOW!
THIS IS A REALLY IMPORTANT THING TO DISCUSS! I MEAN, WE'RE ***PARTNERS*** AFTER ALL...
WE NEED TO GET TO KNOW EACH OTHER AS QUICKLY AS POSSIBLE SO WE CAN START SOLVING CASES, *AM I RIGHT?*
PAT
PAT
WHAT CASES?
RIGHT! I KNOW YOU WROTE IN YOUR REPORT THAT THERE WEREN'T ANY PROBLEMS HERE...
BUT UNDER THE SEEMINGLY PEACEFUL EXTERIOR...
THERE MUST BE *SOMETHING* ROTTEN GOING ON AT THIS SCHOOL!
CLENCH
WHATEVER IT IS, THE TWO OF US ARE ***GONNA TAKE IT DOWN!***
TAKE DOWN...
WHAT EXACTLY?
EH?

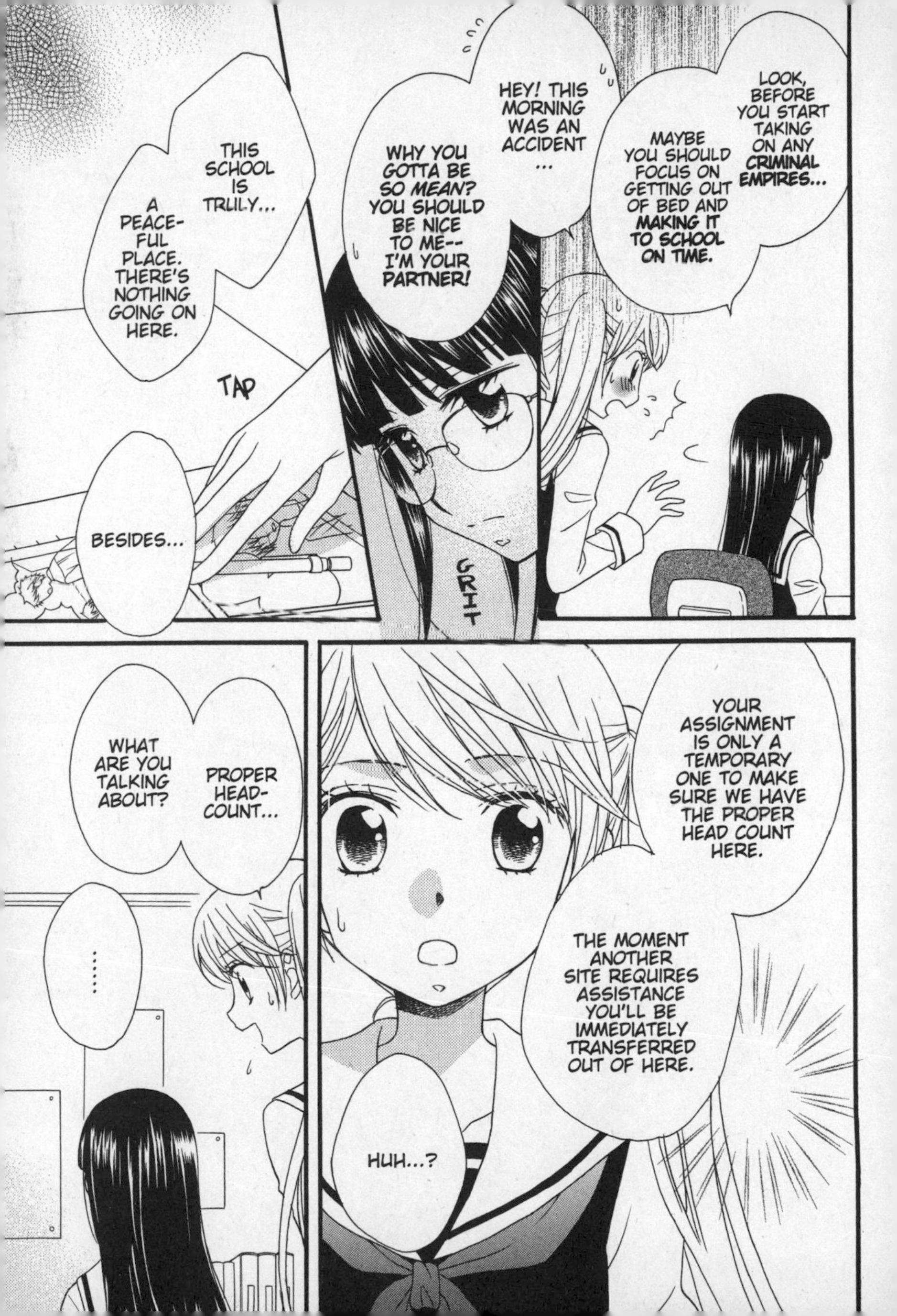
LOOK, BEFORE YOU START TAKING ON ANY **CRIMINAL EMPIRES...**
MAYBE YOU SHOULD FOCUS ON GETTING OUT OF BED AND **MAKING IT TO SCHOOL ON TIME.**
HEY! THIS MORNING WAS AN ACCIDENT ...
WHY YOU GOTTA BE SO *MEAN?* YOU SHOULD BE NICE TO ME-- I'M YOUR PARTNER!
GRIT
THIS SCHOOL IS TRULY...
A PEACE-FUL PLACE. THERE'S NOTHING GOING ON HERE.
TAP
BESIDES...
YOUR ASSIGNMENT IS ONLY A TEMPORARY ONE TO MAKE SURE WE HAVE THE PROPER HEAD COUNT HERE.
THE MOMENT ANOTHER SITE REQUIRES ASSISTANCE YOU'LL BE IMMEDIATELY TRANSFERRED OUT OF HERE.
HUH...?
PROPER HEAD-COUNT...
WHAT ARE YOU TALKING ABOUT?
......

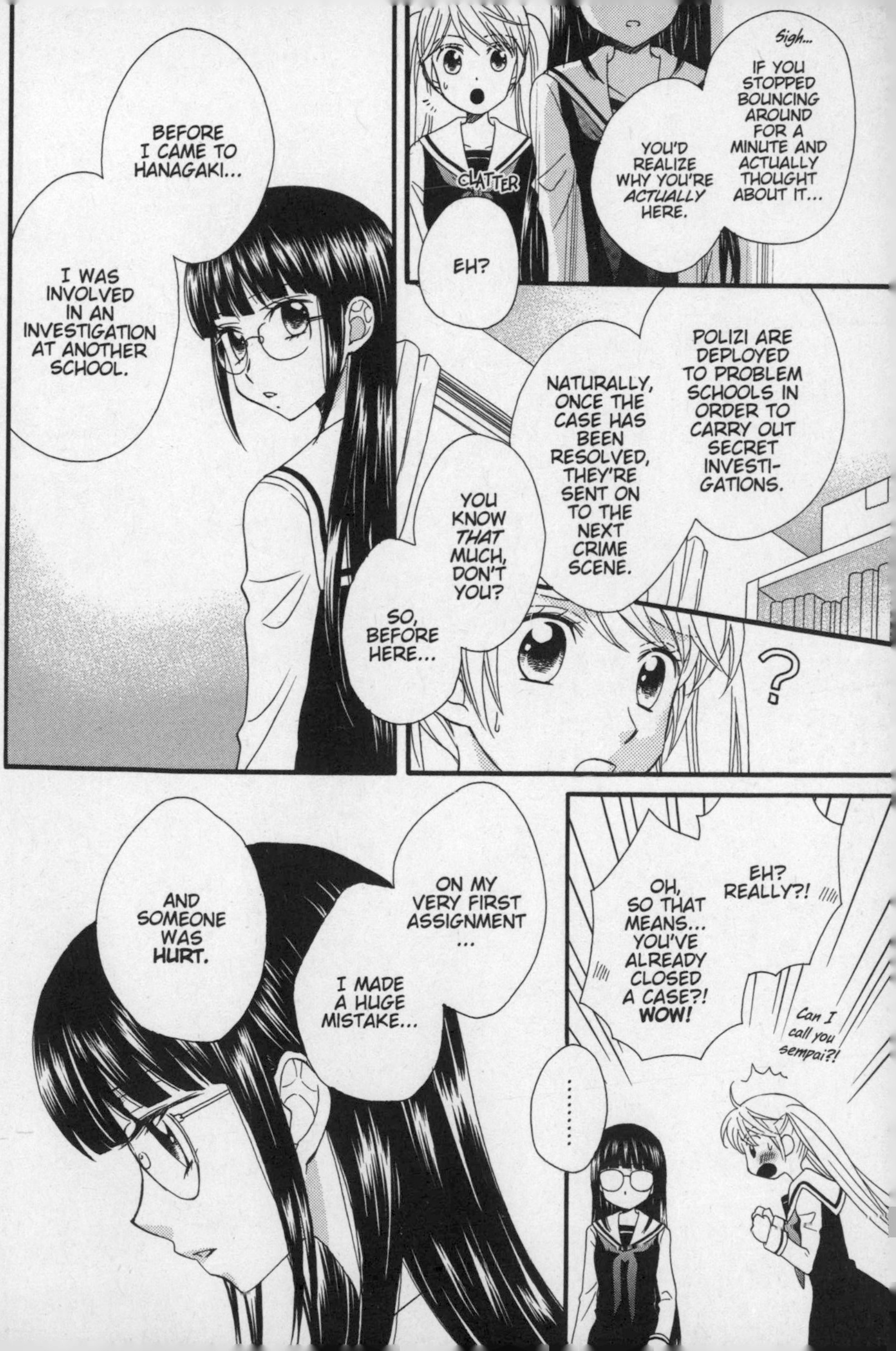
Sigh...
IF YOU STOPPED BOUNCING AROUND FOR A MINUTE AND ACTUALLY THOUGHT ABOUT IT...
YOU'D REALIZE WHY YOU'RE *ACTUALLY* HERE.
CLATTER
EH?
POLIZI ARE DEPLOYED TO PROBLEM SCHOOLS IN ORDER TO CARRY OUT SECRET INVESTI-GATIONS.
NATURALLY, ONCE THE CASE HAS BEEN RESOLVED, THEY'RE SENT ON TO THE NEXT CRIME SCENE.
YOU KNOW *THAT* MUCH, DON'T YOU?
SO, BEFORE HERE...
?
BEFORE I CAME TO HANAGAKI...
I WAS INVOLVED IN AN INVESTIGATION AT ANOTHER SCHOOL.
EH? REALLY?!
OH, SO THAT MEANS... YOU'VE ALREADY CLOSED A CASE?! **WOW!**
Can I call you sempai?!
......
ON MY VERY FIRST ASSIGNMENT ...
I MADE A HUGE MISTAKE...
AND SOMEONE WAS **HURT.**

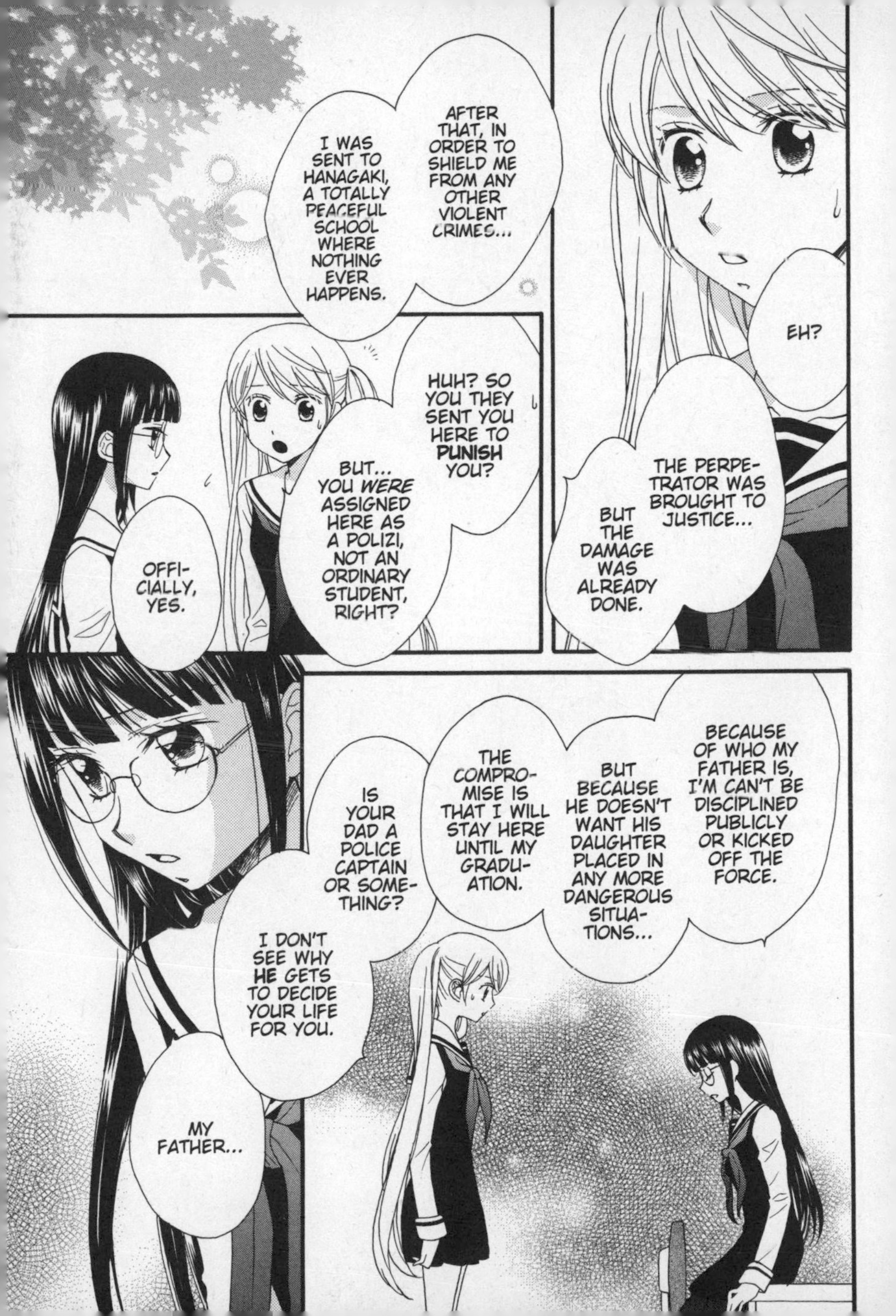
EH?
THE PERPE-TRATOR WAS BROUGHT TO JUSTICE...
BUT THE DAMAGE WAS ALREADY DONE.
AFTER THAT, IN ORDER TO SHIELD ME FROM ANY OTHER VIOLENT CRIMES...
I WAS SENT TO HANAGAKI, A TOTALLY PEACEFUL SCHOOL WHERE NOTHING EVER HAPPENS.
HUH? SO YOU THEY SENT YOU HERE TO PUNISH YOU?
BUT... YOU WERE ASSIGNED HERE AS A POLIZI, NOT AN ORDINARY STUDENT, RIGHT?
OFFI-CIALLY, YES.
BECAUSE OF WHO MY FATHER IS, I'M CAN'T BE DISCIPLINED PUBLICLY OR KICKED OFF THE FORCE.
BUT BECAUSE HE DOESN'T WANT HIS DAUGHTER PLACED IN ANY MORE DANGEROUS SITUA-TIONS...
THE COMPRO-MISE IS THAT I WILL STAY HERE UNTIL MY GRADU-ATION.
IS YOUR DAD A POLICE CAPTAIN OR SOME-THING?
I DON'T SEE WHY HE GETS TO DECIDE YOUR LIFE FOR YOU.
MY FATHER...

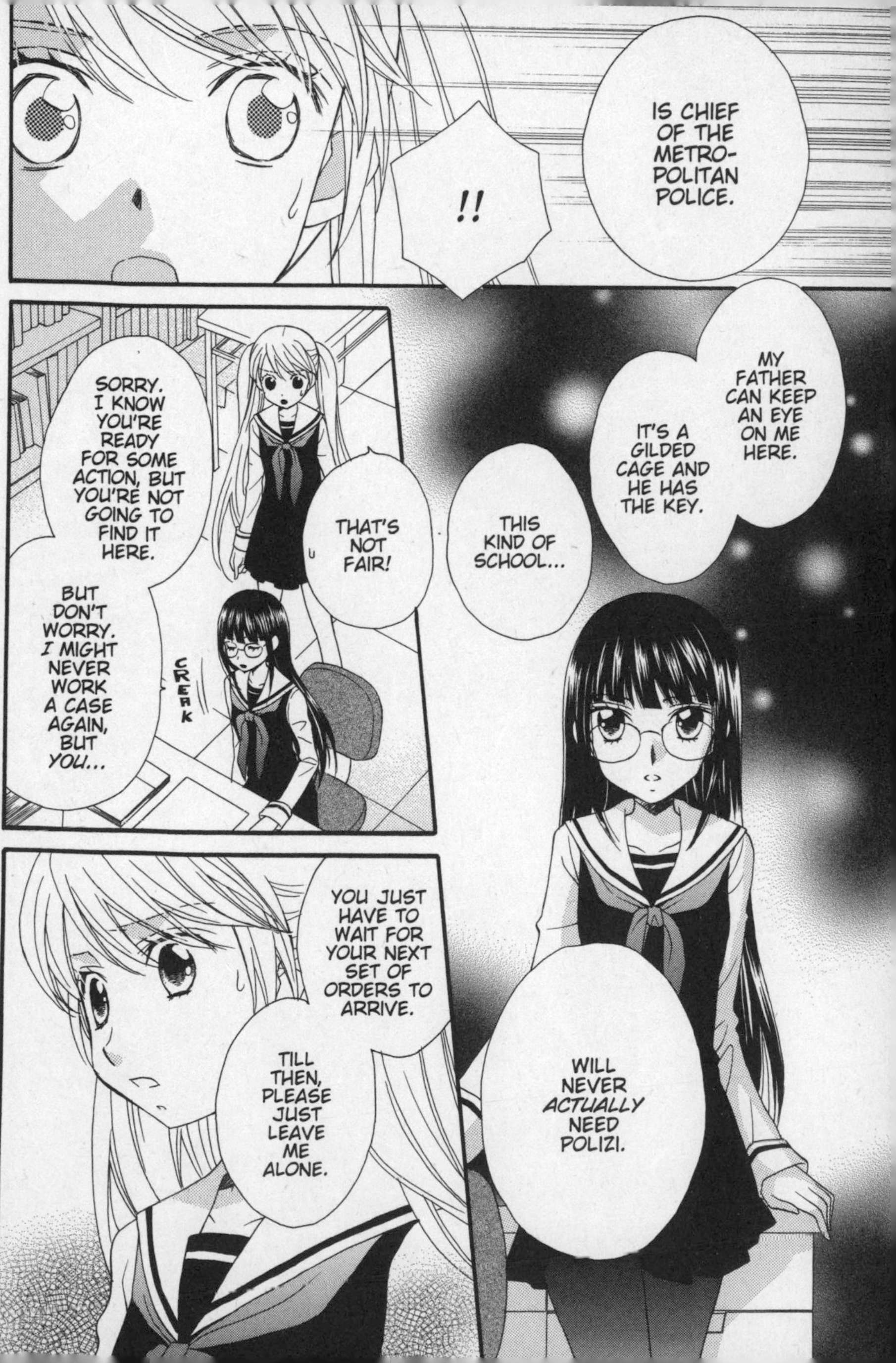
IS CHIEF OF THE METRO-POLITAN POLICE.
!!
MY FATHER CAN KEEP AN EYE ON ME HERE.
IT'S A GILDED CAGE AND HE HAS THE KEY.
THIS KIND OF SCHOOL...
WILL NEVER *ACTUALLY* NEED POLIZI.
THAT'S NOT FAIR!
SORRY. I KNOW YOU'RE READY FOR SOME ACTION, BUT YOU'RE NOT GOING TO FIND IT HERE.
CREAK
BUT DON'T WORRY. *I* MIGHT NEVER WORK A CASE AGAIN, BUT *YOU*...
YOU JUST HAVE TO WAIT FOR YOUR NEXT SET OF ORDERS TO ARRIVE.
TILL THEN, PLEASE JUST LEAVE ME ALONE.

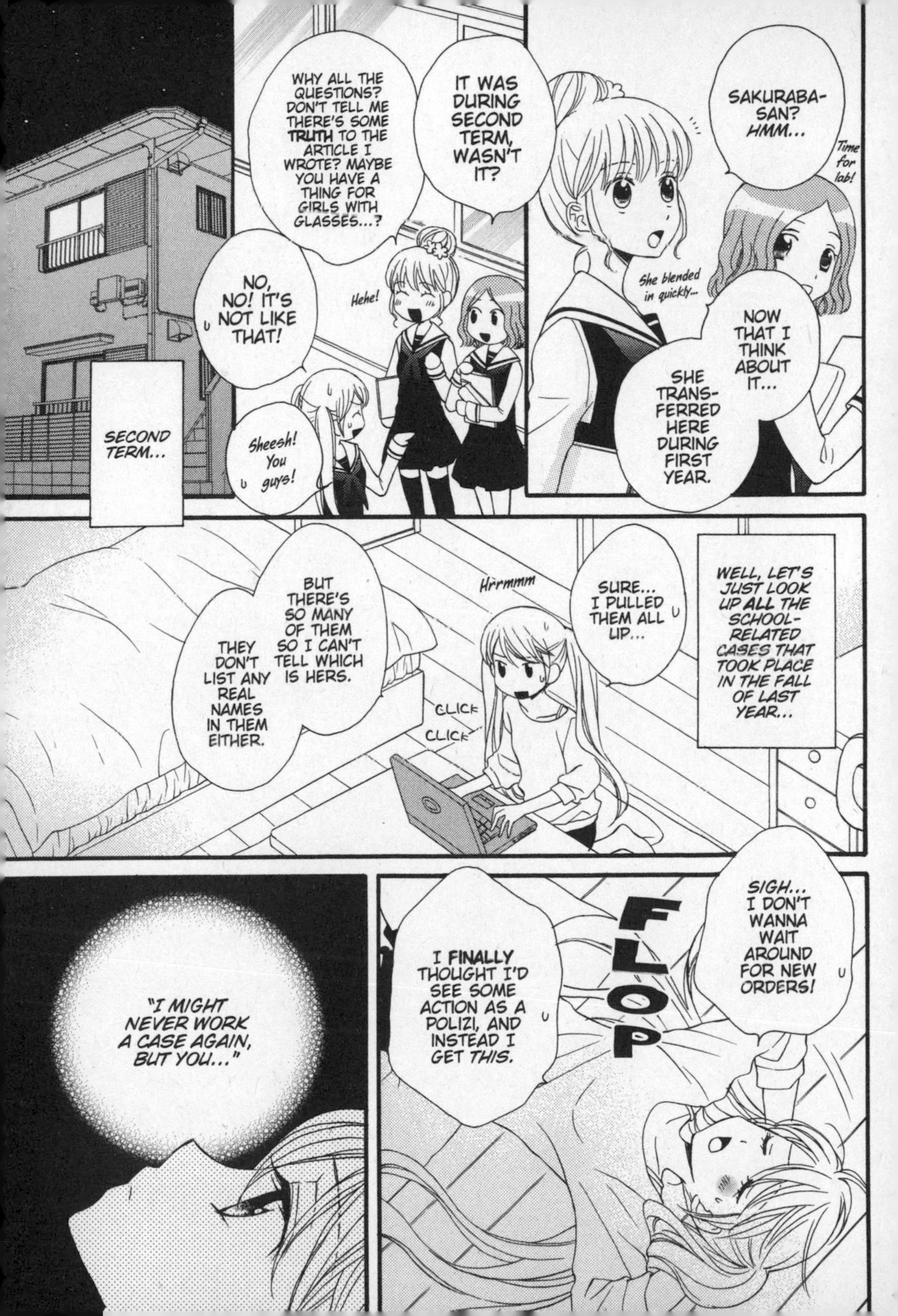
SAKURABA-SAN? HMM...
Time for lab!
She blended in quickly...
NOW THAT I THINK ABOUT IT...
SHE TRANSFERRED HERE DURING FIRST YEAR.
IT WAS DURING SECOND TERM, WASN'T IT?
WHY ALL THE QUESTIONS? DON'T TELL ME THERE'S SOME TRUTH TO THE ARTICLE I WROTE? MAYBE YOU HAVE A THING FOR GIRLS WITH GLASSES...?
Hehe!
NO, NO! IT'S NOT LIKE THAT!
Sheesh! You guys!
SECOND TERM...
WELL, LET'S JUST LOOK UP ALL THE SCHOOL-RELATED CASES THAT TOOK PLACE IN THE FALL OF LAST YEAR...
SURE... I PULLED THEM ALL UP...
Hrrmmm
BUT THERE'S SO MANY OF THEM SO I CAN'T TELL WHICH IS HERS.
THEY DON'T LIST ANY REAL NAMES IN THEM EITHER.
CLICK
CLICK
SIGH... I DON'T WANNA WAIT AROUND FOR NEW ORDERS!
FLOP
I FINALLY THOUGHT I'D SEE SOME ACTION AS A POLIZI, AND INSTEAD I GET THIS.
"I MIGHT NEVER WORK A CASE AGAIN, BUT YOU..."

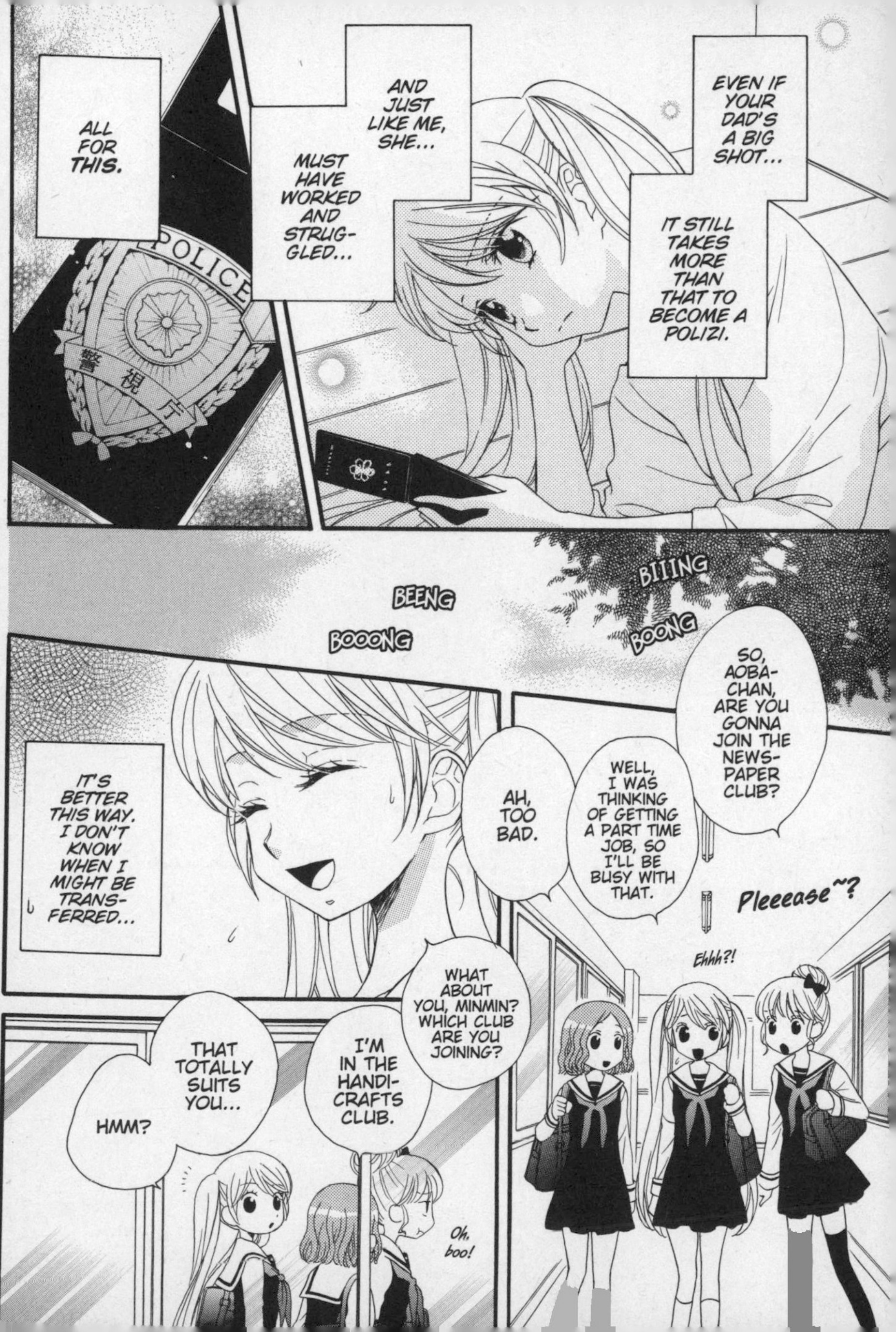
EVEN IF YOUR DAD'S A BIG SHOT...
IT STILL TAKES MORE THAN THAT TO BECOME A POLIZI.
AND JUST LIKE ME, SHE...
MUST HAVE WORKED AND STRUG-GLED...
ALL FOR THIS.
BIIING
BOONG
BEENG
BOOONG
SO, AOBA-CHAN, ARE YOU GONNA JOIN THE NEWS-PAPER CLUB?
Pleeease~?
WELL, I WAS THINKING OF GETTING A PART TIME JOB, SO I'LL BE BUSY WITH THAT.
Ehhh?!
AH, TOO BAD.
IT'S BETTER THIS WAY. I DON'T KNOW WHEN I MIGHT BE TRANS-FERRED...
WHAT ABOUT YOU, MINMIN? WHICH CLUB ARE YOU JOINING?
I'M IN THE HANDI-CRAFTS CLUB.
Oh, boo!
THAT TOTALLY SUITS YOU...
HMM?

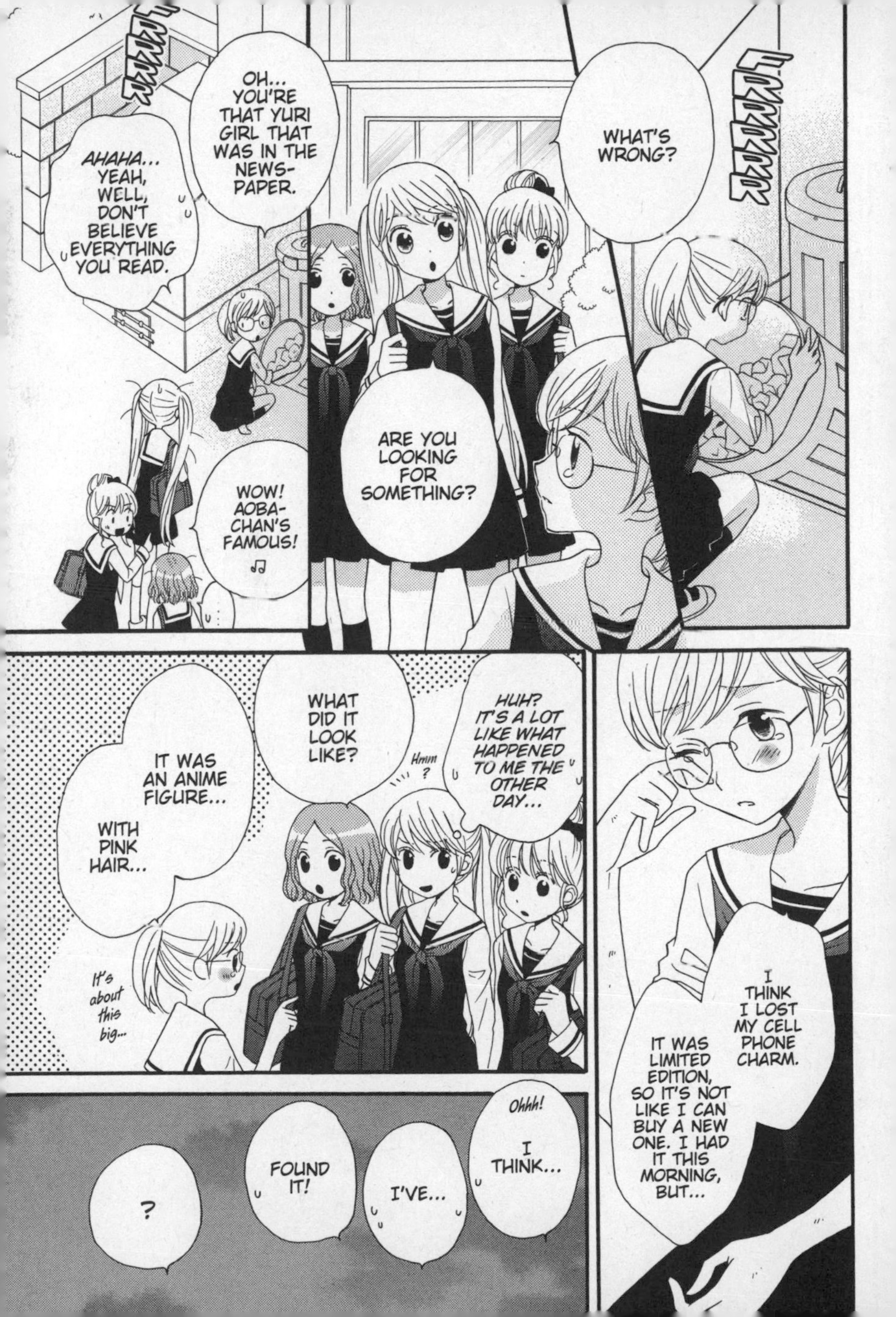
WHAT'S WRONG?
ARE YOU LOOKING FOR SOMETHING?
OH... YOU'RE THAT YURI GIRL THAT WAS IN THE NEWS-PAPER.
AHAHA... YEAH, WELL, DON'T BELIEVE EVERYTHING YOU READ.
WOW! AOBA-CHAN'S FAMOUS! ♫
I THINK I LOST MY CELL PHONE CHARM.
IT WAS LIMITED EDITION, SO IT'S NOT LIKE I CAN BUY A NEW ONE. I HAD IT THIS MORNING, BUT...
WHAT DID IT LOOK LIKE?
IT WAS AN ANIME FIGURE...
WITH PINK HAIR...
It's about this big...
Hmm ?
HUH? IT'S A LOT LIKE WHAT HAPPENED TO ME THE OTHER DAY...
Ohhh!
I THINK...
I'VE...
FOUND IT!
?

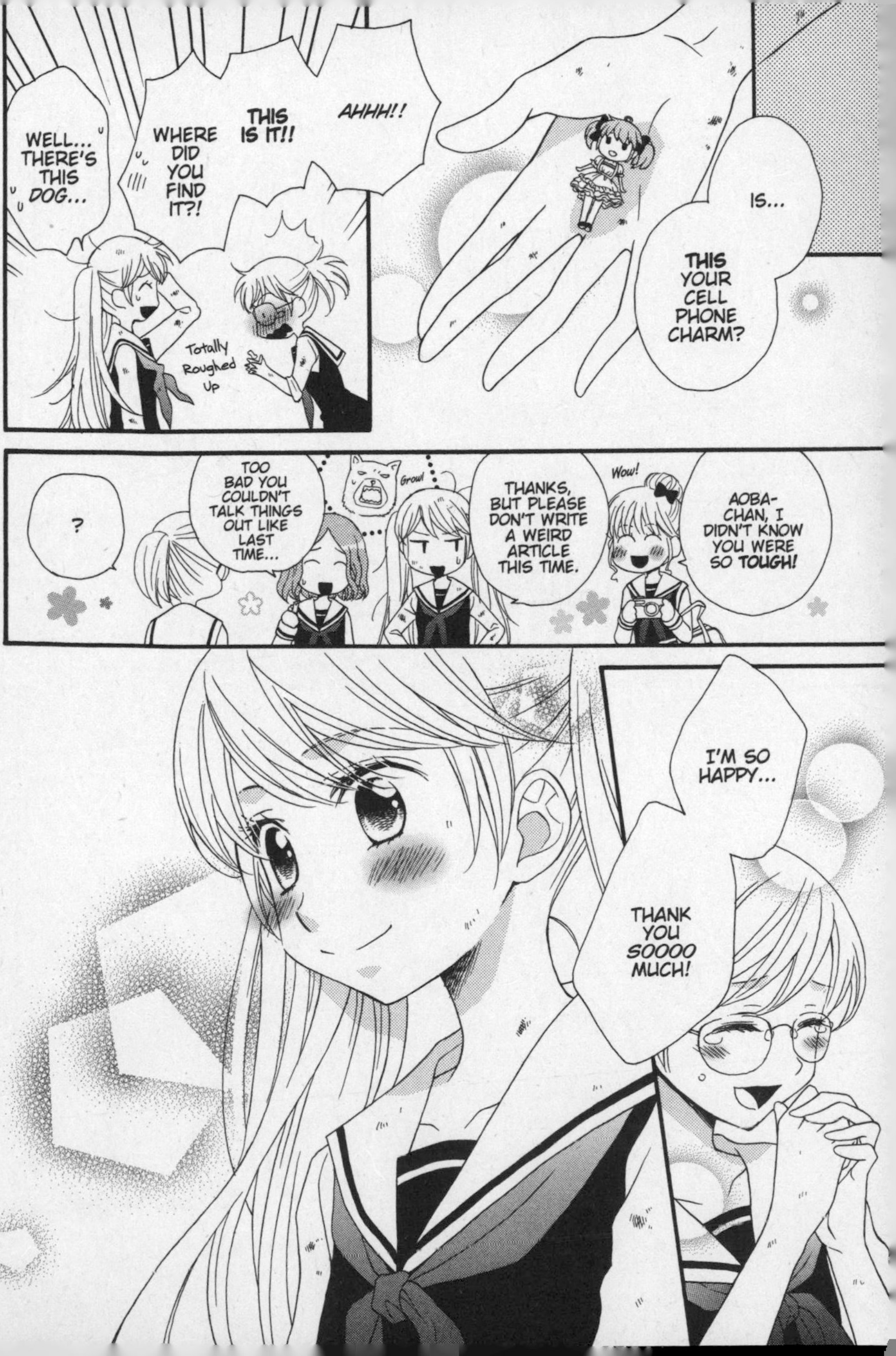
IS...
THIS YOUR CELL PHONE CHARM?
AHHH!!
THIS IS IT!!
WHERE DID YOU FIND IT?!
WELL... THERE'S THIS DOG...
Totally Roughed Up
AOBA-CHAN, I DIDN'T KNOW YOU WERE SO TOUGH!
Wow!
THANKS, BUT PLEASE DON'T WRITE A WEIRD ARTICLE THIS TIME.
Growl
TOO BAD YOU COULDN'T TALK THINGS OUT LIKE LAST TIME...
?
I'M SO HAPPY...
THANK YOU SOOOO MUCH!

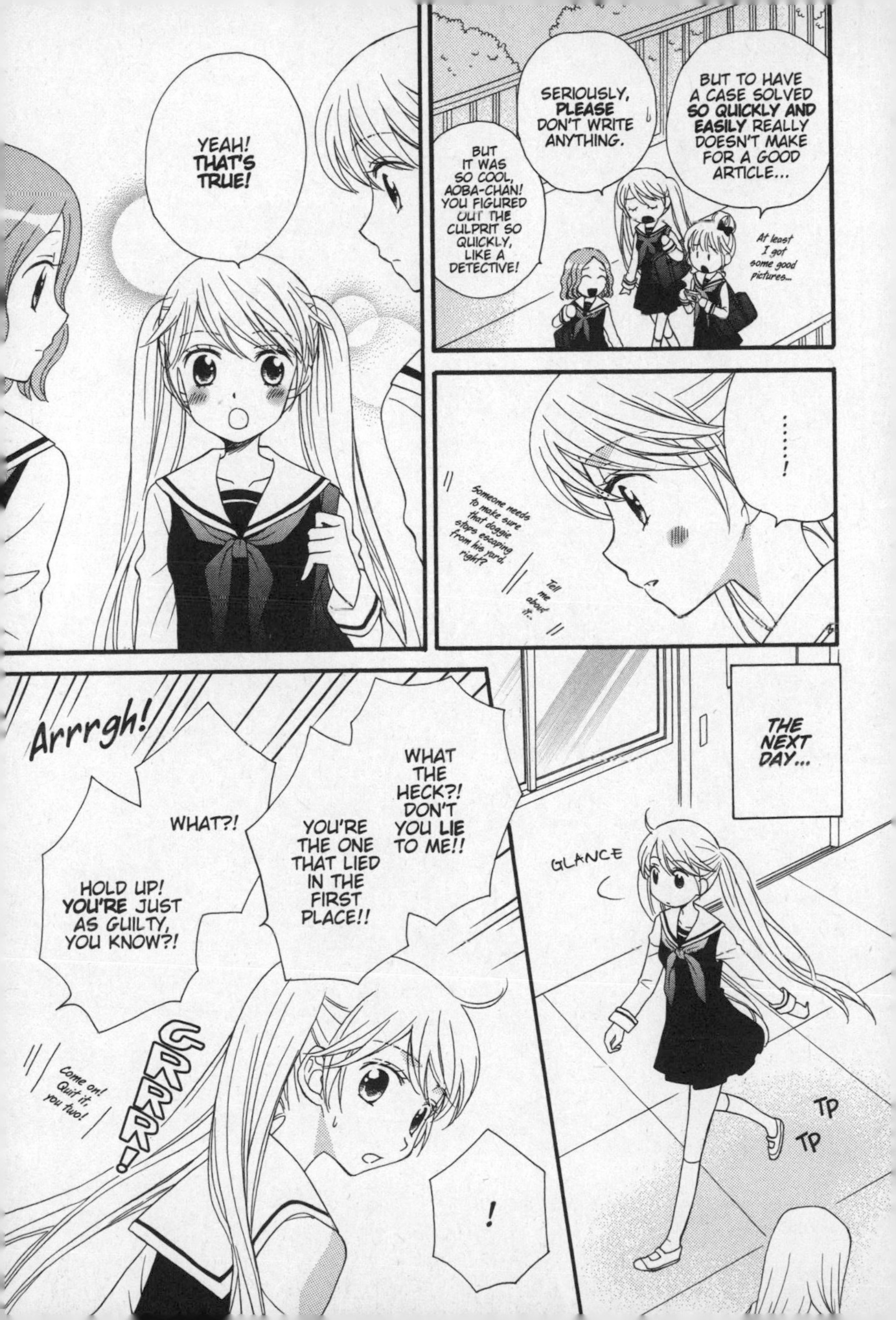
BUT TO HAVE A CASE SOLVED SO QUICKLY AND EASILY REALLY DOESN'T MAKE FOR A GOOD ARTICLE...
SERIOUSLY, PLEASE DON'T WRITE ANYTHING.
BUT IT WAS SO COOL, AOBA-CHAN! YOU FIGURED OUT THE CULPRIT SO QUICKLY, LIKE A DETECTIVE!
At least I got some good pictures...
......!
Someone needs to make sure that doggie stops escaping from his yard, right?
Tell me about it...
YEAH! THAT'S TRUE!
THE NEXT DAY...
GLANCE
TP TP
WHAT THE HECK?! DON'T YOU LIE TO ME!!
YOU'RE THE ONE THAT LIED IN THE FIRST PLACE!!
WHAT?!
HOLD UP! YOU'RE JUST AS GUILTY, YOU KNOW?!
Arrrgh!
!
GRRR!
Come on! Quit it, you two!

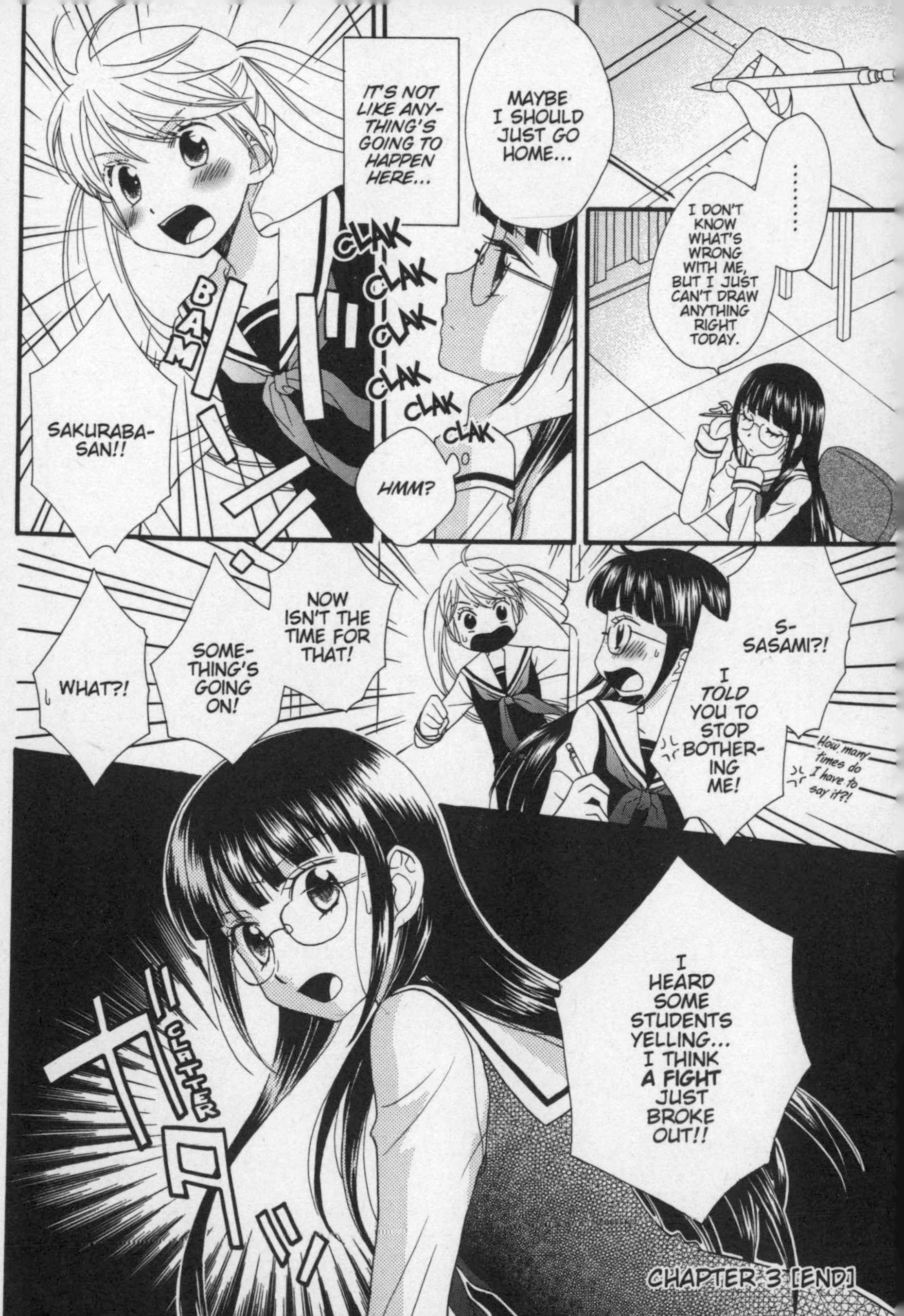
......
I DON'T KNOW WHAT'S WRONG WITH ME, BUT I JUST CAN'T DRAW ANYTHING RIGHT TODAY.
MAYBE I SHOULD JUST GO HOME...
IT'S NOT LIKE ANYTHING'S GOING TO HAPPEN HERE...
CLAK CLAK CLAK CLAK CLAK CLAK
HMM?
BAM
SAKURABA-SAN!!
S-SASAMI?!
I TOLD YOU TO STOP BOTHERING ME!
How many times do I have to say it?!
NOW ISN'T THE TIME FOR THAT!
SOMETHING'S GOING ON!
WHAT?!
I HEARD SOME STUDENTS YELLING... I THINK A FIGHT JUST BROKE OUT!!
CLATTER
CHAPTER 3 [END]

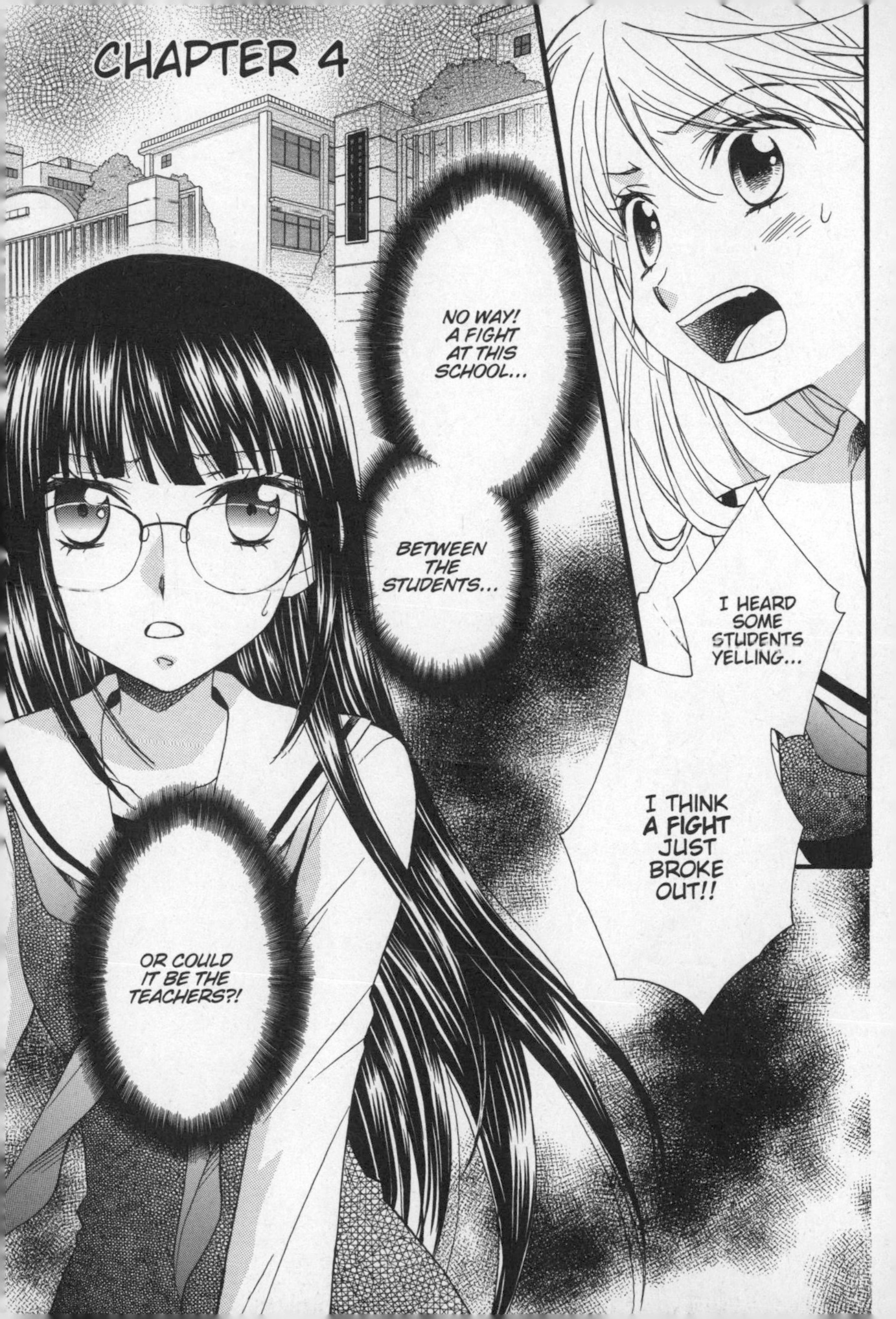
CHAPTER 4
I HEARD SOME STUDENTS YELLING...
I THINK A FIGHT JUST BROKE OUT!!
NO WAY! A FIGHT AT THIS SCHOOL...
BETWEEN THE STUDENTS...
OR COULD IT BE THE TEACHERS?!

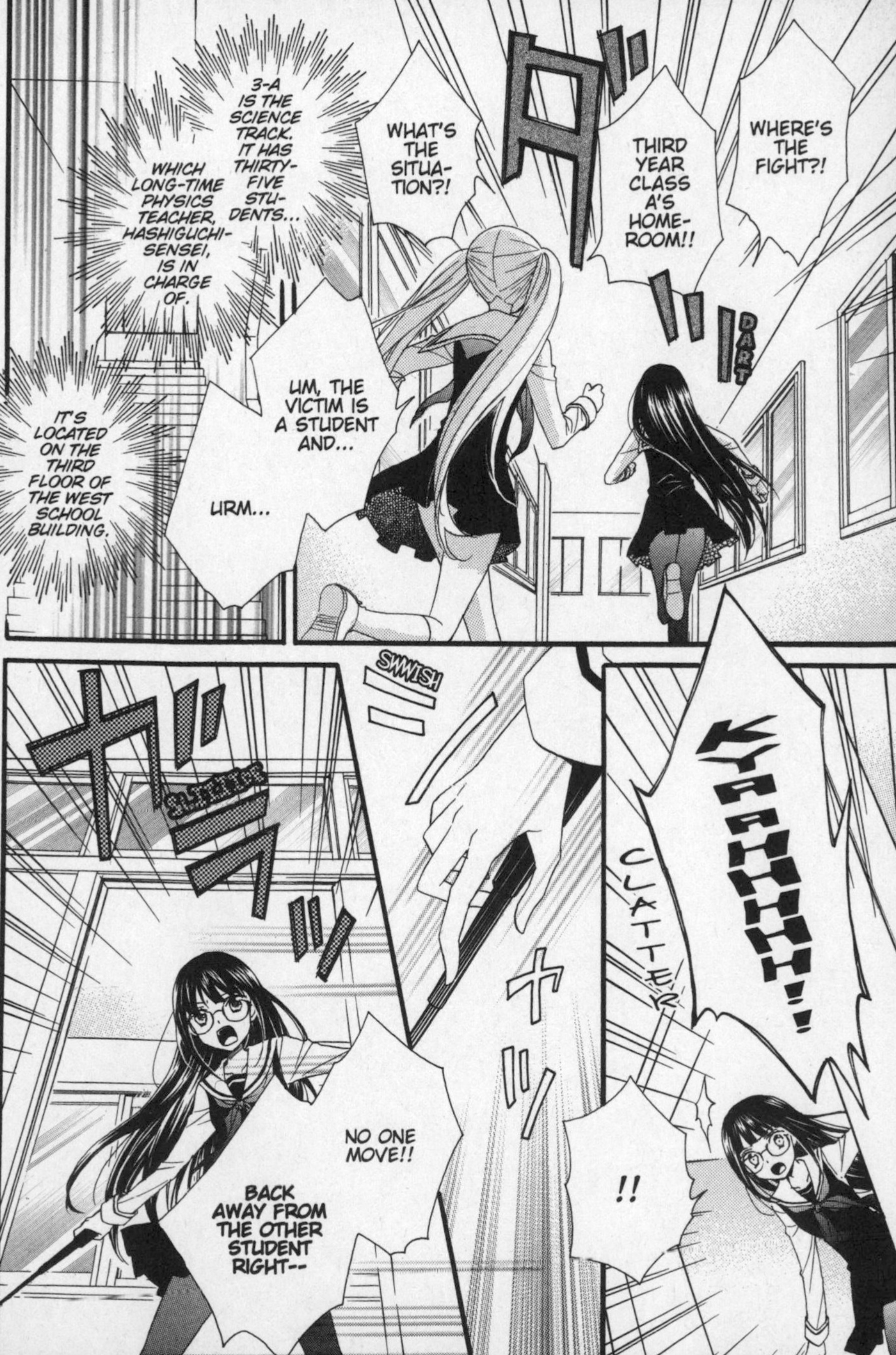
WHERE'S THE FIGHT?!
THIRD YEAR CLASS A'S HOME-ROOM!!
WHAT'S THE SITUA-TION?!
DART
UM, THE VICTIM IS A STUDENT AND...
URM...
3-A IS THE SCIENCE TRACK. IT HAS THIRTY-FIVE STU-DENTS...
WHICH LONG-TIME PHYSICS TEACHER, HASHIGUCHI-SENSEI, IS IN CHARGE OF.
IT'S LOCATED ON THE THIRD FLOOR OF THE WEST SCHOOL BUILDING.
KYAAAHHH!!
CLATTER
!!
SWISH
NO ONE MOVE!!
BACK AWAY FROM THE OTHER STUDENT RIGHT--

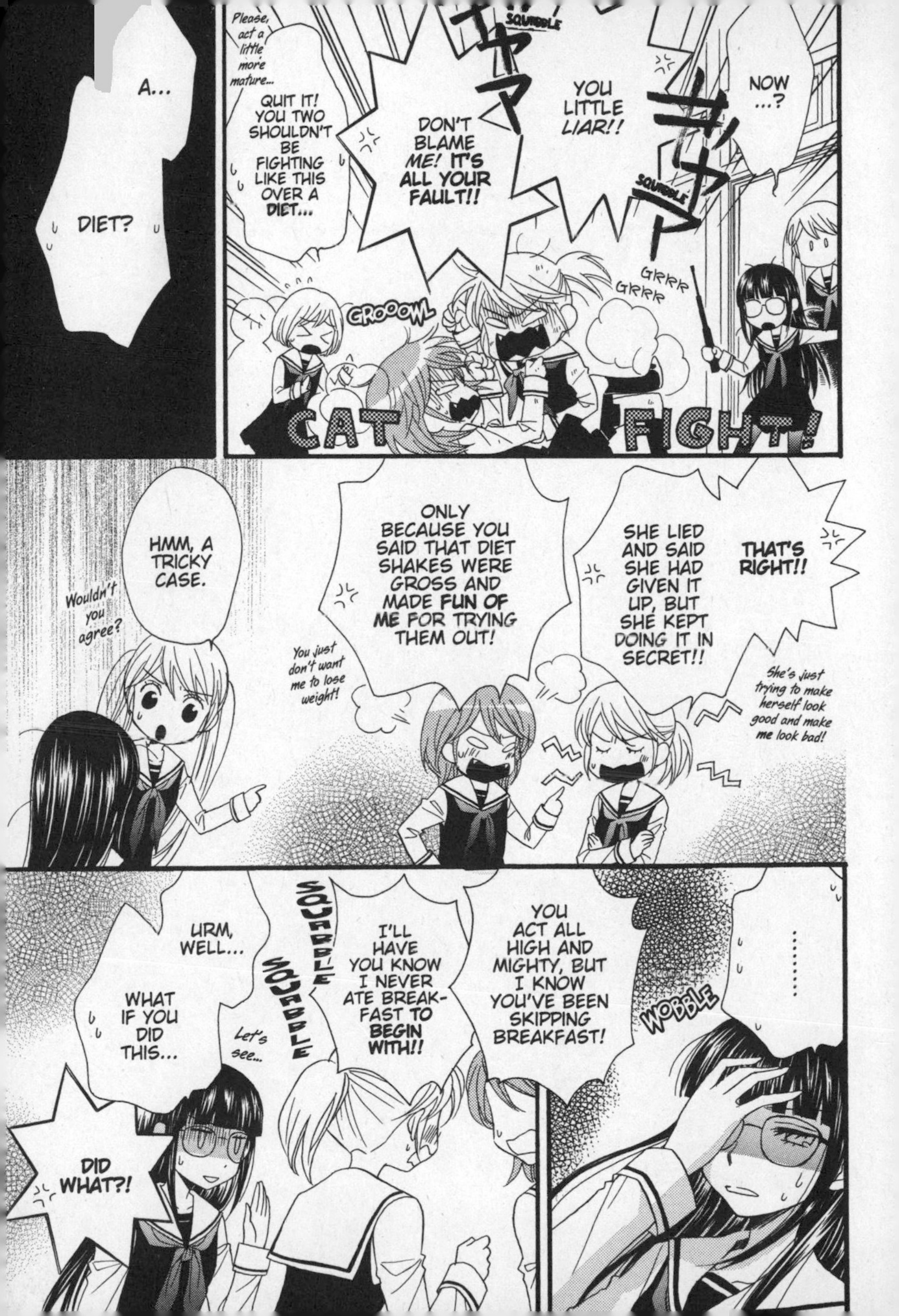
NOW...?
YOU LITTLE LIAR!!
SQUABBLE
SQUABBLE
DON'T BLAME ME! IT'S ALL YOUR FAULT!!
Please, act a little more mature...
QUIT IT! YOU TWO SHOULDN'T BE FIGHTING LIKE THIS OVER A DIET...
GRRR GRRR
GROOOWL
CAT FIGHT!
A...
DIET?
THAT'S RIGHT!!
SHE LIED AND SAID SHE HAD GIVEN IT UP, BUT SHE KEPT DOING IT IN SECRET!!
She's just trying to make herself look good and make me look bad!
ONLY BECAUSE YOU SAID THAT DIET SHAKES WERE GROSS AND MADE FUN OF ME FOR TRYING THEM OUT!
You just don't want me to lose weight!
HMM, A TRICKY CASE.
Wouldn't you agree?
....
WOBBLE
YOU ACT ALL HIGH AND MIGHTY, BUT I KNOW YOU'VE BEEN SKIPPING BREAKFAST!
I'LL HAVE YOU KNOW I NEVER ATE BREAK-FAST TO BEGIN WITH!!
SQUABBLE
SQUABBLE
Let's see...
URM, WELL...
WHAT IF YOU DID THIS...
DID WHAT?!

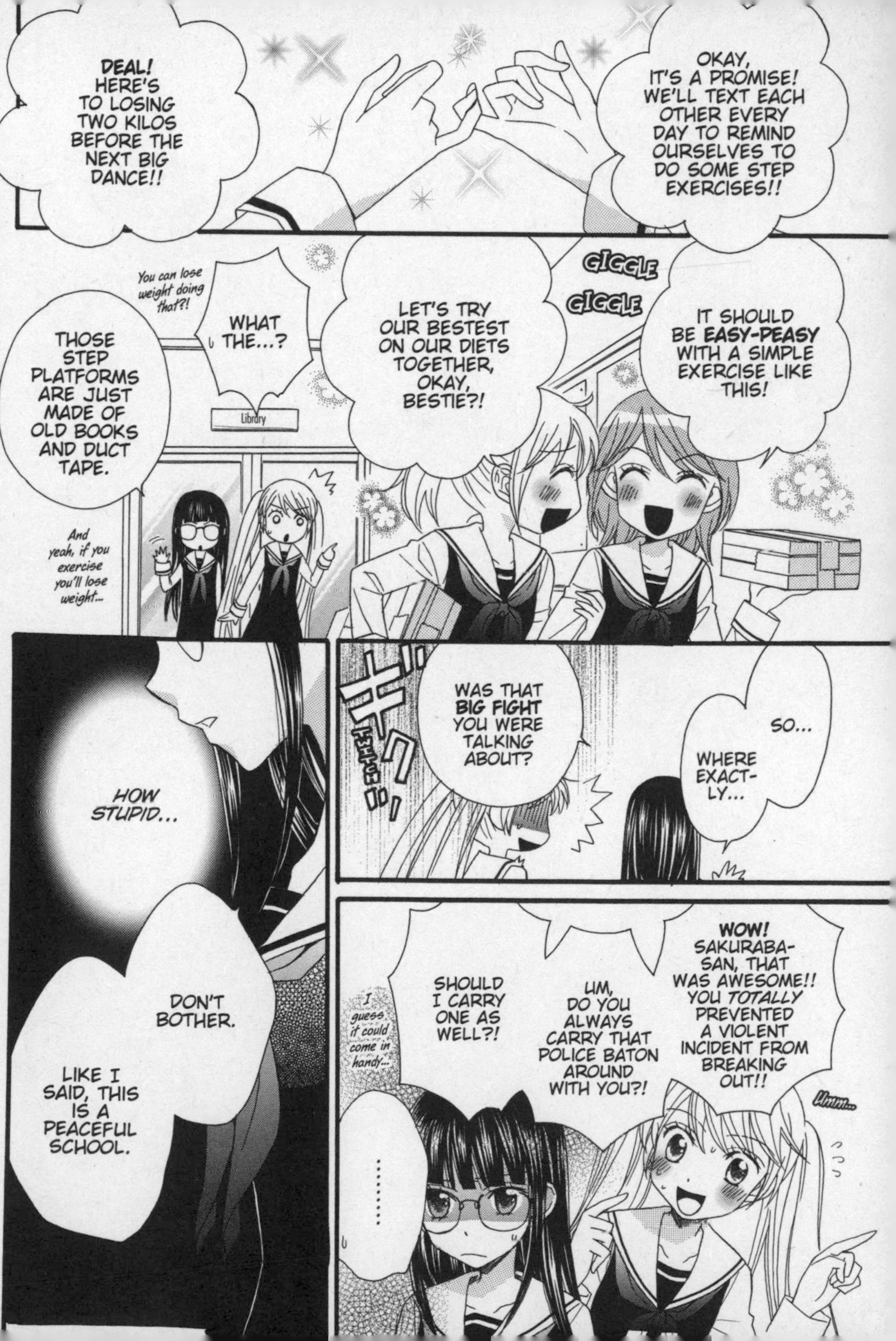
OKAY, IT'S A PROMISE! WE'LL TEXT EACH OTHER EVERY DAY TO REMIND OURSELVES TO DO SOME STEP EXERCISES!!
DEAL! HERE'S TO LOSING TWO KILOS BEFORE THE NEXT BIG DANCE!!
IT SHOULD BE EASY-PEASY WITH A SIMPLE EXERCISE LIKE THIS!
GIGGLE
GIGGLE
LET'S TRY OUR BESTEST ON OUR DIETS TOGETHER, OKAY, BESTIE?!
WHAT THE...?
You can lose weight doing that?!
THOSE STEP PLATFORMS ARE JUST MADE OF OLD BOOKS AND DUCT TAPE.
Library
And yeah, if you exercise you'll lose weight...
SO... WHERE EXACTLY...
WAS THAT BIG FIGHT YOU WERE TALKING ABOUT?
WOW! SAKURABA-SAN, THAT WAS AWESOME!! YOU TOTALLY PREVENTED A VIOLENT INCIDENT FROM BREAKING OUT!!
UM, DO YOU ALWAYS CARRY THAT POLICE BATON AROUND WITH YOU?!
SHOULD I CARRY ONE AS WELL?!
Ummm...
I guess it could come in handy...
......
HOW STUPID...
DON'T BOTHER.
LIKE I SAID, THIS IS A PEACEFUL SCHOOL.

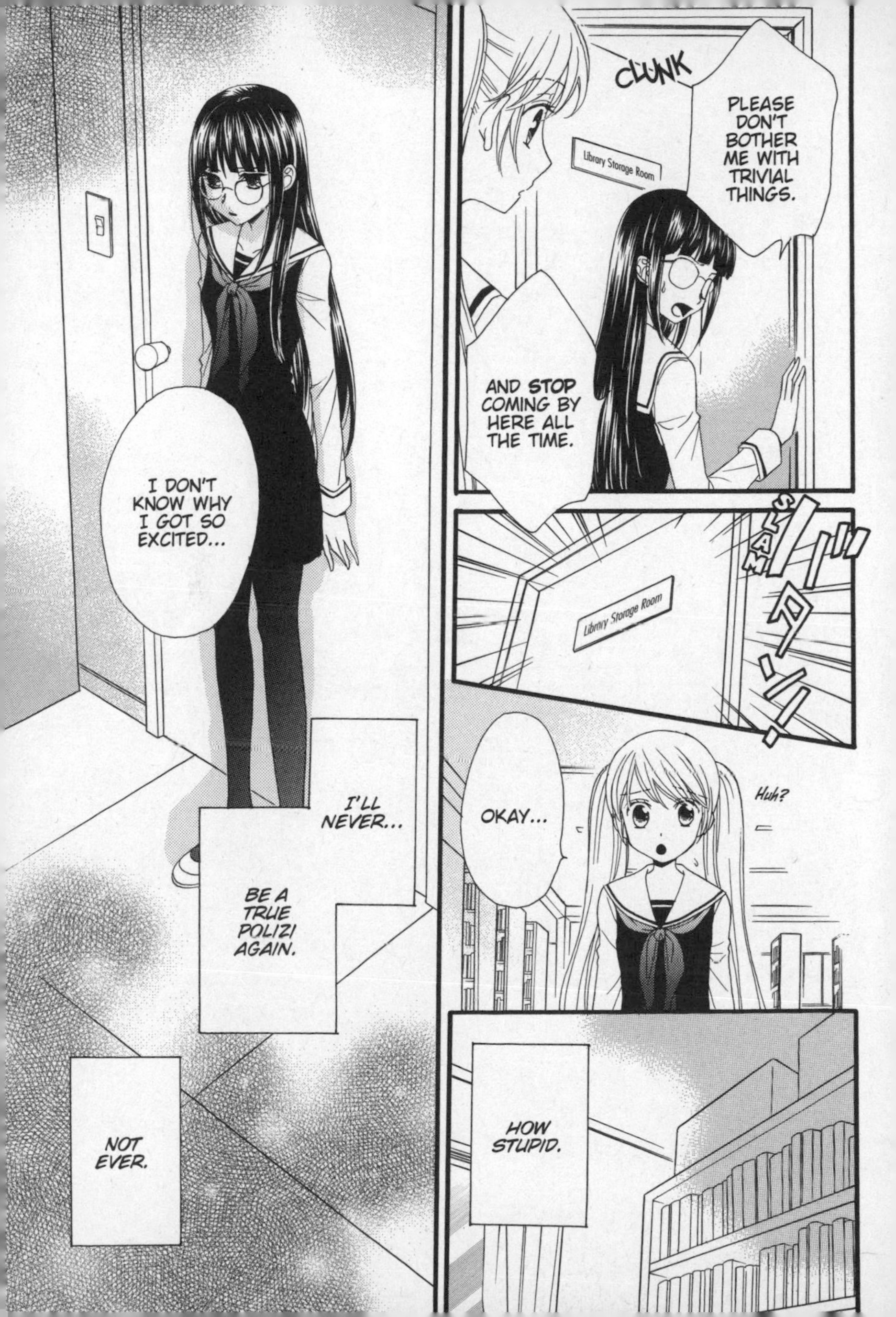
CLUNK
Library Storage Room
PLEASE DON'T BOTHER ME WITH TRIVIAL THINGS.
AND STOP COMING BY HERE ALL THE TIME.
SLAM
Library Storage Room
Huh?
OKAY...
HOW STUPID.
I DON'T KNOW WHY I GOT SO EXCITED...
I'LL NEVER...
BE A TRUE POLIZI AGAIN.
NOT EVER.

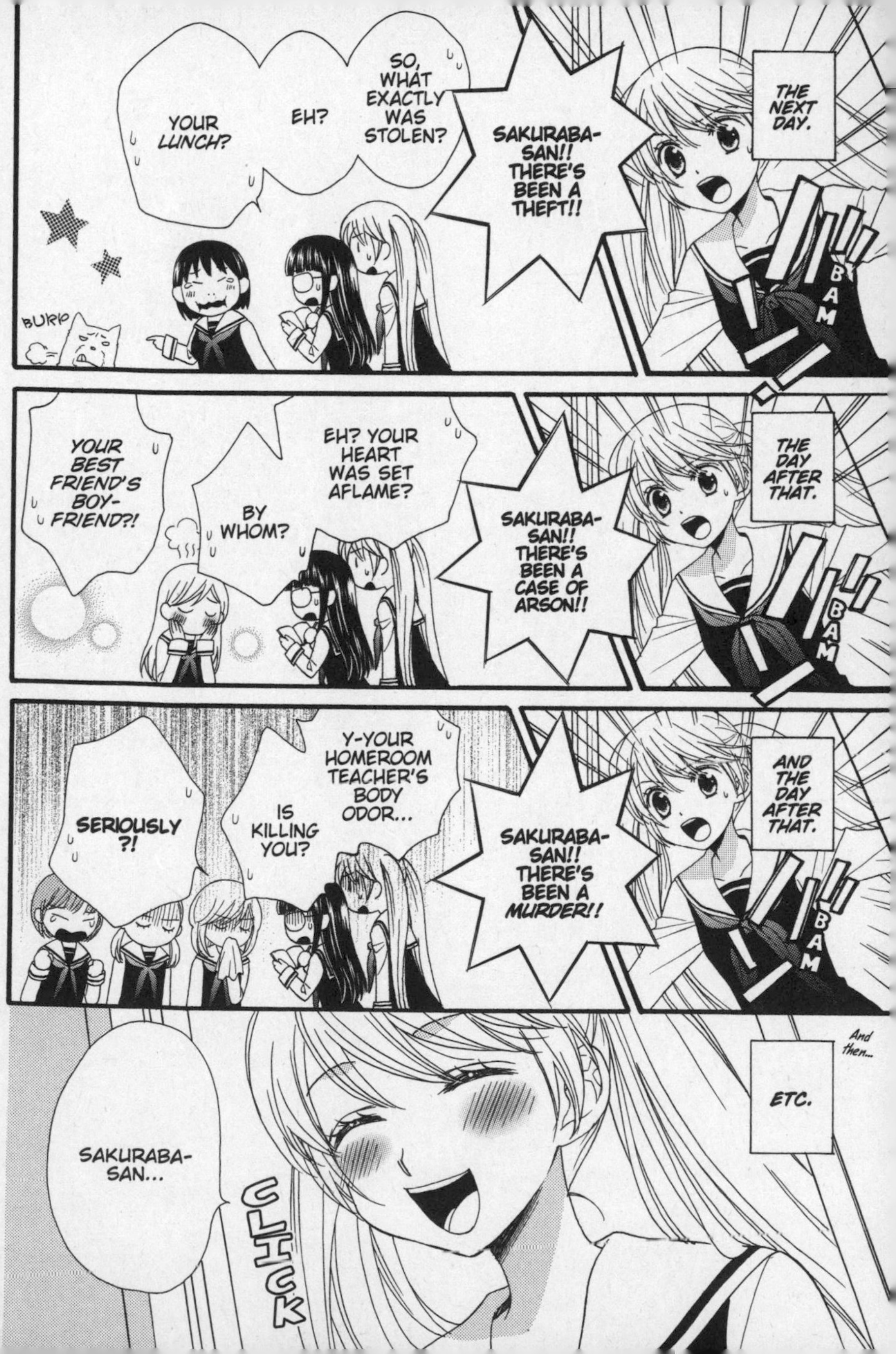
THE NEXT DAY.
SAKURABA-SAN!! THERE'S BEEN A THEFT!!
BAM
SO, WHAT EXACTLY WAS STOLEN?
EH?
YOUR LUNCH?
BURP
THE DAY AFTER THAT.
SAKURABA-SAN!! THERE'S BEEN A CASE OF ARSON!!
BAM
EH? YOUR HEART WAS SET AFLAME?
BY WHOM?
YOUR BEST FRIEND'S BOY-FRIEND?!
AND THE DAY AFTER THAT.
SAKURABA-SAN!! THERE'S BEEN A MURDER!!
BAM
Y-YOUR HOMEROOM TEACHER'S BODY ODOR...
IS KILLING YOU?
SERIOUSLY?!
And then...
ETC.
SAKURABA-SAN...
CLICK

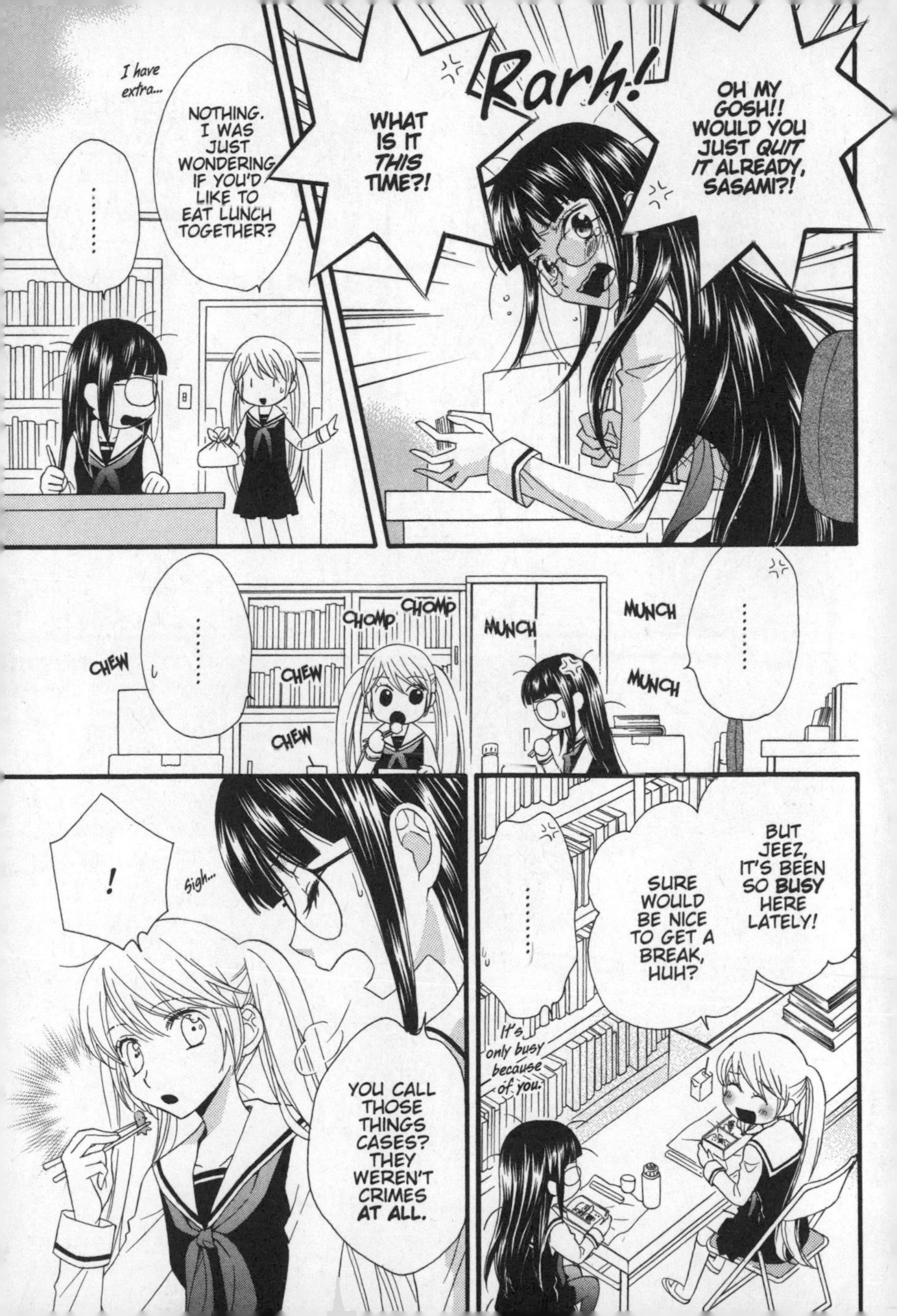
Rarh!
OH MY GOSH!! WOULD YOU JUST QUIT IT ALREADY, SASAMI?!
WHAT IS IT THIS TIME?!
NOTHING. I WAS JUST WONDERING IF YOU'D LIKE TO EAT LUNCH TOGETHER?
I have extra...
......
......
MUNCH
MUNCH
MUNCH
CHOMP
CHOMP
CHEW
CHEW
CHEW
......
BUT JEEZ, IT'S BEEN SO BUSY HERE LATELY!
SURE WOULD BE NICE TO GET A BREAK, HUH?
......
It's only busy because of you.
Sigh...
!
YOU CALL THOSE THINGS CASES? THEY WEREN'T CRIMES AT ALL.

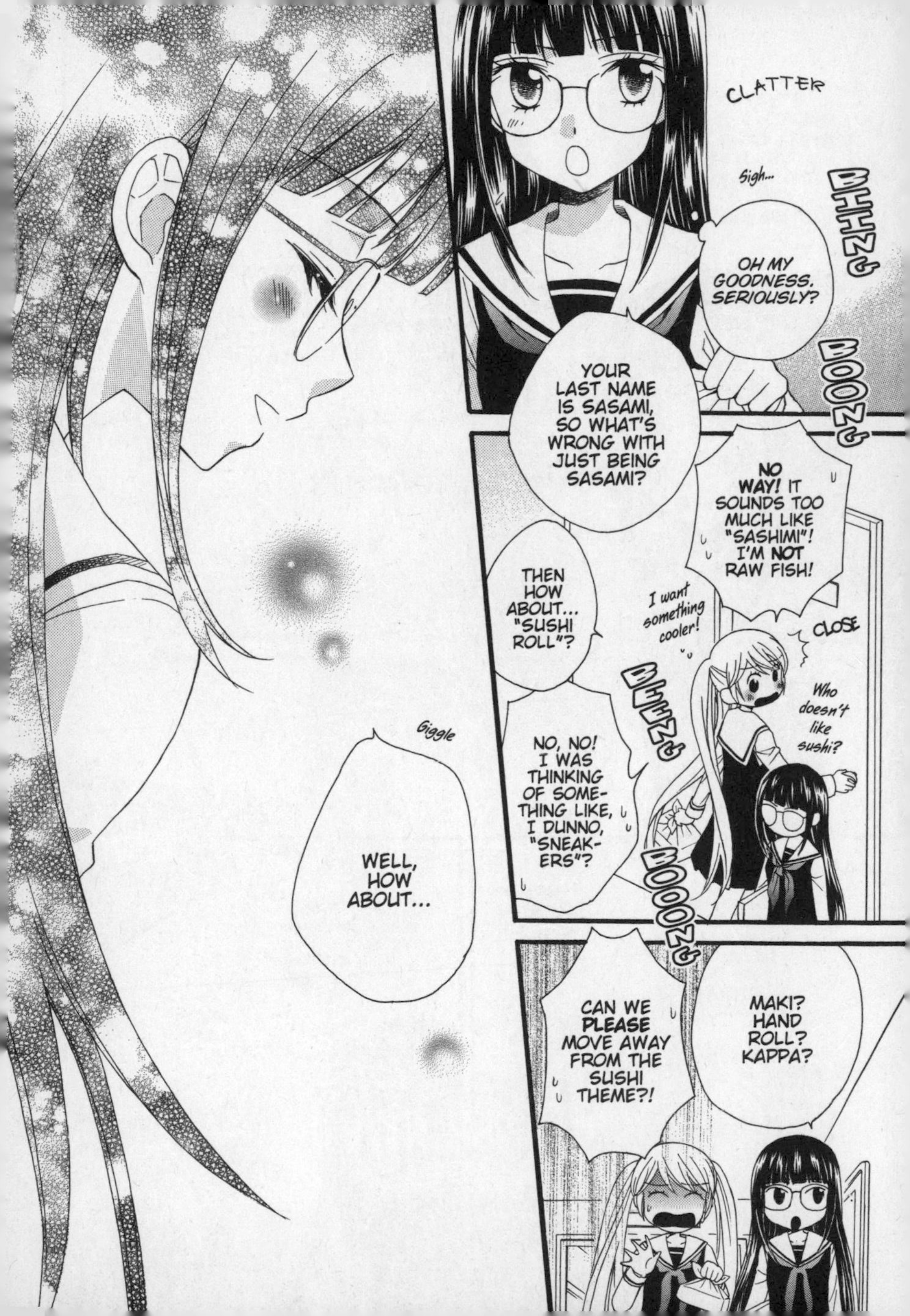
CLATTER
Sigh...
BIHNG
OH MY GOODNESS. SERIOUSLY?
BOONG
YOUR LAST NAME IS SASAMI, SO WHAT'S WRONG WITH JUST BEING SASAMI?
NO WAY! IT SOUNDS TOO MUCH LIKE "SASHIMI"! I'M NOT RAW FISH!
THEN HOW ABOUT... "SUSHI ROLL"?
I want something cooler!
CLOSE
Who doesn't like sushi?
BEENG
NO, NO! I WAS THINKING OF SOME-THING LIKE, I DUNNO, "SNEAK-ERS"?
BOOONG
MAKI? HAND ROLL? KAPPA?
CAN WE PLEASE MOVE AWAY FROM THE SUSHI THEME?!
Giggle
WELL, HOW ABOUT...

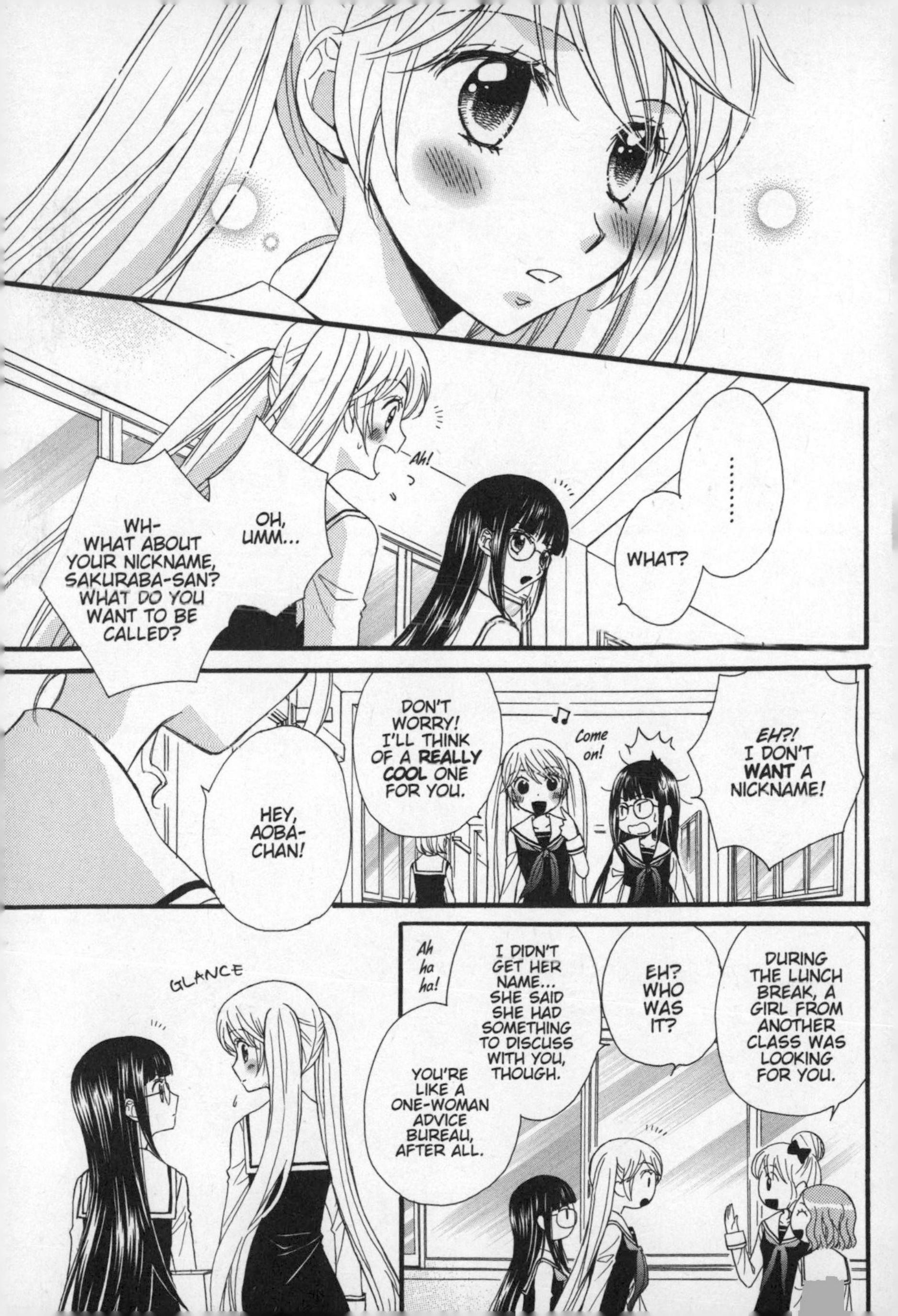
......
WHAT?
Ah!
OH, UMM...
WH- WHAT ABOUT YOUR NICKNAME, SAKURABA-SAN? WHAT DO YOU WANT TO BE CALLED?
EH?! I DON'T WANT A NICKNAME!
Come on!
DON'T WORRY! I'LL THINK OF A REALLY COOL ONE FOR YOU.
HEY, AOBA-CHAN!
DURING THE LUNCH BREAK, A GIRL FROM ANOTHER CLASS WAS LOOKING FOR YOU.
EH? WHO WAS IT?
I DIDN'T GET HER NAME... SHE SAID SHE HAD SOMETHING TO DISCUSS WITH YOU, THOUGH.
Ah ha ha!
YOU'RE LIKE A ONE-WOMAN ADVICE BUREAU, AFTER ALL.
GLANCE

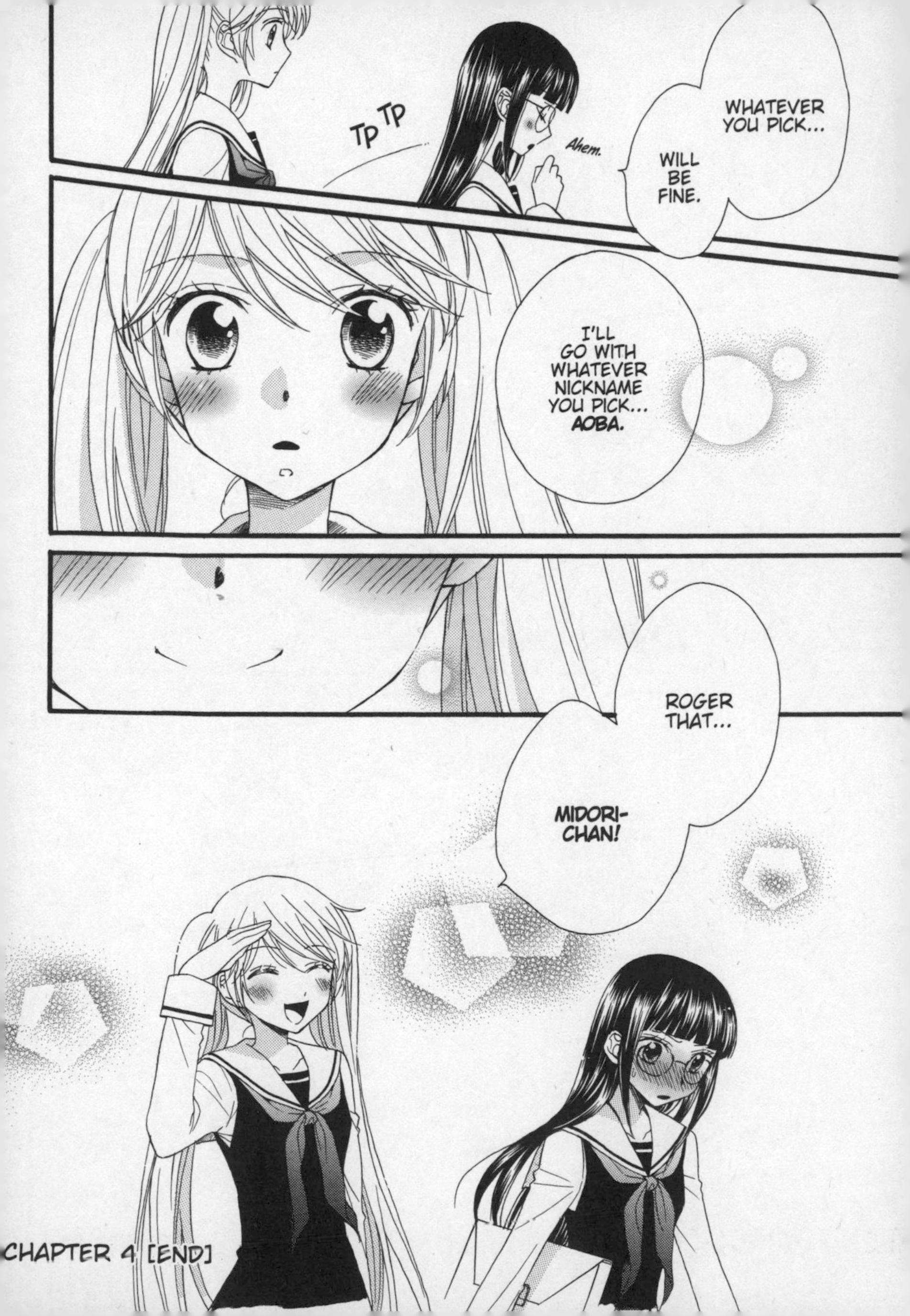
WHATEVER YOU PICK... WILL BE FINE.
Ahem.
Tp Tp
I'LL GO WITH WHATEVER NICKNAME YOU PICK... AOBA.
ROGER THAT... MIDORI-CHAN!

CHAPTER 4 [END]

GAKUEN
POLIZI

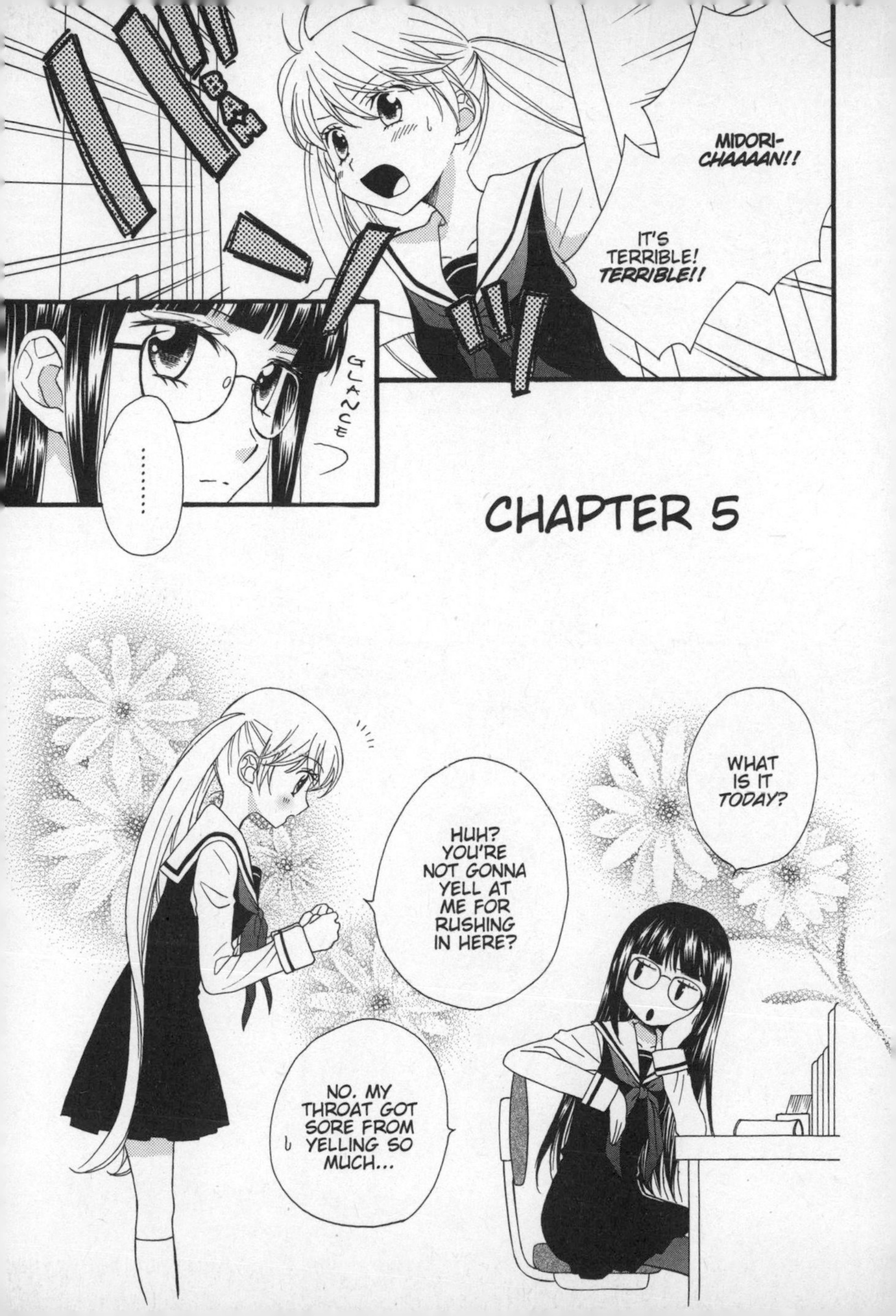
MIDORI-CHAAAAN!!
IT'S TERRIBLE! TERRIBLE!!
BAM
GLANCE
......
CHAPTER 5
WHAT IS IT TODAY?
HUH? YOU'RE NOT GONNA YELL AT ME FOR RUSHING IN HERE?
NO. MY THROAT GOT SORE FROM YELLING SO MUCH...

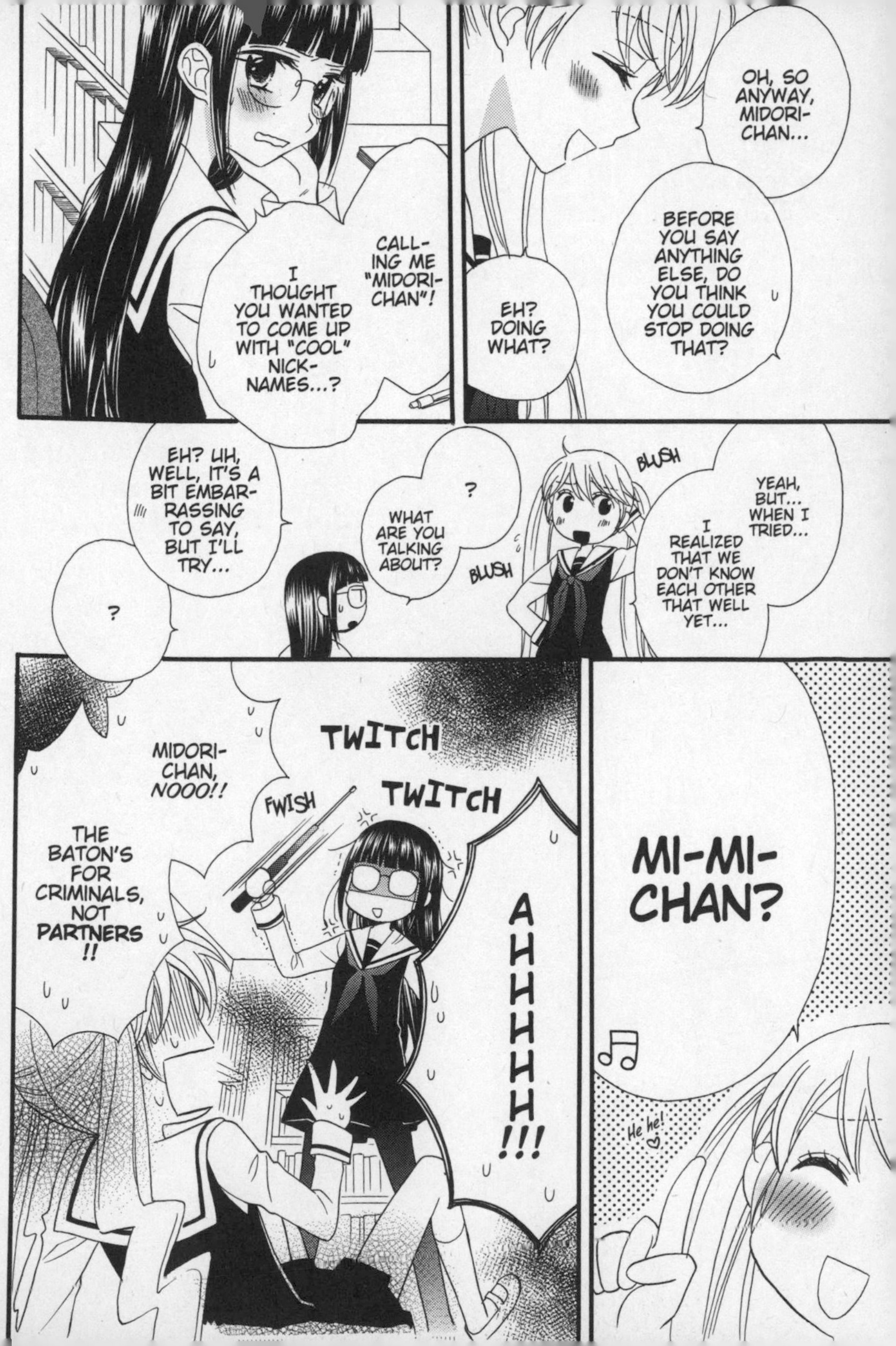
OH, SO ANYWAY, MIDORI-CHAN...
BEFORE YOU SAY ANYTHING ELSE, DO YOU THINK YOU COULD STOP DOING THAT?
EH? DOING WHAT?
CALLING ME "MIDORI-CHAN"!
I THOUGHT YOU WANTED TO COME UP WITH "COOL" NICKNAMES...?
BLUSH
YEAH, BUT... WHEN I TRIED...
I REALIZED THAT WE DON'T KNOW EACH OTHER THAT WELL YET...
BLUSH
?
WHAT ARE YOU TALKING ABOUT?
EH? UH, WELL, IT'S A BIT EMBARRASSING TO SAY, BUT I'LL TRY...
?
MI-MI-CHAN?
He he!
TWITCH
TWITCH
FWISH
AHHHHH!!!
MIDORI-CHAN, NOOO!!
THE BATON'S FOR CRIMINALS, NOT PARTNERS!!

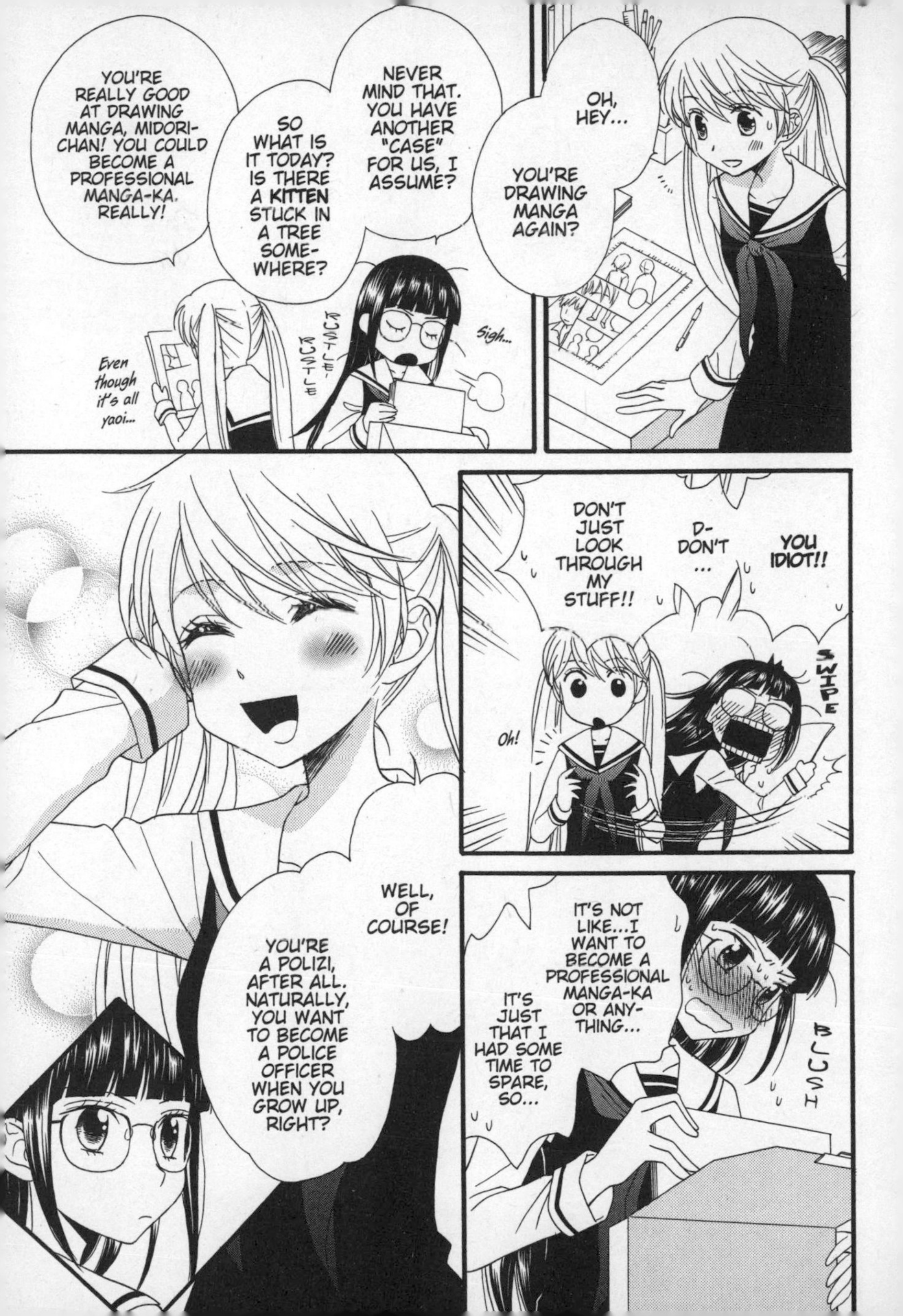
OH, HEY...
YOU'RE DRAWING MANGA AGAIN?
NEVER MIND THAT. YOU HAVE ANOTHER "CASE" FOR US, I ASSUME?
SO WHAT IS IT TODAY? IS THERE A **KITTEN** STUCK IN A TREE SOME-WHERE?
YOU'RE REALLY GOOD AT DRAWING MANGA, MIDORI-CHAN! YOU COULD BECOME A PROFESSIONAL MANGA-KA. REALLY!
Sigh...
RUSTLE RUSTLE
Even though it's all yaoi...
YOU IDIOT!!
D-DON'T...
DON'T JUST LOOK THROUGH MY STUFF!!
SWIPE
Oh!
IT'S NOT LIKE...I WANT TO BECOME A PROFESSIONAL MANGA-KA OR ANY-THING...
IT'S JUST THAT I HAD SOME TIME TO SPARE, SO...
BLUSH
WELL, OF COURSE!
YOU'RE A POLIZI, AFTER ALL. NATURALLY, YOU WANT TO BECOME A POLICE OFFICER WHEN YOU GROW UP, RIGHT?

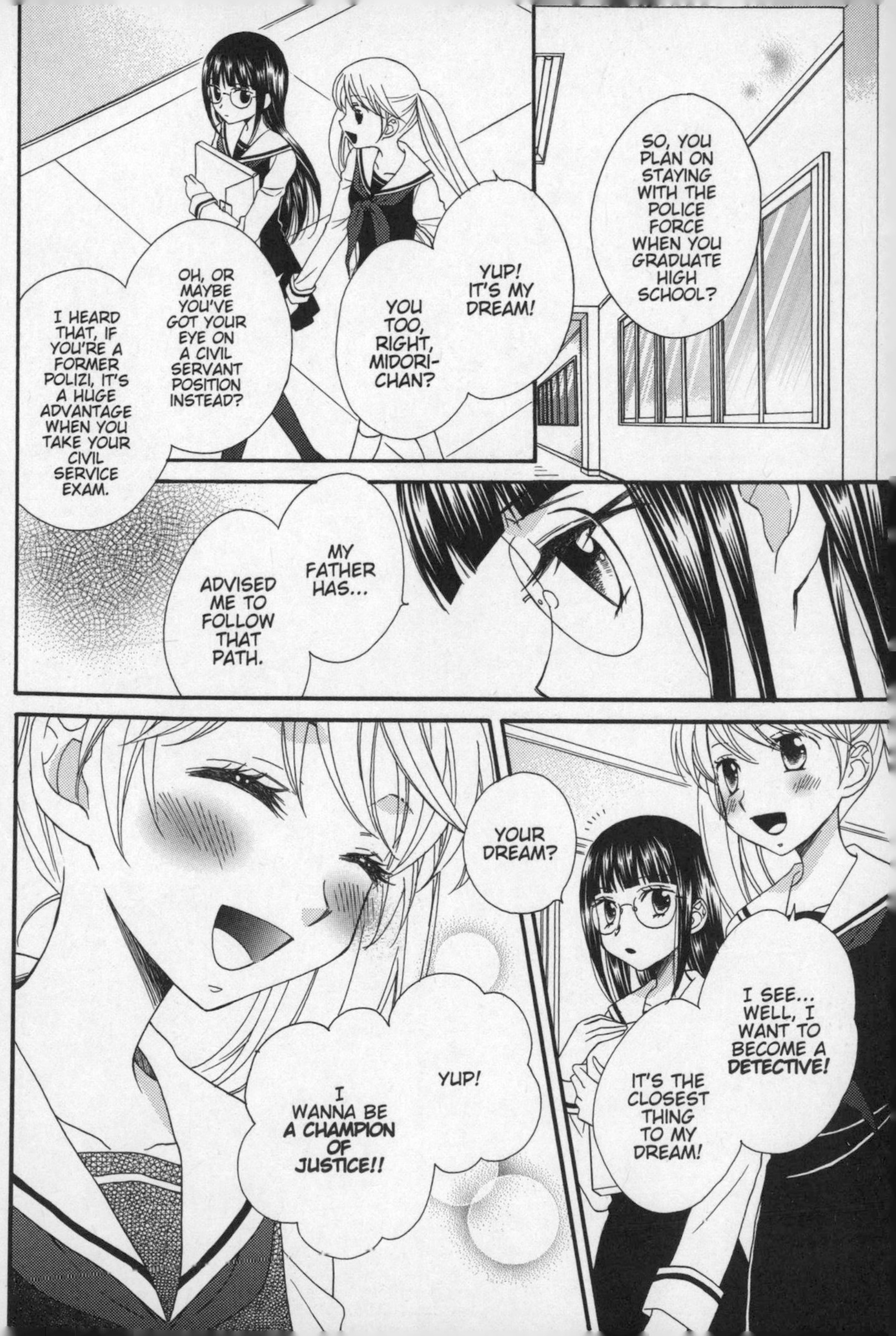
SO, YOU PLAN ON STAYING WITH THE POLICE FORCE WHEN YOU GRADUATE HIGH SCHOOL?
YUP! IT'S MY DREAM!
YOU TOO, RIGHT, MIDORI-CHAN?
OH, OR MAYBE YOU'VE GOT YOUR EYE ON A CIVIL SERVANT POSITION INSTEAD?
I HEARD THAT, IF YOU'RE A FORMER POLIZI, IT'S A HUGE ADVANTAGE WHEN YOU TAKE YOUR CIVIL SERVICE EXAM.
MY FATHER HAS...
ADVISED ME TO FOLLOW THAT PATH.
I SEE... WELL, I WANT TO BECOME A **DETECTIVE**!
IT'S THE CLOSEST THING TO MY DREAM!
YOUR DREAM?
YUP!
I WANNA BE **A CHAMPION OF JUSTICE!!**

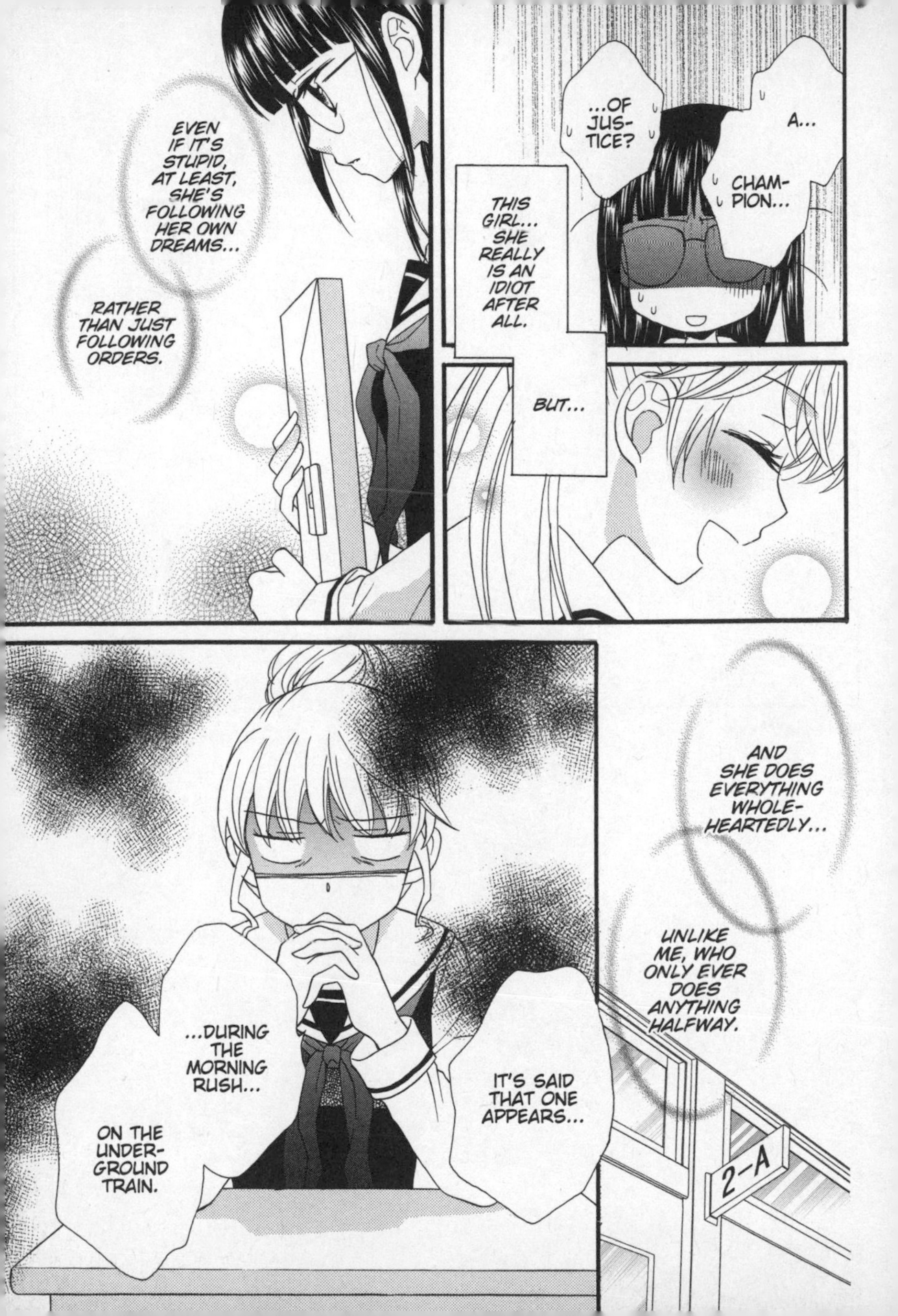
A... CHAMPION...
...OF JUSTICE?
THIS GIRL... SHE REALLY IS AN IDIOT AFTER ALL.
BUT...
EVEN IF IT'S STUPID, AT LEAST, SHE'S FOLLOWING HER OWN DREAMS...
RATHER THAN JUST FOLLOWING ORDERS.
AND SHE DOES EVERYTHING WHOLE-HEARTEDLY...
UNLIKE ME, WHO ONLY EVER DOES ANYTHING HALFWAY.
2-A
IT'S SAID THAT ONE APPEARS...
...DURING THE MORNING RUSH...
ON THE UNDER-GROUND TRAIN.

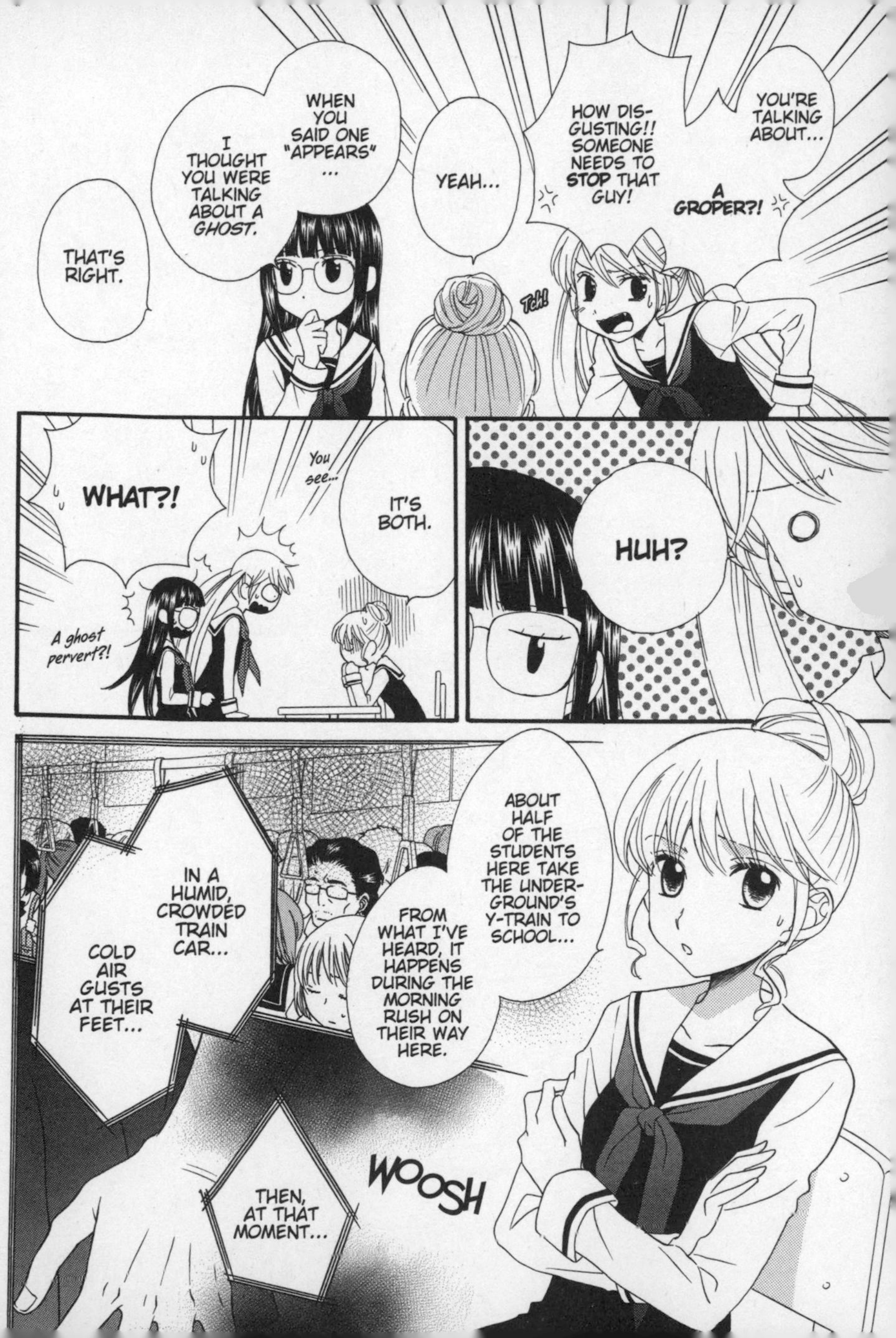
YOU'RE TALKING ABOUT...
A GROPER?!
HOW DIS-GUSTING!! SOMEONE NEEDS TO STOP THAT GUY!
Tch!
YEAH...
WHEN YOU SAID ONE "APPEARS" ...
I THOUGHT YOU WERE TALKING ABOUT A GHOST.
THAT'S RIGHT.
HUH?
IT'S BOTH.
You see...
WHAT?!
A ghost pervert?!
ABOUT HALF OF THE STUDENTS HERE TAKE THE UNDER-GROUND'S Y-TRAIN TO SCHOOL...
FROM WHAT I'VE HEARD, IT HAPPENS DURING THE MORNING RUSH ON THEIR WAY HERE.
IN A HUMID, CROWDED TRAIN CAR...
COLD AIR GUSTS AT THEIR FEET...
WOOSH
THEN, AT THAT MOMENT...

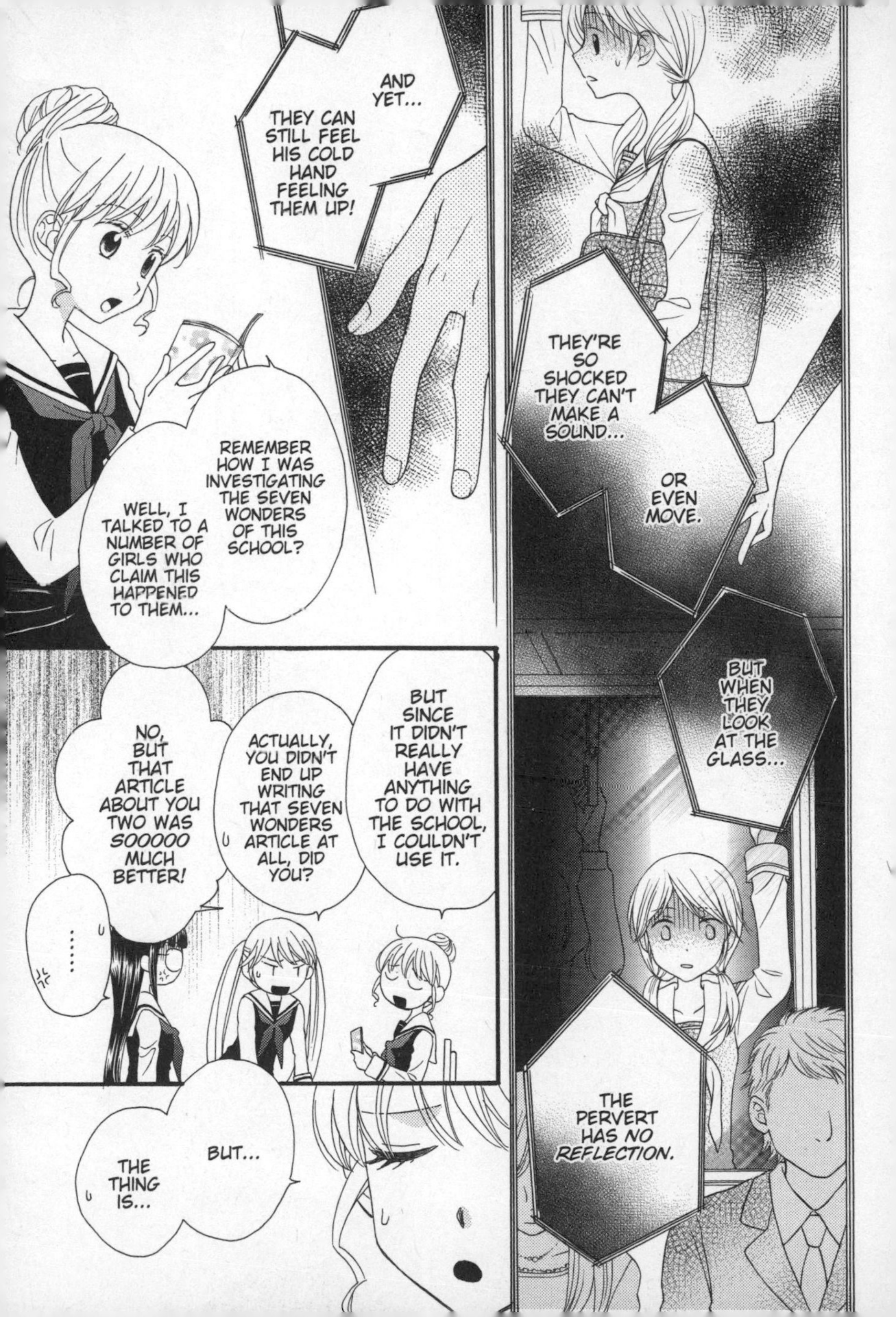
THEY'RE SO SHOCKED THEY CAN'T MAKE A SOUND...
OR EVEN MOVE.
BUT WHEN THEY LOOK AT THE GLASS...
THE PERVERT HAS *NO REFLECTION*.
AND YET...
THEY CAN STILL FEEL HIS COLD HAND FEELING THEM UP!
REMEMBER HOW I WAS INVESTIGATING THE SEVEN WONDERS OF THIS SCHOOL?
WELL, I TALKED TO A NUMBER OF GIRLS WHO CLAIM THIS HAPPENED TO THEM...
BUT SINCE IT DIDN'T REALLY HAVE ANYTHING TO DO WITH THE SCHOOL, I COULDN'T USE IT.
ACTUALLY, YOU DIDN'T END UP WRITING THAT SEVEN WONDERS ARTICLE AT ALL, DID YOU?
NO, BUT THAT ARTICLE ABOUT YOU TWO WAS *SOOOOO* MUCH BETTER!
......
BUT...
THE THING IS...

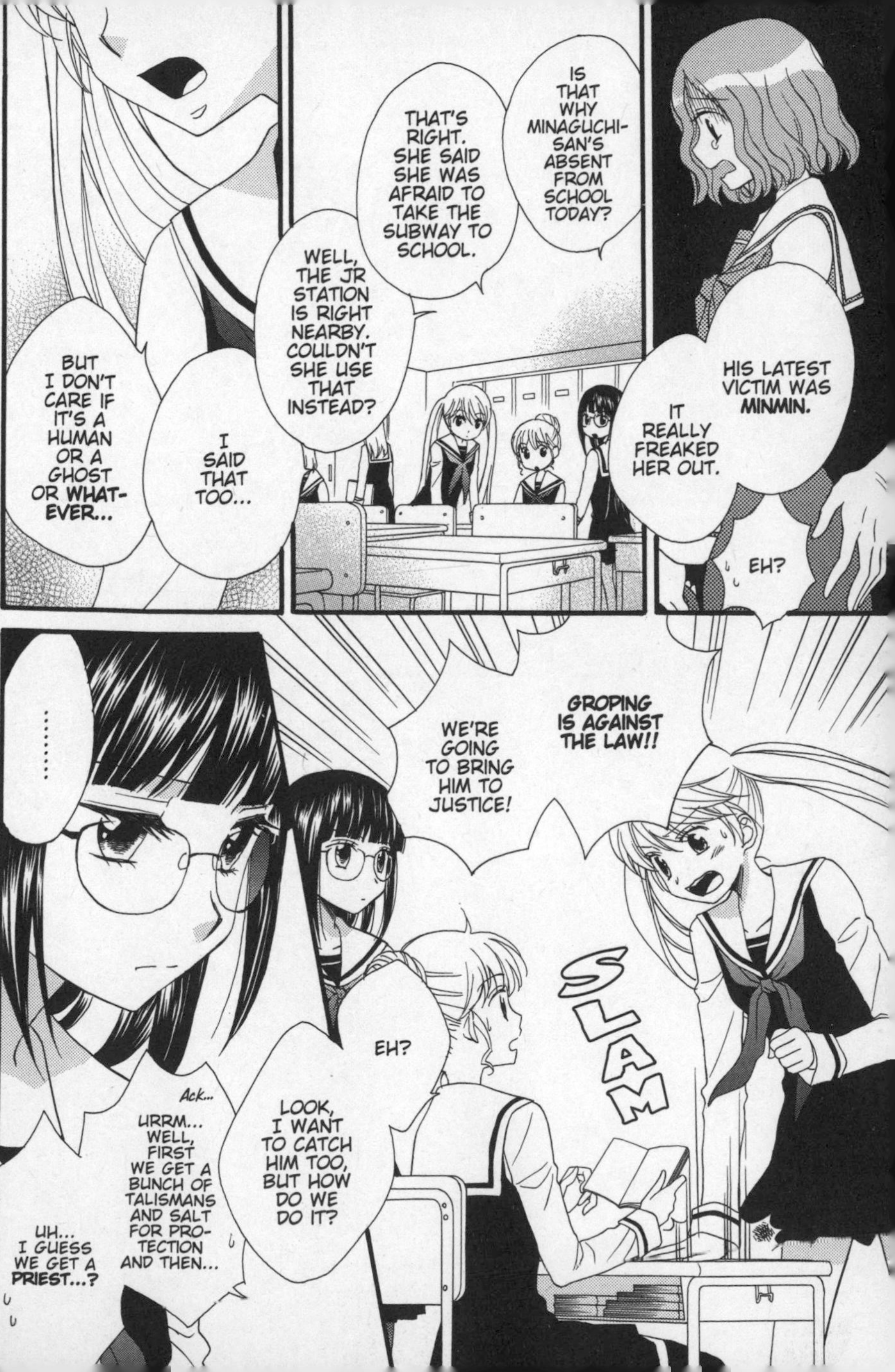
HIS LATEST VICTIM WAS MINMIN.
IT REALLY FREAKED HER OUT.
EH?
IS THAT WHY MINAGUCHI-SAN'S ABSENT FROM SCHOOL TODAY?
THAT'S RIGHT. SHE SAID SHE WAS AFRAID TO TAKE THE SUBWAY TO SCHOOL.
WELL, THE JR STATION IS RIGHT NEARBY. COULDN'T SHE USE THAT INSTEAD?
I SAID THAT TOO...
BUT I DON'T CARE IF IT'S A HUMAN OR A GHOST OR WHAT-EVER...
GROPING IS AGAINST THE LAW!!
WE'RE GOING TO BRING HIM TO JUSTICE!
SLAM
......
EH?
LOOK, I WANT TO CATCH HIM TOO, BUT HOW DO WE DO IT?
Ack...
URRM... WELL, FIRST WE GET A BUNCH OF TALISMANS AND SALT FOR PRO-TECTION AND THEN...
UH... I GUESS WE GET A PRIEST...?

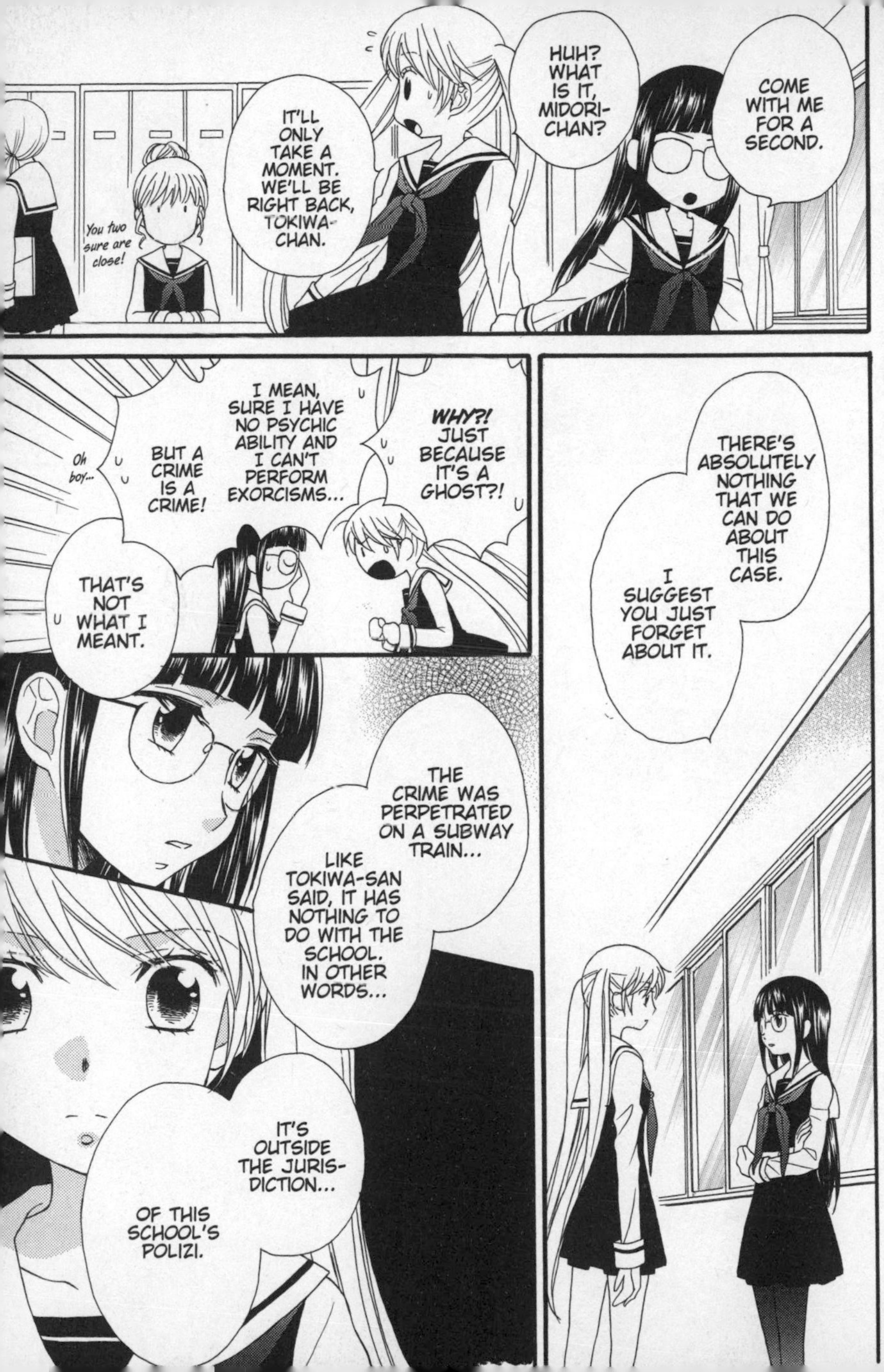
COME WITH ME FOR A SECOND.
HUH? WHAT IS IT, MIDORI-CHAN?
IT'LL ONLY TAKE A MOMENT. WE'LL BE RIGHT BACK, TOKIWA-CHAN.
You two sure are close!
THERE'S ABSOLUTELY NOTHING THAT WE CAN DO ABOUT THIS CASE.
I SUGGEST YOU JUST FORGET ABOUT IT.
WHY?! JUST BECAUSE IT'S A GHOST?!
I MEAN, SURE I HAVE NO PSYCHIC ABILITY AND I CAN'T PERFORM EXORCISMS...
BUT A CRIME IS A CRIME!
Oh boy...
THAT'S NOT WHAT I MEANT.
THE CRIME WAS PERPETRATED ON A SUBWAY TRAIN...
LIKE TOKIWA-SAN SAID, IT HAS NOTHING TO DO WITH THE SCHOOL. IN OTHER WORDS...
IT'S OUTSIDE THE JURIS-DICTION...
OF THIS SCHOOL'S POLIZI.

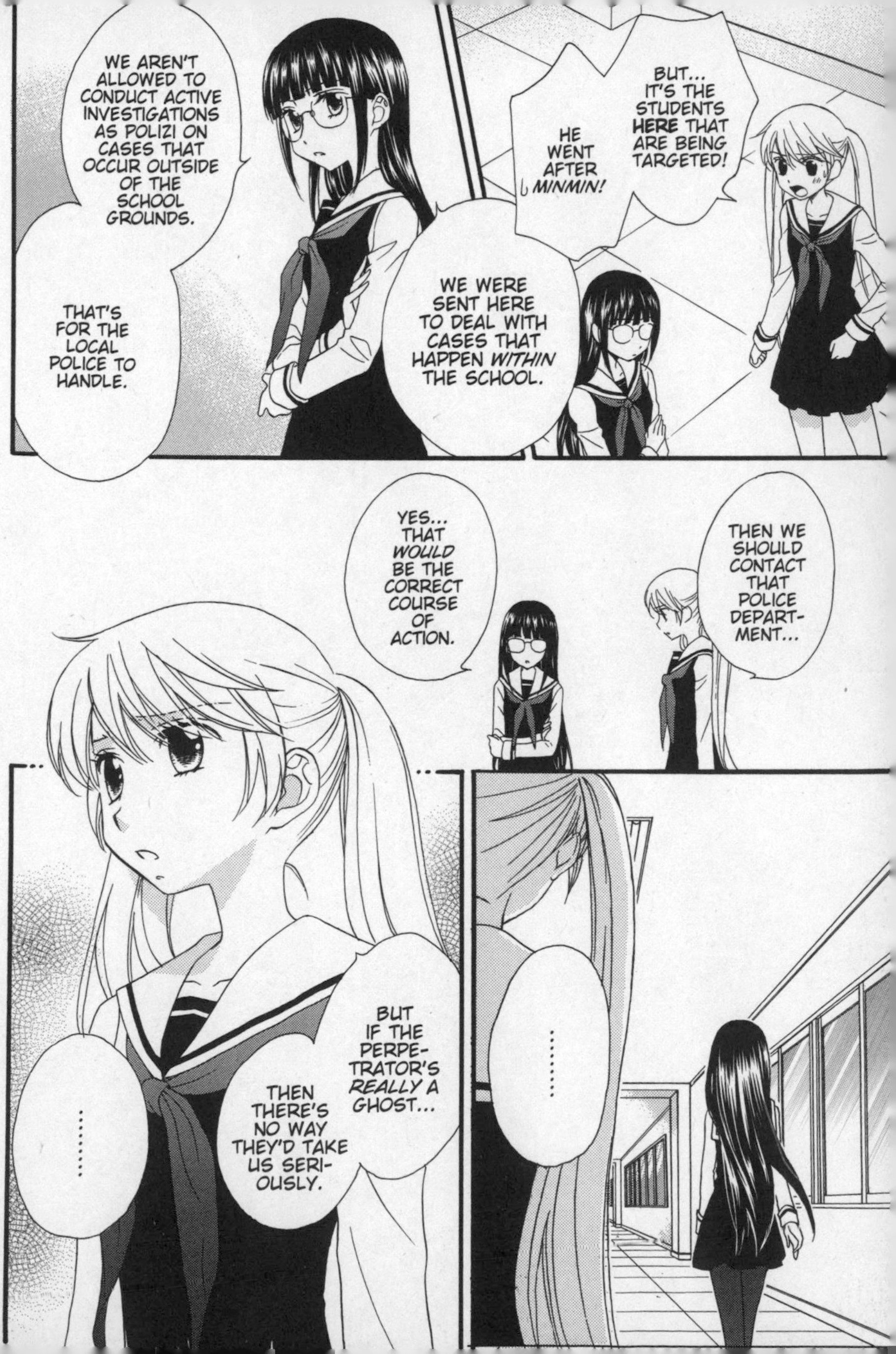
BUT... IT'S THE STUDENTS **HERE** THAT ARE BEING TARGETED!
HE WENT AFTER *MINMIN!*
WE WERE SENT HERE TO DEAL WITH CASES THAT HAPPEN *WITHIN* THE SCHOOL.
WE AREN'T ALLOWED TO CONDUCT ACTIVE INVESTIGATIONS AS POLIZI ON CASES THAT OCCUR OUTSIDE OF THE SCHOOL GROUNDS.
THAT'S FOR THE LOCAL POLICE TO HANDLE.
THEN WE SHOULD CONTACT THAT POLICE DEPART-MENT...
YES... THAT *WOULD* BE THE CORRECT COURSE OF ACTION.
......
BUT IF THE PERPE-TRATOR'S *REALLY* A GHOST...
THEN THERE'S NO WAY THEY'D TAKE US SERI-OUSLY.
......

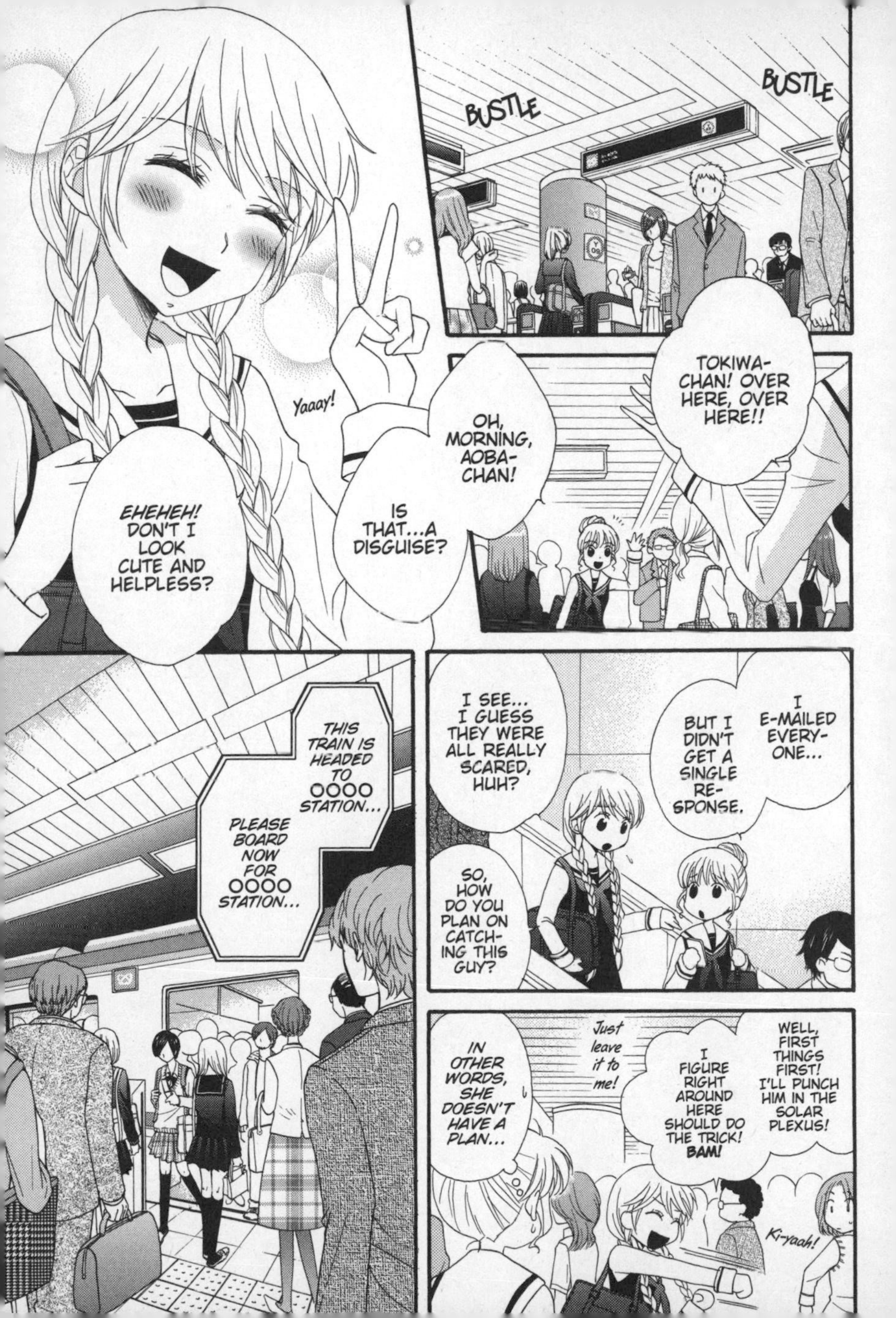
BUSTLE
BUSTLE
TOKIWA-CHAN! OVER HERE, OVER HERE!!
OH, MORNING, AOBA-CHAN!
IS THAT...A DISGUISE?
Yaaay!
EHEHEH! DON'T I LOOK CUTE AND HELPLESS?
I E-MAILED EVERYONE...
BUT I DIDN'T GET A SINGLE RESPONSE.
I SEE... I GUESS THEY WERE ALL REALLY SCARED, HUH?
SO, HOW DO YOU PLAN ON CATCHING THIS GUY?
WELL, FIRST THINGS FIRST! I'LL PUNCH HIM IN THE SOLAR PLEXUS!
I FIGURE RIGHT AROUND HERE SHOULD DO THE TRICK! BAM!
Ki-yaah!
Just leave it to me!
IN OTHER WORDS, SHE DOESN'T HAVE A PLAN...
THIS TRAIN IS HEADED TO OOOO STATION...
PLEASE BOARD NOW FOR OOOO STATION...

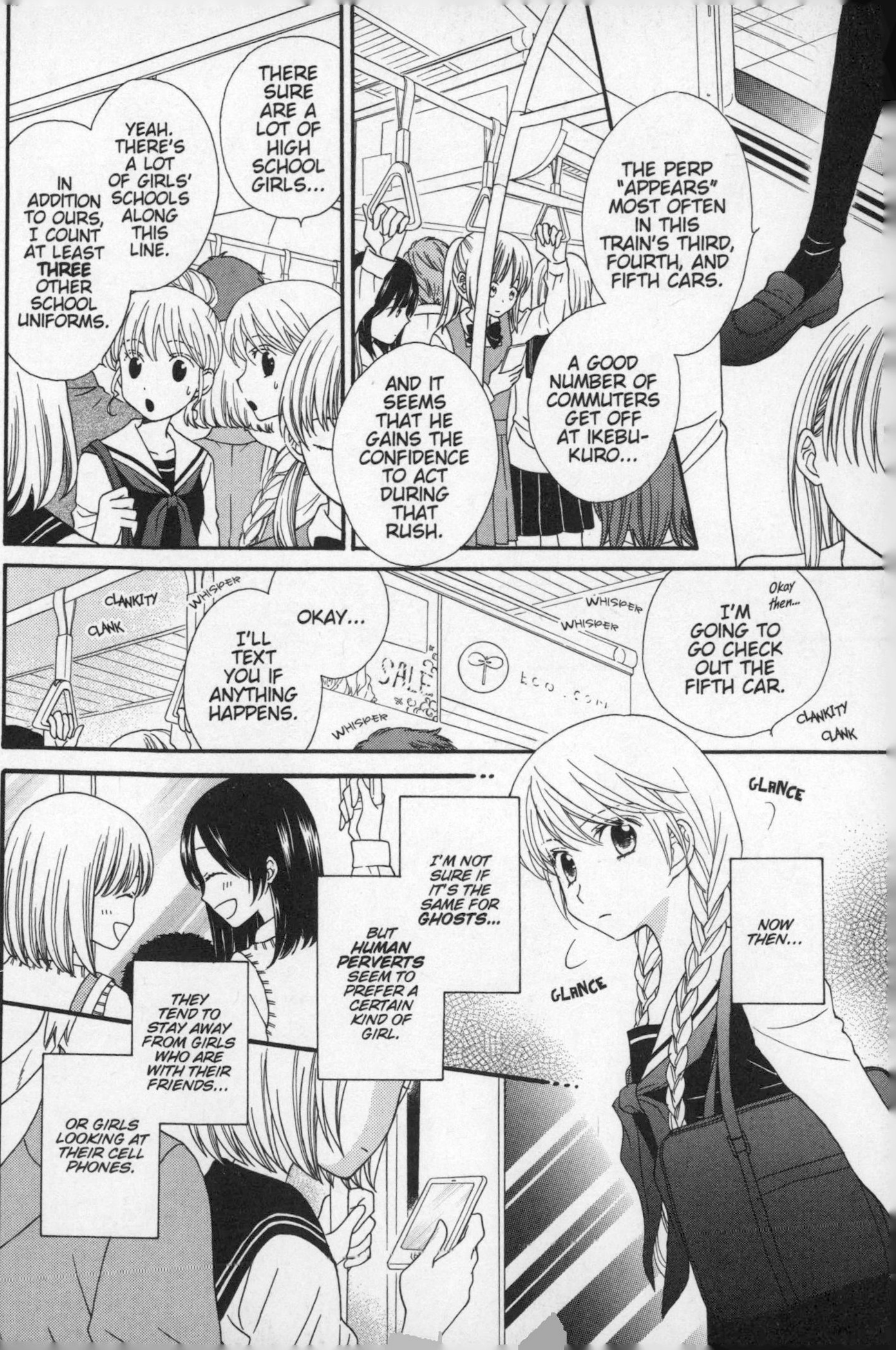
THE PERP "APPEARS" MOST OFTEN IN THIS TRAIN'S THIRD, FOURTH, AND FIFTH CARS.
A GOOD NUMBER OF COMMUTERS GET OFF AT IKEBUKURO...
AND IT SEEMS THAT HE GAINS THE CONFIDENCE TO ACT DURING THAT RUSH.
THERE SURE ARE A LOT OF HIGH SCHOOL GIRLS...
YEAH. THERE'S A LOT OF GIRLS' SCHOOLS ALONG THIS LINE.
IN ADDITION TO OURS, I COUNT AT LEAST THREE OTHER SCHOOL UNIFORMS.
Okay then...
I'M GOING TO GO CHECK OUT THE FIFTH CAR.
CLANKITY CLANK
WHISPER
WHISPER
OKAY... I'LL TEXT YOU IF ANYTHING HAPPENS.
WHISPER
WHISPER
CLANKITY CLANK
SALE
GLANCE
NOW THEN...
GLANCE
I'M NOT SURE IF IT'S THE SAME FOR GHOSTS...
BUT HUMAN PERVERTS SEEM TO PREFER A CERTAIN KIND OF GIRL.
THEY TEND TO STAY AWAY FROM GIRLS WHO ARE WITH THEIR FRIENDS...
OR GIRLS LOOKING AT THEIR CELL PHONES.

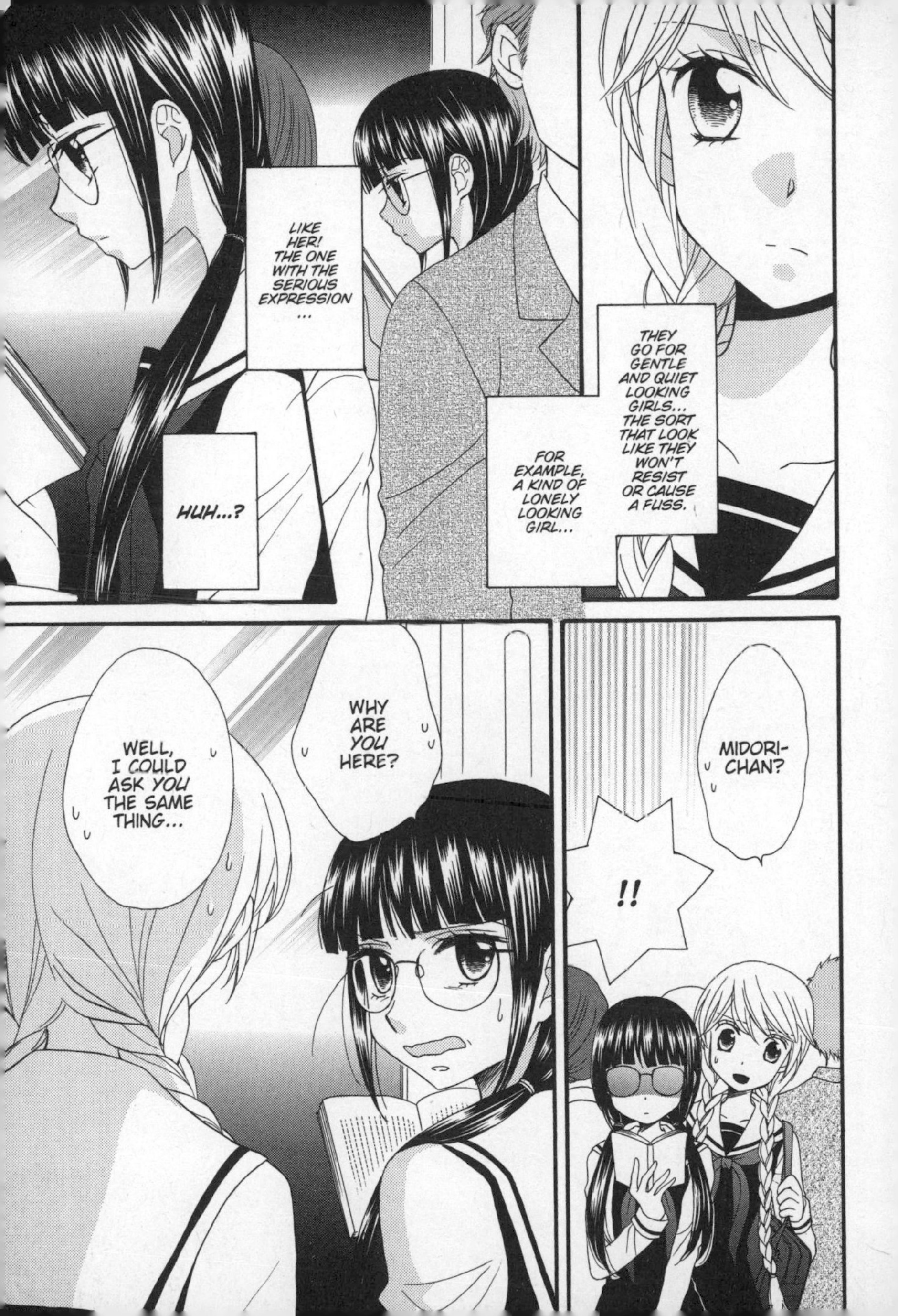
THEY GO FOR GENTLE AND QUIET LOOKING GIRLS... THE SORT THAT LOOK LIKE THEY WON'T RESIST OR CAUSE A FUSS.
FOR EXAMPLE, A KIND OF LONELY LOOKING GIRL...
LIKE HER! THE ONE WITH THE SERIOUS EXPRESSION...
HUH...?
MIDORI-CHAN?
!!
WHY ARE YOU HERE?
WELL, I COULD ASK YOU THE SAME THING...

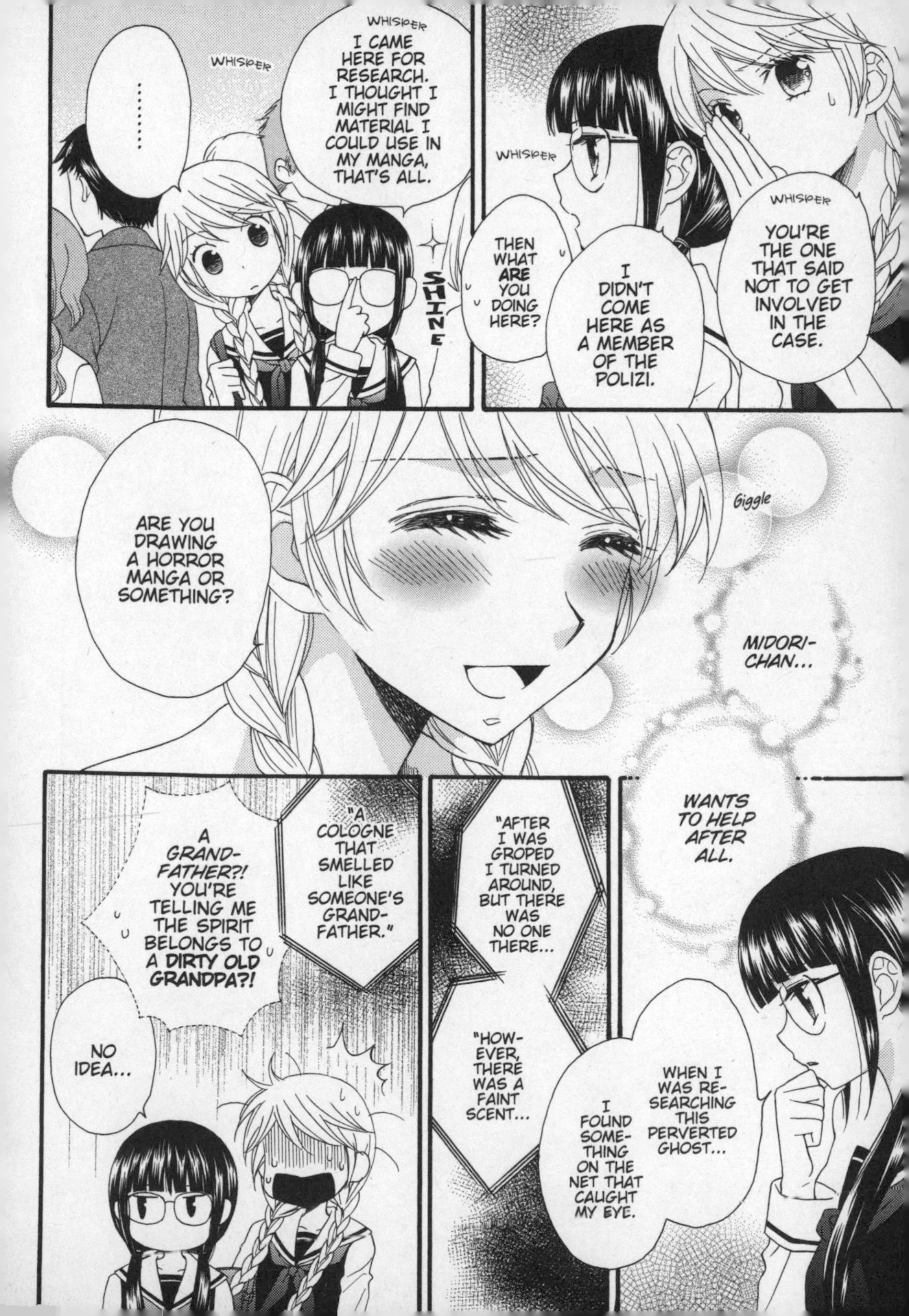
WHISPER
YOU'RE THE ONE THAT SAID NOT TO GET INVOLVED IN THE CASE.
WHISPER
I DIDN'T COME HERE AS A MEMBER OF THE POLIZI.
THEN WHAT **ARE** YOU DOING HERE?
WHISPER
I CAME HERE FOR RESEARCH. I THOUGHT I MIGHT FIND MATERIAL I COULD USE IN MY MANGA, THAT'S ALL.
SHINE
WHISPER
......
Giggle
ARE YOU DRAWING A HORROR MANGA OR SOMETHING?
MIDORI-CHAN...
WANTS TO HELP AFTER ALL.
WHEN I WAS RE-SEARCHING THIS PERVERTED GHOST...
I FOUND SOME-THING ON THE NET THAT CAUGHT MY EYE.
"AFTER I WAS GROPED I TURNED AROUND, BUT THERE WAS NO ONE THERE...
"HOW-EVER, THERE WAS A FAINT SCENT...
"A COLOGNE THAT SMELLED LIKE SOMEONE'S GRAND-FATHER."
A GRAND-FATHER?! YOU'RE TELLING ME THE SPIRIT BELONGS TO A **DIRTY OLD GRANDPA?!**
NO IDEA...

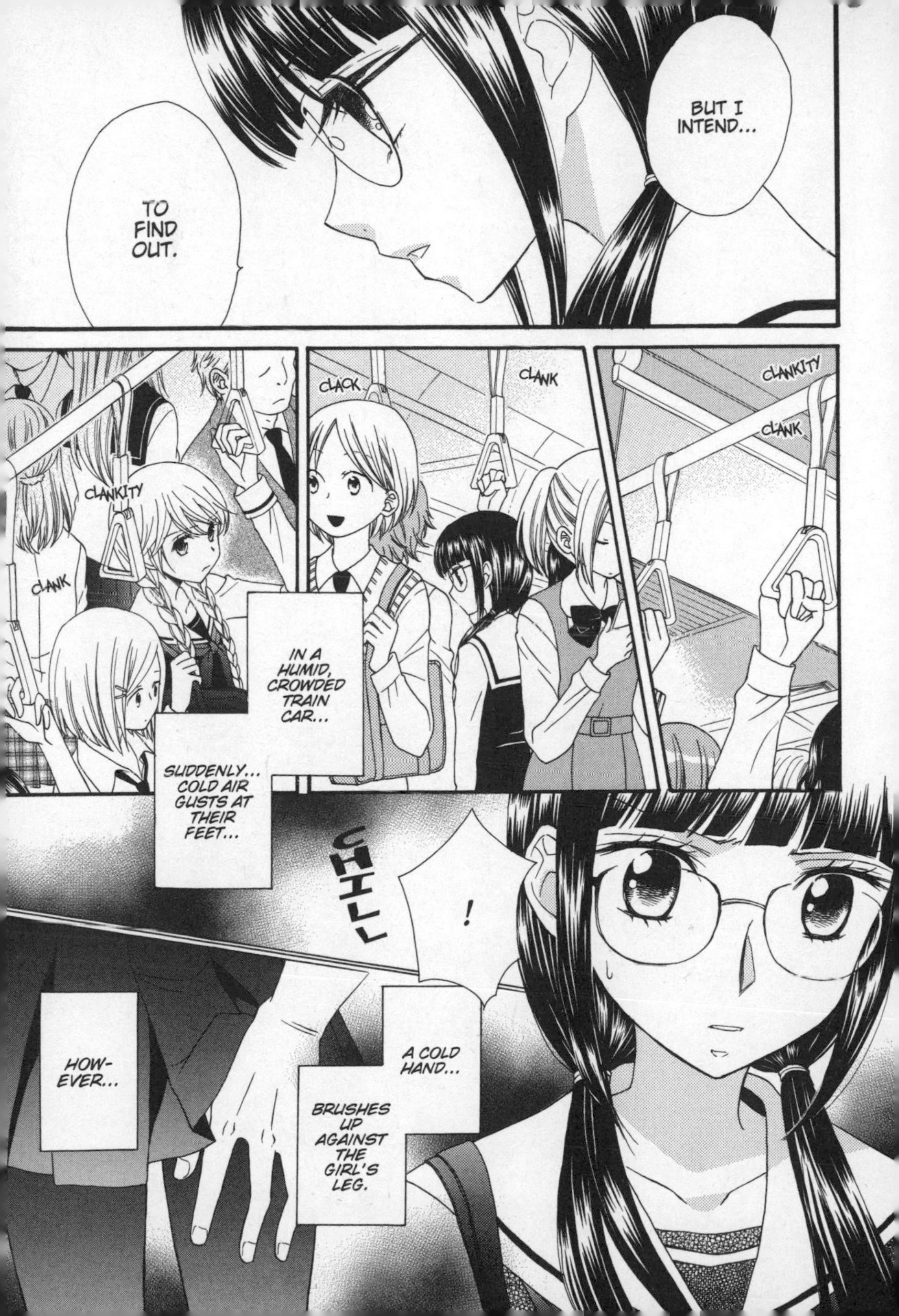
BUT I INTEND...
TO FIND OUT.
CLANKITY
CLANK
CLACK
CLANK
CLANKITY
CLANK
IN A HUMID, CROWDED TRAIN CAR...
SUDDENLY... COLD AIR GUSTS AT THEIR FEET...
!
CHILL
HOW-EVER...
A COLD HAND...
BRUSHES UP AGAINST THE GIRL'S LEG.

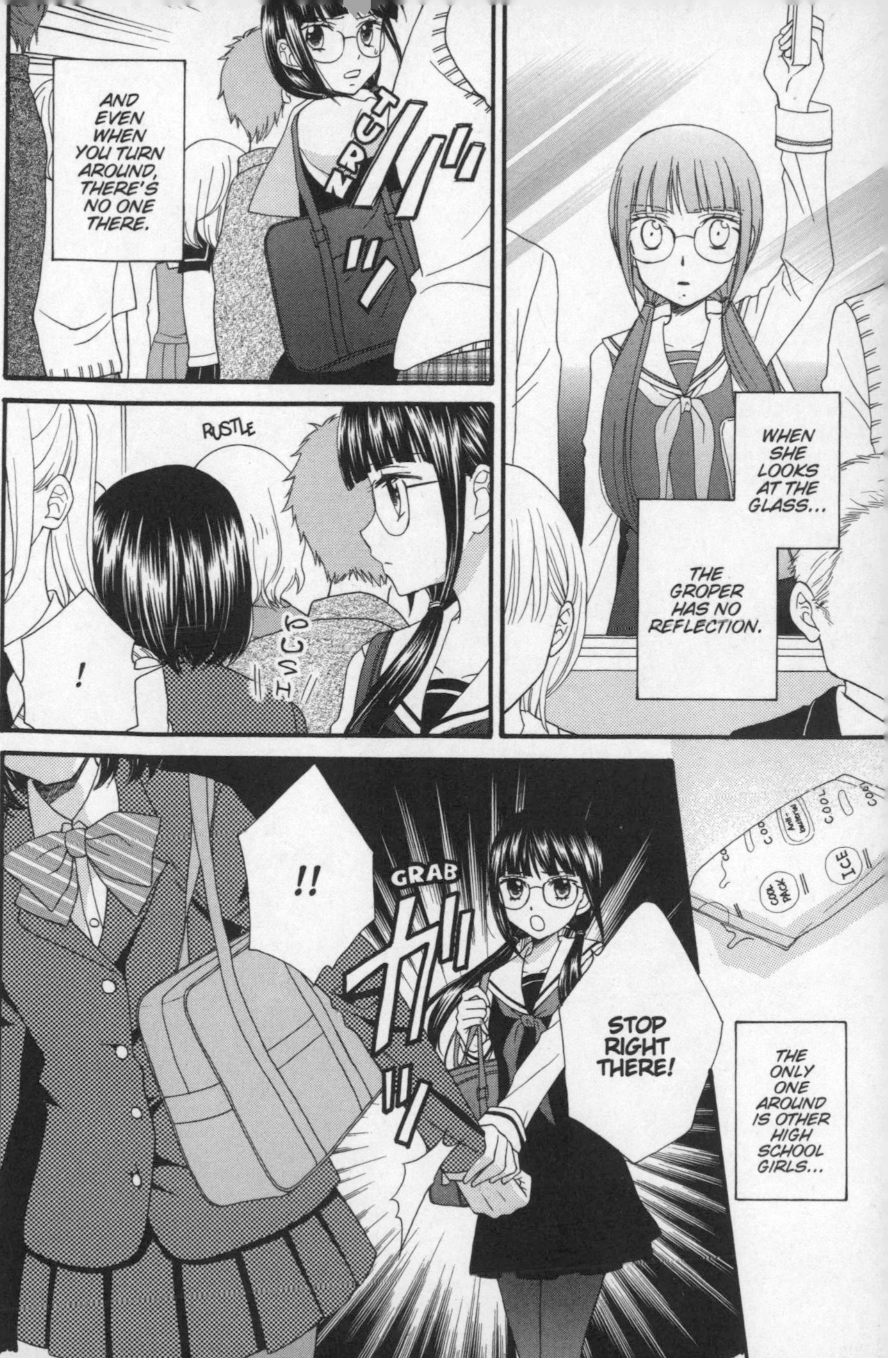
WHEN SHE LOOKS AT THE GLASS...
THE GROPER HAS NO REFLECTION.
AND EVEN WHEN YOU TURN AROUND, THERE'S NO ONE THERE.
TURN
RUSTLE
!
THE ONLY ONE AROUND IS OTHER HIGH SCHOOL GIRLS...
COOL
ICE
COOL PACK
STOP RIGHT THERE!
GRAB
!!

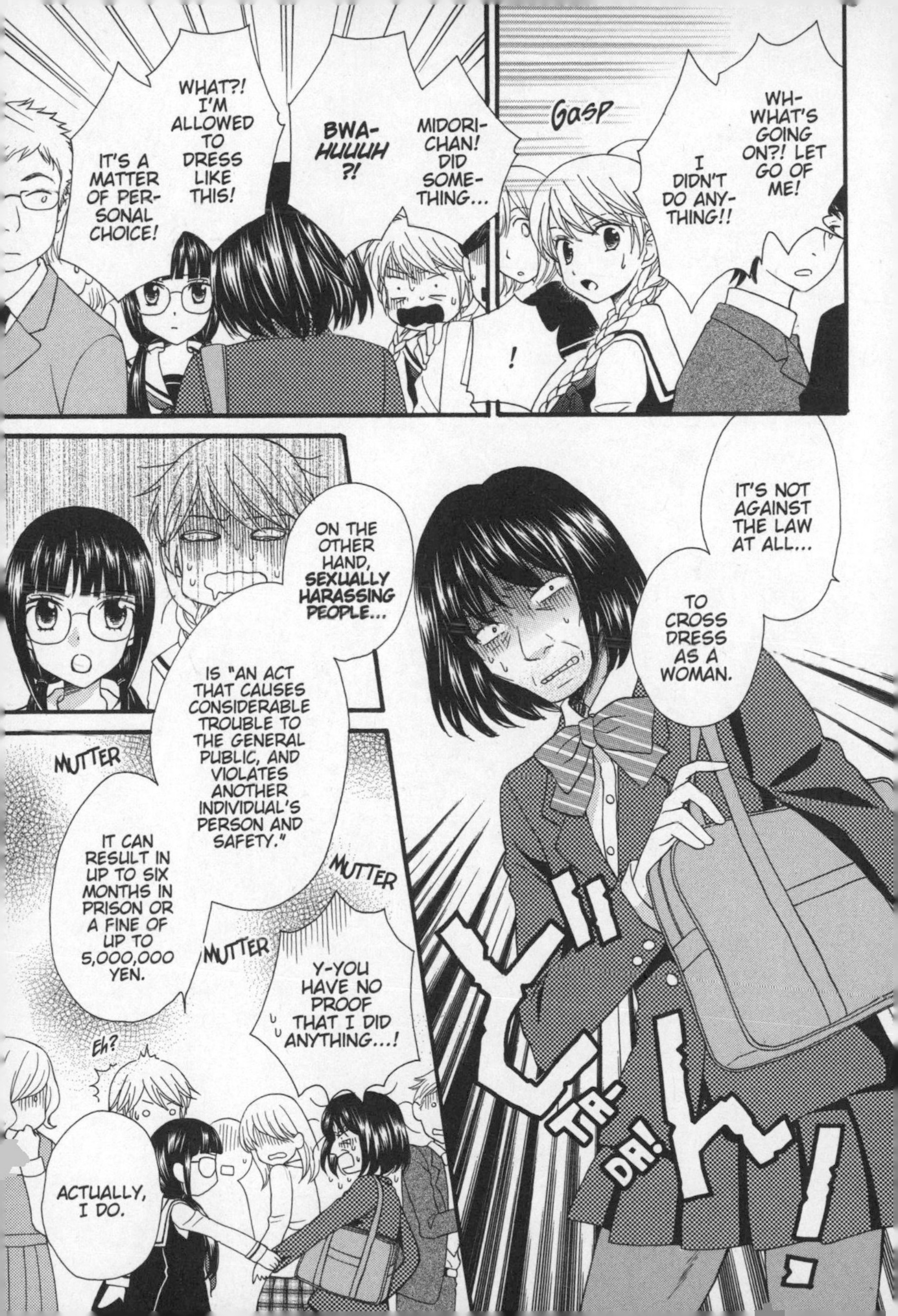
WH-WHAT'S GOING ON?! LET GO OF ME!
I DIDN'T DO ANY-THING!!
Gasp
!
MIDORI-CHAN! DID SOME-THING...
BWA-HUUUH?!
WHAT?! I'M ALLOWED TO DRESS LIKE THIS!
IT'S A MATTER OF PER-SONAL CHOICE!
IT'S NOT AGAINST THE LAW AT ALL...
TO CROSS DRESS AS A WOMAN.
TA-DA!
ON THE OTHER HAND, SEXUALLY HARASSING PEOPLE...
IS "AN ACT THAT CAUSES CONSIDERABLE TROUBLE TO THE GENERAL PUBLIC, AND VIOLATES ANOTHER INDIVIDUAL'S PERSON AND SAFETY."
MUTTER
IT CAN RESULT IN UP TO SIX MONTHS IN PRISON OR A FINE OF UP TO 5,000,000 YEN.
MUTTER
MUTTER
Y-YOU HAVE NO PROOF THAT I DID ANYTHING...!
Eh?
ACTUALLY, I DO.

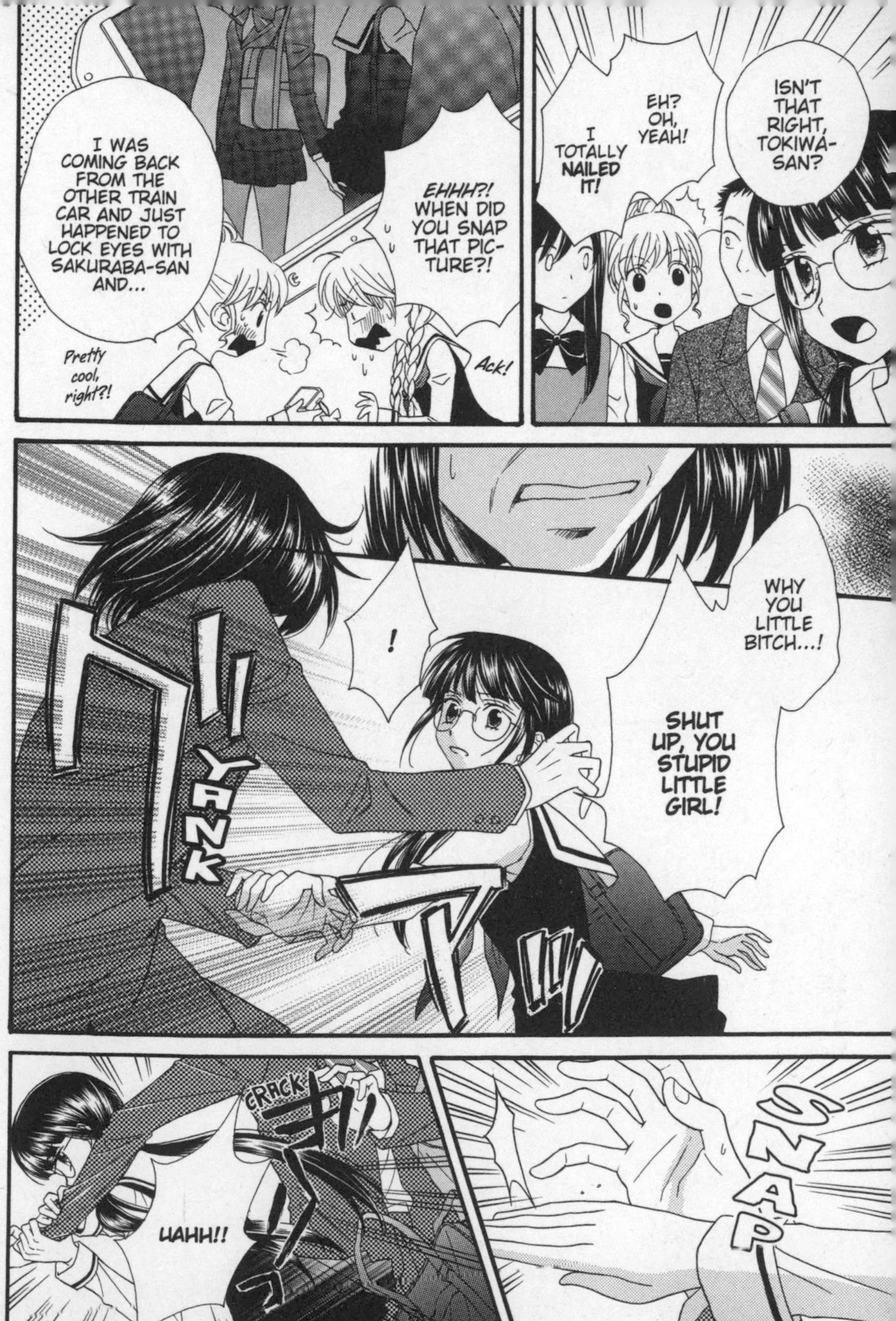
ISN'T THAT RIGHT, TOKIWA-SAN?
EH? OH, YEAH!
I TOTALLY NAILED IT!
EHHH?! WHEN DID YOU SNAP THAT PICTURE?!
Ack!
I WAS COMING BACK FROM THE OTHER TRAIN CAR AND JUST HAPPENED TO LOCK EYES WITH SAKURABA-SAN AND...
Pretty cool, right?!
WHY YOU LITTLE BITCH...!
SHUT UP, YOU STUPID LITTLE GIRL!
!
YANK
SNAP
CRACK
UAHH!!

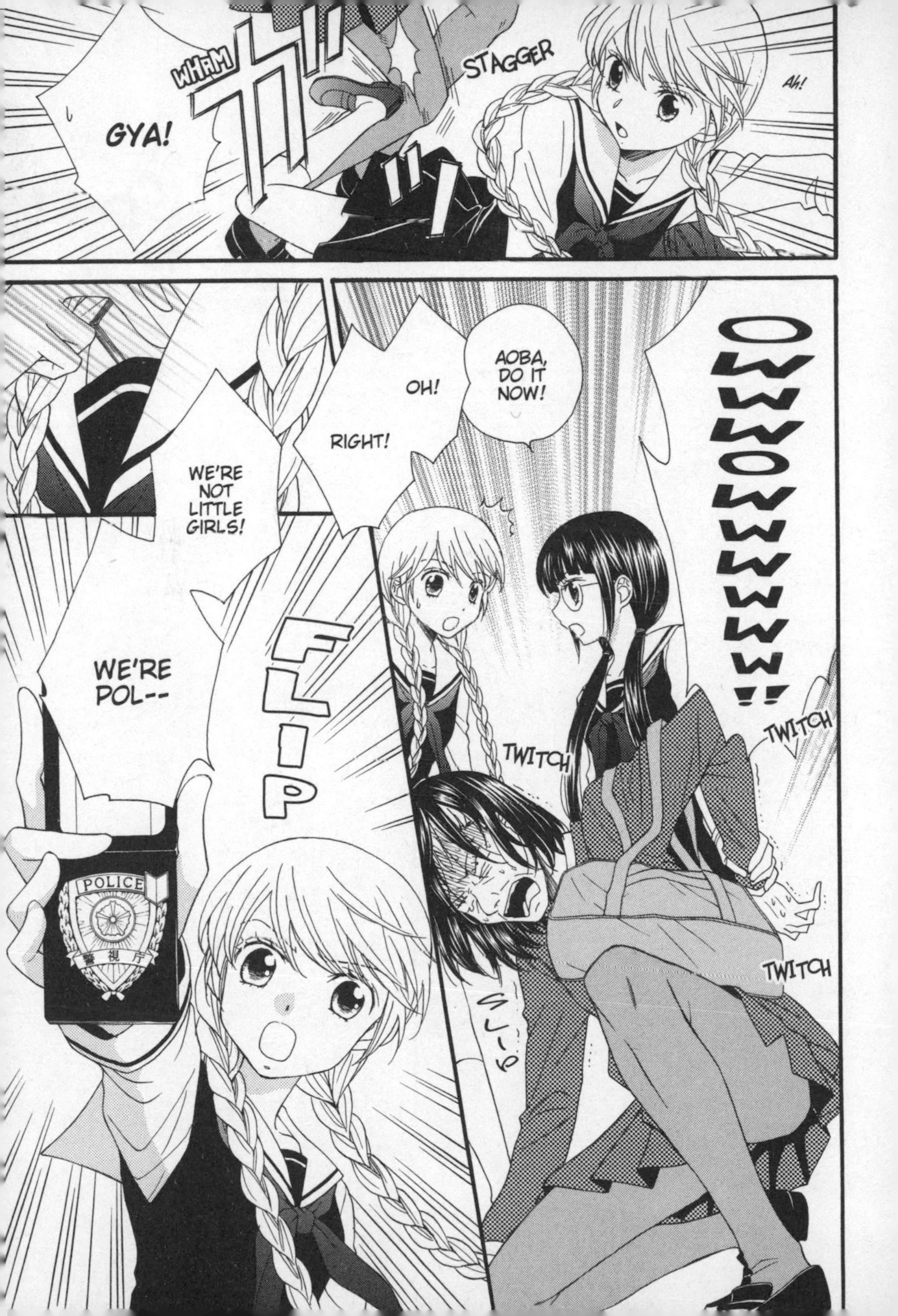
Ah!
STAGGER
WHAM
GYA!
OWWWOWWWWWW!!
AOBA, DO IT NOW!
OH!
RIGHT!
TWITCH
TWITCH
TWITCH
WE'RE NOT LITTLE GIRLS!
WE'RE POL--
FLIP
POLICE

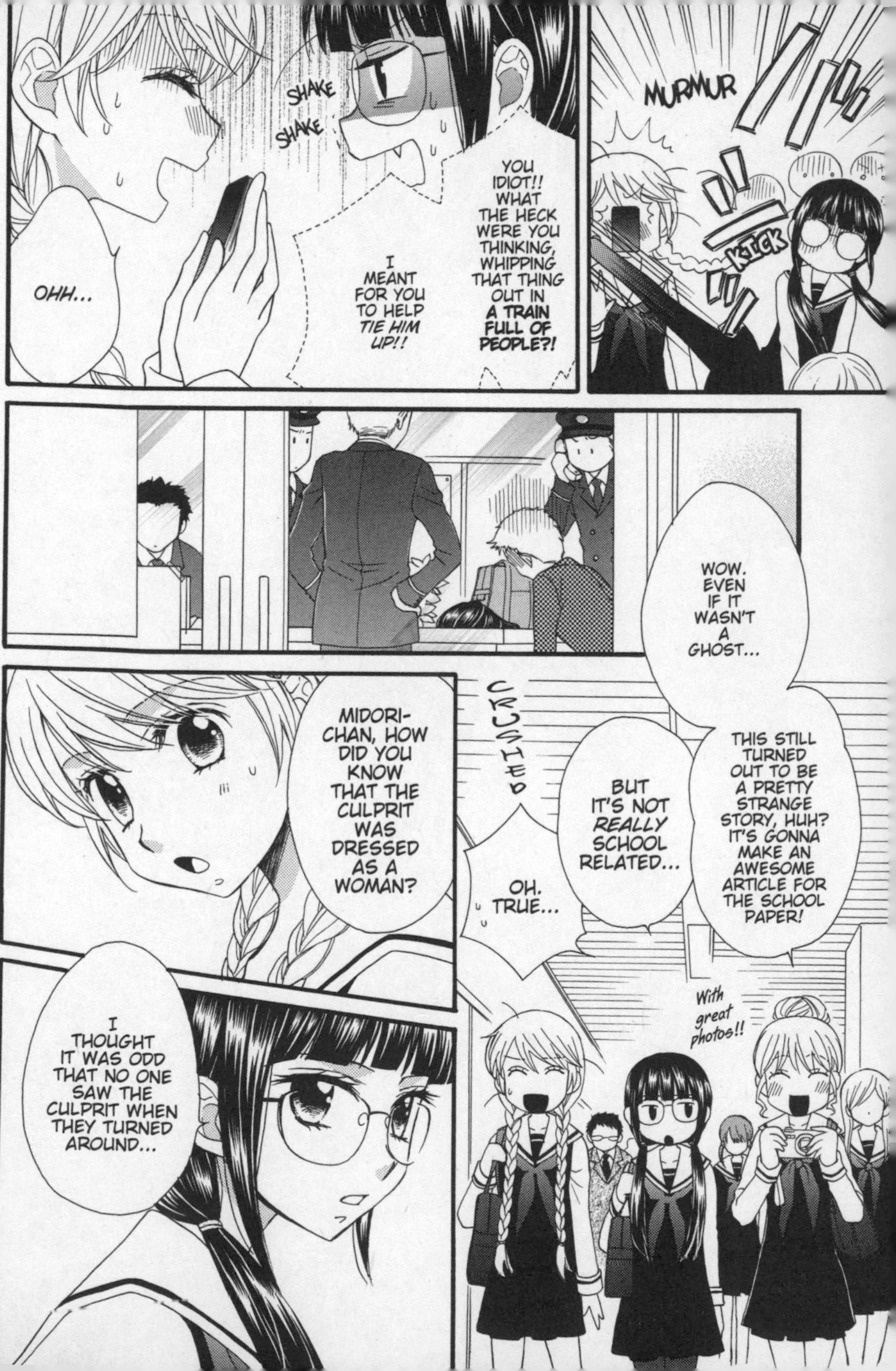
MURMUR
KICK
SHAKE
SHAKE
YOU IDIOT!! WHAT THE HECK WERE YOU THINKING, WHIPPING THAT THING OUT IN A TRAIN FULL OF PEOPLE?!
I MEANT FOR YOU TO HELP TIE HIM UP!!
OHH...
WOW. EVEN IF IT WASN'T A GHOST...
THIS STILL TURNED OUT TO BE A PRETTY STRANGE STORY, HUH? IT'S GONNA MAKE AN AWESOME ARTICLE FOR THE SCHOOL PAPER!
With great photos!!
BUT IT'S NOT REALLY SCHOOL RELATED...
OH. TRUE...
CRUSHED
MIDORI-CHAN, HOW DID YOU KNOW THAT THE CULPRIT WAS DRESSED AS A WOMAN?
I THOUGHT IT WAS ODD THAT NO ONE SAW THE CULPRIT WHEN THEY TURNED AROUND...

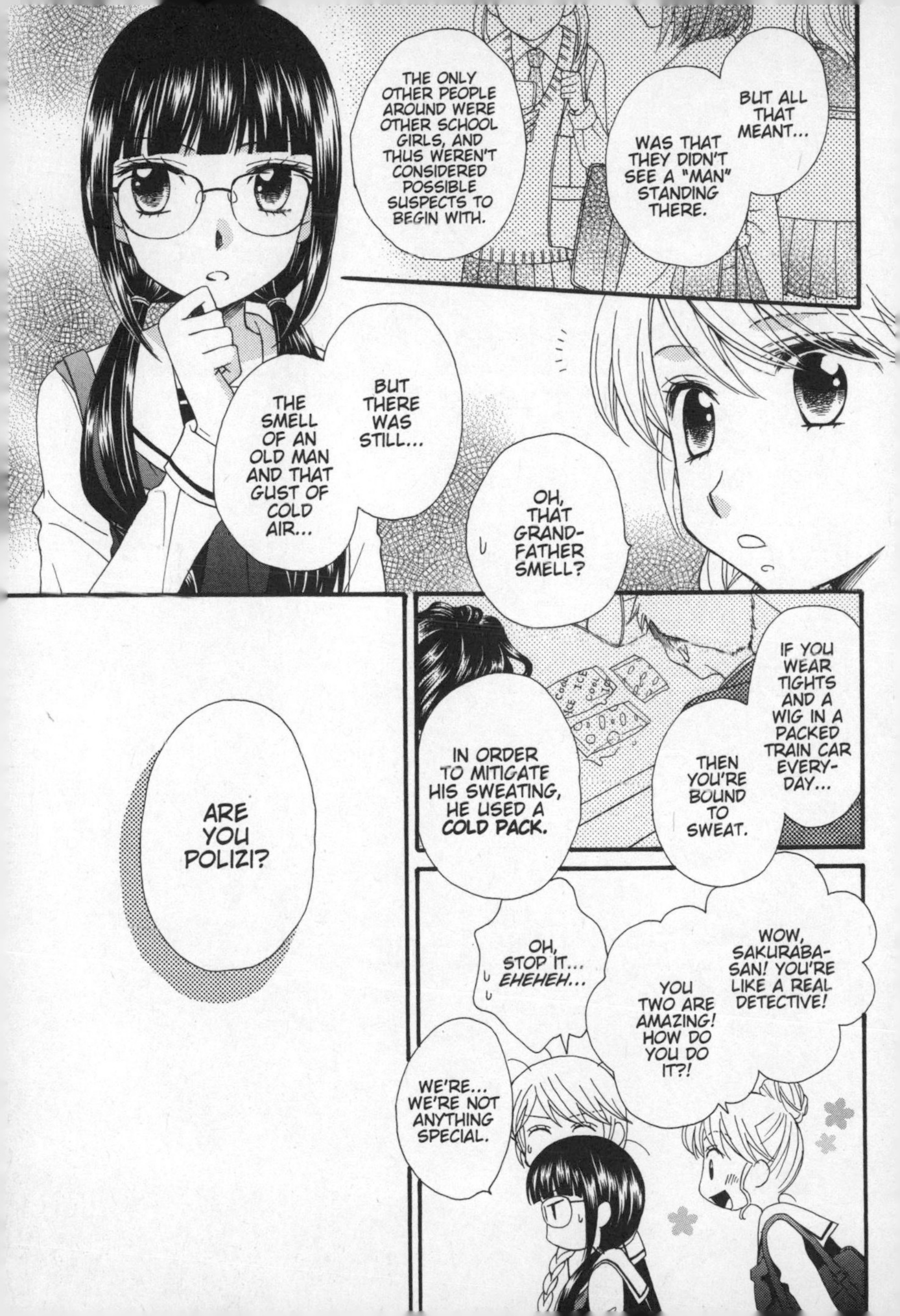

THE ONLY OTHER PEOPLE AROUND WERE OTHER SCHOOL GIRLS, AND THUS WEREN'T CONSIDERED POSSIBLE SUSPECTS TO BEGIN WITH.
BUT ALL THAT MEANT...
WAS THAT THEY DIDN'T SEE A "MAN" STANDING THERE.
BUT THERE WAS STILL...
THE SMELL OF AN OLD MAN AND THAT GUST OF COLD AIR...
OH, THAT GRAND-FATHER SMELL?
IF YOU WEAR TIGHTS AND A WIG IN A PACKED TRAIN CAR EVERY-DAY...
THEN YOU'RE BOUND TO SWEAT.
IN ORDER TO MITIGATE HIS SWEATING, HE USED A **COLD PACK.**
WOW, SAKURABA-SAN! YOU'RE LIKE A REAL DETECTIVE!
YOU TWO ARE AMAZING! HOW DO YOU DO IT?!
OH, STOP IT... *EHEHEH...*
WE'RE... WE'RE NOT ANYTHING SPECIAL.
ARE YOU POLIZI?

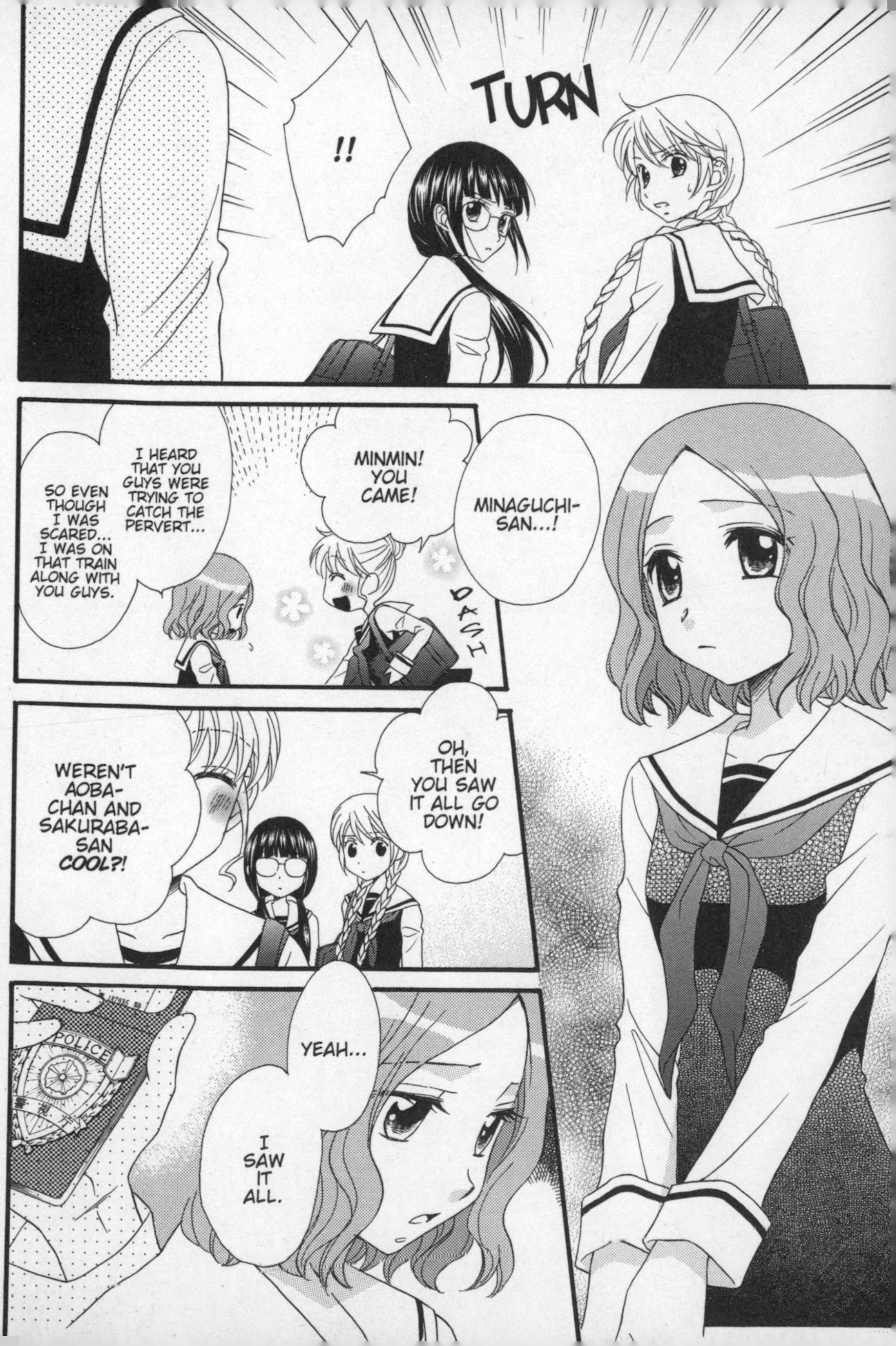
TURN
!!
MINAGUCHI-SAN...!
MINMIN! YOU CAME!
DASH
I HEARD THAT YOU GUYS WERE TRYING TO CATCH THE PERVERT...
SO EVEN THOUGH I WAS SCARED... I WAS ON THAT TRAIN ALONG WITH YOU GUYS.
OH, THEN YOU SAW IT ALL GO DOWN!
WEREN'T AOBA-CHAN AND SAKURABA-SAN *COOL*?!
POLICE
YEAH...
I SAW IT ALL.

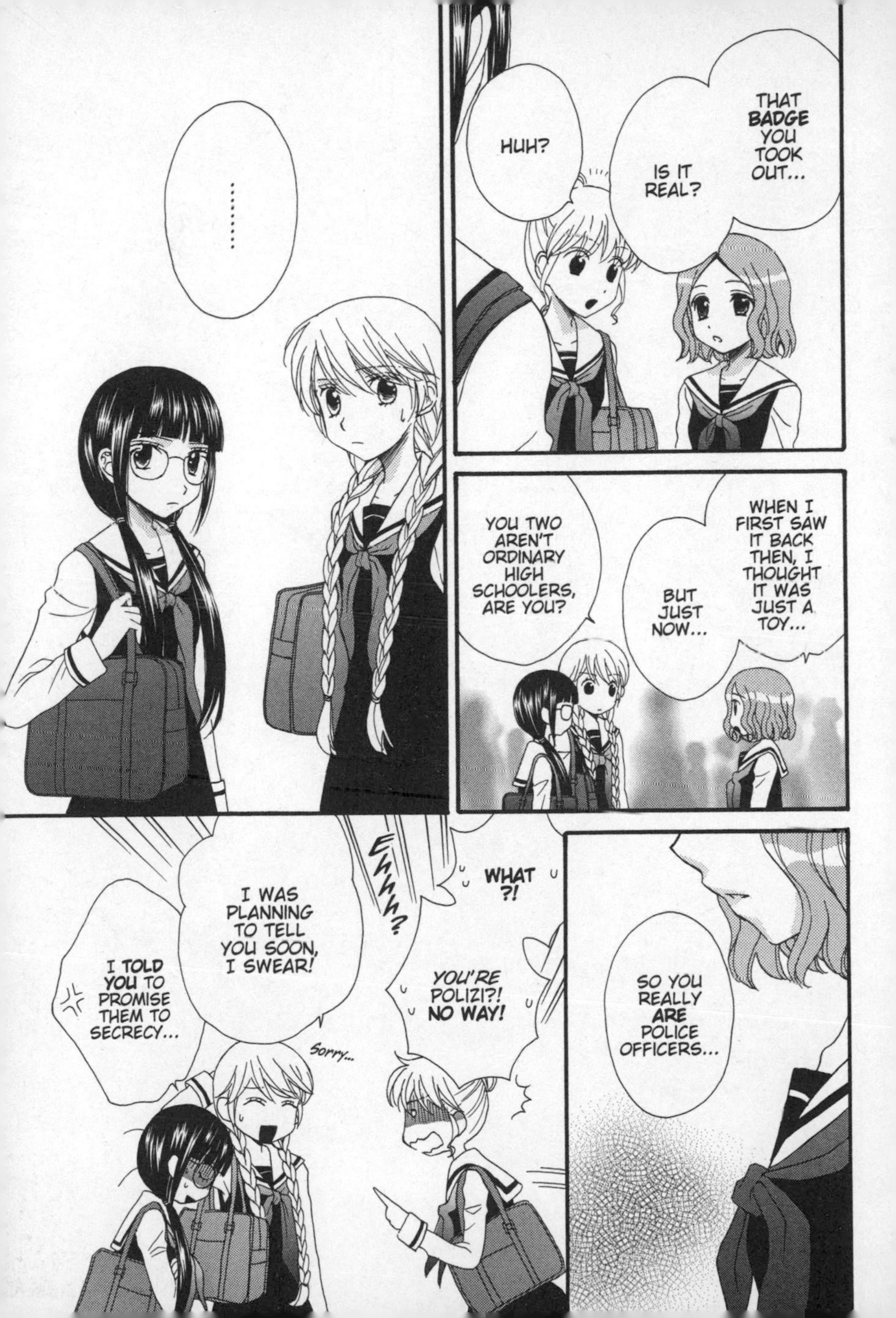
THAT BADGE YOU TOOK OUT...
IS IT REAL?
HUH?
WHEN I FIRST SAW IT BACK THEN, I THOUGHT IT WAS JUST A TOY...
BUT JUST NOW...
YOU TWO AREN'T ORDINARY HIGH SCHOOLERS, ARE YOU?
......
SO YOU REALLY ARE POLICE OFFICERS...
WHAT?!
EHHHH?
YOU'RE POLIZI?! NO WAY!
I WAS PLANNING TO TELL YOU SOON, I SWEAR!
I TOLD YOU TO PROMISE THEM TO SECRECY...
Sorry...

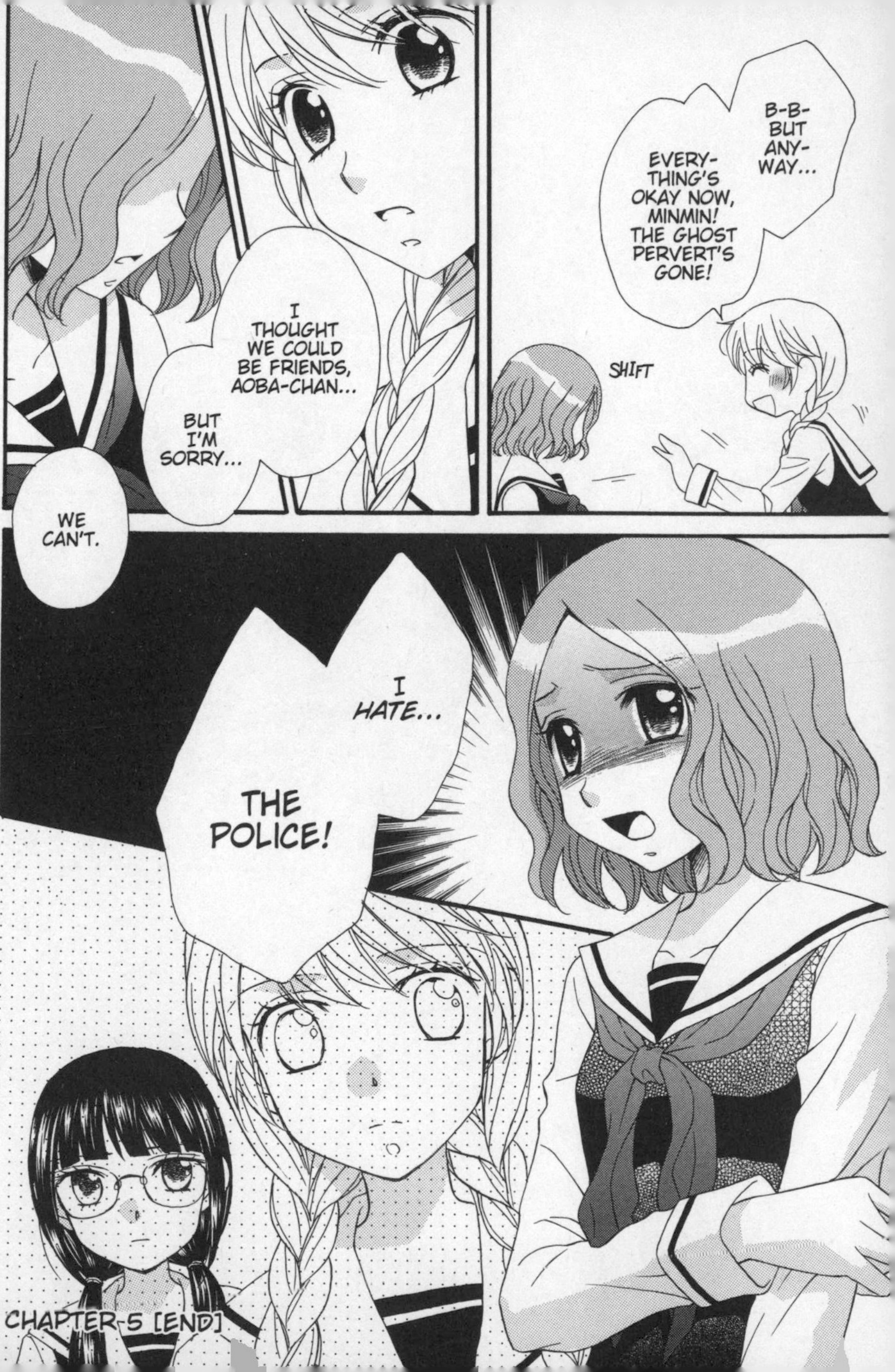
B-B-BUT ANYWAY...
EVERYTHING'S OKAY NOW, MINMIN! THE GHOST PERVERT'S GONE!
SHIFT
I THOUGHT WE COULD BE FRIENDS, AOBA-CHAN...
BUT I'M SORRY...
WE CAN'T.
I HATE...
THE POLICE!
CHAPTER 5 [END]

GAKUEN POLIZI

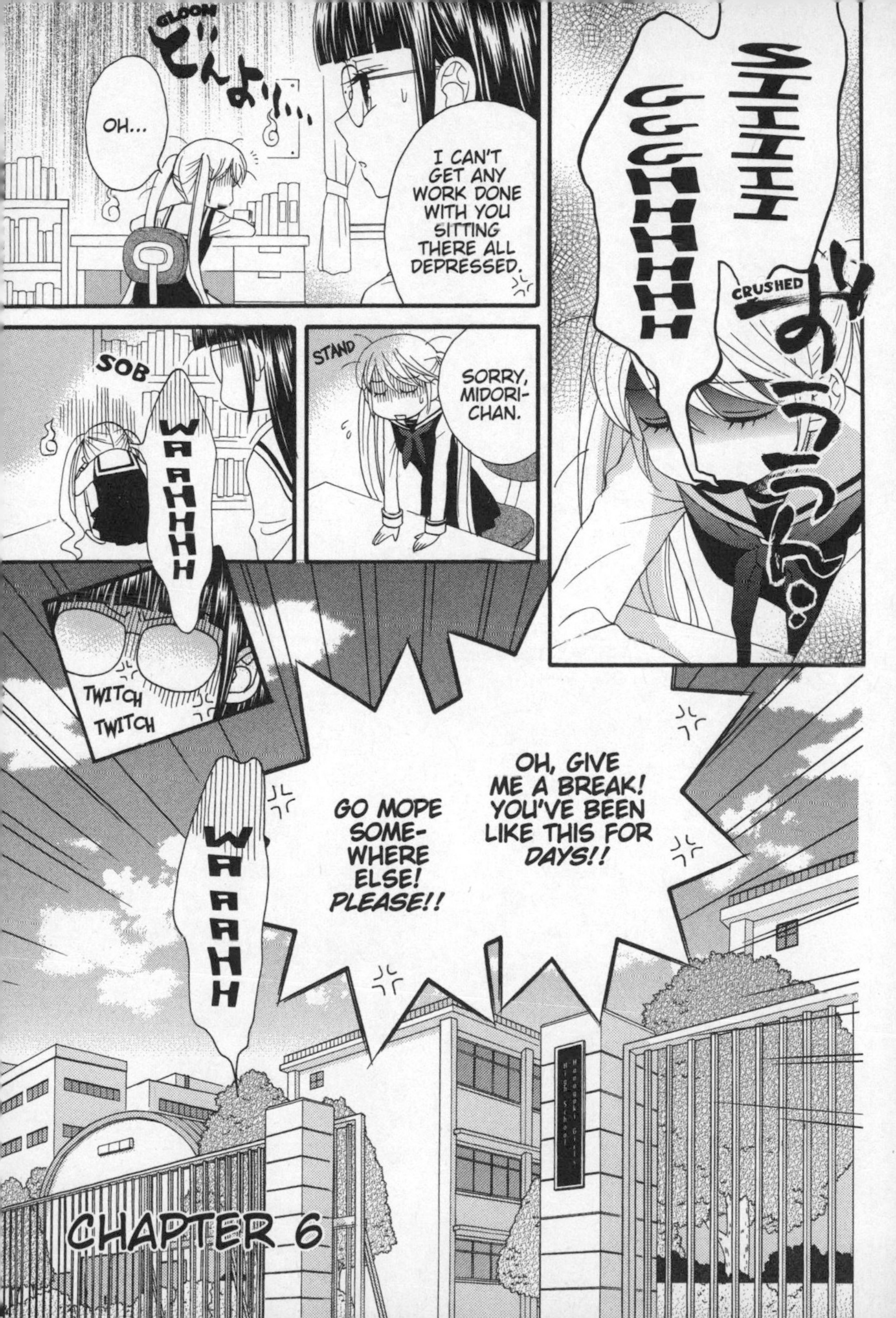
SIIIIIGGGHHHHHH
CRUSHED
I CAN'T GET ANY WORK DONE WITH YOU SITTING THERE ALL DEPRESSED.
GLOOM
OH...
STAND
SORRY, MIDORI-CHAN.
SOB
WAAHHHHH
TWITCH
TWITCH
OH, GIVE ME A BREAK! YOU'VE BEEN LIKE THIS FOR DAYS!!
GO MOPE SOME-WHERE ELSE! PLEASE!!
WAAAAHH
CHAPTER 6

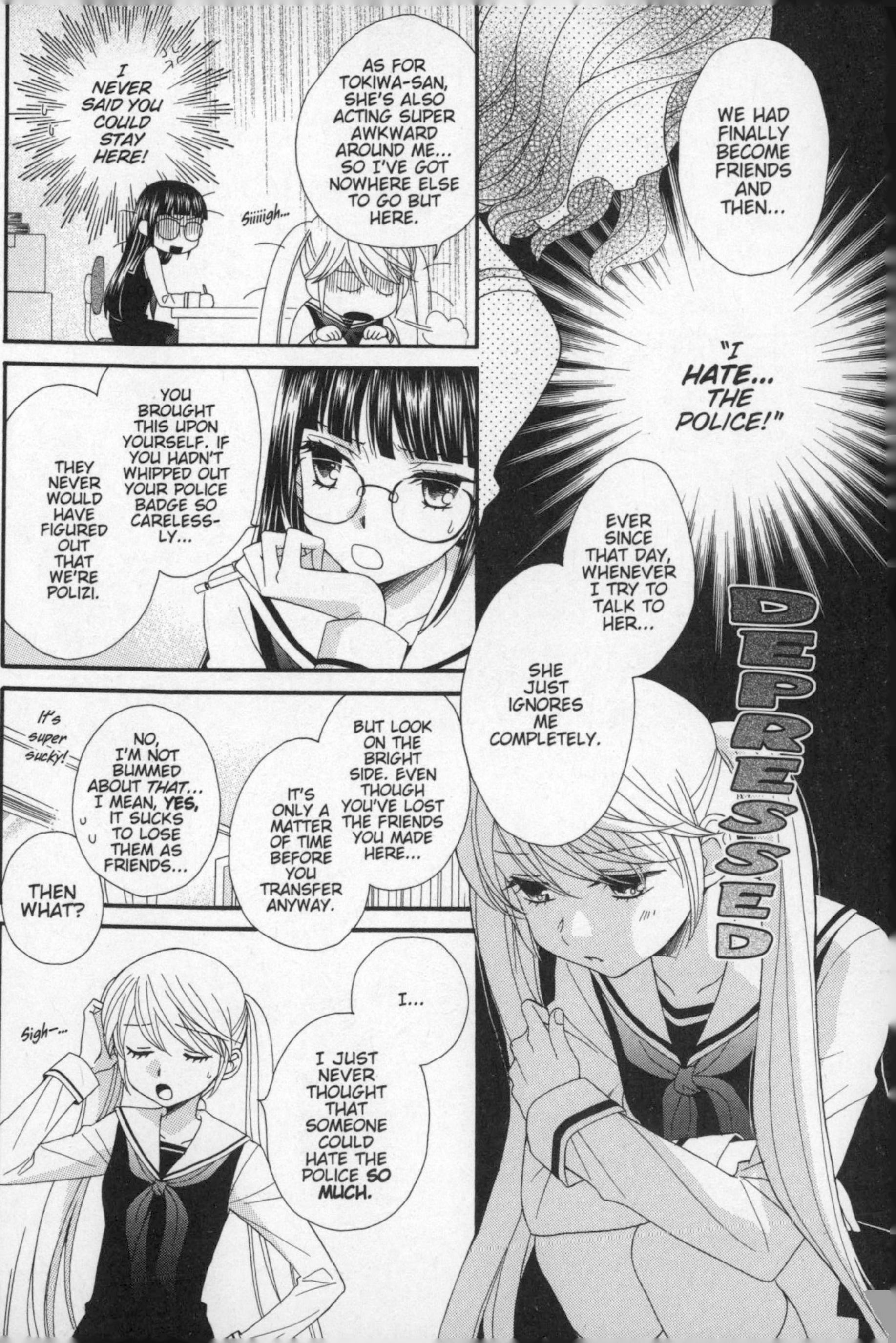
WE HAD FINALLY BECOME FRIENDS AND THEN...
"I HATE... THE POLICE!"
EVER SINCE THAT DAY, WHENEVER I TRY TO TALK TO HER...
SHE JUST IGNORES ME COMPLETELY.
DEPRESSED
AS FOR TOKIWA-SAN, SHE'S ALSO ACTING SUPER AWKWARD AROUND ME... SO I'VE GOT NOWHERE ELSE TO GO BUT HERE.
Siiiiigh...
I NEVER SAID YOU COULD STAY HERE!
YOU BROUGHT THIS UPON YOURSELF. IF YOU HADN'T WHIPPED OUT YOUR POLICE BADGE SO CARELESS-LY...
THEY NEVER WOULD HAVE FIGURED OUT THAT WE'RE POLIZI.
BUT LOOK ON THE BRIGHT SIDE. EVEN THOUGH YOU'VE LOST THE FRIENDS YOU MADE HERE...
IT'S ONLY A MATTER OF TIME BEFORE YOU TRANSFER ANYWAY.
NO, I'M NOT BUMMED ABOUT *THAT*... I MEAN, **YES,** IT SUCKS TO LOSE THEM AS FRIENDS...
It's super sucky!
THEN WHAT?
I...
I JUST NEVER THOUGHT THAT SOMEONE COULD HATE THE POLICE **SO MUCH.**
Sigh—...

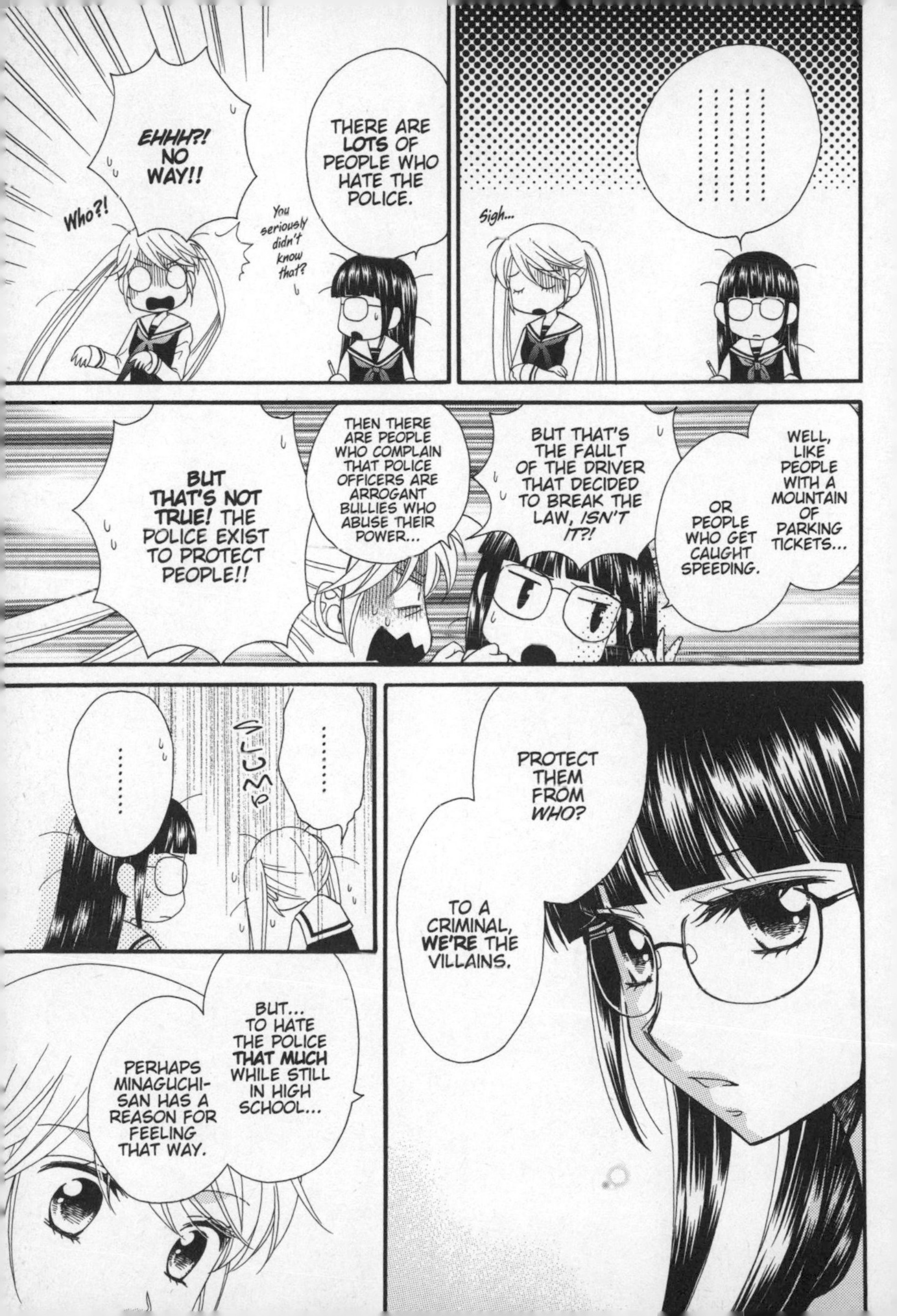
......
Sigh...
THERE ARE LOTS OF PEOPLE WHO HATE THE POLICE.
You seriously didn't know that?
EHHH?! NO WAY!!
Who?!
WELL, LIKE PEOPLE WITH A MOUNTAIN OF PARKING TICKETS...
OR PEOPLE WHO GET CAUGHT SPEEDING.
BUT THAT'S THE FAULT OF THE DRIVER THAT DECIDED TO BREAK THE LAW, ISN'T IT?!
THEN THERE ARE PEOPLE WHO COMPLAIN THAT POLICE OFFICERS ARE ARROGANT BULLIES WHO ABUSE THEIR POWER...
BUT THAT'S NOT TRUE! THE POLICE EXIST TO PROTECT PEOPLE!!
PROTECT THEM FROM WHO?
TO A CRIMINAL, WE'RE THE VILLAINS.
......
SLUMP
......
BUT... TO HATE THE POLICE THAT MUCH WHILE STILL IN HIGH SCHOOL...
PERHAPS MINAGUCHI-SAN HAS A REASON FOR FEELING THAT WAY.

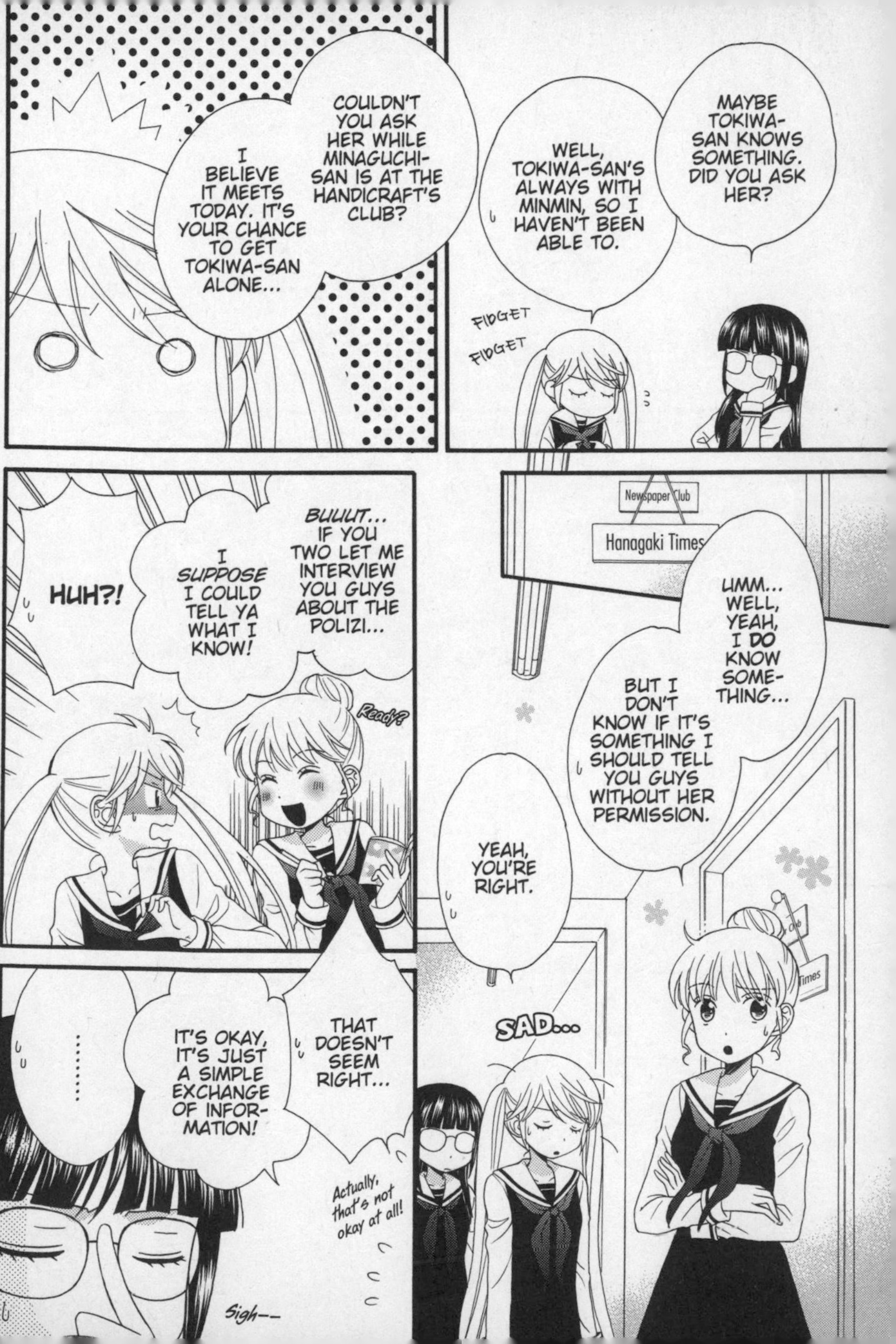
MAYBE TOKIWA-SAN KNOWS SOMETHING. DID YOU ASK HER?
WELL, TOKIWA-SAN'S ALWAYS WITH MINMIN, SO I HAVEN'T BEEN ABLE TO.
FIDGET
FIDGET
COULDN'T YOU ASK HER WHILE MINAGUCHI-SAN IS AT THE HANDICRAFT'S CLUB?
I BELIEVE IT MEETS TODAY. IT'S YOUR CHANCE TO GET TOKIWA-SAN ALONE...
Newspaper Club
Hanagaki Times
UMM... WELL, YEAH, I DO KNOW SOME-THING...
BUT I DON'T KNOW IF IT'S SOMETHING I SHOULD TELL YOU GUYS WITHOUT HER PERMISSION.
YEAH, YOU'RE RIGHT.
SAD...
BUUUT... IF YOU TWO LET ME INTERVIEW YOU GUYS ABOUT THE POLIZI...
I SUPPOSE I COULD TELL YA WHAT I KNOW!
HUH?!
Ready?
THAT DOESN'T SEEM RIGHT...
IT'S OKAY, IT'S JUST A SIMPLE EXCHANGE OF INFOR-MATION!
......
Actually, that's not okay at all!
Sigh--

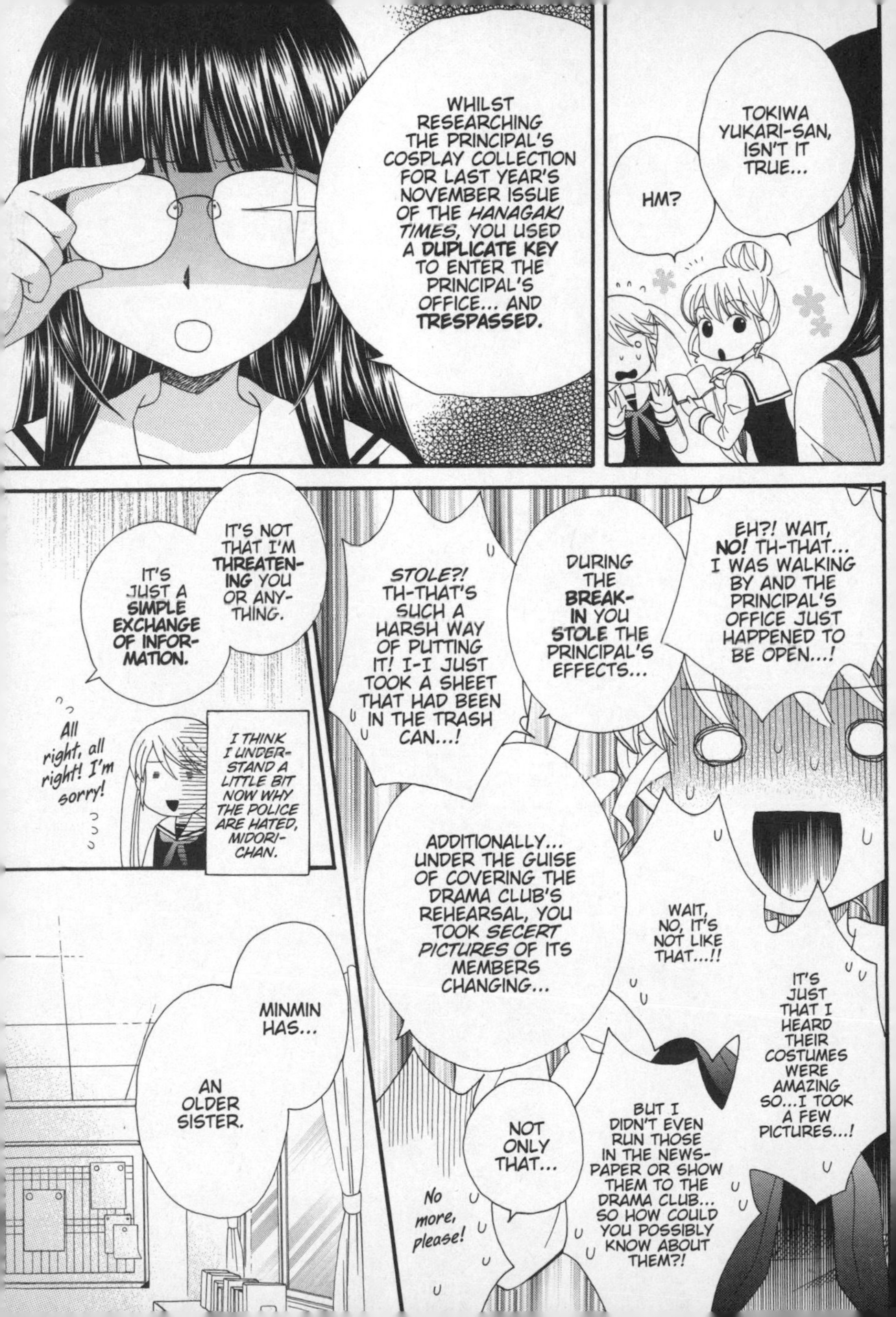
TOKIWA YUKARI-SAN, ISN'T IT TRUE...
HM?
WHILST RESEARCHING THE PRINCIPAL'S COSPLAY COLLECTION FOR LAST YEAR'S NOVEMBER ISSUE OF THE *HANAGAKI TIMES*, YOU USED A **DUPLICATE KEY** TO ENTER THE PRINCIPAL'S OFFICE... AND **TRESPASSED.**
EH?! WAIT, **NO!** TH-THAT... I WAS WALKING BY AND THE PRINCIPAL'S OFFICE JUST HAPPENED TO BE OPEN...!
DURING THE **BREAK-IN** YOU **STOLE** THE PRINCIPAL'S EFFECTS...
STOLE?! TH-THAT'S SUCH A HARSH WAY OF PUTTING IT! I-I JUST TOOK A SHEET THAT HAD BEEN IN THE TRASH CAN...!
IT'S NOT THAT I'M **THREATENING** YOU OR ANYTHING.
IT'S JUST A **SIMPLE EXCHANGE OF INFORMATION.**
I THINK I UNDERSTAND A LITTLE BIT NOW WHY THE POLICE ARE HATED, MIDORI-CHAN.
All right, all right! I'm sorry!
ADDITIONALLY... UNDER THE GUISE OF COVERING THE DRAMA CLUB'S REHEARSAL, YOU TOOK *SECERT PICTURES* OF ITS MEMBERS CHANGING...
WAIT, NO, IT'S NOT LIKE THAT...!!
IT'S JUST THAT I HEARD THEIR COSTUMES WERE AMAZING SO...I TOOK A FEW PICTURES...!
BUT I DIDN'T EVEN RUN THOSE IN THE NEWS-PAPER OR SHOW THEM TO THE DRAMA CLUB... SO HOW COULD YOU POSSIBLY KNOW ABOUT THEM?!
NOT ONLY THAT...
No more, please!
MINMIN HAS...
AN OLDER SISTER.

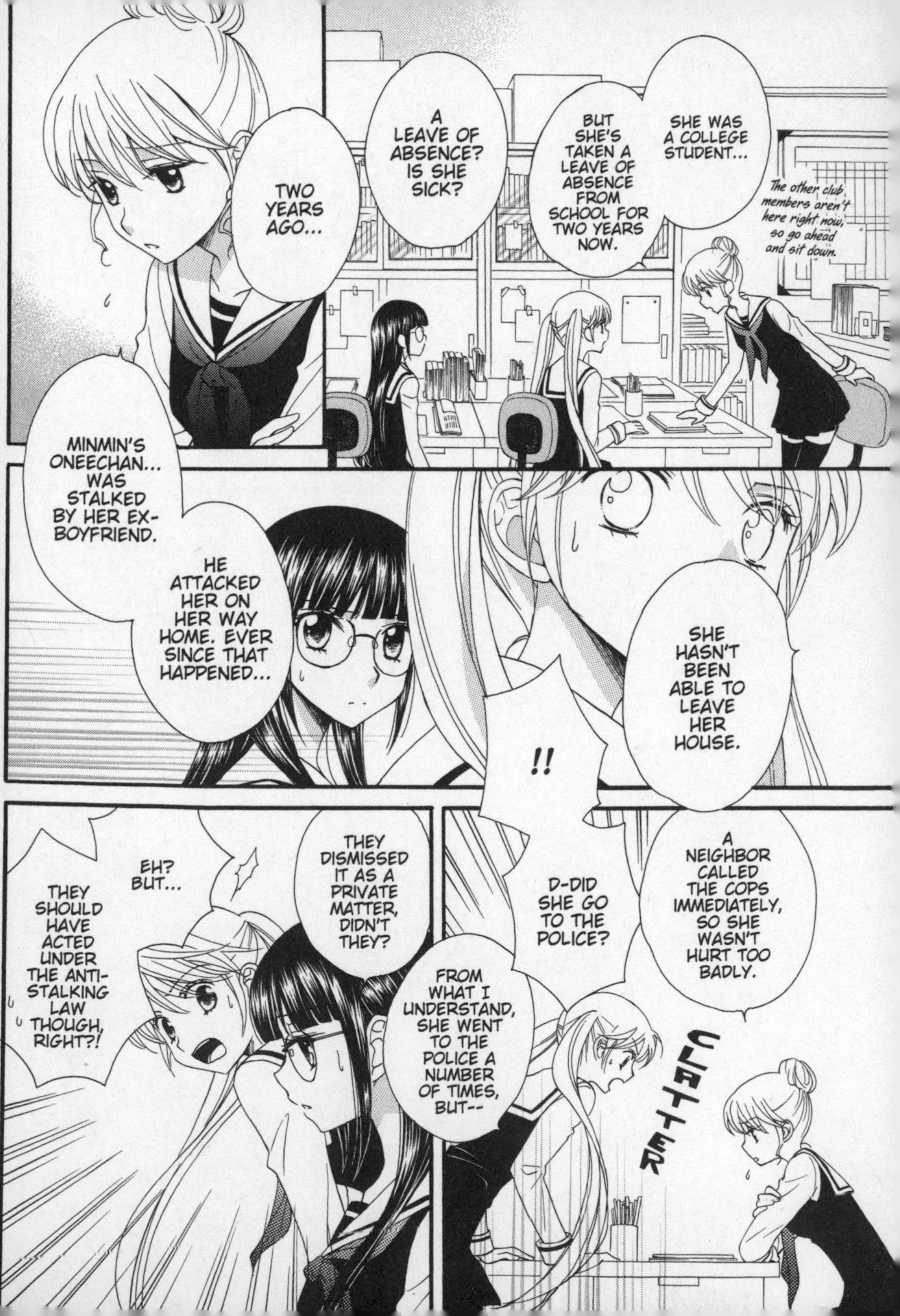
The other club members aren't here right now, so go ahead and sit down.
SHE WAS A COLLEGE STUDENT...
BUT SHE'S TAKEN A LEAVE OF ABSENCE FROM SCHOOL FOR TWO YEARS NOW.
A LEAVE OF ABSENCE? IS SHE SICK?
TWO YEARS AGO...
MINMIN'S ONEECHAN... WAS STALKED BY HER EX-BOYFRIEND.
HE ATTACKED HER ON HER WAY HOME. EVER SINCE THAT HAPPENED...
SHE HASN'T BEEN ABLE TO LEAVE HER HOUSE.
!!
A NEIGHBOR CALLED THE COPS IMMEDIATELY, SO SHE WASN'T HURT TOO BADLY.
D-DID SHE GO TO THE POLICE?
CLATTER
FROM WHAT I UNDERSTAND, SHE WENT TO THE POLICE A NUMBER OF TIMES, BUT--
THEY DISMISSED IT AS A PRIVATE MATTER, DIDN'T THEY?
EH? BUT...
THEY SHOULD HAVE ACTED UNDER THE ANTI-STALKING LAW THOUGH, RIGHT?!

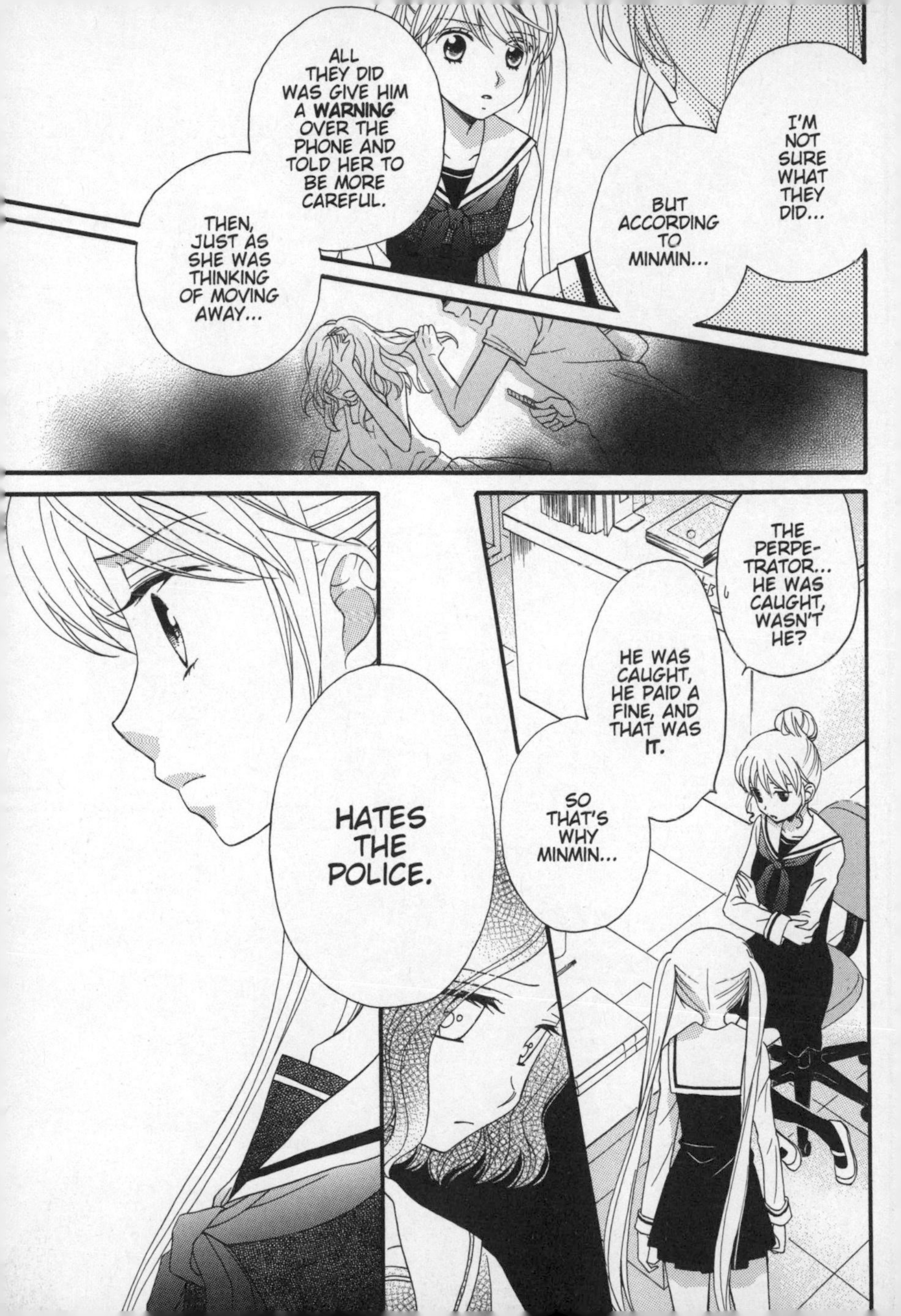
I'M NOT SURE WHAT THEY DID...
BUT ACCORDING TO MINMIN...
ALL THEY DID WAS GIVE HIM A **WARNING** OVER THE PHONE AND TOLD HER TO BE MORE CAREFUL.
THEN, JUST AS SHE WAS THINKING OF MOVING AWAY...
THE PERPE-TRATOR... HE WAS CAUGHT, WASN'T HE?
HE WAS CAUGHT, HE PAID A FINE, AND THAT WAS IT.
SO THAT'S WHY MINMIN...
HATES THE POLICE.

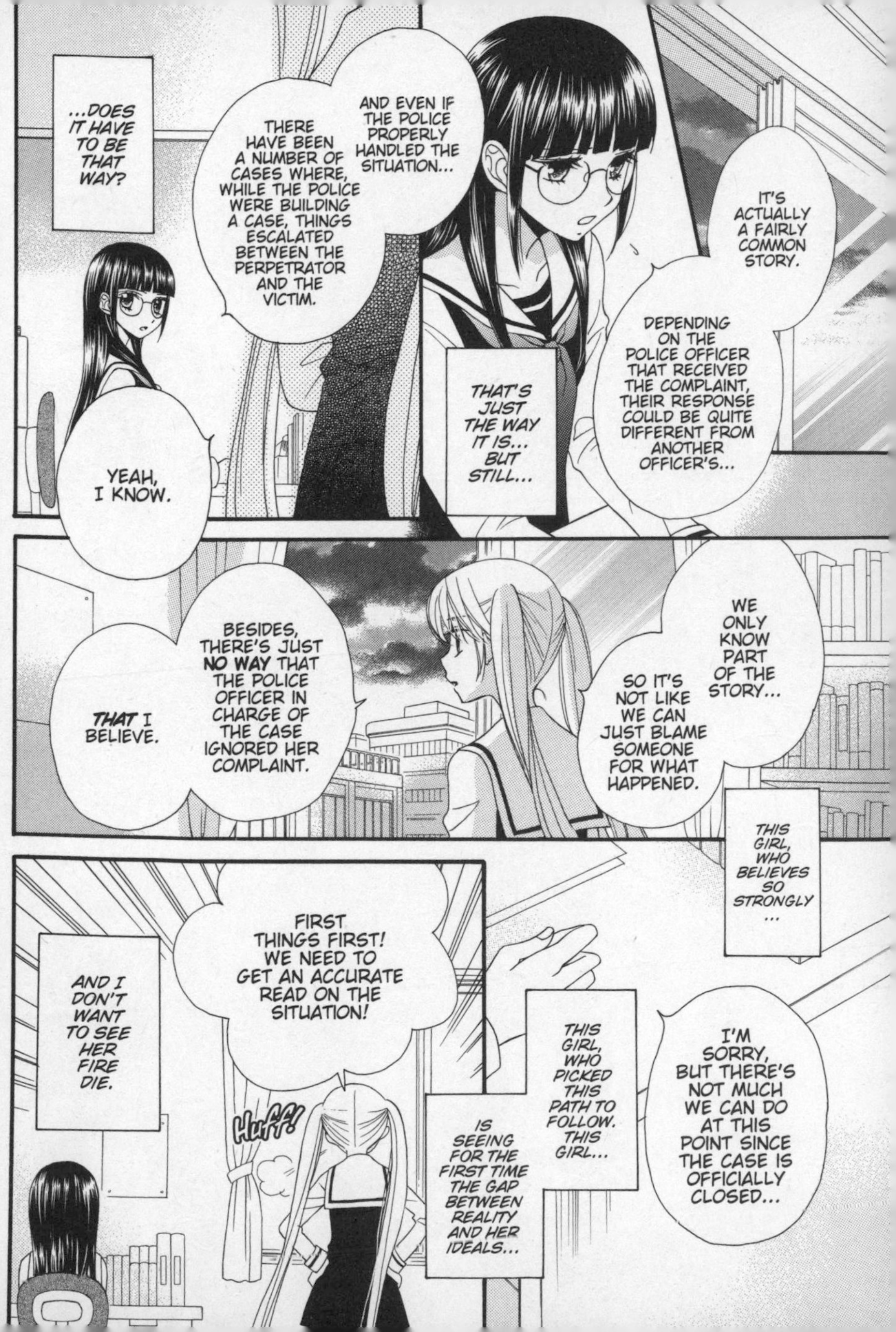
IT'S ACTUALLY A FAIRLY COMMON STORY.
DEPENDING ON THE POLICE OFFICER THAT RECEIVED THE COMPLAINT, THEIR RESPONSE COULD BE QUITE DIFFERENT FROM ANOTHER OFFICER'S...
THAT'S JUST THE WAY IT IS... BUT STILL...
AND EVEN IF THE POLICE PROPERLY HANDLED THE SITUATION...
THERE HAVE BEEN A NUMBER OF CASES WHERE, WHILE THE POLICE WERE BUILDING A CASE, THINGS ESCALATED BETWEEN THE PERPETRATOR AND THE VICTIM.
...DOES IT HAVE TO BE THAT WAY?
YEAH, I KNOW.
WE ONLY KNOW PART OF THE STORY...
SO IT'S NOT LIKE WE CAN JUST BLAME SOMEONE FOR WHAT HAPPENED.
BESIDES, THERE'S JUST NO WAY THAT THE POLICE OFFICER IN CHARGE OF THE CASE IGNORED HER COMPLAINT.
THAT I BELIEVE.
THIS GIRL, WHO BELIEVES SO STRONGLY ...
I'M SORRY, BUT THERE'S NOT MUCH WE CAN DO AT THIS POINT SINCE THE CASE IS OFFICIALLY CLOSED...
THIS GIRL, WHO PICKED THIS PATH TO FOLLOW. THIS GIRL...
IS SEEING FOR THE FIRST TIME THE GAP BETWEEN REALITY AND HER IDEALS...
FIRST THINGS FIRST! WE NEED TO GET AN ACCURATE READ ON THE SITUATION!
Huff!
AND I DON'T WANT TO SEE HER FIRE DIE.

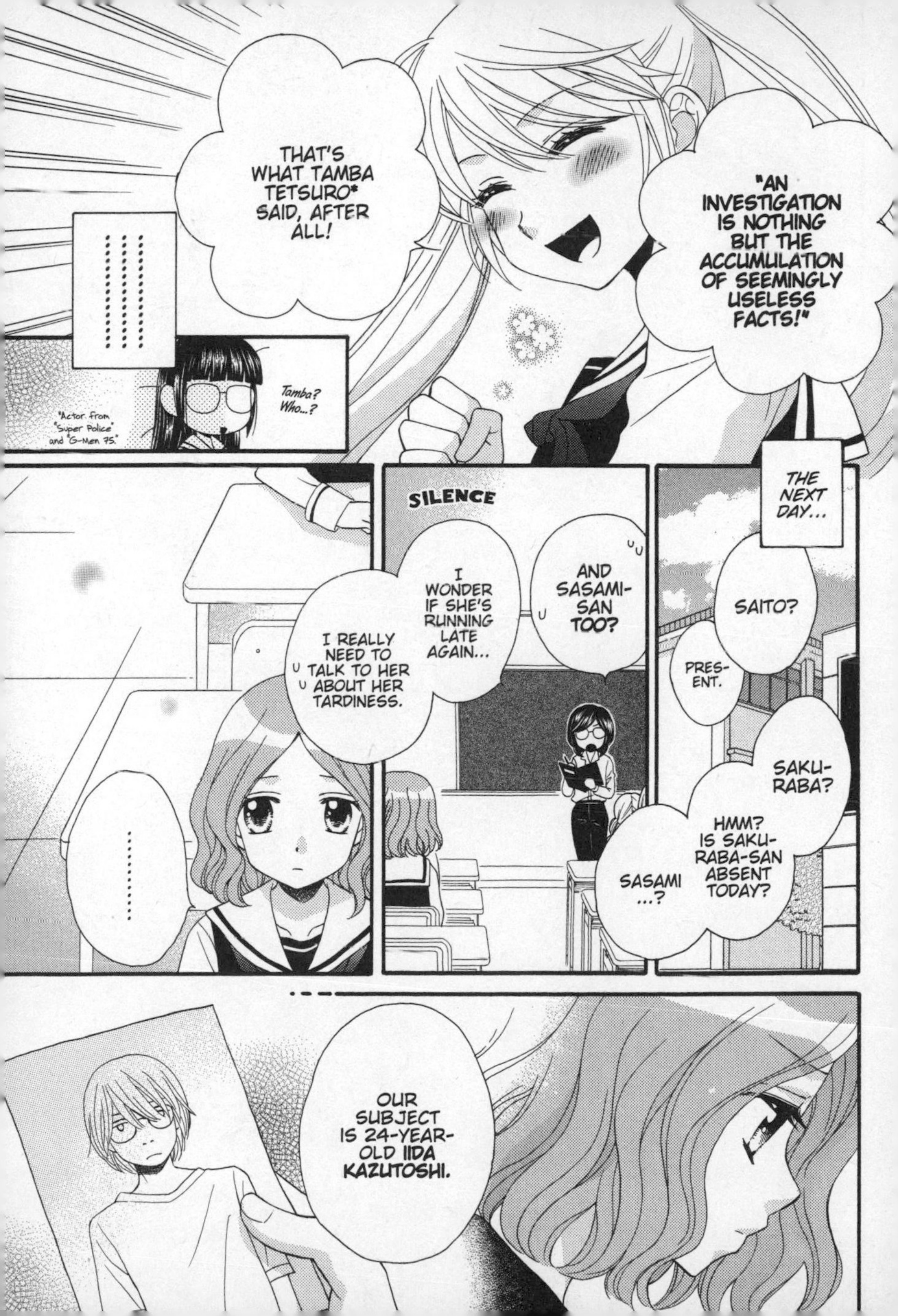
"AN INVESTIGATION IS NOTHING BUT THE ACCUMULATION OF SEEMINGLY USELESS FACTS!"
THAT'S WHAT TAMBA TETSURO* SAID, AFTER ALL!
......
Tamba? Who...?
*Actor from "Super Police" and "G-Men 75."
THE NEXT DAY...
SAITO?
PRESENT.
SAKURABA?
HMM? IS SAKURABA-SAN ABSENT TODAY?
SASAMI ...?
SILENCE
AND SASAMI-SAN TOO?
I WONDER IF SHE'S RUNNING LATE AGAIN...
I REALLY NEED TO TALK TO HER ABOUT HER TARDINESS.
......
OUR SUBJECT IS 24-YEAR-OLD IIDA KAZUTOSHI.

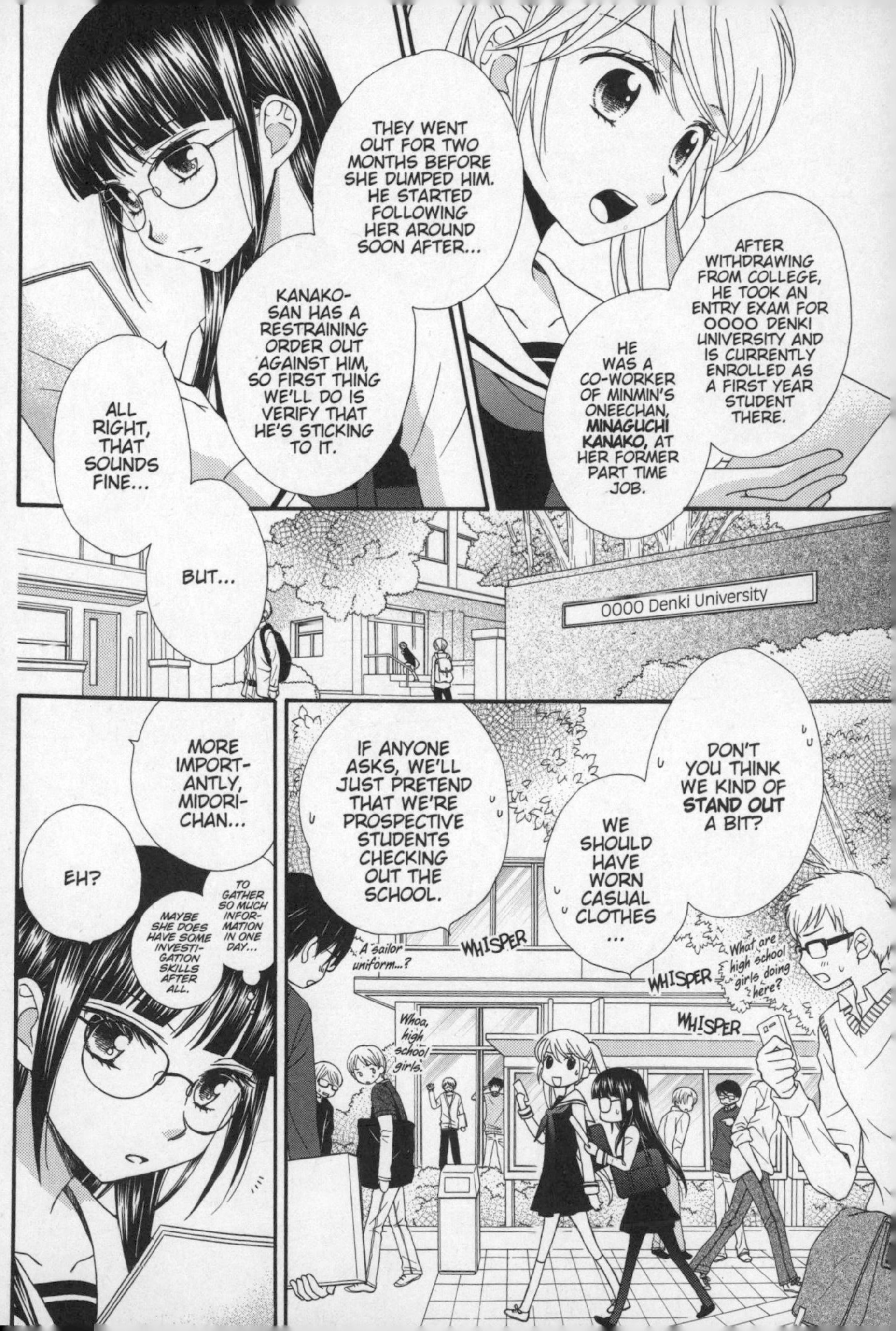
HE WAS A CO-WORKER OF MINMIN'S ONEECHAN, **MINAGUCHI KANAKO,** AT HER FORMER PART TIME JOB.
THEY WENT OUT FOR TWO MONTHS BEFORE SHE DUMPED HIM. HE STARTED FOLLOWING HER AROUND SOON AFTER...
AFTER WITHDRAWING FROM COLLEGE, HE TOOK AN ENTRY EXAM FOR OOOO DENKI UNIVERSITY AND IS CURRENTLY ENROLLED AS A FIRST YEAR STUDENT THERE.
KANAKO-SAN HAS A RESTRAINING ORDER OUT AGAINST HIM, SO FIRST THING WE'LL DO IS VERIFY THAT HE'S STICKING TO IT.
ALL RIGHT, THAT SOUNDS FINE...
BUT...
OOOO Denki University
DON'T YOU THINK WE KIND OF **STAND OUT** A BIT?
WE SHOULD HAVE WORN CASUAL CLOTHES ...
IF ANYONE ASKS, WE'LL JUST PRETEND THAT WE'RE PROSPECTIVE STUDENTS CHECKING OUT THE SCHOOL.
What are high school girls doing here?
WHISPER
A sailor uniform...?
WHISPER
Whoa, high school girls.
WHISPER
MORE IMPORT-ANTLY, MIDORI-CHAN...
EH?
TO GATHER SO MUCH INFORMATION IN ONE DAY...
MAYBE SHE DOES HAVE SOME INVESTIGATION SKILLS AFTER ALL.

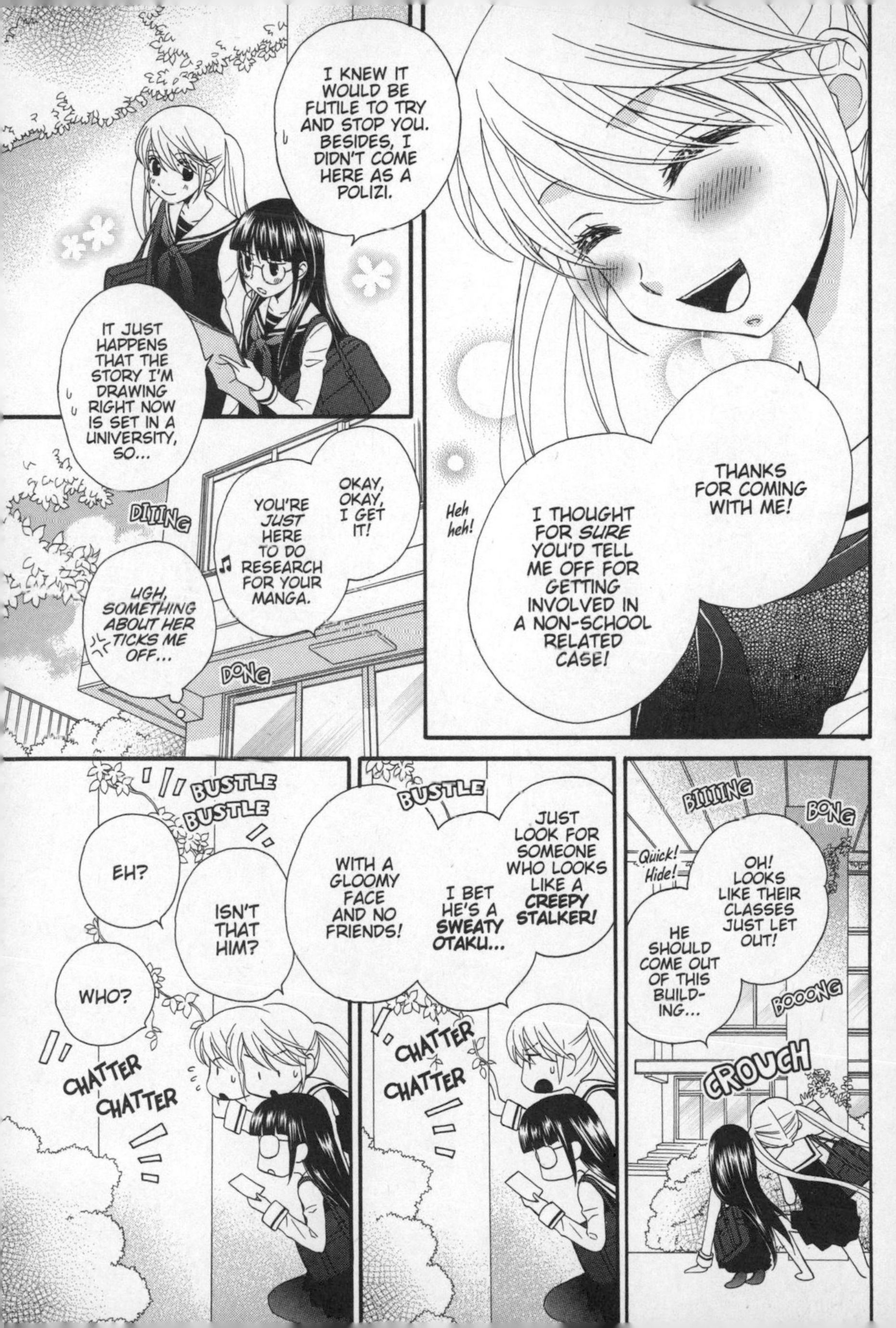
THANKS FOR COMING WITH ME!
I THOUGHT FOR *SURE* YOU'D TELL ME OFF FOR GETTING INVOLVED IN A NON-SCHOOL RELATED CASE!
Heh heh!
I KNEW IT WOULD BE FUTILE TO TRY AND STOP YOU. BESIDES, I DIDN'T COME HERE AS A POLIZI.
IT JUST HAPPENS THAT THE STORY I'M DRAWING RIGHT NOW IS SET IN A UNIVERSITY, SO...
OKAY, OKAY, I GET IT!
YOU'RE *JUST* HERE TO DO RESEARCH FOR YOUR MANGA.
DIIING
UGH, SOMETHING ABOUT HER TICKS ME OFF...
DONG
BIIIING
BONG
OH! LOOKS LIKE THEIR CLASSES JUST LET OUT!
Quick! Hide!
HE SHOULD COME OUT OF THIS BUILDING...
BOOONG
CROUCH
BUSTLE
JUST LOOK FOR SOMEONE WHO LOOKS LIKE A **CREEPY STALKER!**
I BET HE'S A **SWEATY OTAKU...**
WITH A GLOOMY FACE AND NO FRIENDS!
CHATTER CHATTER
BUSTLE BUSTLE
ISN'T THAT HIM?
EH?
WHO?
CHATTER CHATTER

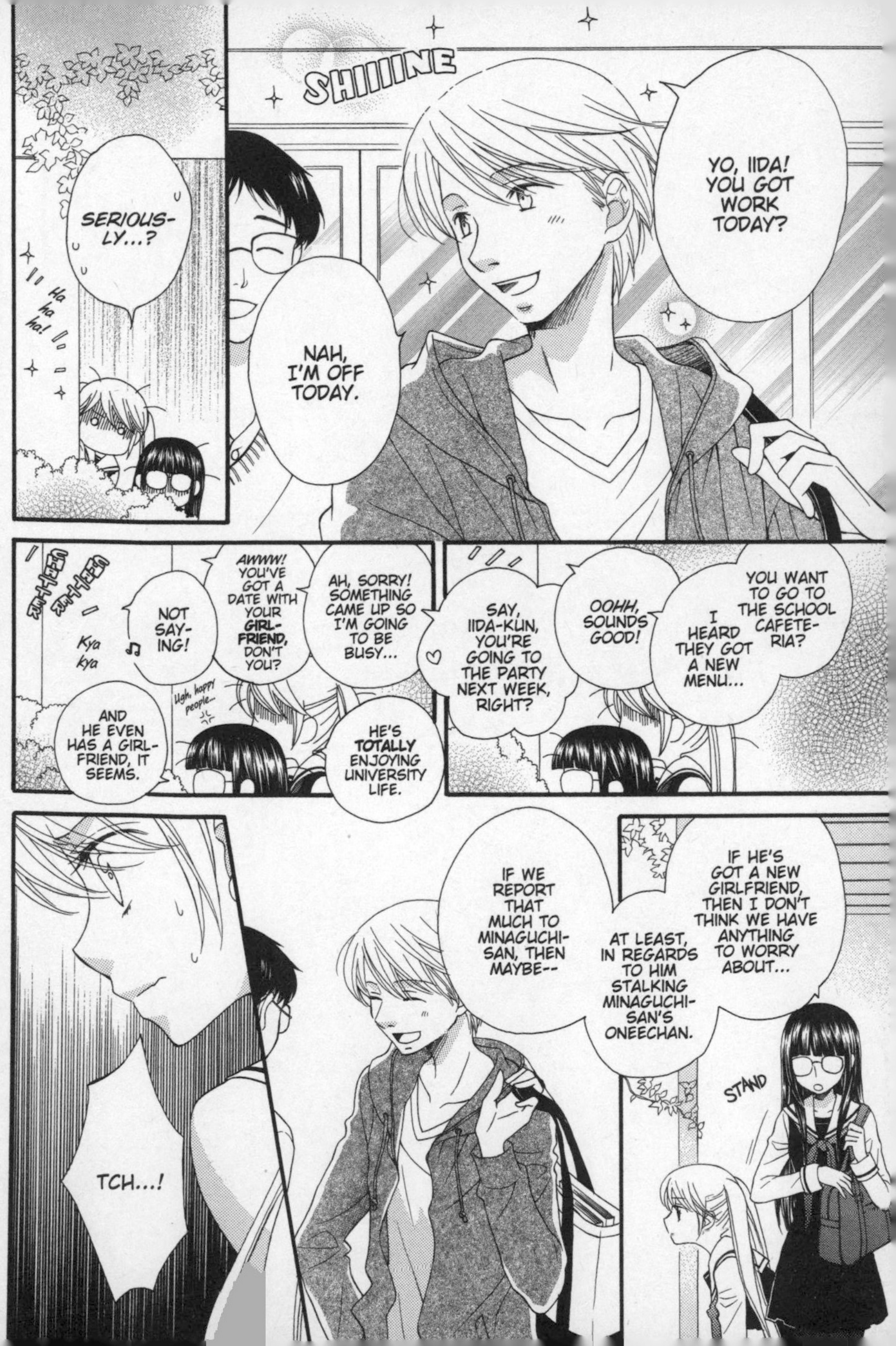
SHIIIINE
YO, IIDA! YOU GOT WORK TODAY?
NAH, I'M OFF TODAY.
SERIOUSLY...?
Ha ha ha!
YOU WANT TO GO TO THE SCHOOL CAFETERIA?
I HEARD THEY GOT A NEW MENU...
OOHH, SOUNDS GOOD!
SAY, IIDA-KUN, YOU'RE GOING TO THE PARTY NEXT WEEK, RIGHT?
AH, SORRY! SOMETHING CAME UP SO I'M GOING TO BE BUSY...
AWWW! YOU'VE GOT A DATE WITH YOUR GIRLFRIEND, DON'T YOU?
NOT SAYING!
Kya kya
Ugh, happy people...
HE'S TOTALLY ENJOYING UNIVERSITY LIFE.
AND HE EVEN HAS A GIRLFRIEND, IT SEEMS.
IF HE'S GOT A NEW GIRLFRIEND, THEN I DON'T THINK WE HAVE ANYTHING TO WORRY ABOUT...
AT LEAST, IN REGARDS TO HIM STALKING MINAGUCHI-SAN'S ONEECHAN.
STAND
IF WE REPORT THAT MUCH TO MINAGUCHI-SAN, THEN MAYBE--
TCH...!

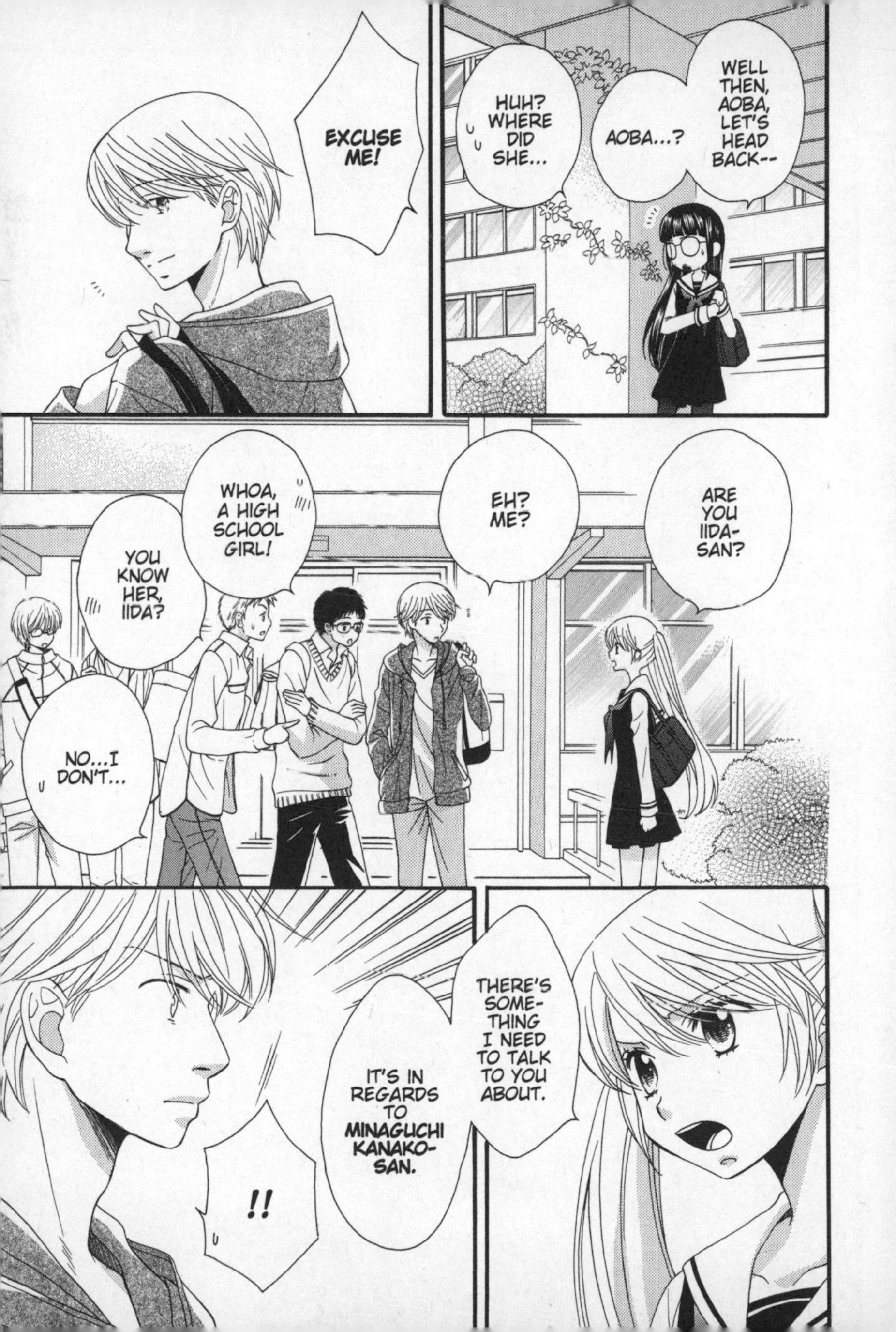
WELL THEN, AOBA, LET'S HEAD BACK--
AOBA...?
HUH? WHERE DID SHE...
EXCUSE ME!
ARE YOU IIDA-SAN?
EH? ME?
WHOA, A HIGH SCHOOL GIRL!
YOU KNOW HER, IIDA?
NO...I DON'T...
THERE'S SOMETHING I NEED TO TALK TO YOU ABOUT.
IT'S IN REGARDS TO MINAGUCHI KANAKO-SAN.
!!

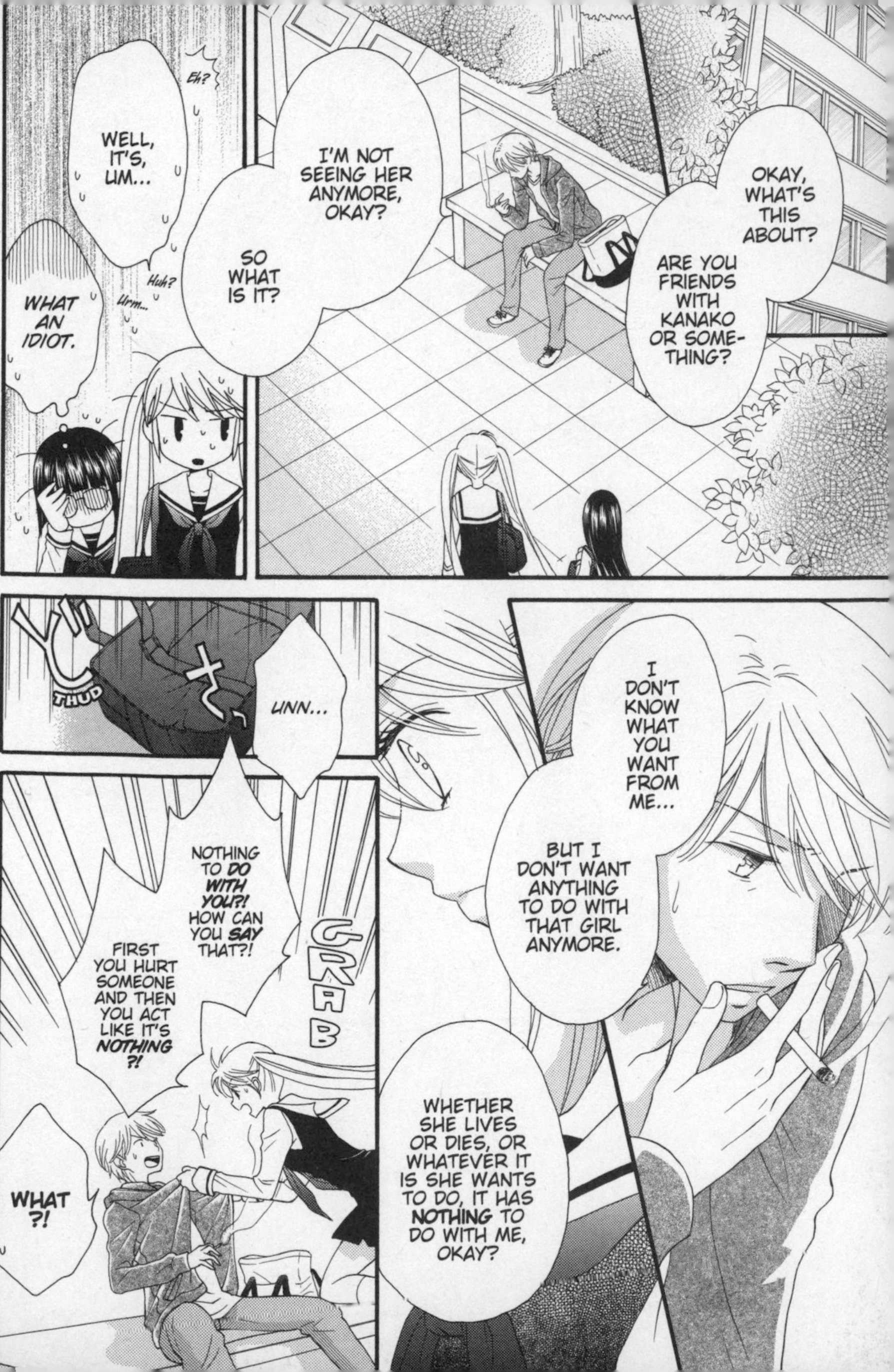
OKAY, WHAT'S THIS ABOUT?
ARE YOU FRIENDS WITH KANAKO OR SOME-THING?
I'M NOT SEEING HER ANYMORE, OKAY?
SO WHAT IS IT?
Eh?
WELL, IT'S, UM...
Huh?
Urm...
WHAT AN IDIOT.
I DON'T KNOW WHAT YOU WANT FROM ME...
BUT I DON'T WANT ANYTHING TO DO WITH THAT GIRL ANYMORE.
WHETHER SHE LIVES OR DIES, OR WHATEVER IT IS SHE WANTS TO DO, IT HAS NOTHING TO DO WITH ME, OKAY?
THUD
UNN...
GRAB
NOTHING TO DO WITH YOU?! HOW CAN YOU SAY THAT?!
FIRST YOU HURT SOMEONE AND THEN YOU ACT LIKE IT'S NOTHING?!
WHAT?!

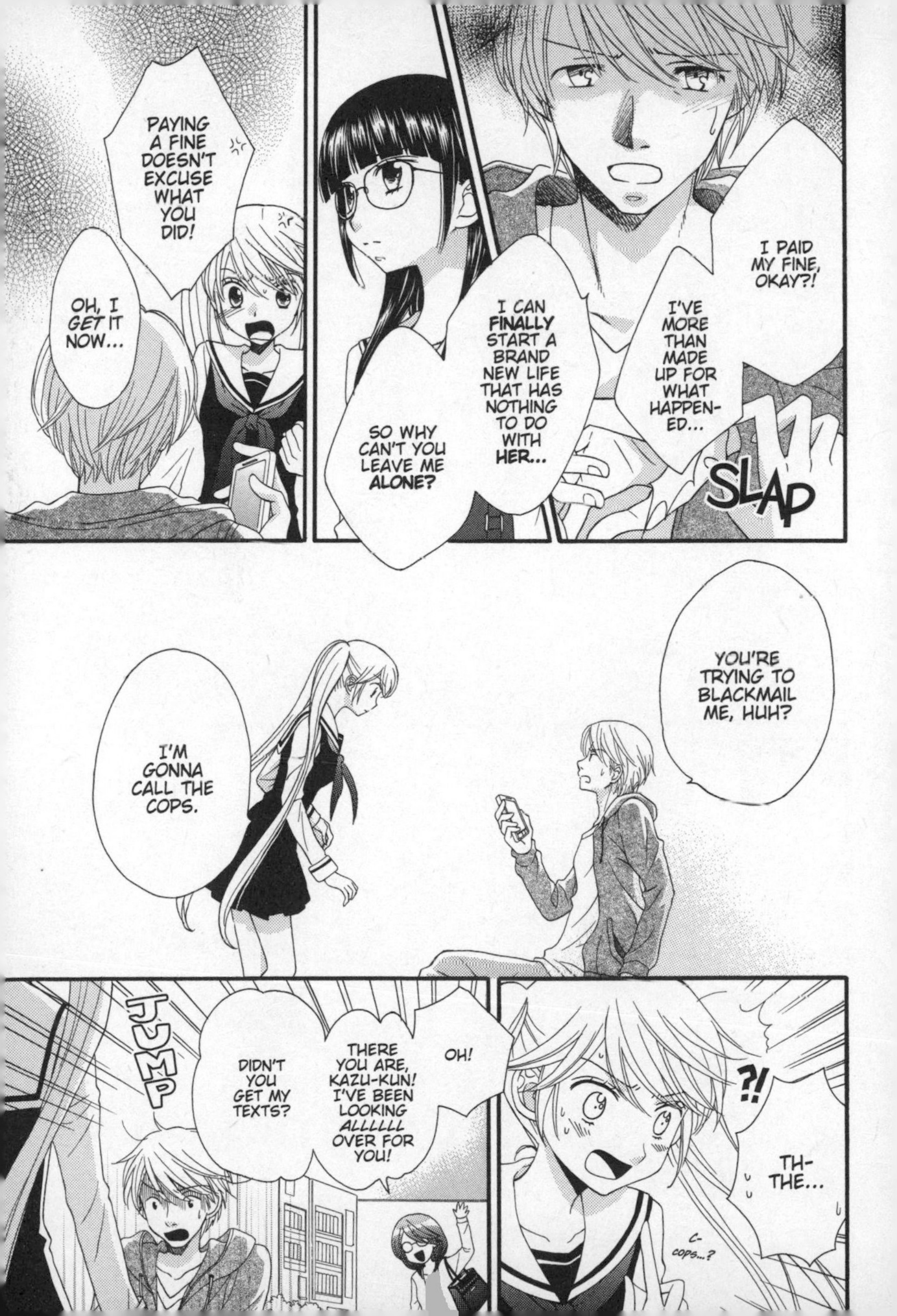
I PAID MY FINE, OKAY?!
SLAP
I'VE MORE THAN MADE UP FOR WHAT HAPPEN-ED...
I CAN FINALLY START A BRAND NEW LIFE THAT HAS NOTHING TO DO WITH HER...
SO WHY CAN'T YOU LEAVE ME ALONE?
PAYING A FINE DOESN'T EXCUSE WHAT YOU DID!
OH, I GET IT NOW...
YOU'RE TRYING TO BLACKMAIL ME, HUH?
I'M GONNA CALL THE COPS.
?!
TH- THE...
C- cops...?
OH!
THERE YOU ARE, KAZU-KUN! I'VE BEEN LOOKING ALLLLLL OVER FOR YOU!
DIDN'T YOU GET MY TEXTS?
JUMP

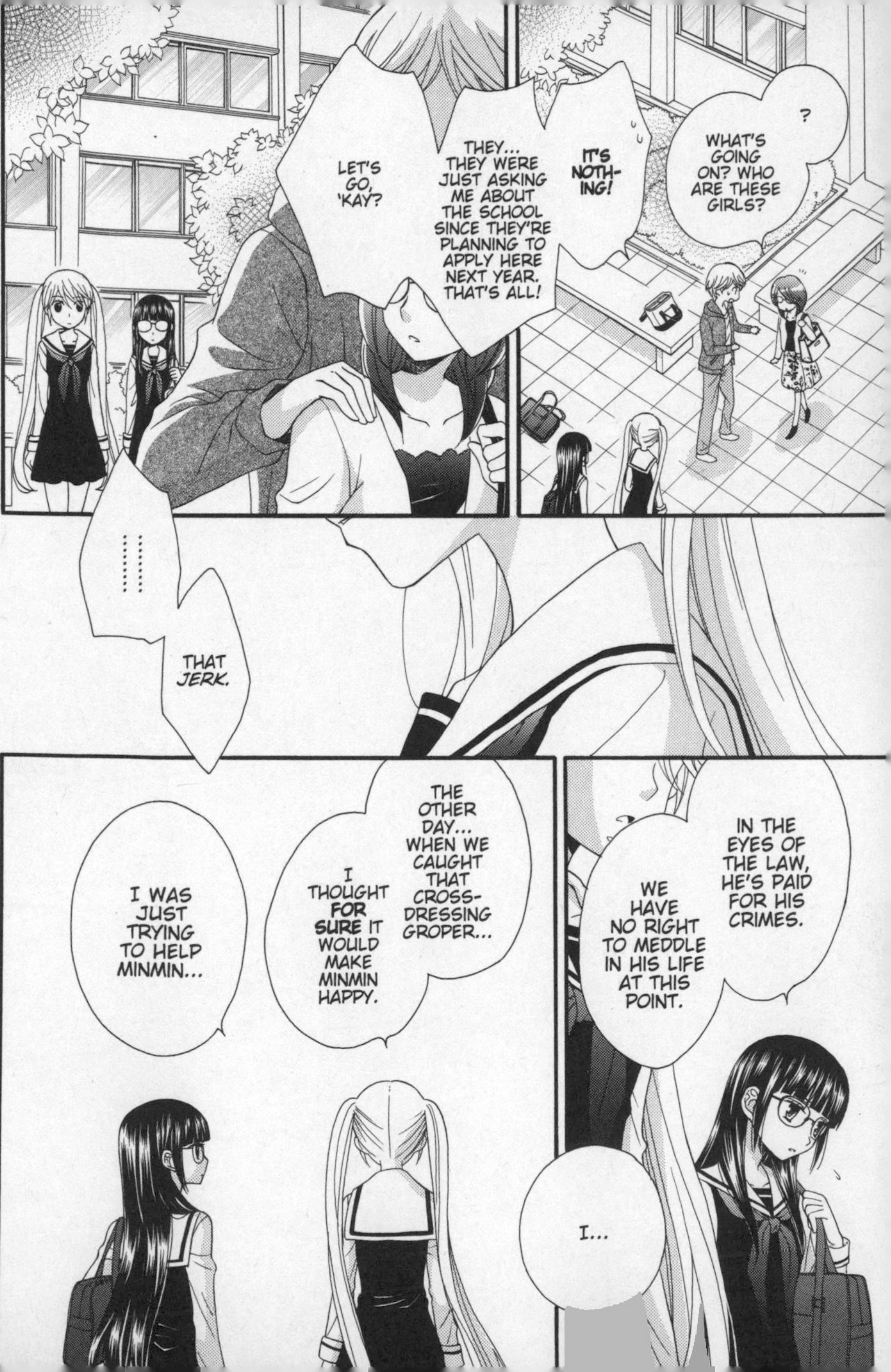
?
WHAT'S GOING ON? WHO ARE THESE GIRLS?
IT'S NOTHING!
THEY... THEY WERE JUST ASKING ME ABOUT THE SCHOOL SINCE THEY'RE PLANNING TO APPLY HERE NEXT YEAR. THAT'S ALL!
LET'S GO, 'KAY?
......
THAT JERK.
IN THE EYES OF THE LAW, HE'S PAID FOR HIS CRIMES.
WE HAVE NO RIGHT TO MEDDLE IN HIS LIFE AT THIS POINT.
I...
THE OTHER DAY... WHEN WE CAUGHT THAT CROSS-DRESSING GROPER...
I THOUGHT FOR SURE IT WOULD MAKE MINMIN HAPPY.
I WAS JUST TRYING TO HELP MINMIN...

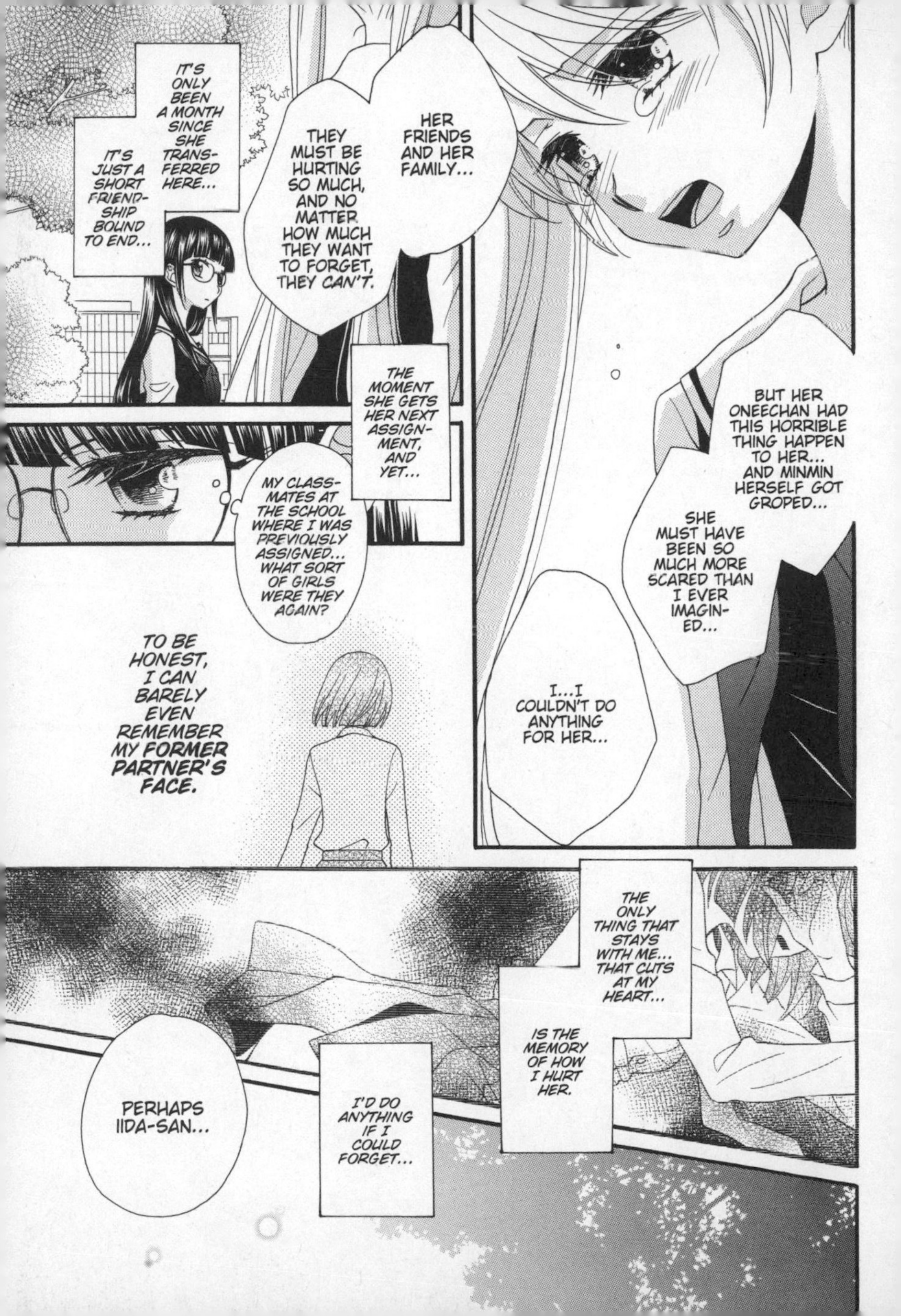

BUT HER ONEECHAN HAD THIS HORRIBLE THING HAPPEN TO HER... AND MINMIN HERSELF GOT GROPED...
SHE MUST HAVE BEEN SO MUCH MORE SCARED THAN I EVER IMAGIN-ED...
I...I COULDN'T DO ANYTHING FOR HER...
HER FRIENDS AND HER FAMILY...
THEY MUST BE HURTING SO MUCH, AND NO MATTER HOW MUCH THEY WANT TO FORGET, THEY CAN'T.
IT'S ONLY BEEN A MONTH SINCE SHE TRANS-FERRED HERE...
IT'S JUST A SHORT FRIEND-SHIP BOUND TO END...
THE MOMENT SHE GETS HER NEXT ASSIGN-MENT, AND YET...
MY CLASS-MATES AT THE SCHOOL WHERE I WAS PREVIOUSLY ASSIGNED... WHAT SORT OF GIRLS WERE THEY AGAIN?
TO BE HONEST, I CAN BARELY EVEN REMEMBER MY FORMER PARTNER'S FACE.
THE ONLY THING THAT STAYS WITH ME... THAT CUTS AT MY HEART...
IS THE MEMORY OF HOW I HURT HER.
I'D DO ANYTHING IF I COULD FORGET...
PERHAPS IIDA-SAN...

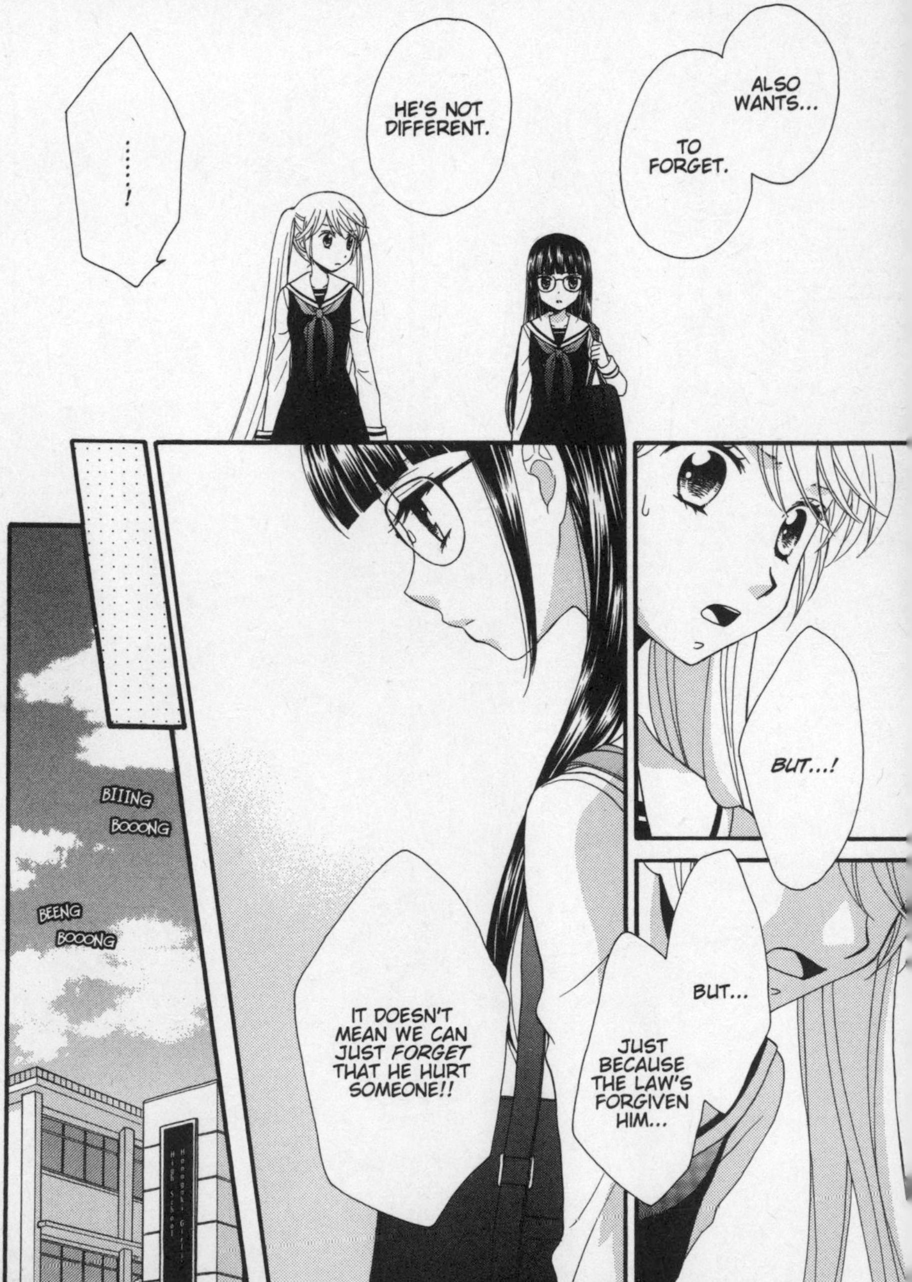
ALSO WANTS... TO FORGET.
HE'S NOT DIFFERENT.
......!
BUT...!
BUT...
JUST BECAUSE THE LAW'S FORGIVEN HIM...
IT DOESN'T MEAN WE CAN JUST *FORGET* THAT HE HURT SOMEONE!!
BIIING
BOOONG
BEENG
BOOONG

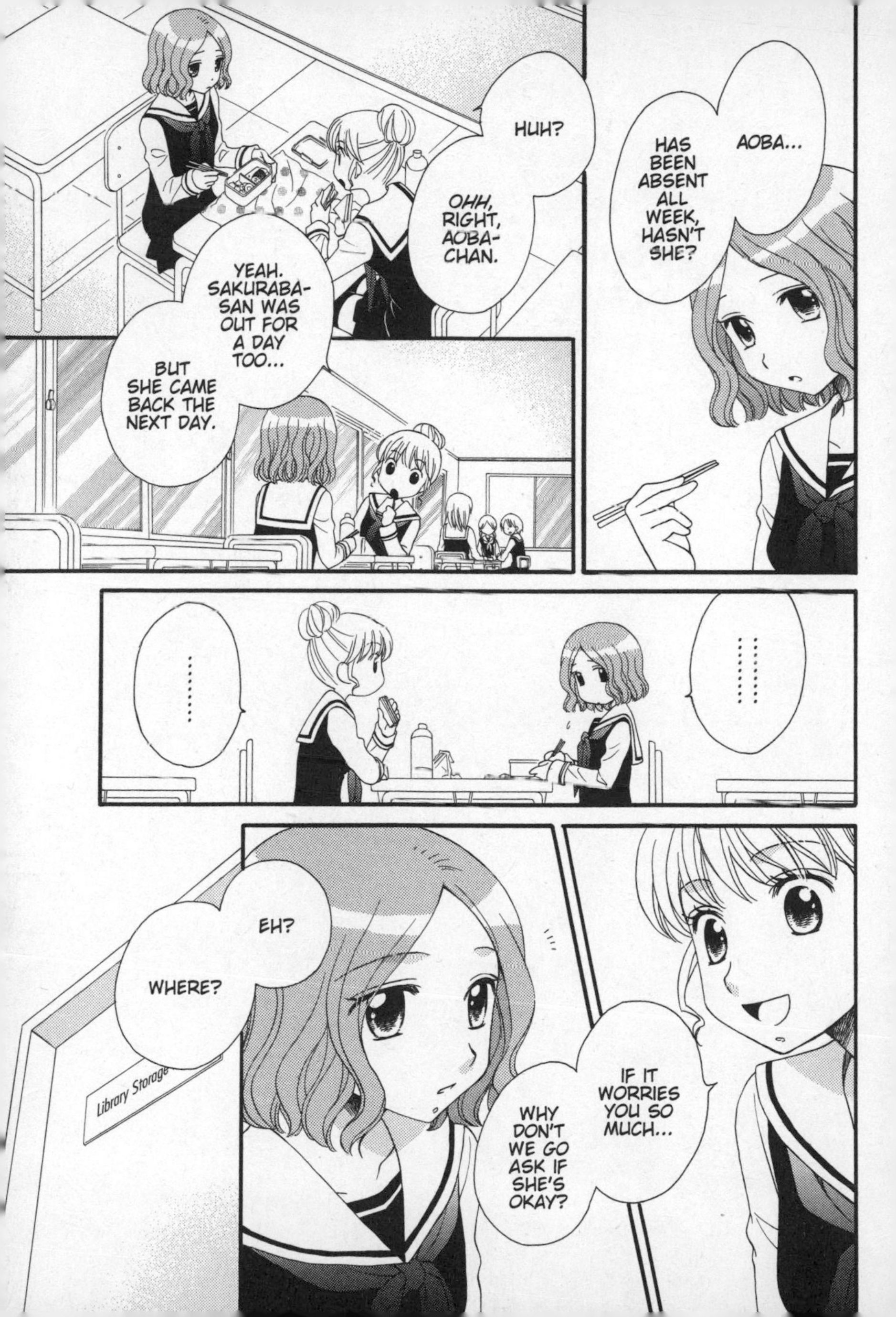
AOBA...
HAS BEEN ABSENT ALL WEEK, HASN'T SHE?
HUH?
OHH, RIGHT, AOBA-CHAN.
YEAH. SAKURABA-SAN WAS OUT FOR A DAY TOO...
BUT SHE CAME BACK THE NEXT DAY.
......
......
IF IT WORRIES YOU SO MUCH...
WHY DON'T WE GO ASK IF SHE'S OKAY?
EH?
WHERE?
Library Storage

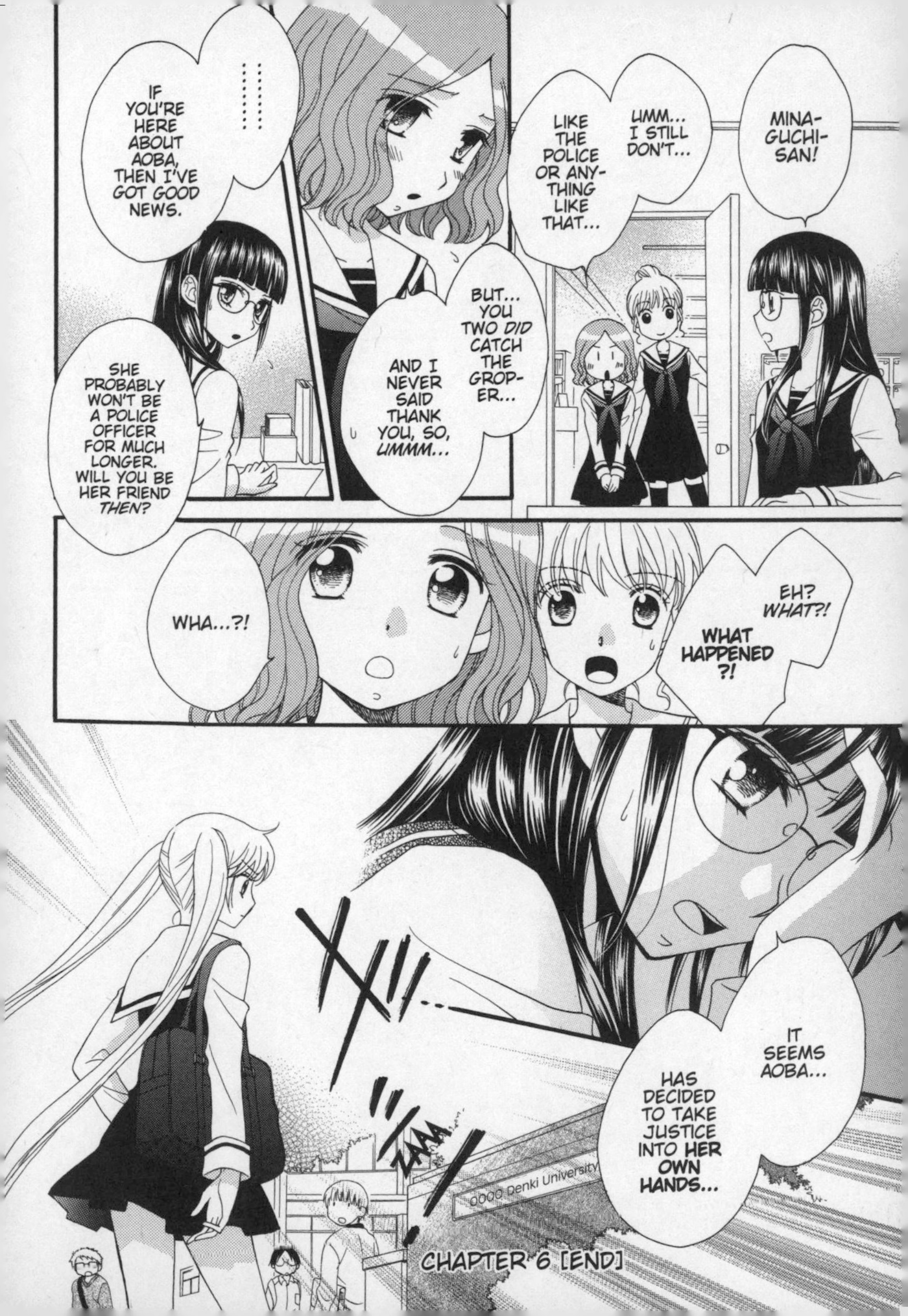
MINA-GUCHI-SAN!
UMM... I STILL DON'T...
LIKE THE POLICE OR ANYTHING LIKE THAT...
BUT... YOU TWO *DID* CATCH THE GROPER...
AND I NEVER SAID THANK YOU, SO, *UMMM...*
......
IF YOU'RE HERE ABOUT AOBA, THEN I'VE GOT GOOD NEWS.
SHE PROBABLY WON'T BE A POLICE OFFICER FOR MUCH LONGER. WILL YOU BE HER FRIEND *THEN?*
EH? *WHAT?!*
WHAT HAPPENED?!
WHA...?!
IT SEEMS AOBA...
HAS DECIDED TO TAKE JUSTICE INTO **HER OWN HANDS...**
ZAAA
OOOO Denki University
CHAPTER 6 [END]

GAKUEN
POLIZI

CHAPTER 7

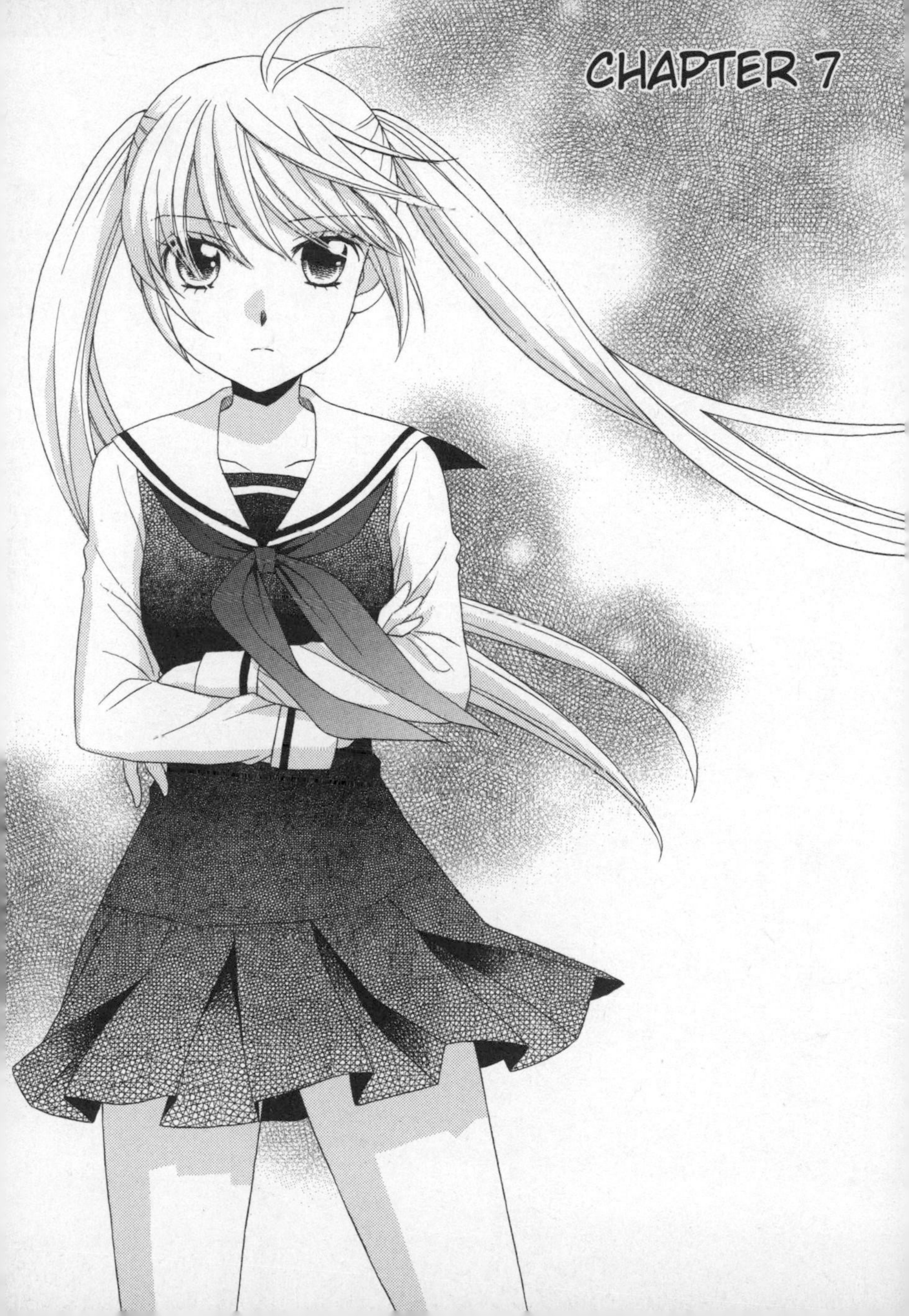

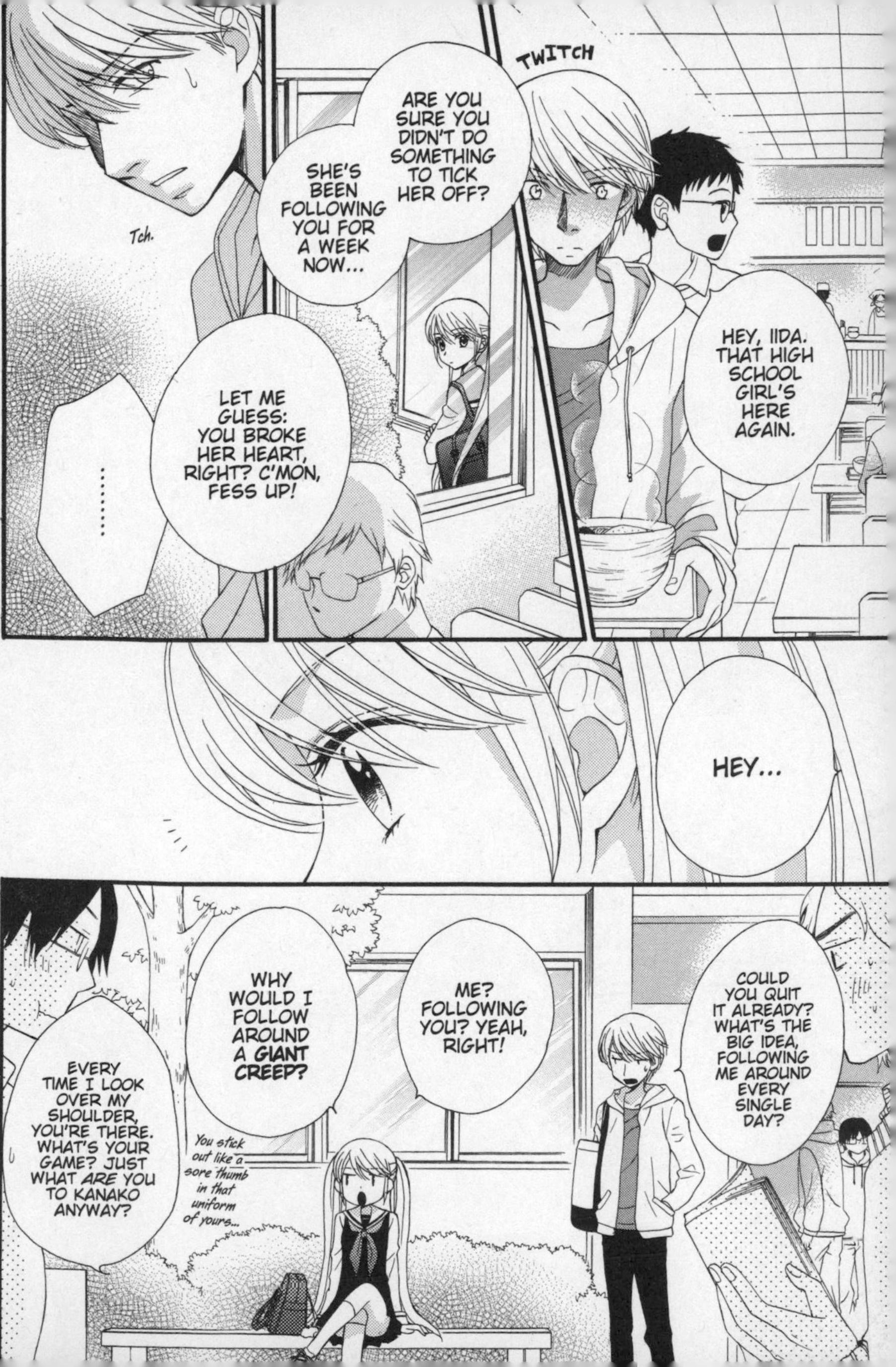

TWITCH
HEY, IIDA. THAT HIGH SCHOOL GIRL'S HERE AGAIN.
ARE YOU SURE YOU DIDN'T DO SOMETHING TO TICK HER OFF?
SHE'S BEEN FOLLOWING YOU FOR A WEEK NOW...
LET ME GUESS: YOU BROKE HER HEART, RIGHT? C'MON, FESS UP!
Tch.
......
HEY...
COULD YOU QUIT IT ALREADY? WHAT'S THE BIG IDEA, FOLLOWING ME AROUND EVERY SINGLE DAY?
ME? FOLLOWING YOU? YEAH, RIGHT!
WHY WOULD I FOLLOW AROUND A **GIANT CREEP**?
You stick out like a sore thumb in that uniform of yours...
EVERY TIME I LOOK OVER MY SHOULDER, YOU'RE THERE. WHAT'S YOUR GAME? JUST WHAT *ARE* YOU TO KANAKO ANYWAY?

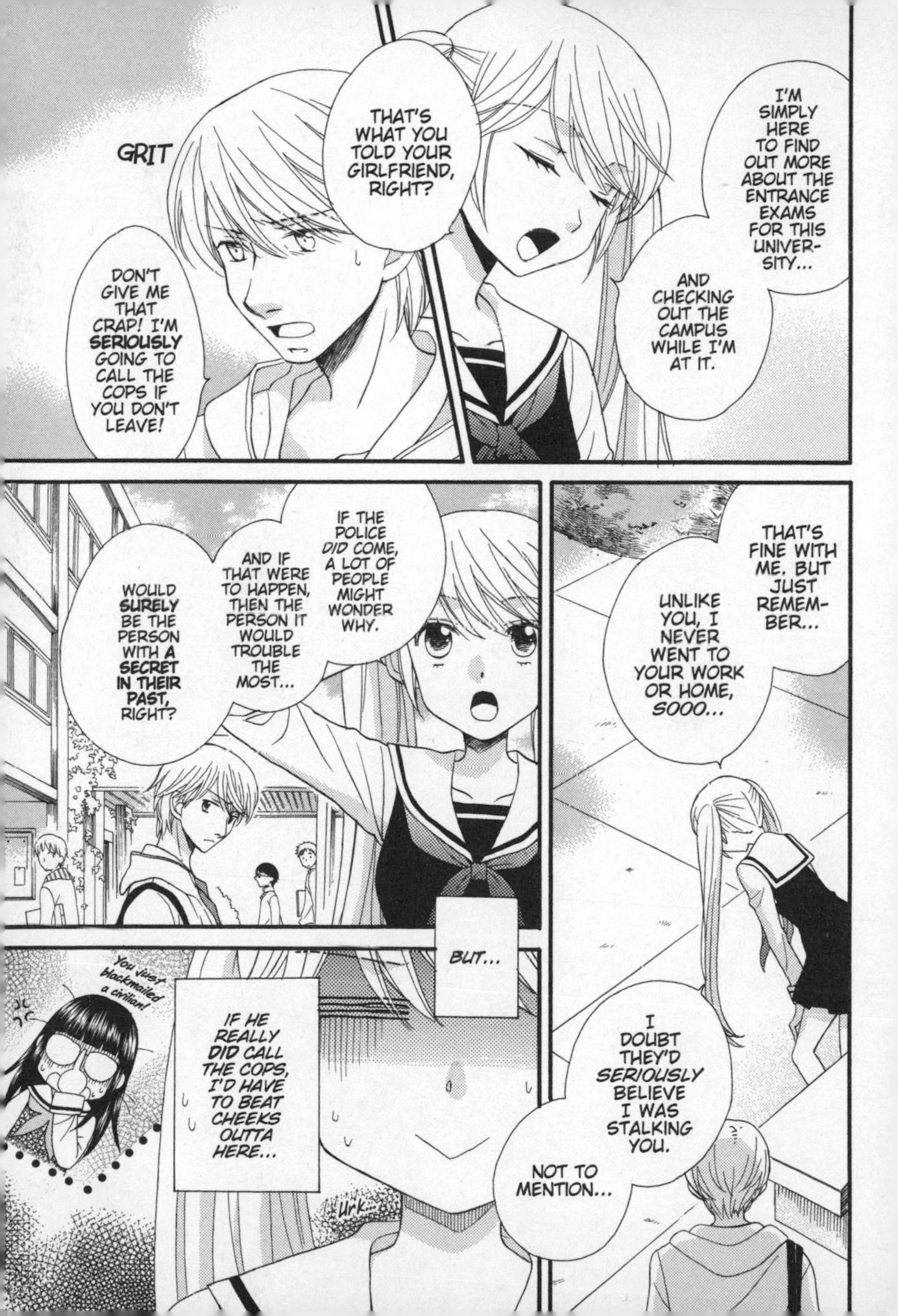
I'M SIMPLY HERE TO FIND OUT MORE ABOUT THE ENTRANCE EXAMS FOR THIS UNIVERSITY...
AND CHECKING OUT THE CAMPUS WHILE I'M AT IT.
THAT'S WHAT YOU TOLD YOUR GIRLFRIEND, RIGHT?
GRIT
DON'T GIVE ME THAT CRAP! I'M **SERIOUSLY** GOING TO CALL THE COPS IF YOU DON'T LEAVE!
THAT'S FINE WITH ME. BUT JUST REMEMBER...
UNLIKE YOU, I NEVER WENT TO YOUR WORK OR HOME, *SOOO...*
I DOUBT THEY'D *SERIOUSLY* BELIEVE I WAS STALKING YOU.
NOT TO MENTION...
IF THE POLICE *DID* COME, A LOT OF PEOPLE MIGHT WONDER WHY.
AND IF THAT WERE TO HAPPEN, THEN THE PERSON IT WOULD TROUBLE THE MOST...
WOULD **SURELY** BE THE PERSON WITH **A SECRET IN THEIR PAST**, RIGHT?
BUT...
IF HE REALLY ***DID*** *CALL THE COPS, I'D HAVE TO BEAT CHEEKS OUTTA HERE...*
You jjust blackmailed a civilian!
Urk...

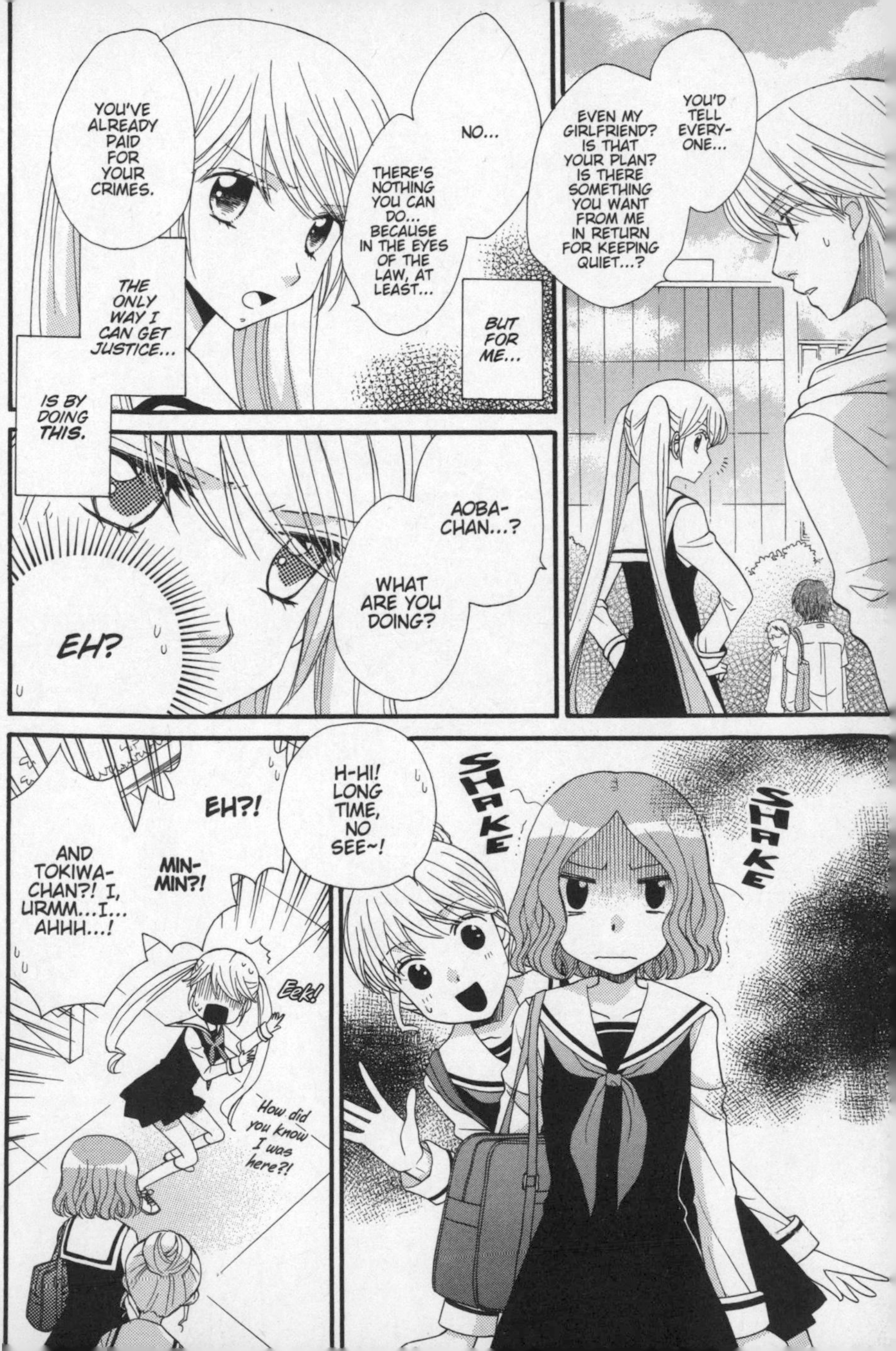
YOU'D TELL EVERY-ONE...
EVEN MY GIRLFRIEND? IS THAT YOUR PLAN? IS THERE SOMETHING YOU WANT FROM ME IN RETURN FOR KEEPING QUIET...?
NO...
THERE'S NOTHING YOU CAN DO... BECAUSE IN THE EYES OF THE LAW, AT LEAST...
YOU'VE ALREADY PAID FOR YOUR CRIMES.
BUT FOR ME...
THE ONLY WAY I CAN GET JUSTICE...
IS BY DOING THIS.
AOBA-CHAN...?
WHAT ARE YOU DOING?
EH?
SHAKE
SHAKE
H-HI! LONG TIME, NO SEE~!
EH?!
MIN-MIN?!
AND TOKIWA-CHAN?! I, URMM...I... AHHH...!
Eek!
How did you know I was here?!

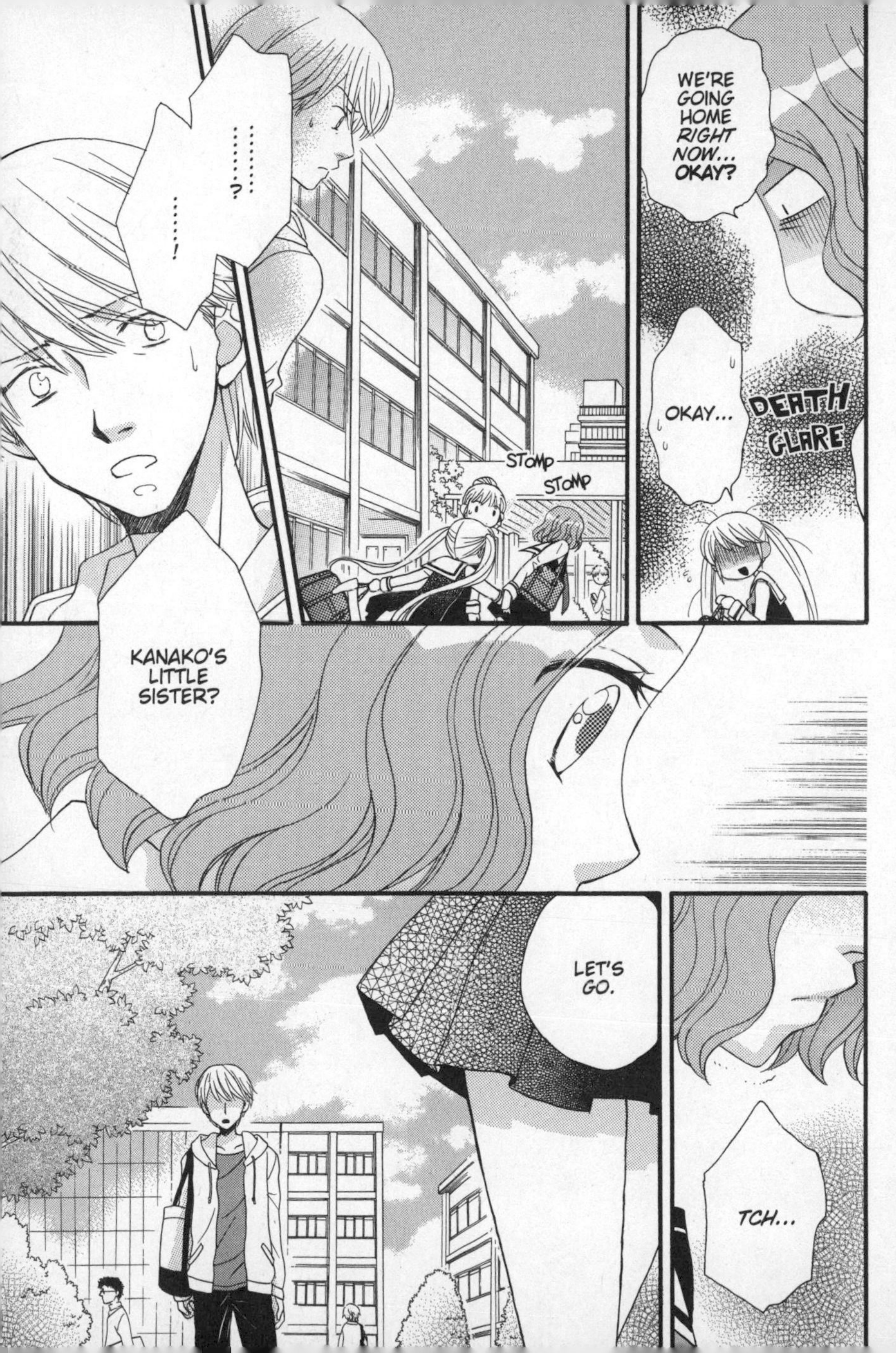
WE'RE GOING HOME RIGHT NOW... OKAY?
OKAY...
DEATH GLARE
......?
......!
STOMP
STOMP
KANAKO'S LITTLE SISTER?
...
TCH...
LET'S GO.

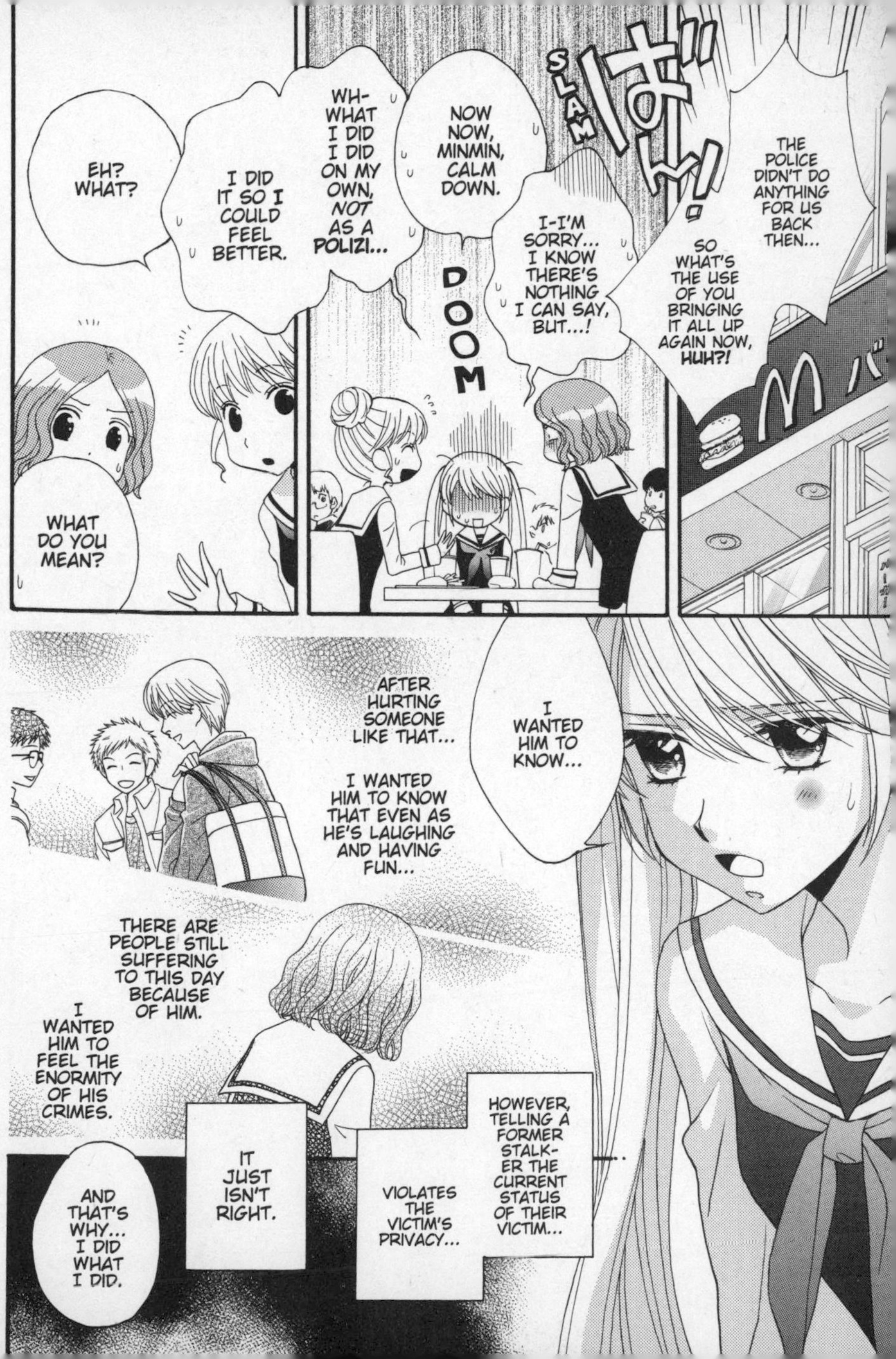
THE POLICE DIDN'T DO ANYTHING FOR US BACK THEN...
SO WHAT'S THE USE OF YOU BRINGING IT ALL UP AGAIN NOW, HUH?!
SLAM
I-I'M SORRY... I KNOW THERE'S NOTHING I CAN SAY, BUT...!
NOW NOW, MINMIN, CALM DOWN.
DOOM
WH- WHAT I DID I DID ON MY OWN, NOT AS A POLIZI...
I DID IT SO I COULD FEEL BETTER.
EH? WHAT?
WHAT DO YOU MEAN?
I WANTED HIM TO KNOW...
AFTER HURTING SOMEONE LIKE THAT...
I WANTED HIM TO KNOW THAT EVEN AS HE'S LAUGHING AND HAVING FUN...
THERE ARE PEOPLE STILL SUFFERING TO THIS DAY BECAUSE OF HIM.
I WANTED HIM TO FEEL THE ENORMITY OF HIS CRIMES.
HOWEVER, TELLING A FORMER STALKER THE CURRENT STATUS OF THEIR VICTIM...
VIOLATES THE VICTIM'S PRIVACY...
IT JUST ISN'T RIGHT.
AND THAT'S WHY... I DID WHAT I DID.

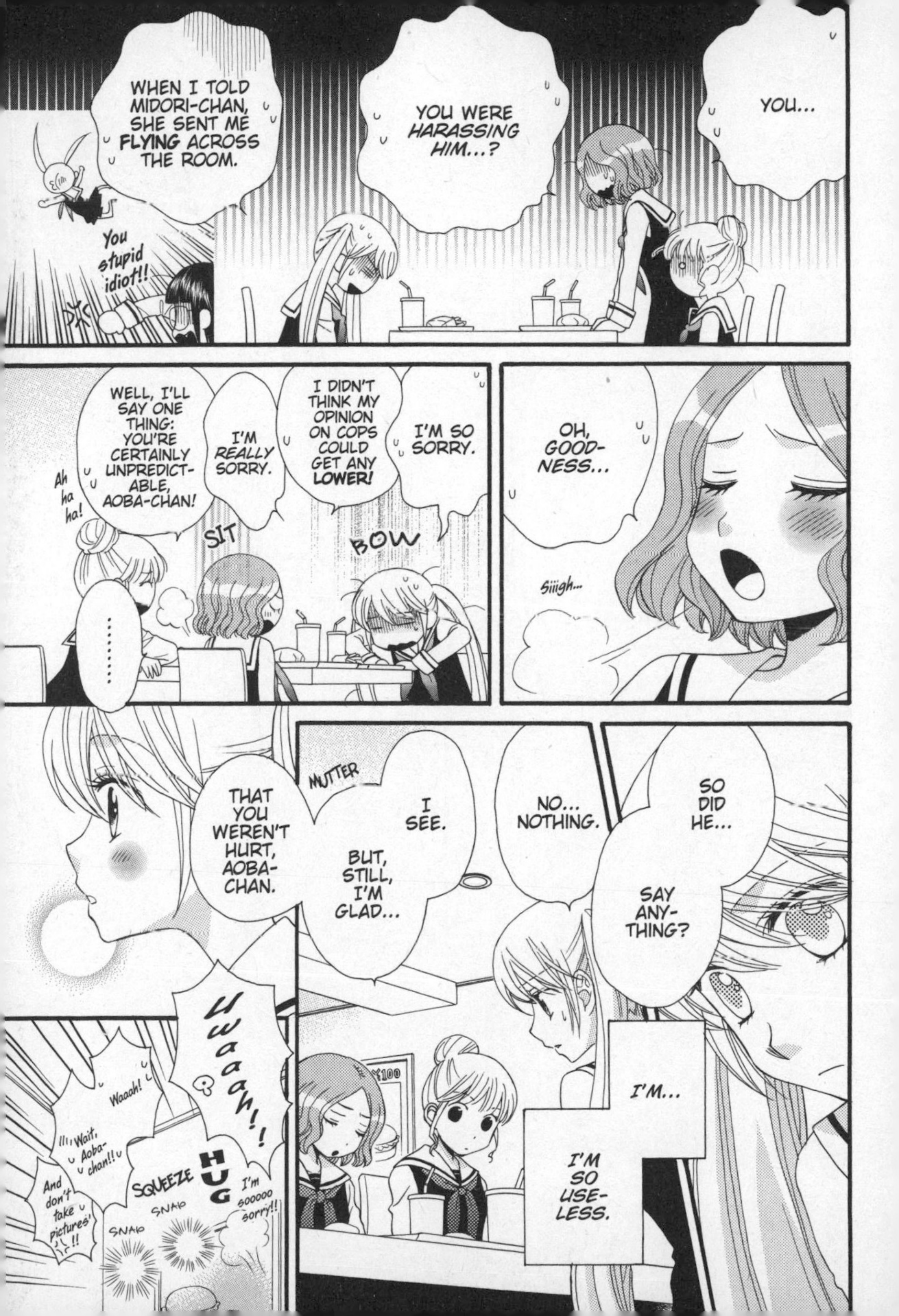

YOU...
YOU WERE HARASSING HIM...?
WHEN I TOLD MIDORI-CHAN, SHE SENT ME FLYING ACROSS THE ROOM.
You stupid idiot!!
OH, GOODNESS...
Siiigh...
I'M SO SORRY.
I DIDN'T THINK MY OPINION ON COPS COULD GET ANY LOWER!
BOW
I'M REALLY SORRY.
SIT
WELL, I'LL SAY ONE THING: YOU'RE CERTAINLY UNPREDICTABLE, AOBA-CHAN!
Ah ha ha!
......
SO DID HE... SAY ANYTHING?
NO... NOTHING.
I SEE.
BUT, STILL, I'M GLAD...
MUTTER
THAT YOU WEREN'T HURT, AOBA-CHAN.
I'M...
I'M SO USELESS.
Uwaaah!!
Waaah!
HUG
SQUEEZE
I'm sooooo sorry!!
Wait, Aoba-chan!!
And don't take pictures!!
SNAP
SNAP

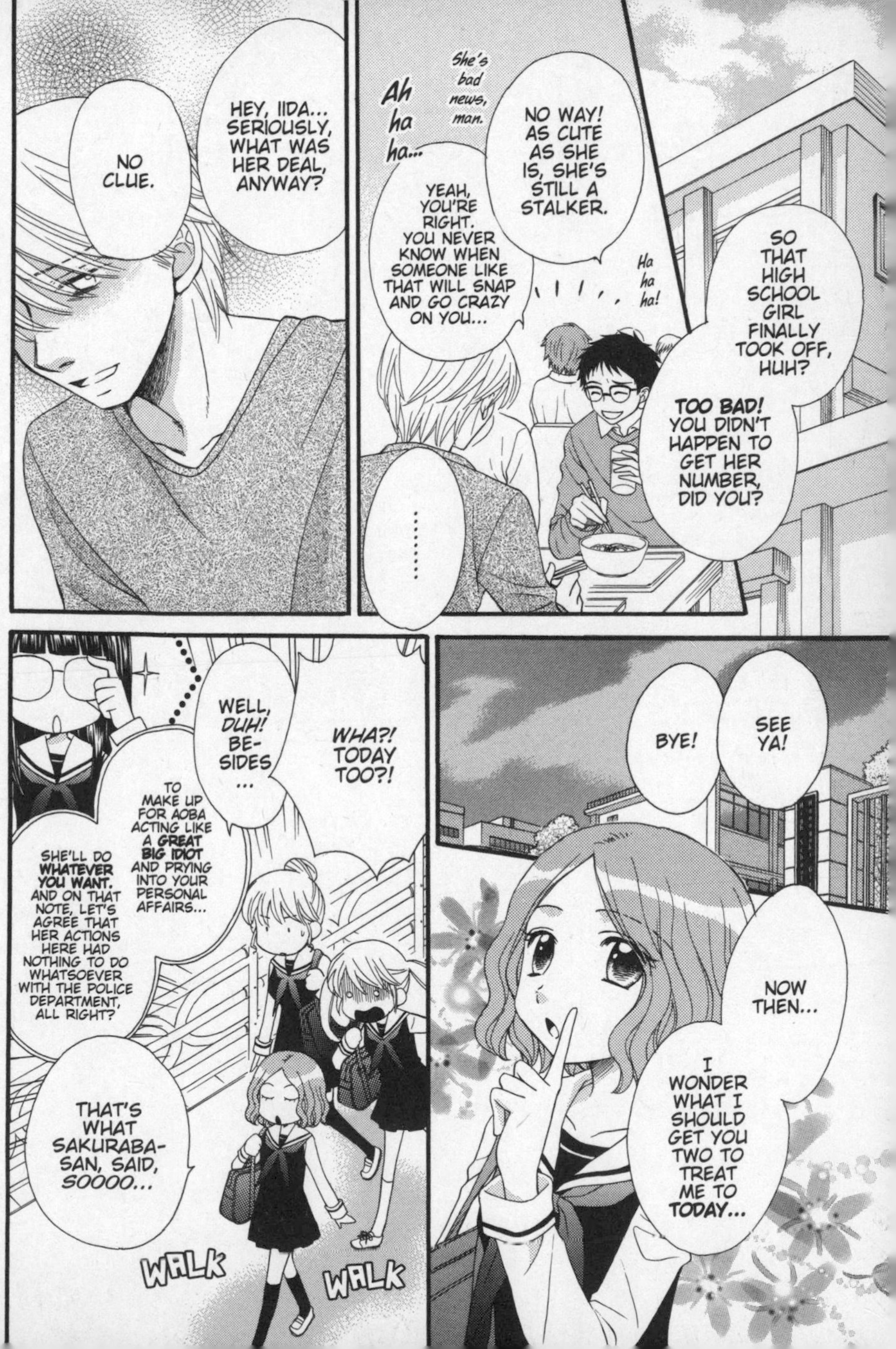

SO THAT HIGH SCHOOL GIRL FINALLY TOOK OFF, HUH?
TOO BAD! YOU DIDN'T HAPPEN TO GET HER NUMBER, DID YOU?
Ha ha ha!
NO WAY! AS CUTE AS SHE IS, SHE'S STILL A STALKER.
She's bad news, man.
Ah ha ha...
YEAH, YOU'RE RIGHT. YOU NEVER KNOW WHEN SOMEONE LIKE THAT WILL SNAP AND GO CRAZY ON YOU...
......
HEY, IIDA... SERIOUSLY, WHAT WAS HER DEAL, ANYWAY?
NO CLUE.
SEE YA!
BYE!
NOW THEN...
I WONDER WHAT I SHOULD GET YOU TWO TO TREAT ME TO TODAY...
WHA?! TODAY TOO?!
WELL, DUH! BE-SIDES...
TO MAKE UP FOR AOBA ACTING LIKE A GREAT BIG IDIOT AND PRYING INTO YOUR PERSONAL AFFAIRS...
SHE'LL DO WHATEVER YOU WANT. AND ON THAT NOTE, LET'S AGREE THAT HER ACTIONS HERE HAD NOTHING TO DO WHATSOEVER WITH THE POLICE DEPARTMENT, ALL RIGHT?
THAT'S WHAT SAKURABA-SAN, SAID, SOOOO...
WALK
WALK

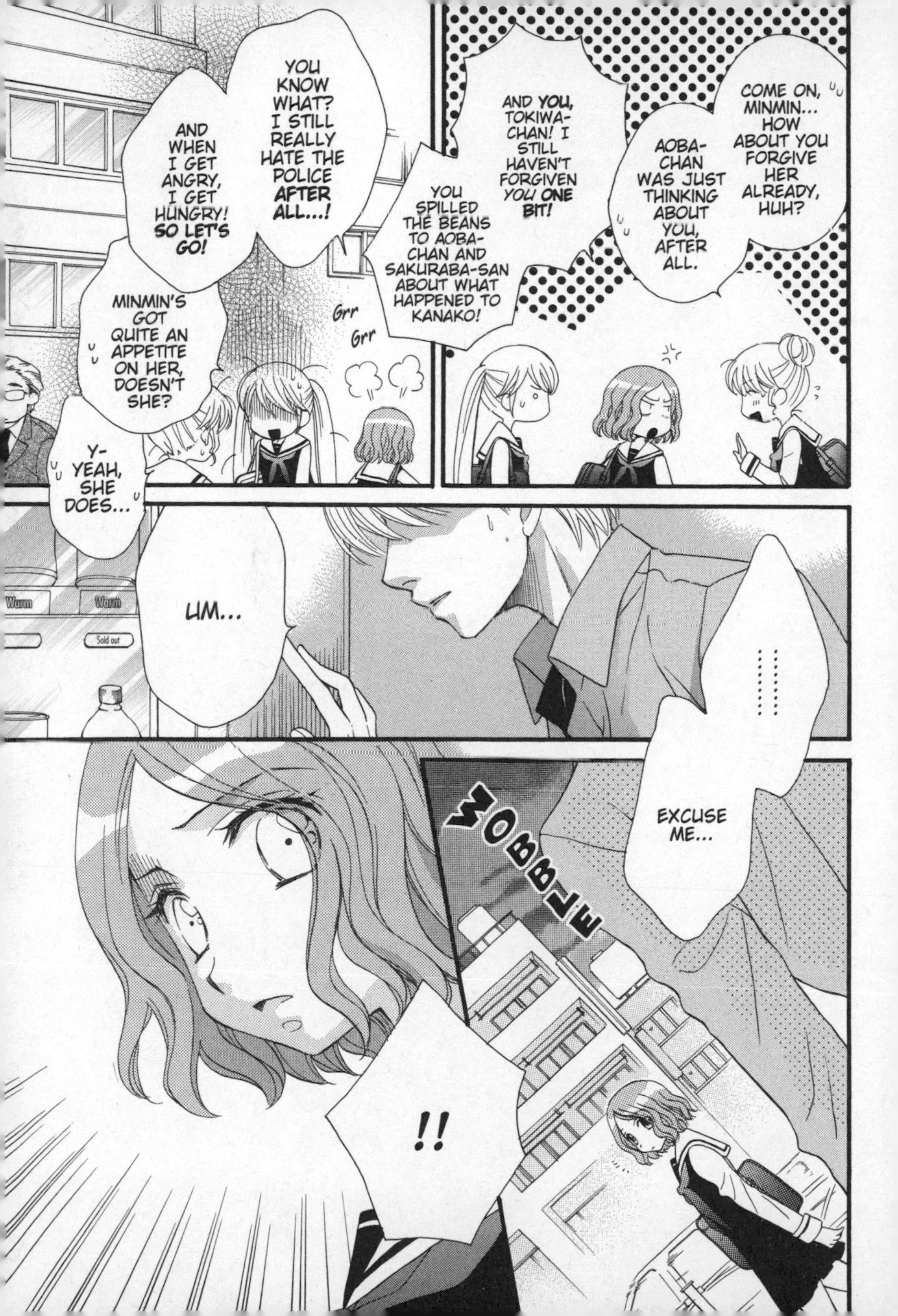
COME ON, MINMIN... HOW ABOUT YOU FORGIVE HER ALREADY, HUH?
AOBA-CHAN WAS JUST THINKING ABOUT YOU, AFTER ALL.
AND YOU, TOKIWA-CHAN! I STILL HAVEN'T FORGIVEN YOU ONE BIT!
YOU SPILLED THE BEANS TO AOBA-CHAN AND SAKURABA-SAN ABOUT WHAT HAPPENED TO KANAKO!
YOU KNOW WHAT? I STILL REALLY HATE THE POLICE AFTER ALL...!
AND WHEN I GET ANGRY, I GET HUNGRY! SO LET'S GO!
Grr
Grr
MINMIN'S GOT QUITE AN APPETITE ON HER, DOESN'T SHE?
Y-YEAH, SHE DOES...
......
UM...
Warm
Warm
Sold out
EXCUSE ME...
WOBBLE
!!

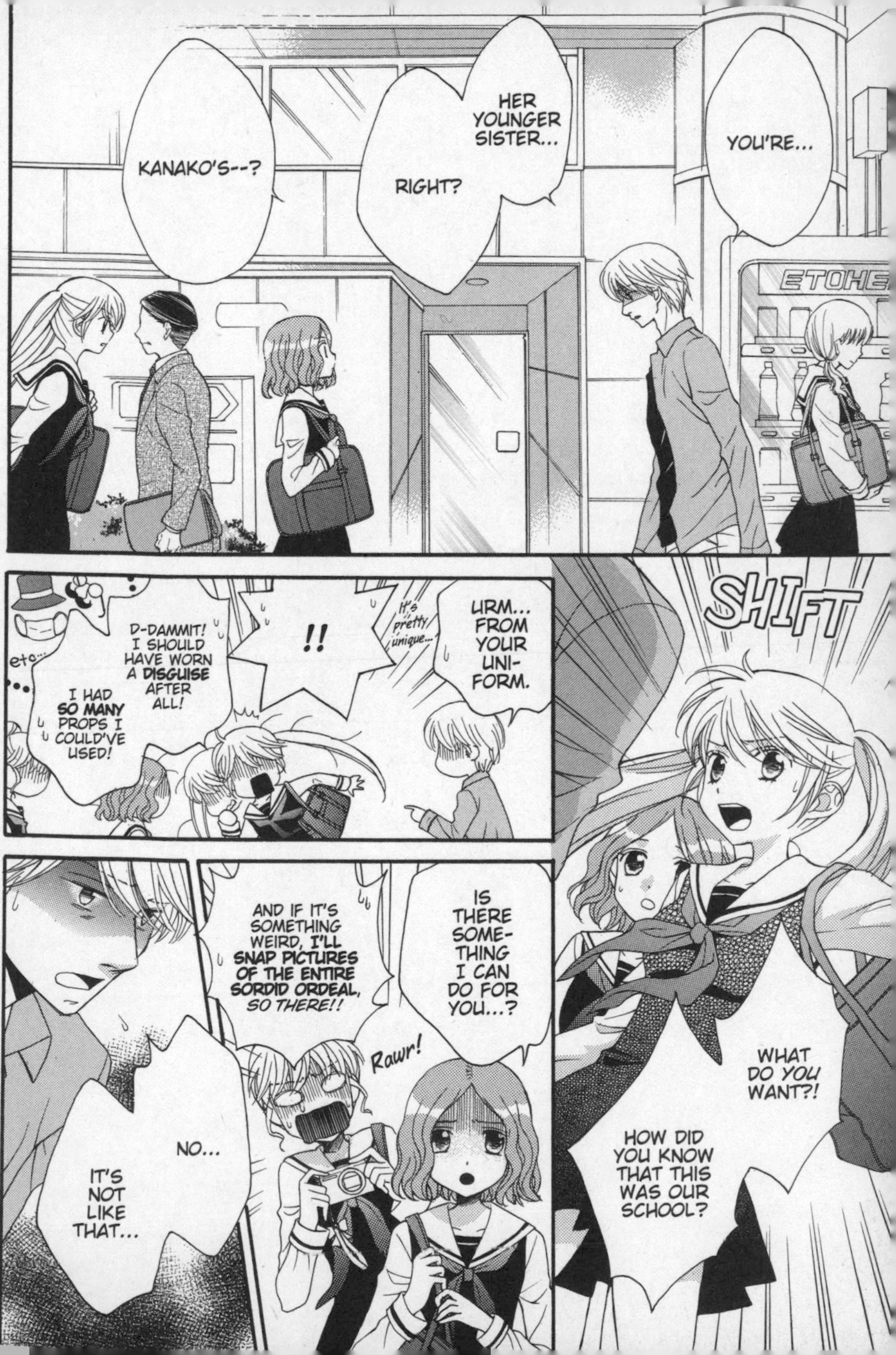
YOU'RE...
HER YOUNGER SISTER...
RIGHT?
KANAKO'S--?
SHIFT
WHAT DO YOU WANT?!
HOW DID YOU KNOW THAT THIS WAS OUR SCHOOL?
URM... FROM YOUR UNI-FORM.
It's pretty unique...
!!
D-DAMMIT! I SHOULD HAVE WORN A DISGUISE AFTER ALL!
I HAD SO MANY PROPS I COULD'VE USED!
etc...
IS THERE SOME-THING I CAN DO FOR YOU...?
AND IF IT'S SOMETHING WEIRD, I'LL SNAP PICTURES OF THE ENTIRE SORDID ORDEAL, SO THERE!!
Rawr!
NO...
IT'S NOT LIKE THAT...

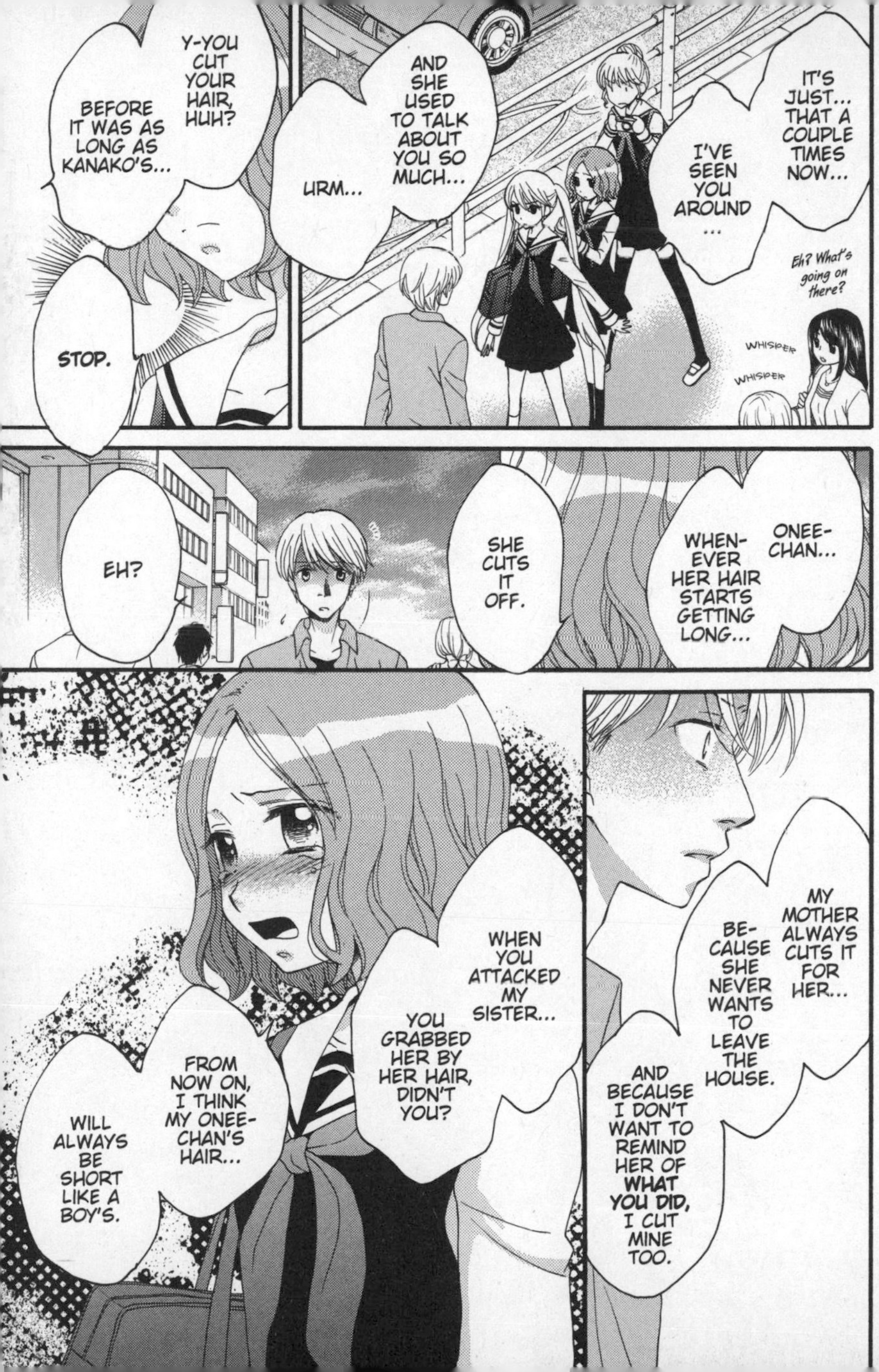

IT'S JUST... THAT A COUPLE TIMES NOW...
I'VE SEEN YOU AROUND...
Eh? What's going on there?
AND SHE USED TO TALK ABOUT YOU SO MUCH...
URM...
WHISPER
WHISPER
Y-YOU CUT YOUR HAIR, HUH?
BEFORE IT WAS AS LONG AS KANAKO'S...
STOP.
ONEE-CHAN...
WHEN-EVER HER HAIR STARTS GETTING LONG...
SHE CUTS IT OFF.
EH?
MY MOTHER ALWAYS CUTS IT FOR HER...
BE-CAUSE SHE NEVER WANTS TO LEAVE THE HOUSE.
AND BECAUSE I DON'T WANT TO REMIND HER OF **WHAT YOU DID,** I CUT MINE TOO.
WHEN YOU ATTACKED MY SISTER...
YOU GRABBED HER BY HER HAIR, DIDN'T YOU?
FROM NOW ON, I THINK MY ONEE-CHAN'S HAIR...
WILL ALWAYS BE SHORT LIKE A BOY'S.

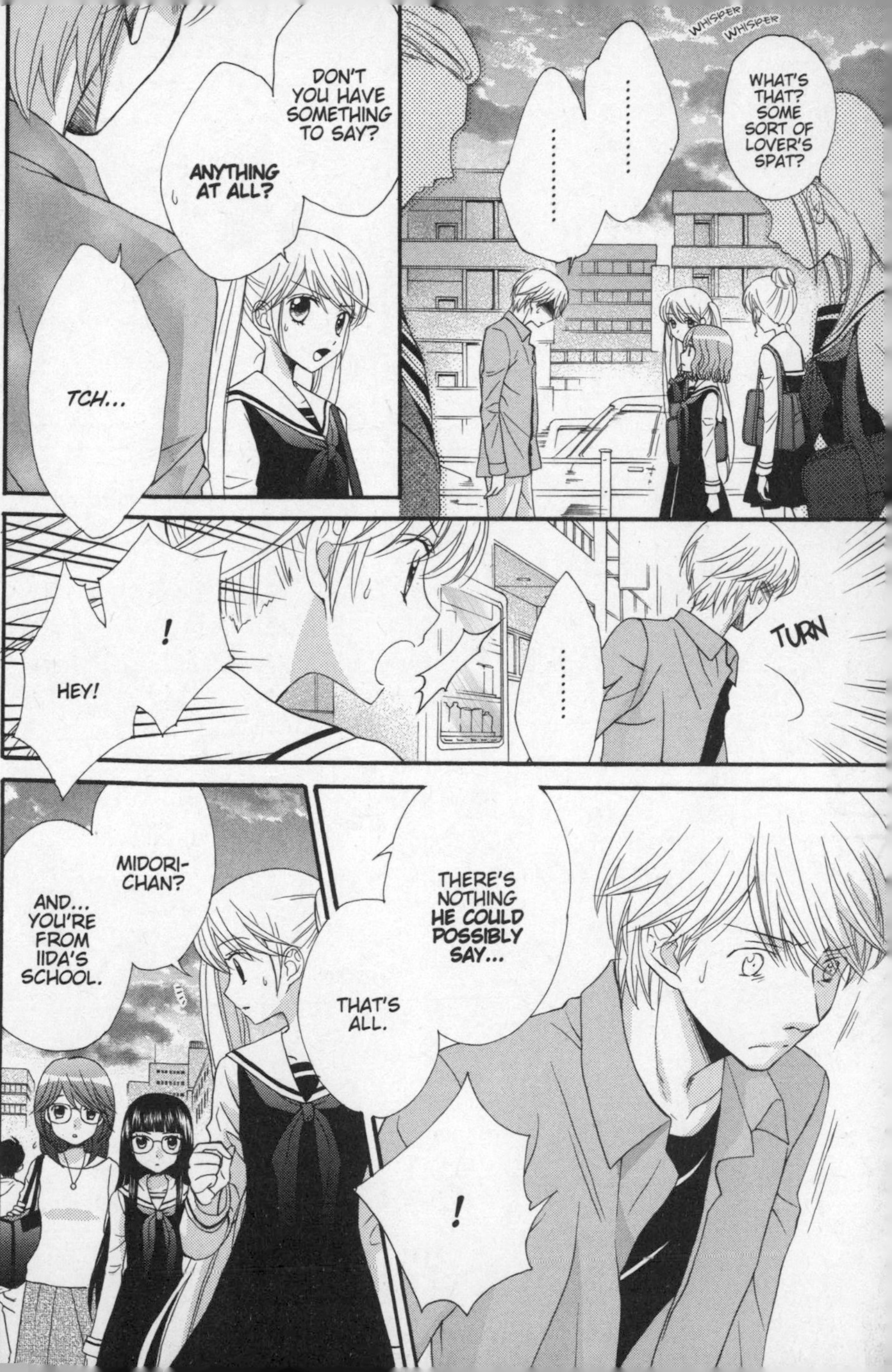
WHISPER
WHISPER
WHAT'S THAT? SOME SORT OF LOVER'S SPAT?
......
......
DON'T YOU HAVE SOMETHING TO SAY?
ANYTHING AT ALL?
TCH...
TURN
......
!
HEY!
THERE'S NOTHING HE COULD POSSIBLY SAY...
THAT'S ALL.
!
MIDORI-CHAN?
AND... YOU'RE FROM IIDA'S SCHOOL.

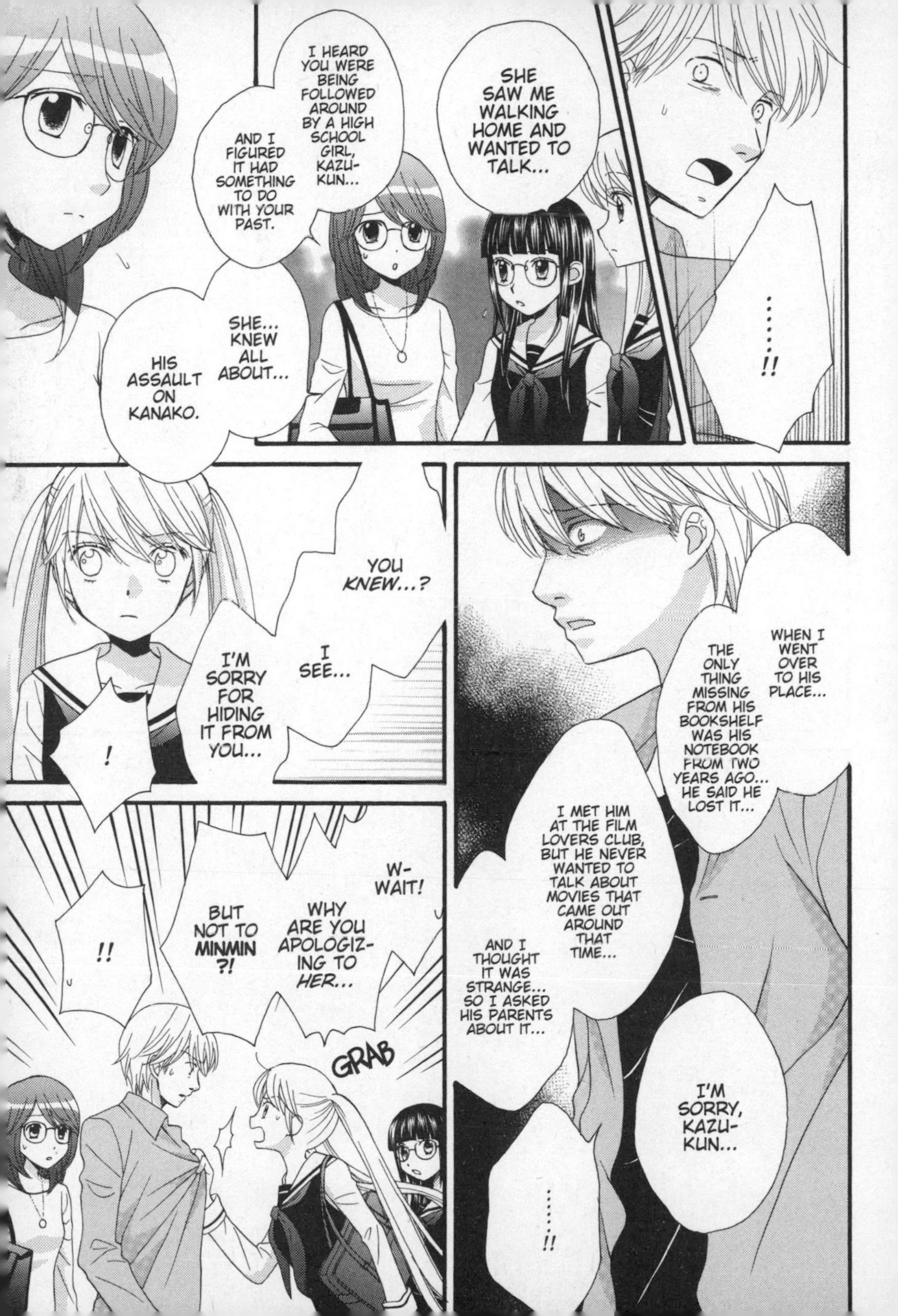
......!!
SHE SAW ME WALKING HOME AND WANTED TO TALK...
I HEARD YOU WERE BEING FOLLOWED AROUND BY A HIGH SCHOOL GIRL, KAZU-KUN...
AND I FIGURED IT HAD SOMETHING TO DO WITH YOUR PAST.
SHE... KNEW ALL ABOUT...
HIS ASSAULT ON KANAKO.
WHEN I WENT OVER TO HIS PLACE...
THE ONLY THING MISSING FROM HIS BOOKSHELF WAS HIS NOTEBOOK FROM TWO YEARS AGO... HE SAID HE LOST IT...
I MET HIM AT THE FILM LOVERS CLUB, BUT HE NEVER WANTED TO TALK ABOUT MOVIES THAT CAME OUT AROUND THAT TIME...
AND I THOUGHT IT WAS STRANGE... SO I ASKED HIS PARENTS ABOUT IT...
I'M SORRY, KAZU-KUN...
......!!
YOU KNEW...?
I SEE...
I'M SORRY FOR HIDING IT FROM YOU...
!
W-WAIT!
WHY ARE YOU APOLOGIZING TO HER...
BUT NOT TO MINMIN?!
!!
GRAB

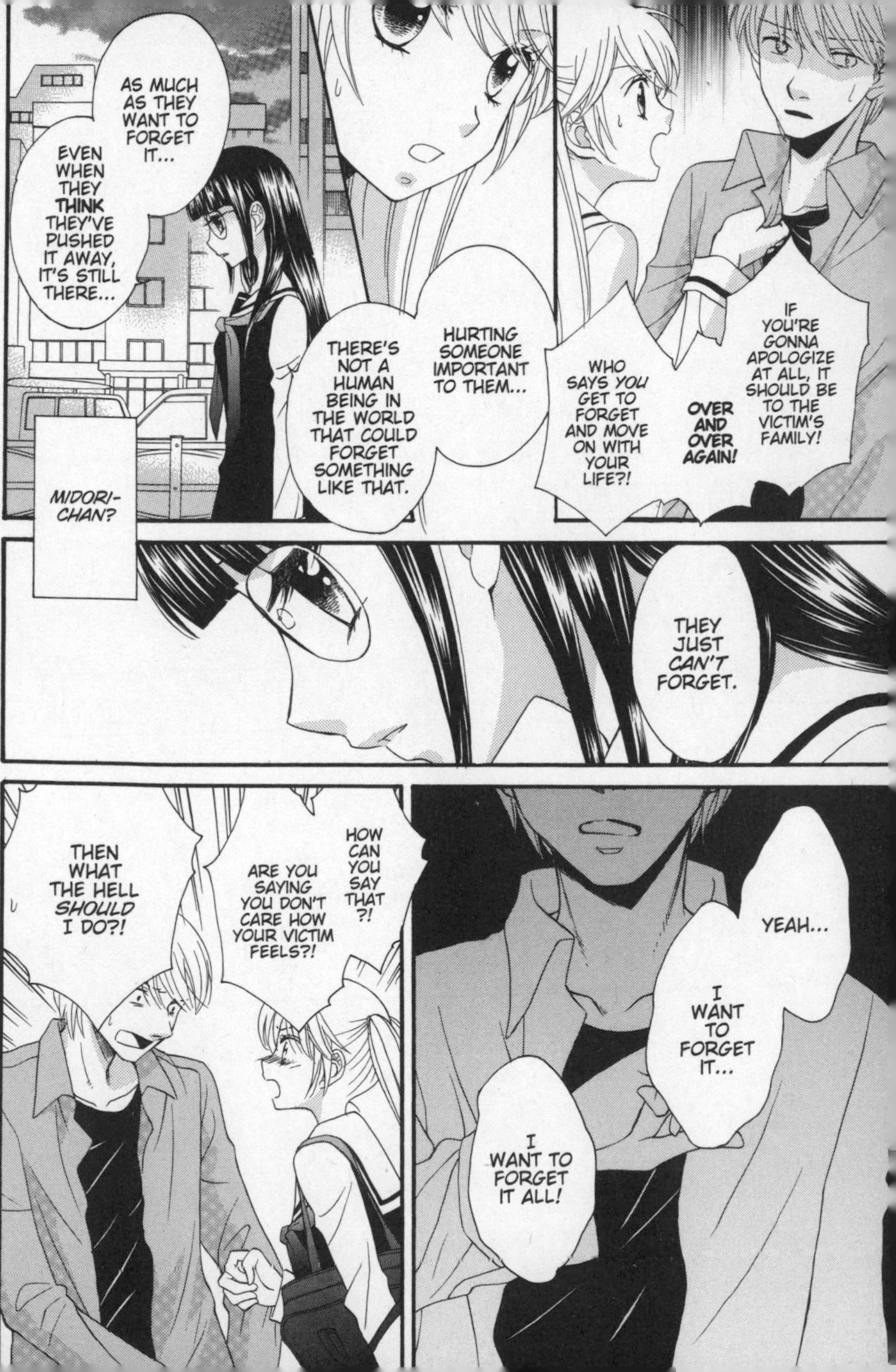
IF YOU'RE GONNA APOLOGIZE AT ALL, IT SHOULD BE TO THE VICTIM'S FAMILY!
OVER AND OVER AGAIN!
WHO SAYS YOU GET TO FORGET AND MOVE ON WITH YOUR LIFE?!
HURTING SOMEONE IMPORTANT TO THEM...
THERE'S NOT A HUMAN BEING IN THE WORLD THAT COULD FORGET SOMETHING LIKE THAT.
AS MUCH AS THEY WANT TO FORGET IT...
EVEN WHEN THEY THINK THEY'VE PUSHED IT AWAY, IT'S STILL THERE...
MIDORI-CHAN?
THEY JUST CAN'T FORGET.
YEAH...
I WANT TO FORGET IT...
I WANT TO FORGET IT ALL!
HOW CAN YOU SAY THAT?!
ARE YOU SAYING YOU DON'T CARE HOW YOUR VICTIM FEELS?!
THEN WHAT THE HELL SHOULD I DO?!

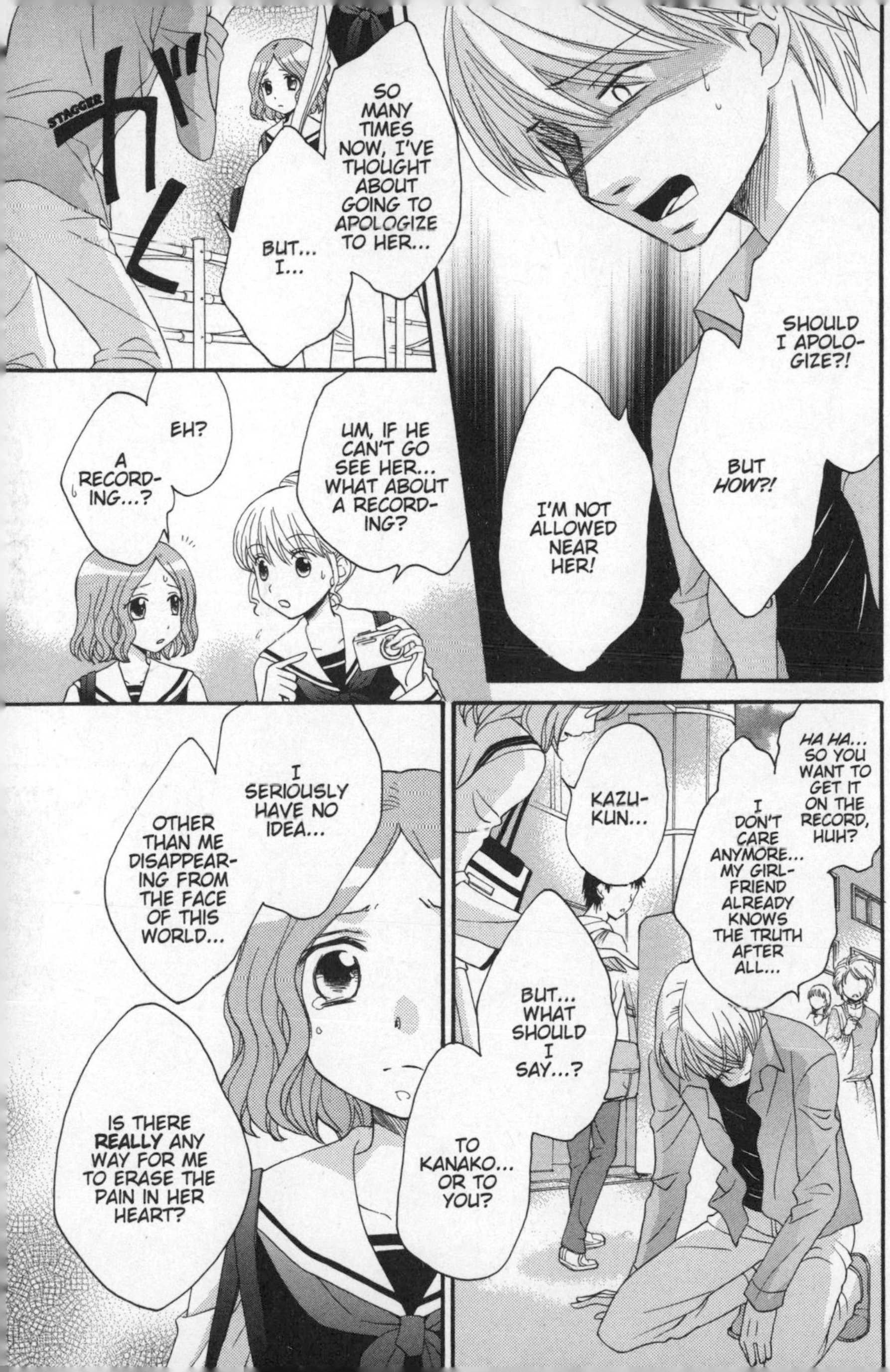
SHOULD I APOLOGIZE?!
BUT *HOW?!*
I'M NOT ALLOWED NEAR HER!
STAGGER
SO MANY TIMES NOW, I'VE THOUGHT ABOUT GOING TO APOLOGIZE TO HER...
BUT... I...
UM, IF HE CAN'T GO SEE HER... WHAT ABOUT A RECORDING?
EH?
A RECORDING...?
HA HA... SO YOU WANT TO GET IT ON THE RECORD, HUH?
I DON'T CARE ANYMORE... MY GIRLFRIEND ALREADY KNOWS THE TRUTH AFTER ALL...
KAZU-KUN...
BUT... WHAT SHOULD I SAY...?
TO KANAKO... OR TO YOU?
I SERIOUSLY HAVE NO IDEA...
OTHER THAN ME DISAPPEARING FROM THE FACE OF THIS WORLD...
IS THERE **REALLY** ANY WAY FOR ME TO ERASE THE PAIN IN HER HEART?

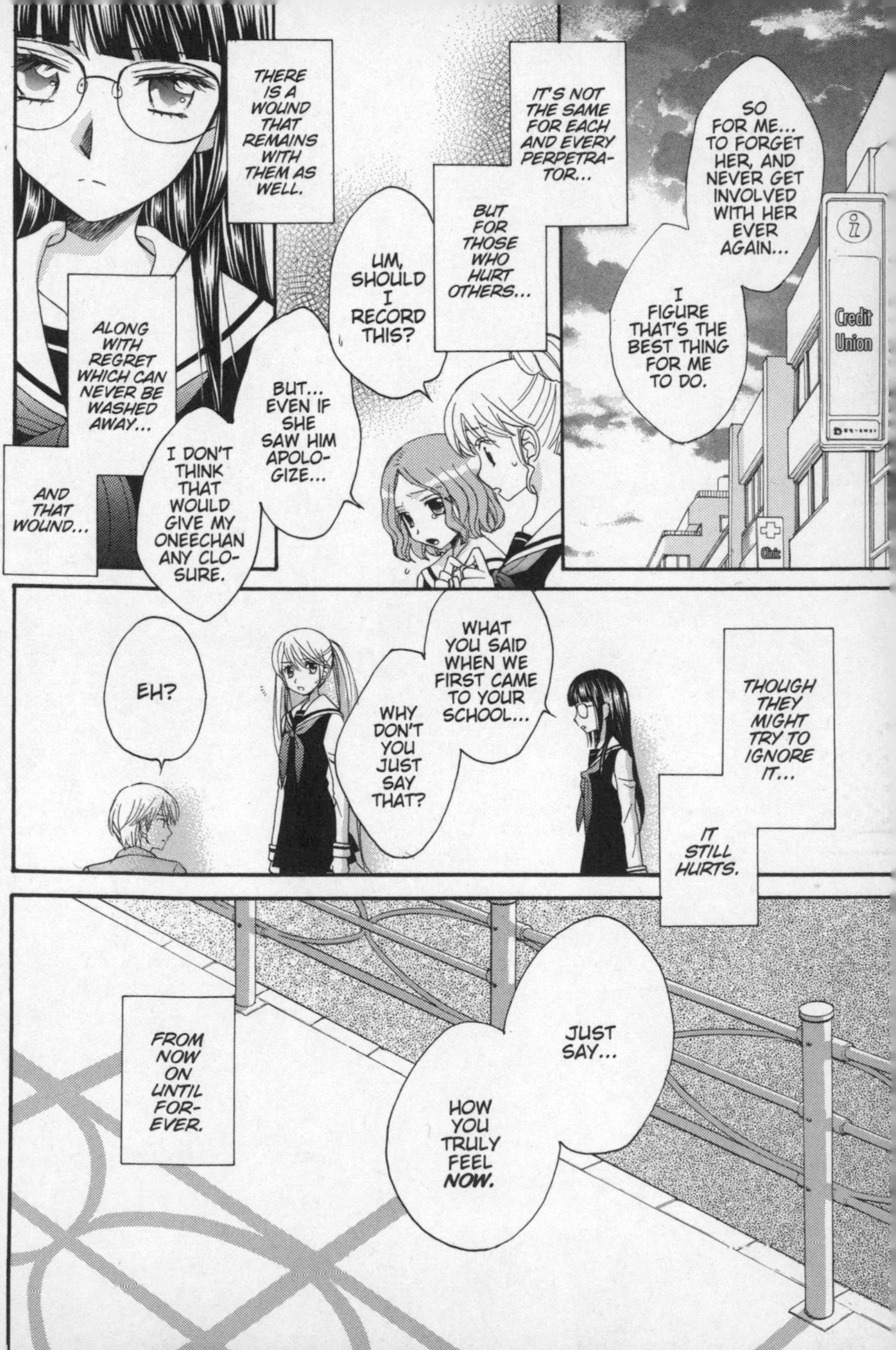
SO FOR ME... TO FORGET HER, AND NEVER GET INVOLVED WITH HER EVER AGAIN...
I FIGURE THAT'S THE BEST THING FOR ME TO DO.
Credit Union
Clinic
IT'S NOT THE SAME FOR EACH AND EVERY PERPETRATOR...
BUT FOR THOSE WHO HURT OTHERS...
UM, SHOULD I RECORD THIS?
BUT... EVEN IF SHE SAW HIM APOLOGIZE...
I DON'T THINK THAT WOULD GIVE MY ONEECHAN ANY CLOSURE.
THERE IS A WOUND THAT REMAINS WITH THEM AS WELL.
ALONG WITH REGRET WHICH CAN NEVER BE WASHED AWAY...
AND THAT WOUND...
THOUGH THEY MIGHT TRY TO IGNORE IT...
IT STILL HURTS.
WHAT YOU SAID WHEN WE FIRST CAME TO YOUR SCHOOL...
WHY DON'T YOU JUST SAY THAT?
EH?
JUST SAY...
HOW YOU TRULY FEEL NOW.
FROM NOW ON UNTIL FOREVER.

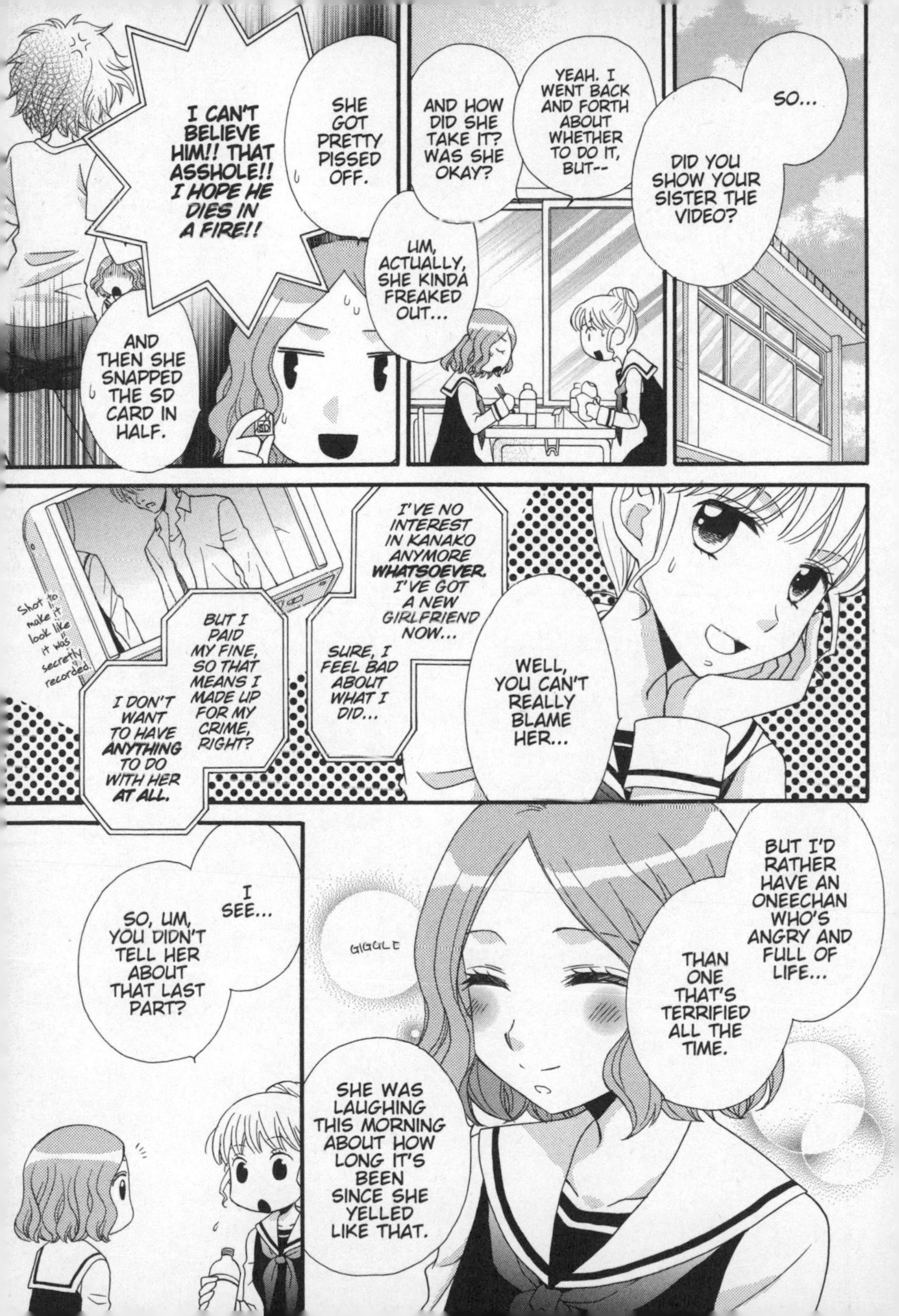
SO...
DID YOU SHOW YOUR SISTER THE VIDEO?
YEAH. I WENT BACK AND FORTH ABOUT WHETHER TO DO IT, BUT--
AND HOW DID SHE TAKE IT? WAS SHE OKAY?
UM, ACTUALLY, SHE KINDA FREAKED OUT...
SHE GOT PRETTY PISSED OFF.
I CAN'T BELIEVE HIM!! THAT ASSHOLE!! I HOPE HE DIES IN A FIRE!!
AND THEN SHE SNAPPED THE SD CARD IN HALF.
WELL, YOU CAN'T REALLY BLAME HER...
I'VE NO INTEREST IN KANAKO ANYMORE WHATSOEVER. I'VE GOT A NEW GIRLFRIEND NOW...
SURE, I FEEL BAD ABOUT WHAT I DID...
BUT I PAID MY FINE, SO THAT MEANS I MADE UP FOR MY CRIME, RIGHT?
I DON'T WANT TO HAVE ANYTHING TO DO WITH HER AT ALL.
Shot to make it look like it was secretly recorded.
BUT I'D RATHER HAVE AN ONEECHAN WHO'S ANGRY AND FULL OF LIFE...
THAN ONE THAT'S TERRIFIED ALL THE TIME.
GIGGLE
SHE WAS LAUGHING THIS MORNING ABOUT HOW LONG IT'S BEEN SINCE SHE YELLED LIKE THAT.
I SEE...
SO, UM, YOU DIDN'T TELL HER ABOUT THAT LAST PART?

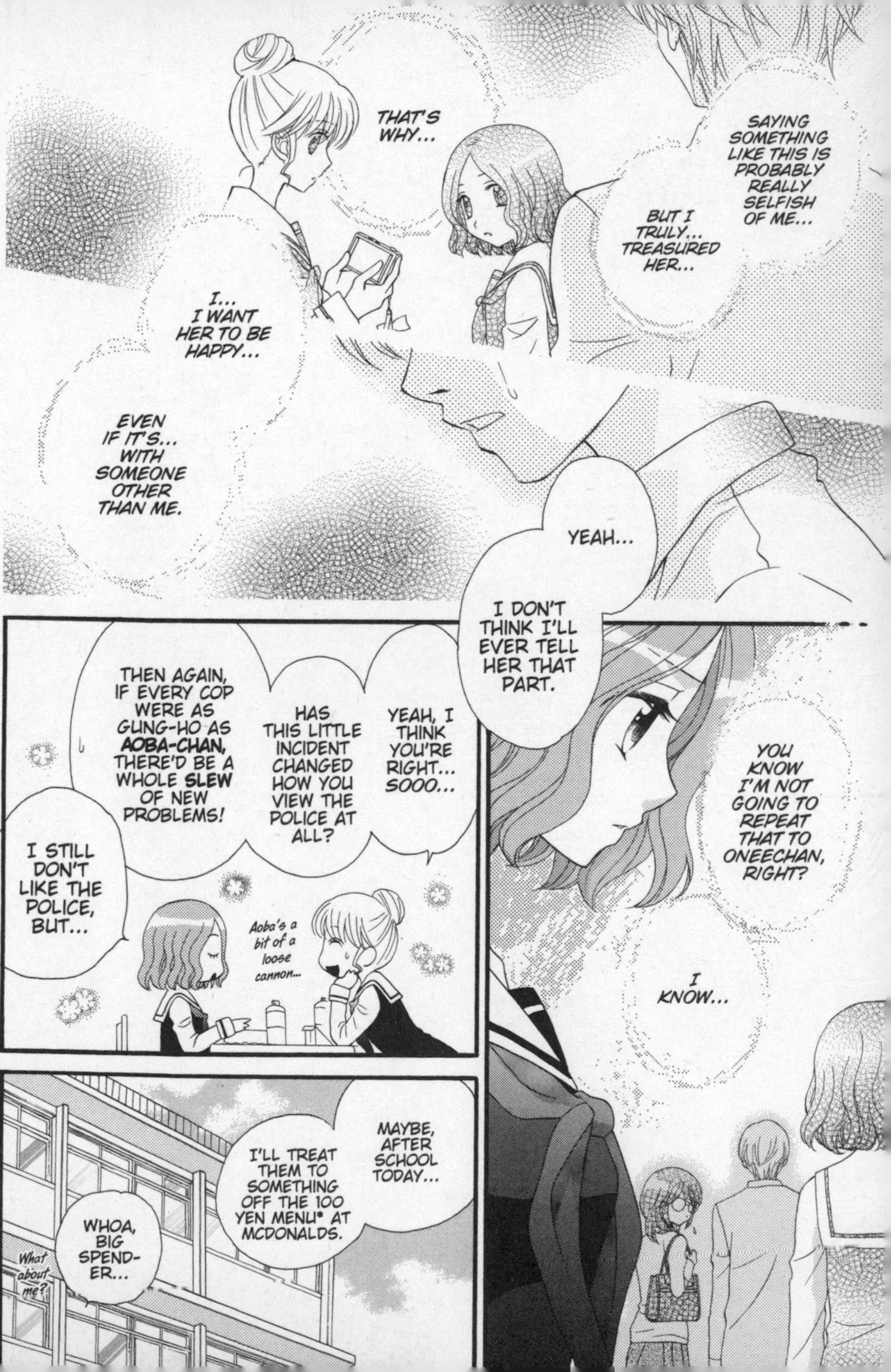
SAYING SOMETHING LIKE THIS IS PROBABLY REALLY SELFISH OF ME...
BUT I TRULY... TREASURED HER...
THAT'S WHY...
I... I WANT HER TO BE HAPPY...
EVEN IF IT'S... WITH SOMEONE OTHER THAN ME.
YEAH...
I DON'T THINK I'LL EVER TELL HER THAT PART.
YOU KNOW I'M NOT GOING TO REPEAT THAT TO ONEECHAN, RIGHT?
I KNOW...
YEAH, I THINK YOU'RE RIGHT... SOOO...
HAS THIS LITTLE INCIDENT CHANGED HOW YOU VIEW THE POLICE AT ALL?
THEN AGAIN, IF EVERY COP WERE AS GUNG-HO AS AOBA-CHAN, THERE'D BE A WHOLE SLEW OF NEW PROBLEMS!
I STILL DON'T LIKE THE POLICE, BUT...
Aoba's a bit of a loose cannon...
MAYBE, AFTER SCHOOL TODAY...
I'LL TREAT THEM TO SOMETHING OFF THE 100 YEN MENU* AT MCDONALDS.
WHOA, BIG SPENDER...
What about me?

*Japan's equivalent of the dollar menu.

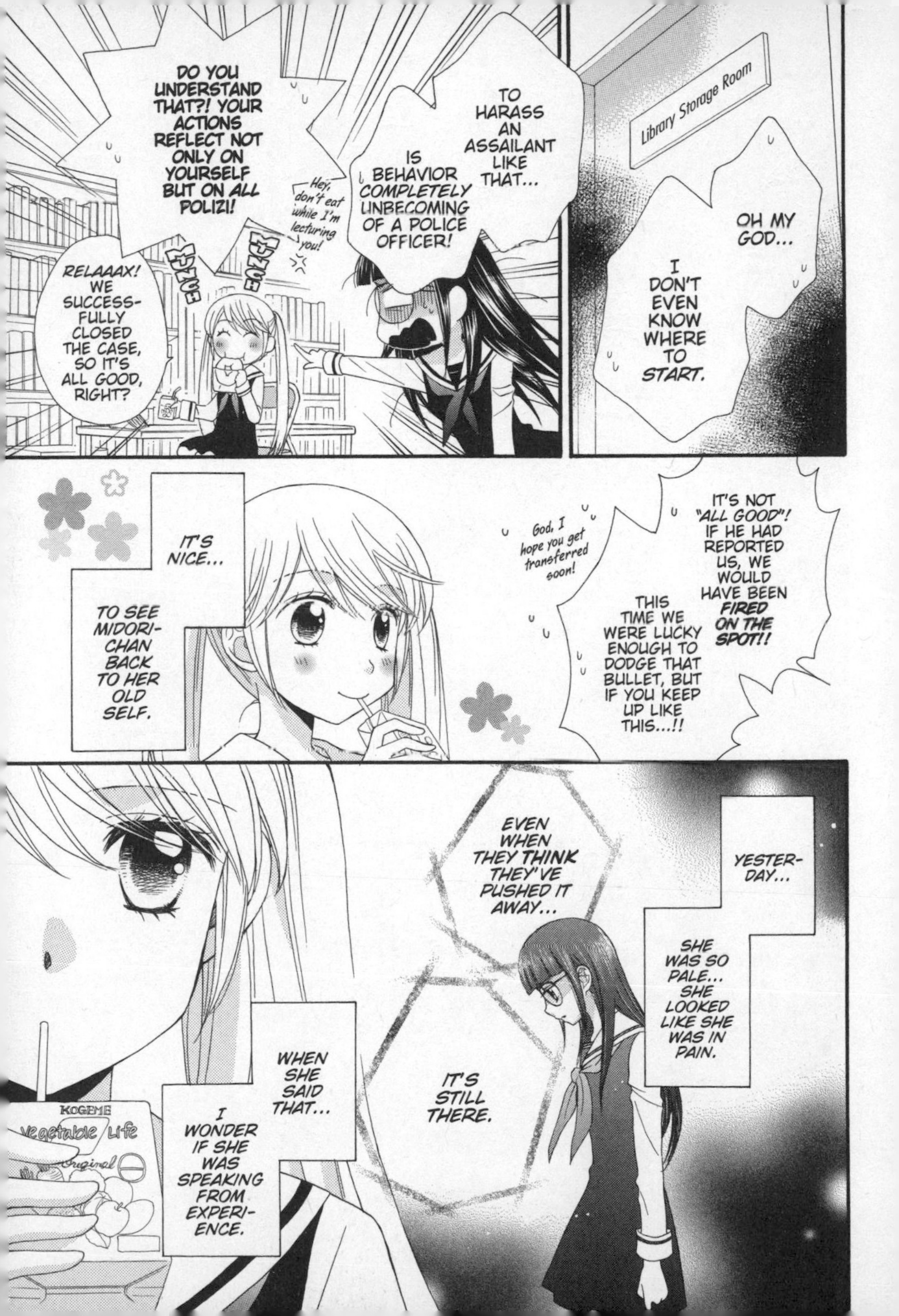

Library Storage Room
OH MY GOD...
I DON'T EVEN KNOW WHERE TO START.
TO HARASS AN ASSAILANT LIKE THAT...
IS BEHAVIOR COMPLETELY UNBECOMING OF A POLICE OFFICER!
Hey, don't eat while I'm lecturing you!
DO YOU UNDERSTAND THAT?! YOUR ACTIONS REFLECT NOT ONLY ON YOURSELF BUT ON ALL POLIZI!
MUNCH
MUNCH
RELAAAX! WE SUCCESSFULLY CLOSED THE CASE, SO IT'S ALL GOOD, RIGHT?
IT'S NOT "ALL GOOD"! IF HE HAD REPORTED US, WE WOULD HAVE BEEN FIRED ON THE SPOT!!
THIS TIME WE WERE LUCKY ENOUGH TO DODGE THAT BULLET, BUT IF YOU KEEP UP LIKE THIS...!!
God, I hope you get transferred soon!
IT'S NICE...
TO SEE MIDORI-CHAN BACK TO HER OLD SELF.
YESTER-DAY...
SHE WAS SO PALE... SHE LOOKED LIKE SHE WAS IN PAIN.
EVEN WHEN THEY THINK THEY'VE PUSHED IT AWAY...
IT'S STILL THERE.
WHEN SHE SAID THAT...
I WONDER IF SHE WAS SPEAKING FROM EXPERI-ENCE.
KOGEME
vegetable Life
Original

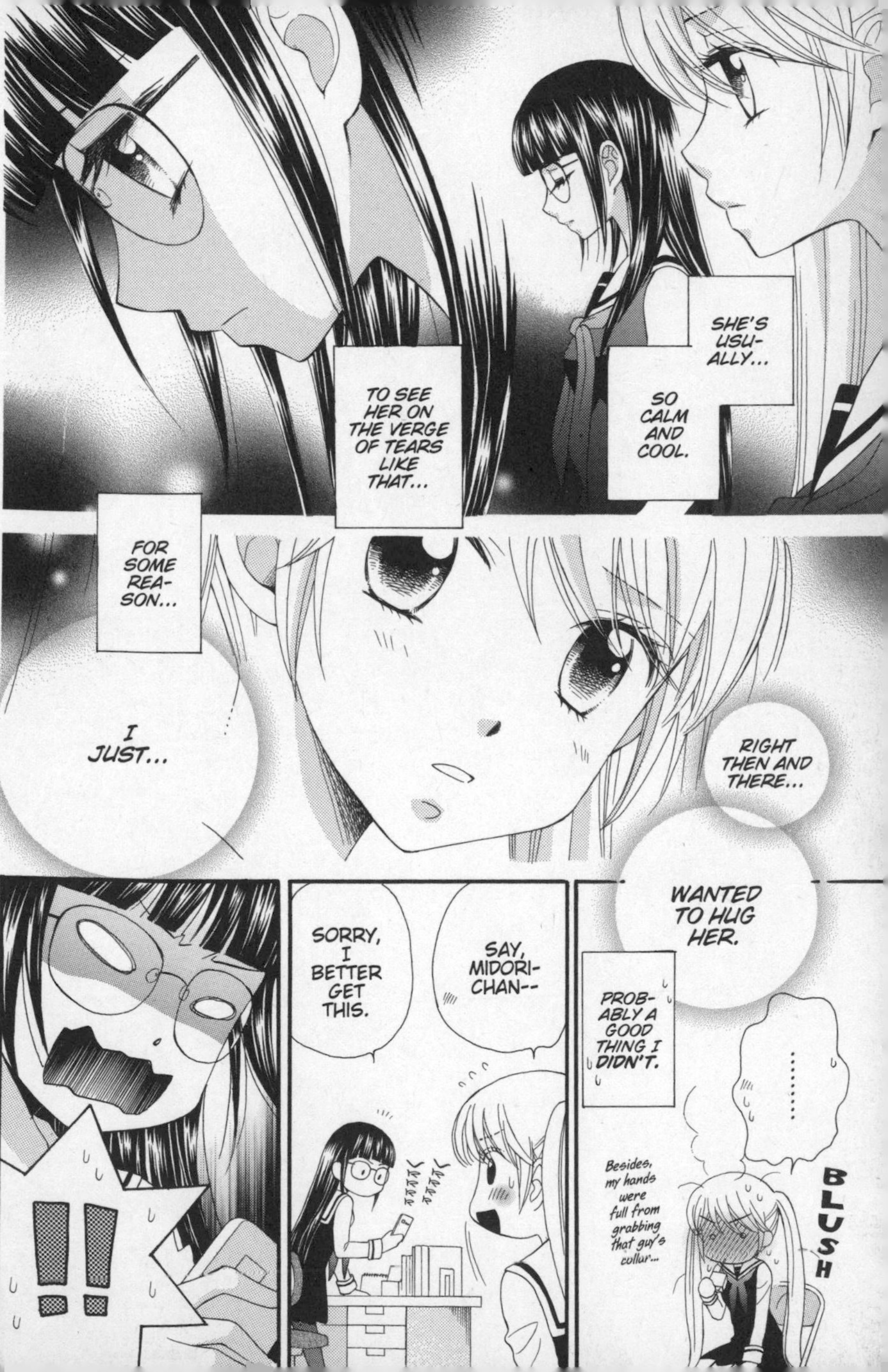
SHE'S USUALLY...
SO CALM AND COOL.
TO SEE HER ON THE VERGE OF TEARS LIKE THAT...
FOR SOME REASON...
RIGHT THEN AND THERE...
I JUST...
WANTED TO HUG HER.
PROBABLY A GOOD THING I DIDN'T.
......
Besides, my hands were full from grabbing that guy's collar...
BLUSH
SAY, MIDORI-CHAN--
SORRY, I BETTER GET THIS.
!!

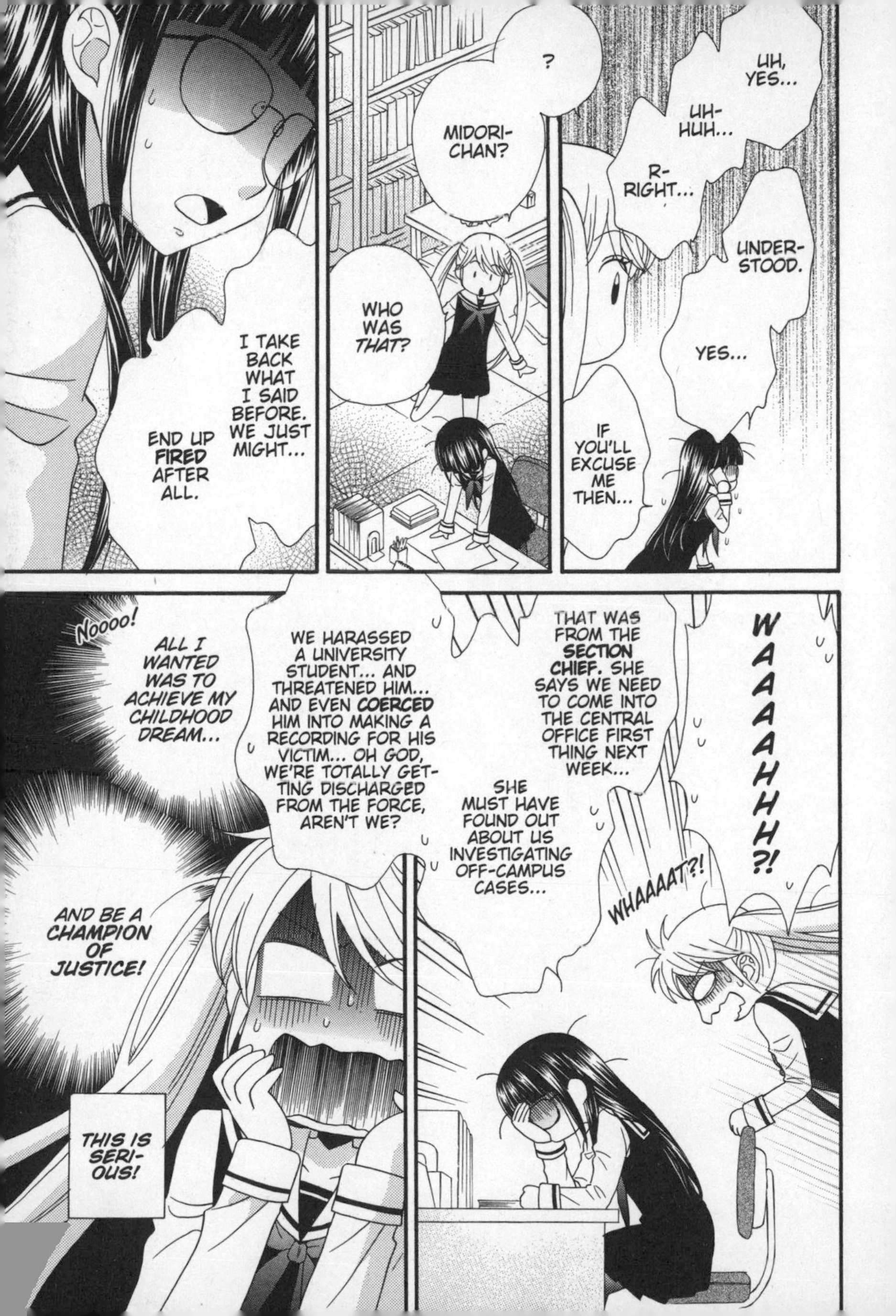
UH, YES...
UH-HUH...
R-RIGHT...
UNDER-STOOD.
YES...
IF YOU'LL EXCUSE ME THEN...
?
MIDORI-CHAN?
WHO WAS *THAT*?
I TAKE BACK WHAT I SAID BEFORE. WE JUST MIGHT...
END UP **FIRED** AFTER ALL.
THAT WAS FROM THE **SECTION CHIEF.** SHE SAYS WE NEED TO COME INTO THE CENTRAL OFFICE FIRST THING NEXT WEEK...
WHAAAAT?!
SHE MUST HAVE FOUND OUT ABOUT US INVESTIGATING OFF-CAMPUS CASES...
WAAAAAHHH?!
WE HARASSED A UNIVERSITY STUDENT... AND THREATENED HIM... AND EVEN **COERCED** HIM INTO MAKING A RECORDING FOR HIS VICTIM... OH GOD, WE'RE TOTALLY GET-TING DISCHARGED FROM THE FORCE, AREN'T WE?
Noooo!
ALL I WANTED WAS TO ACHIEVE MY CHILDHOOD DREAM...
AND BE A CHAMPION OF JUSTICE!
THIS IS SERI-OUS!

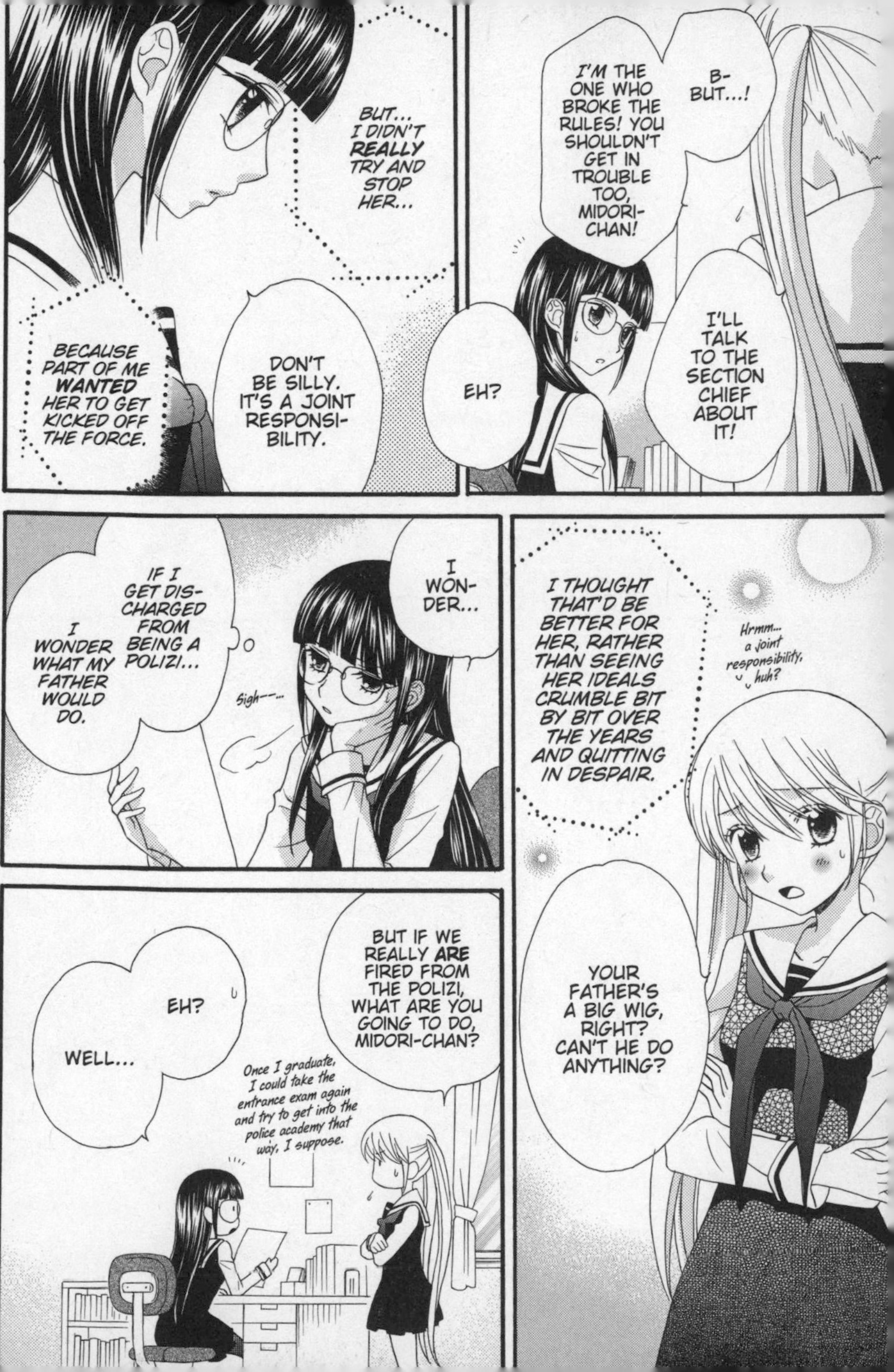
B-BUT...!
I'M THE ONE WHO BROKE THE RULES! YOU SHOULDN'T GET IN TROUBLE TOO, MIDORI-CHAN!
I'LL TALK TO THE SECTION CHIEF ABOUT IT!
EH?
BUT... I DIDN'T REALLY TRY AND STOP HER...
DON'T BE SILLY. IT'S A JOINT RESPONSIBILITY.
BECAUSE PART OF ME WANTED HER TO GET KICKED OFF THE FORCE.
I THOUGHT THAT'D BE BETTER FOR HER, RATHER THAN SEEING HER IDEALS CRUMBLE BIT BY BIT OVER THE YEARS AND QUITTING IN DESPAIR.
Hrmm... a joint responsibility, huh?
YOUR FATHER'S A BIG WIG, RIGHT? CAN'T HE DO ANYTHING?
I WONDER...
IF I GET DISCHARGED FROM BEING A POLIZI...
I WONDER WHAT MY FATHER WOULD DO.
Sigh~...
BUT IF WE REALLY ARE FIRED FROM THE POLIZI, WHAT ARE YOU GOING TO DO, MIDORI-CHAN?
EH?
WELL...
Once I graduate, I could take the entrance exam again and try to get into the police academy that way, I suppose.

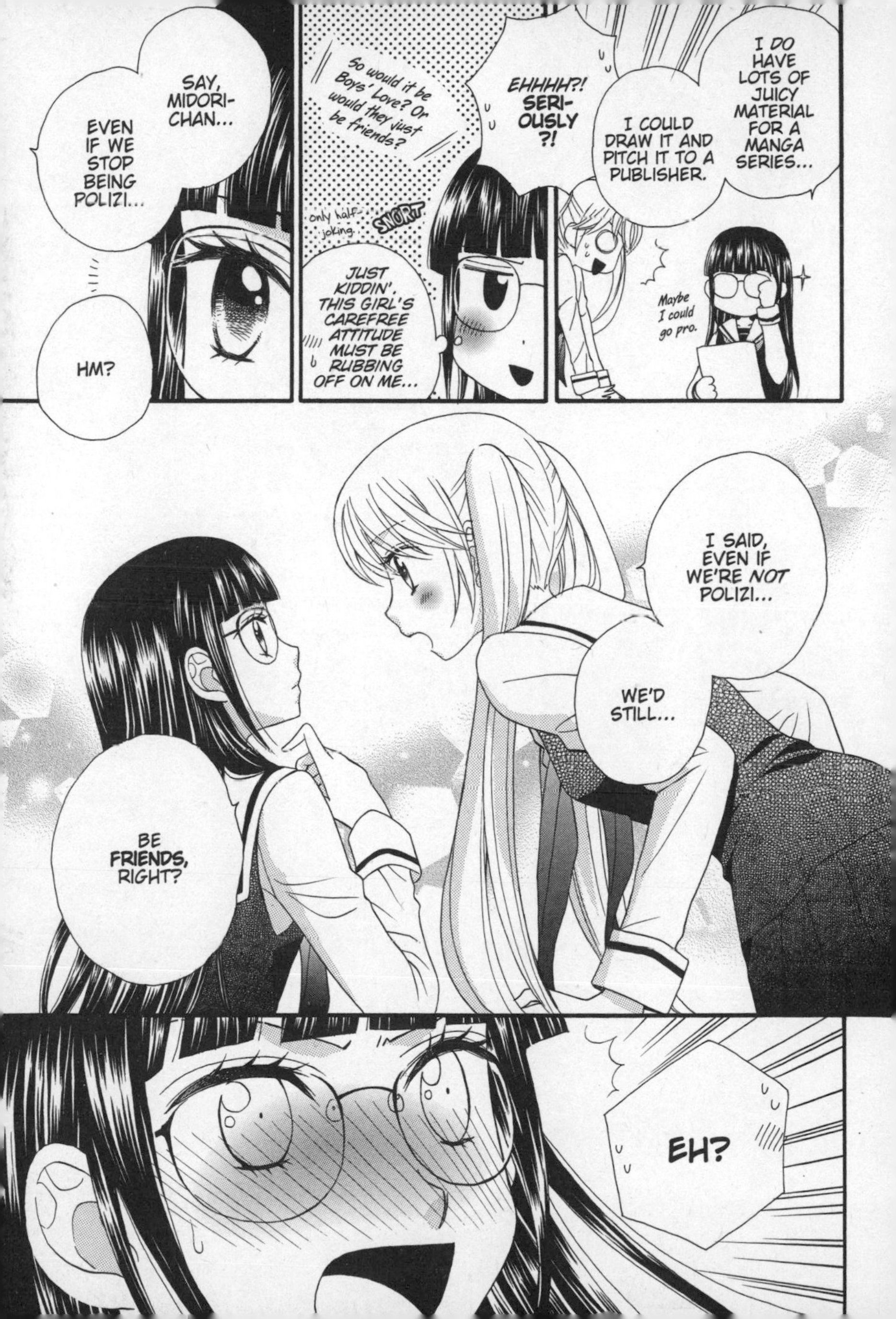
I DO HAVE LOTS OF JUICY MATERIAL FOR A MANGA SERIES...
I COULD DRAW IT AND PITCH IT TO A PUBLISHER.
Maybe I could go pro.
EHHHH?! SERIOUSLY?!
So would it be Boys' Love? Or would they just be friends?
SNORT
only half-joking.
JUST KIDDIN'. THIS GIRL'S CAREFREE ATTITUDE MUST BE RUBBING OFF ON ME...
SAY, MIDORI-CHAN...
EVEN IF WE STOP BEING POLIZI...
HM?
I SAID, EVEN IF WE'RE *NOT* POLIZI...
WE'D STILL...
BE FRIENDS, RIGHT?
EH?

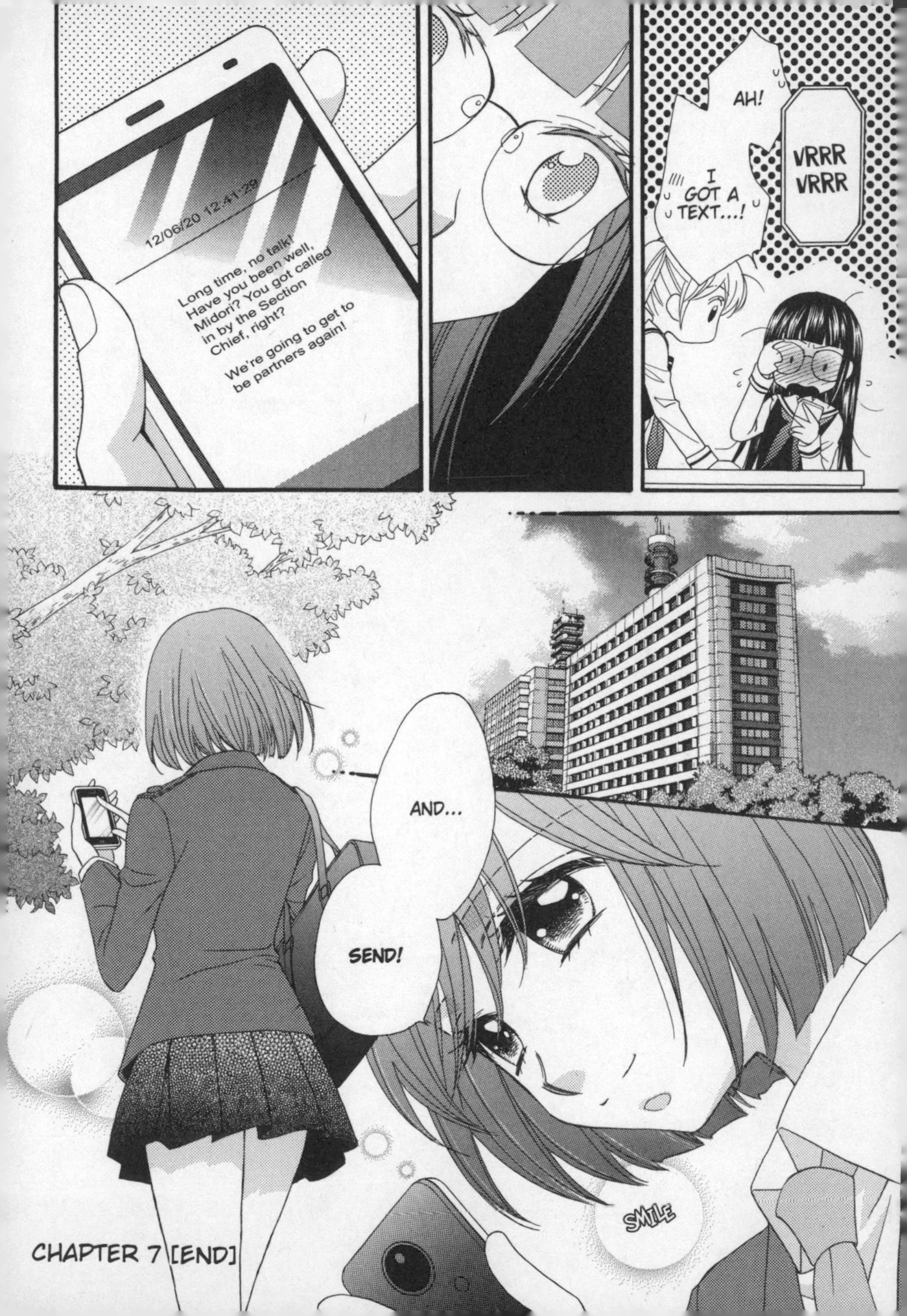
AH!
VRRR VRRR
I GOT A TEXT...!
12/06/20 12:41:29
Long time, no talk! Have you been well, Midori? You got called in by the Section Chief, right?
We're going to get to be partners again!
AND...
SEND!
SMILE
CHAPTER 7 [END]

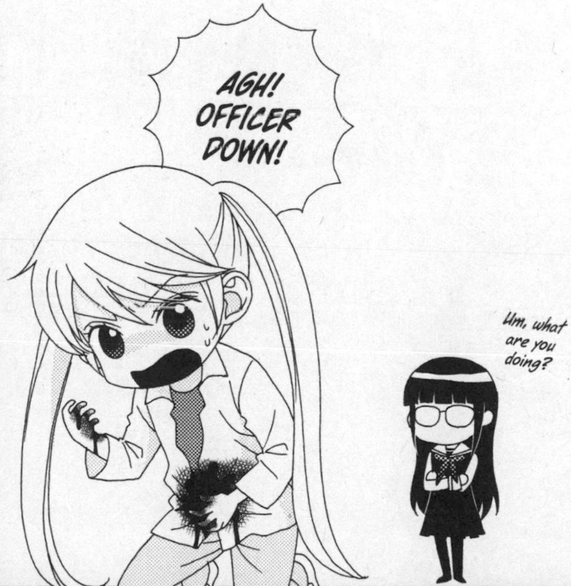
AGH! OFFICER DOWN!
Um, what are you doing?

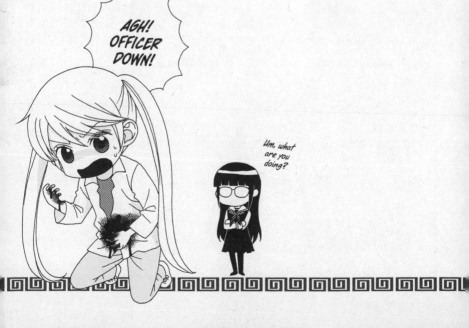

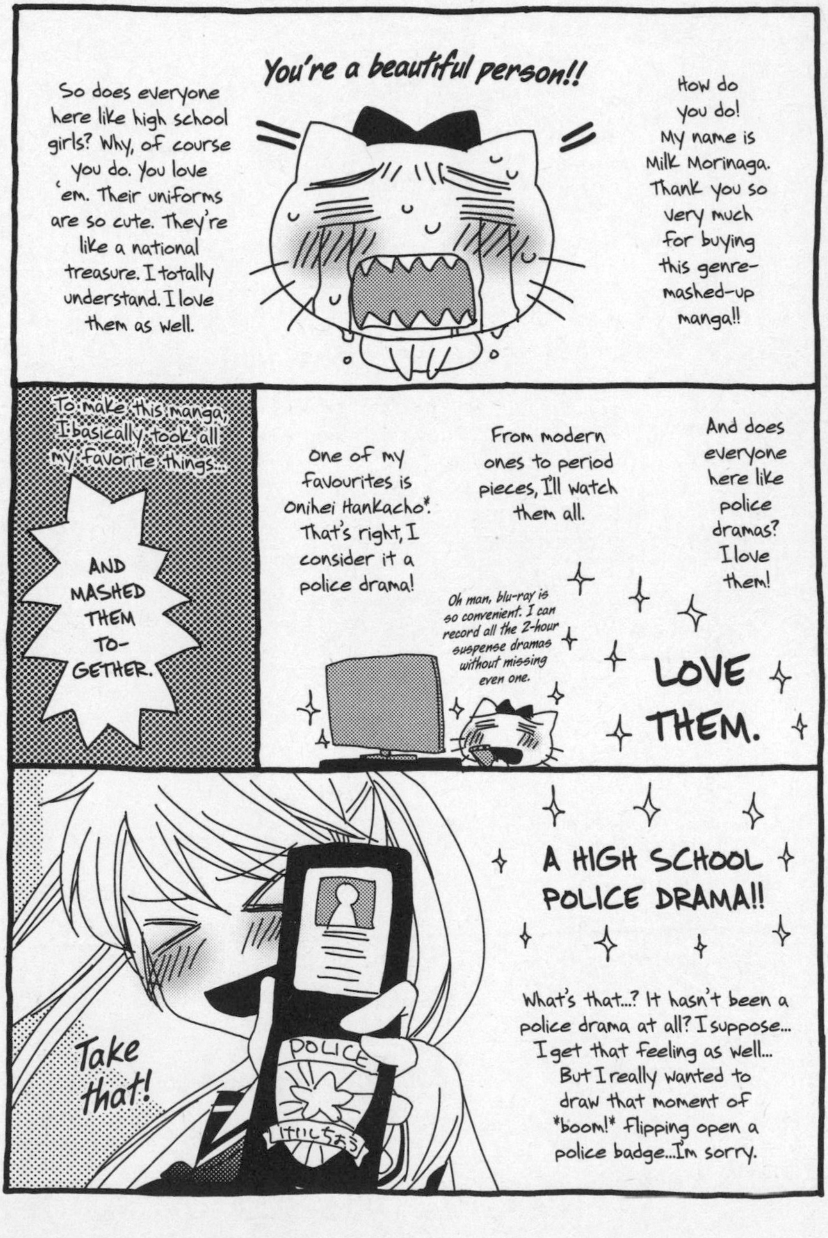
How do you do! My name is Milk Morinaga. Thank you so very much for buying this genre-mashed-up manga!!
You're a beautiful person!!
So does everyone here like high school girls? Why, of course you do. You love 'em. Their uniforms are so cute. They're like a national treasure. I totally understand. I love them as well.
And does everyone here like police dramas? I love them!
From modern ones to period pieces, I'll watch them all.
One of my favourites is Onihei Hankacho*. That's right, I consider it a police drama!
Oh man, blu-ray is so convenient. I can record all the 2-hour suspense dramas without missing even one.
LOVE THEM.
To make this manga, I basically took all my favorite things...
AND MASHED THEM TO-GETHER.
A HIGH SCHOOL POLICE DRAMA!!
What's that...? It hasn't been a police drama at all? I suppose... I get that feeling as well... But I really wanted to draw that moment of *boom!* flipping open a police badge...I'm sorry.
POLICE
Take that!

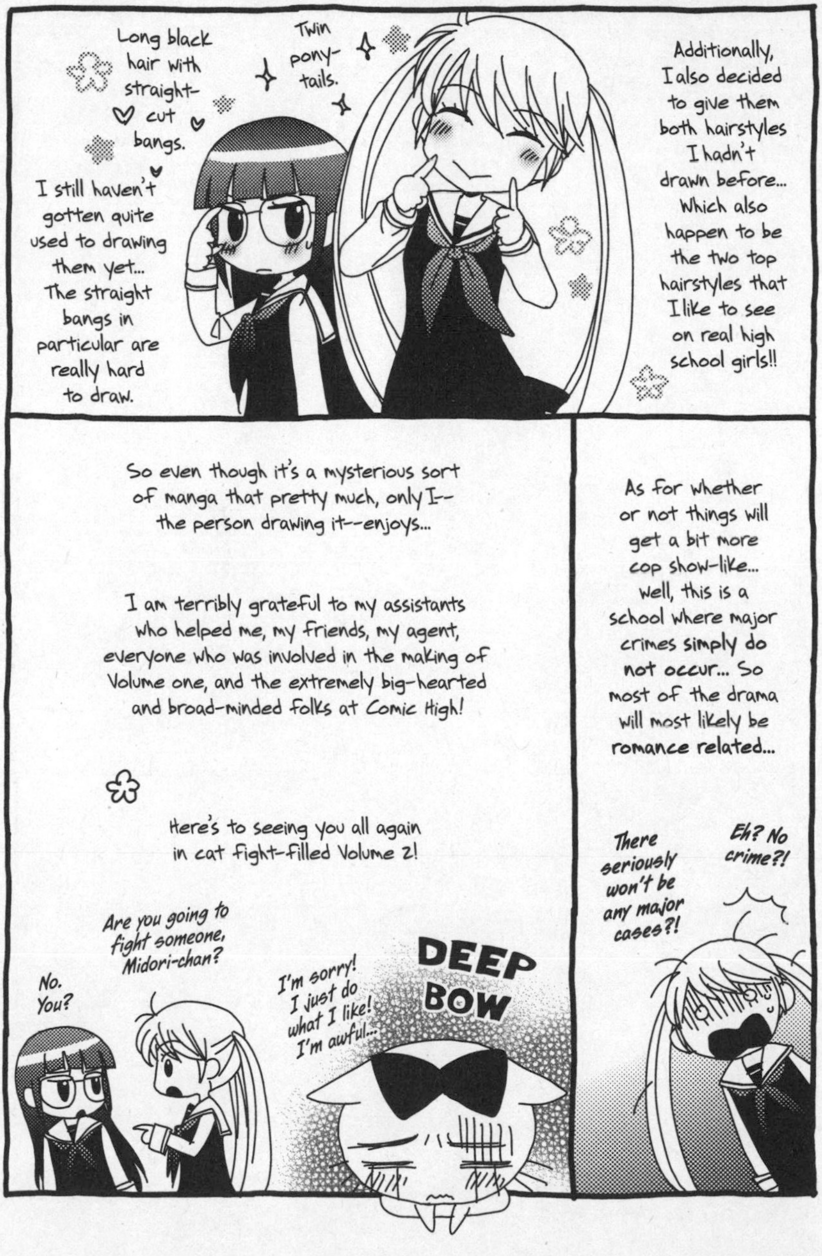
Additionally, I also decided to give them both hairstyles I hadn't drawn before... Which also happen to be the two top hairstyles that I like to see on real high school girls!!
Twin pony-tails.
Long black hair with straight-cut bangs.
I still haven't gotten quite used to drawing them yet... The straight bangs in particular are really hard to draw.
As for whether or not things will get a bit more cop show-like... well, this is a school where major crimes simply do not occur... So most of the drama will most likely be romance related...
Eh? No crime?!
There seriously won't be any major cases?!
So even though it's a mysterious sort of manga that pretty much, only I-- the person drawing it--enjoys...
I am terribly grateful to my assistants who helped me, my friends, my agent, everyone who was involved in the making of Volume one, and the extremely big-hearted and broad-minded folks at Comic High!
Here's to seeing you all again in cat fight-filled Volume 2!
DEEP BOW
I'm sorry! I just do what I like! I'm awful...
Are you going to fight someone, Midori-chan?
No. You?

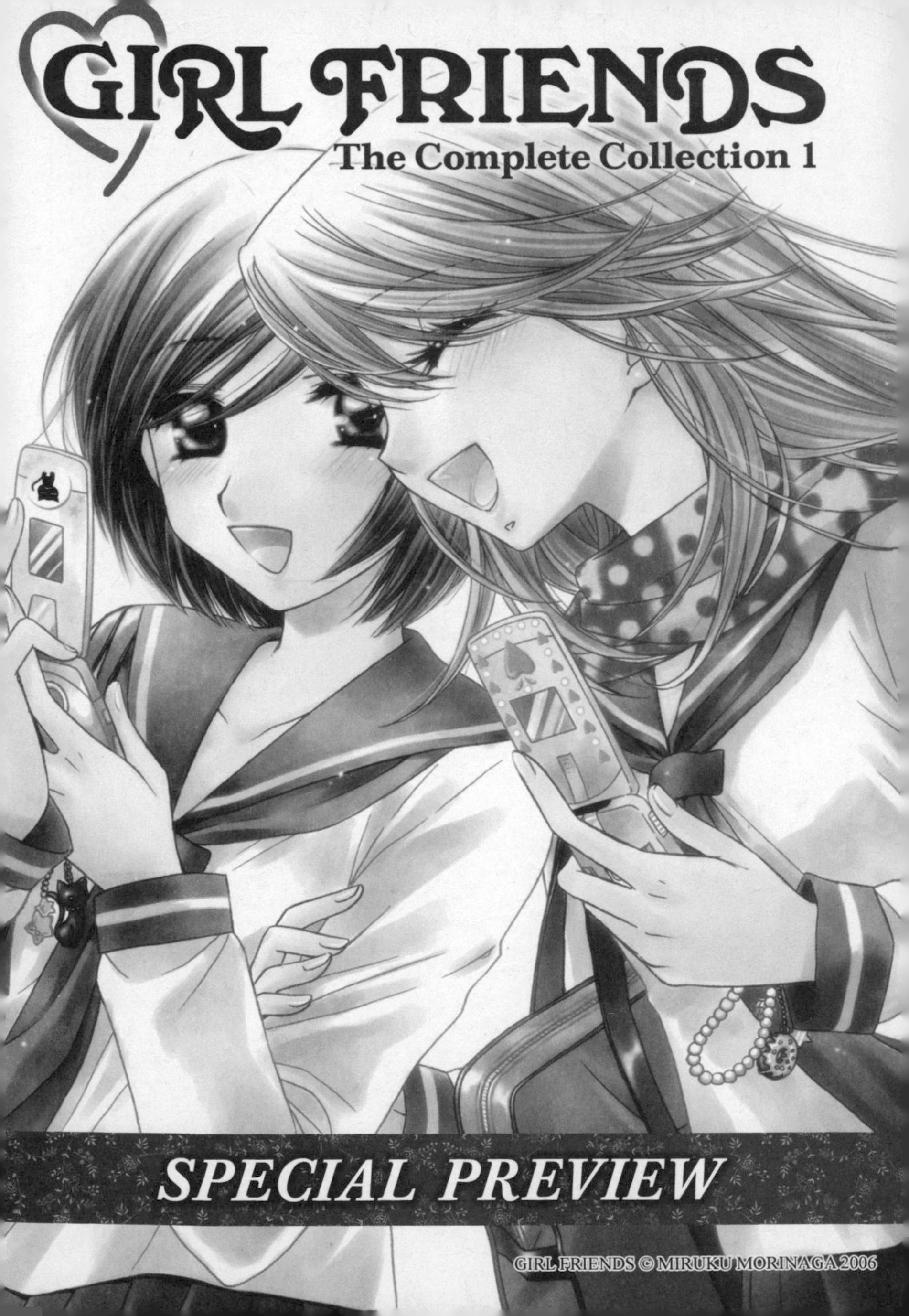
GIRL FRIENDS
The Complete Collection 1
SPECIAL PREVIEW

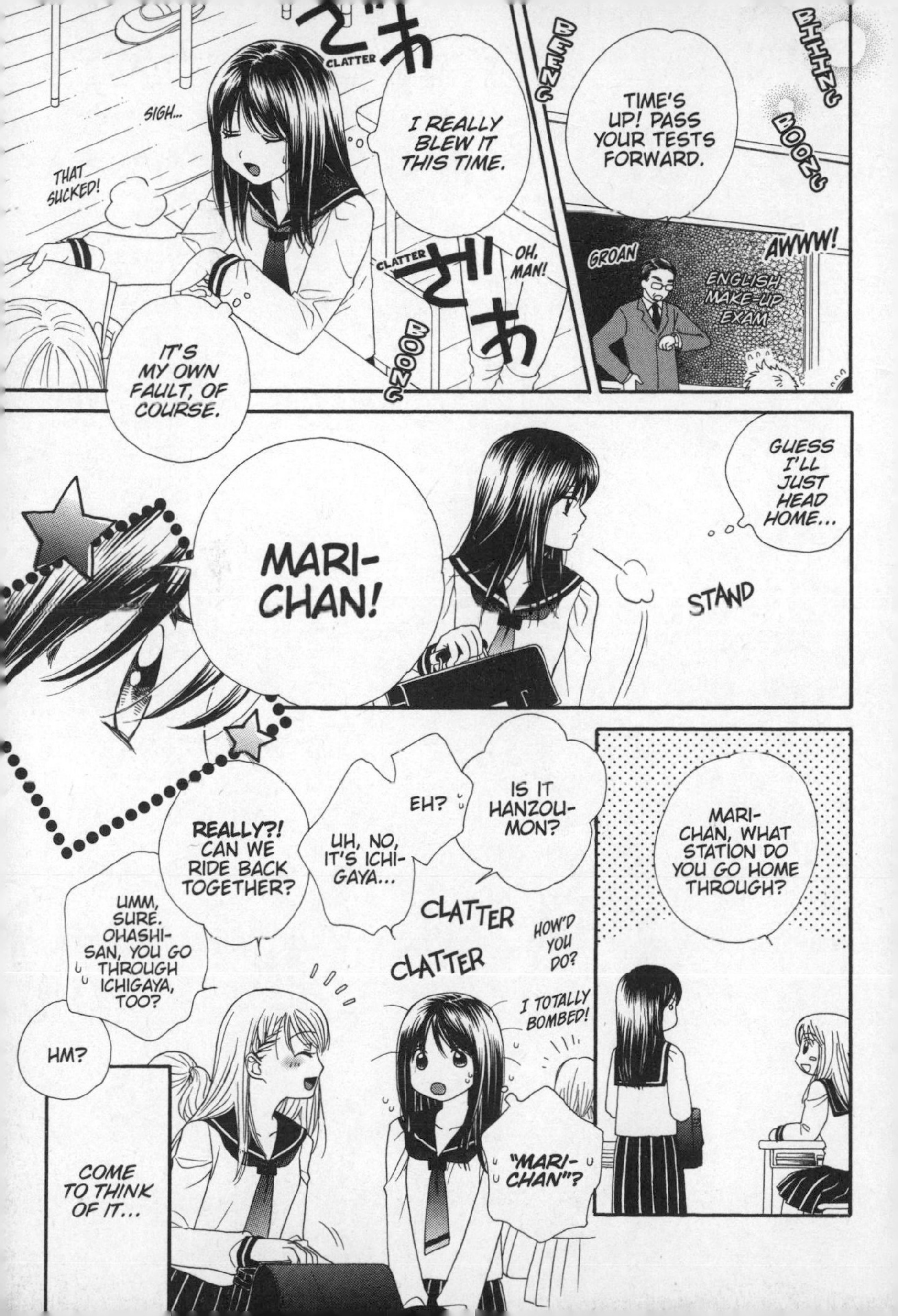
BEEENG
BIIING
BOOZU
TIME'S UP! PASS YOUR TESTS FORWARD.
AWWW!
GROAN
ENGLISH MAKE-UP EXAM
I REALLY BLEW IT THIS TIME.
CLATTER
OH, MAN!
CLATTER
BOONG
SIGH...
THAT SUCKED!
IT'S MY OWN FAULT, OF COURSE.
GUESS I'LL JUST HEAD HOME...
STAND
MARI-CHAN!
MARI-CHAN, WHAT STATION DO YOU GO HOME THROUGH?
IS IT HANZOUMON?
EH?
UH, NO, IT'S ICHIGAYA...
REALLY?! CAN WE RIDE BACK TOGETHER?
CLATTER
CLATTER
HOW'D YOU DO?
I TOTALLY BOMBED!
UMM, SURE. OHASHI-SAN, YOU GO THROUGH ICHIGAYA, TOO?
"MARI-CHAN"?
HM?
COME TO THINK OF IT...

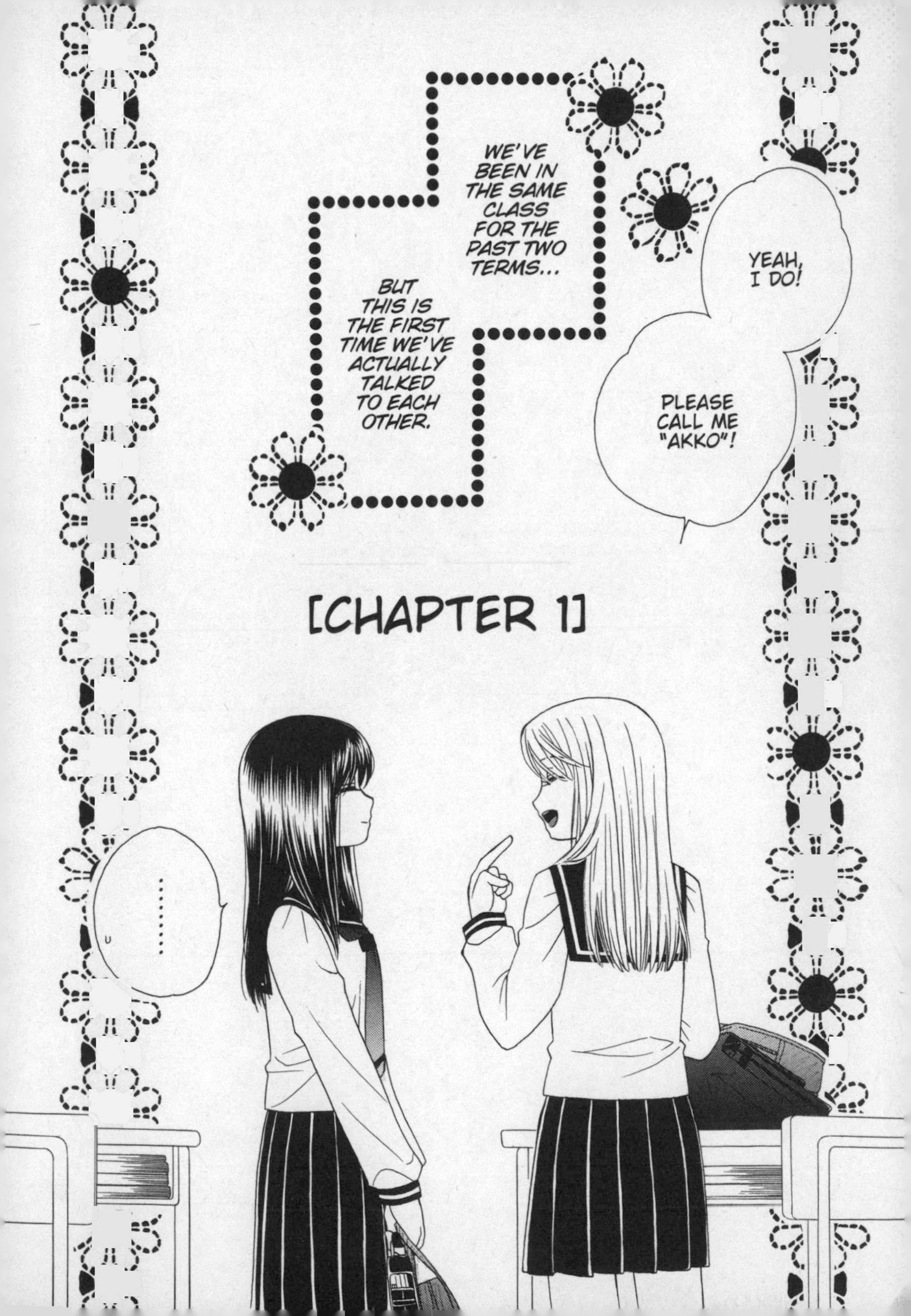
YEAH, I DO!
PLEASE CALL ME "AKKO"!
WE'VE BEEN IN THE SAME CLASS FOR THE PAST TWO TERMS...
BUT THIS IS THE FIRST TIME WE'VE ACTUALLY TALKED TO EACH OTHER.
[CHAPTER 1]
......

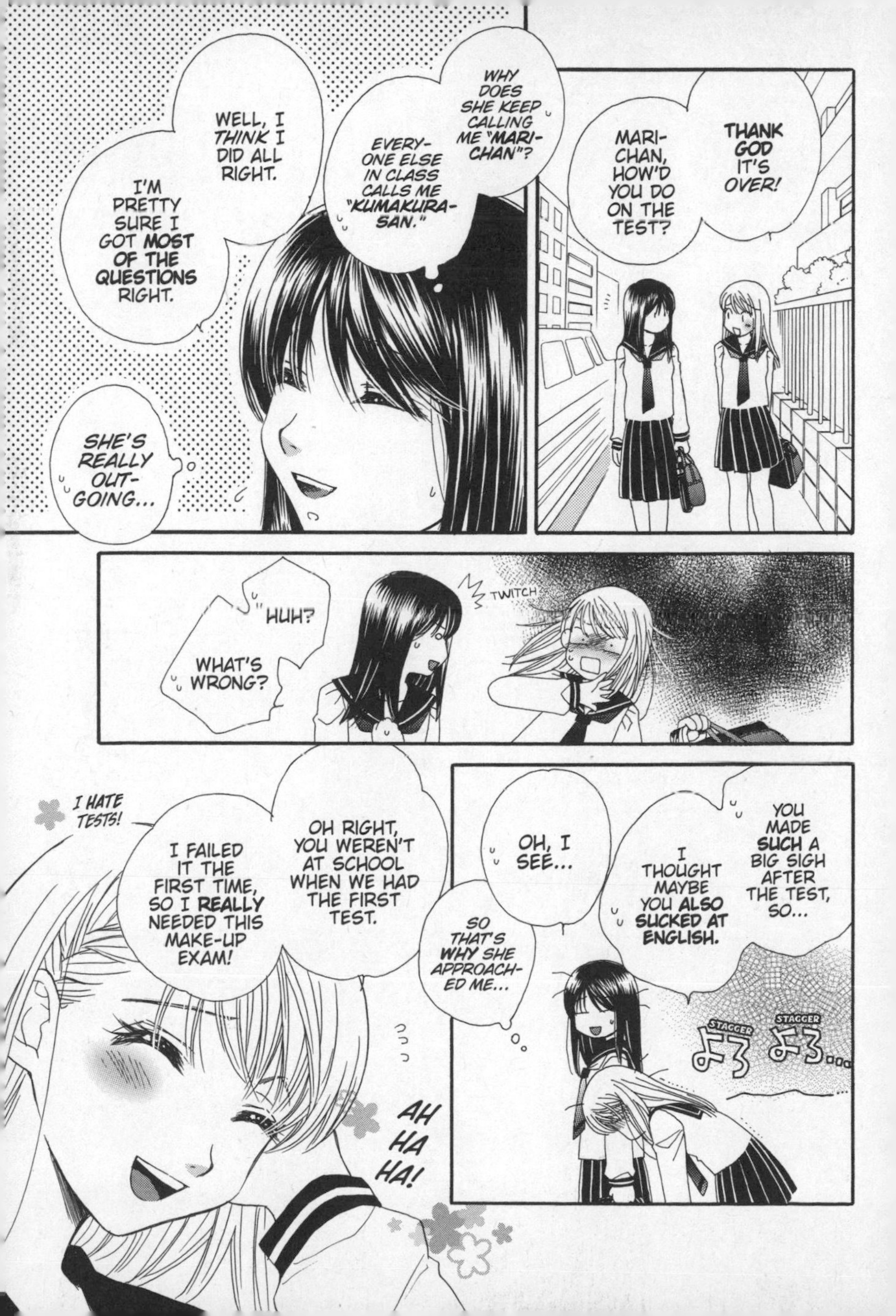
THANK GOD IT'S OVER!
MARI-CHAN, HOW'D YOU DO ON THE TEST?
WHY DOES SHE KEEP CALLING ME "MARI-CHAN"?
EVERY-ONE ELSE IN CLASS CALLS ME "KUMAKURA-SAN."
WELL, I THINK I DID ALL RIGHT.
I'M PRETTY SURE I GOT MOST OF THE QUESTIONS RIGHT.
SHE'S REALLY OUT-GOING...
TWITCH
HUH?
WHAT'S WRONG?
YOU MADE SUCH A BIG SIGH AFTER THE TEST, SO...
I THOUGHT MAYBE YOU ALSO SUCKED AT ENGLISH.
STAGGER STAGGER
よろよろ...
OH, I SEE...
SO THAT'S WHY SHE APPROACHED ME...
OH RIGHT, YOU WEREN'T AT SCHOOL WHEN WE HAD THE FIRST TEST.
I FAILED IT THE FIRST TIME, SO I REALLY NEEDED THIS MAKE-UP EXAM!
I HATE TESTS!
AH HA HA!

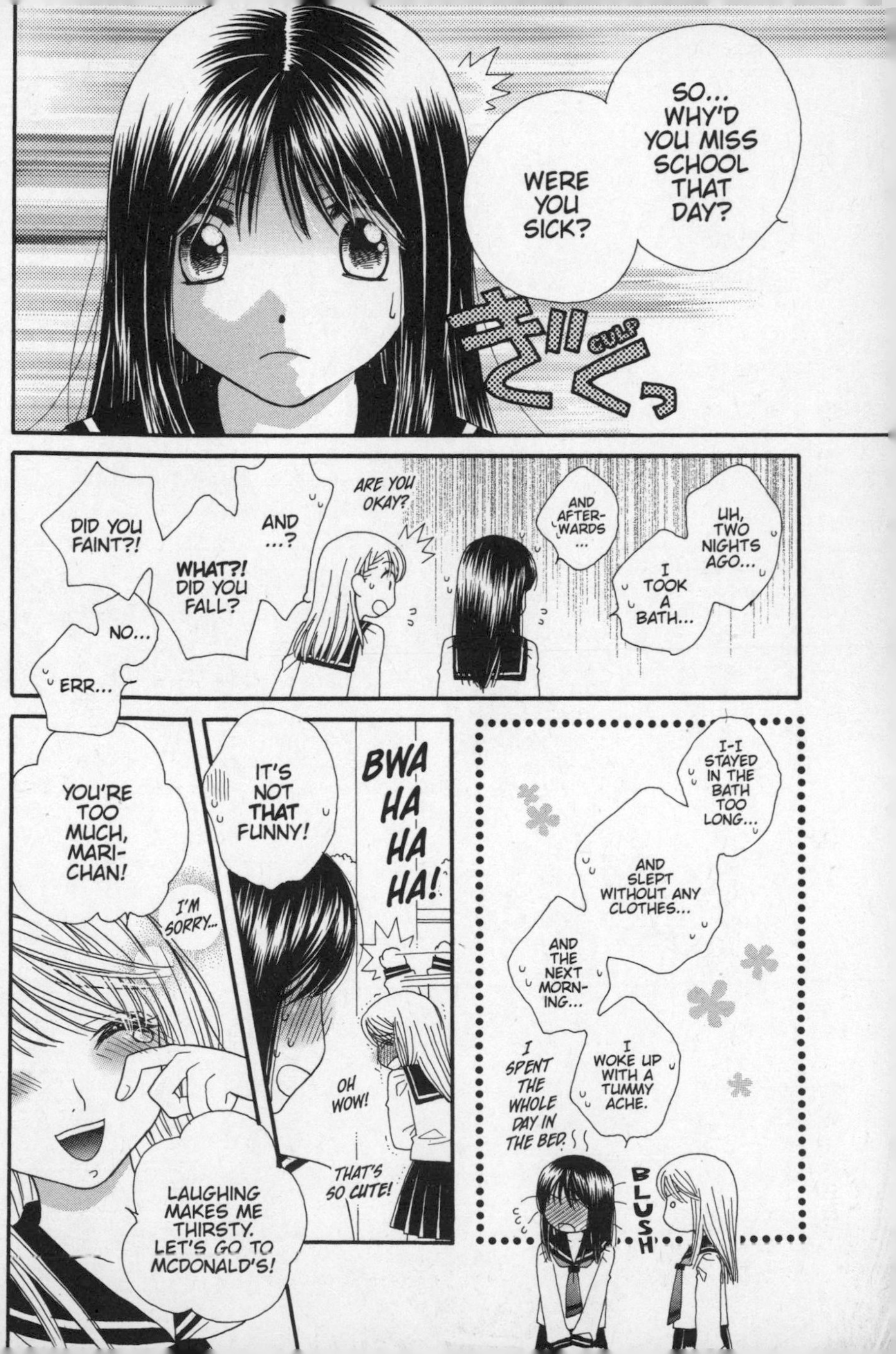
SO... WHY'D YOU MISS SCHOOL THAT DAY?
WERE YOU SICK?
ぎくっ
GULP
UH, TWO NIGHTS AGO...
I TOOK A BATH...
AND AFTER-WARDS...
ARE YOU OKAY?
AND ...?
WHAT?! DID YOU FALL?
DID YOU FAINT?!
NO...
ERR...
I-I STAYED IN THE BATH TOO LONG...
AND SLEPT WITHOUT ANY CLOTHES...
AND THE NEXT MORNING...
I WOKE UP WITH A TUMMY ACHE.
I SPENT THE WHOLE DAY IN THE BED.
BLUSH
BWA HA HA HA!
IT'S NOT THAT FUNNY!
OH WOW!
THAT'S SO CUTE!
YOU'RE TOO MUCH, MARI-CHAN!
I'M SORRY...
LAUGHING MAKES ME THIRSTY. LET'S GO TO MCDONALD'S!

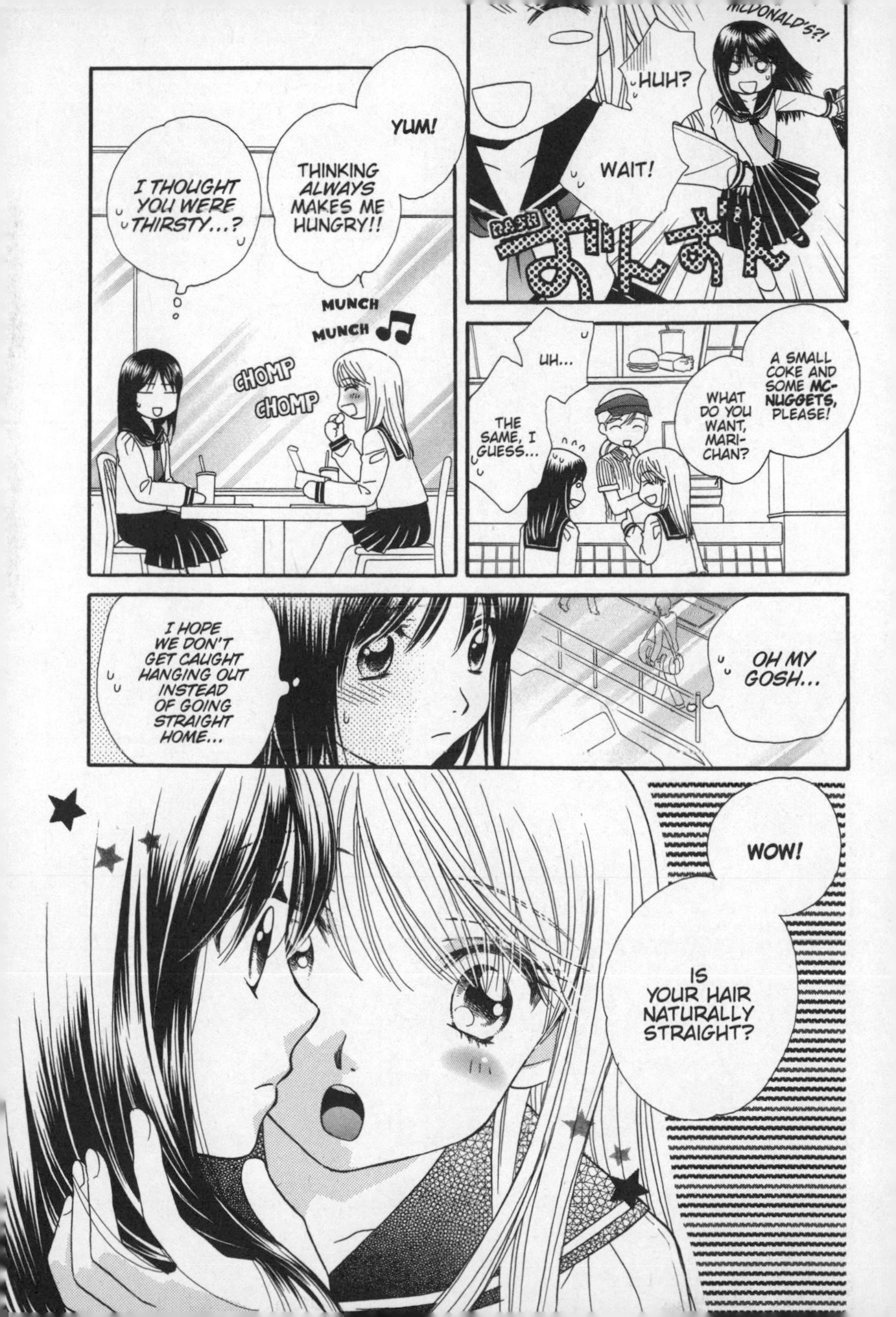
MCDONALD'S?!
HUH?
WAIT!
A SMALL COKE AND SOME MC-NUGGETS, PLEASE!
WHAT DO YOU WANT, MARI-CHAN?
UH...
THE SAME, I GUESS...
YUM!
THINKING ALWAYS MAKES ME HUNGRY!!
I THOUGHT YOU WERE THIRSTY...?
MUNCH MUNCH
CHOMP CHOMP
OH MY GOSH...
I HOPE WE DON'T GET CAUGHT HANGING OUT INSTEAD OF GOING STRAIGHT HOME...
WOW!
IS YOUR HAIR NATURALLY STRAIGHT?

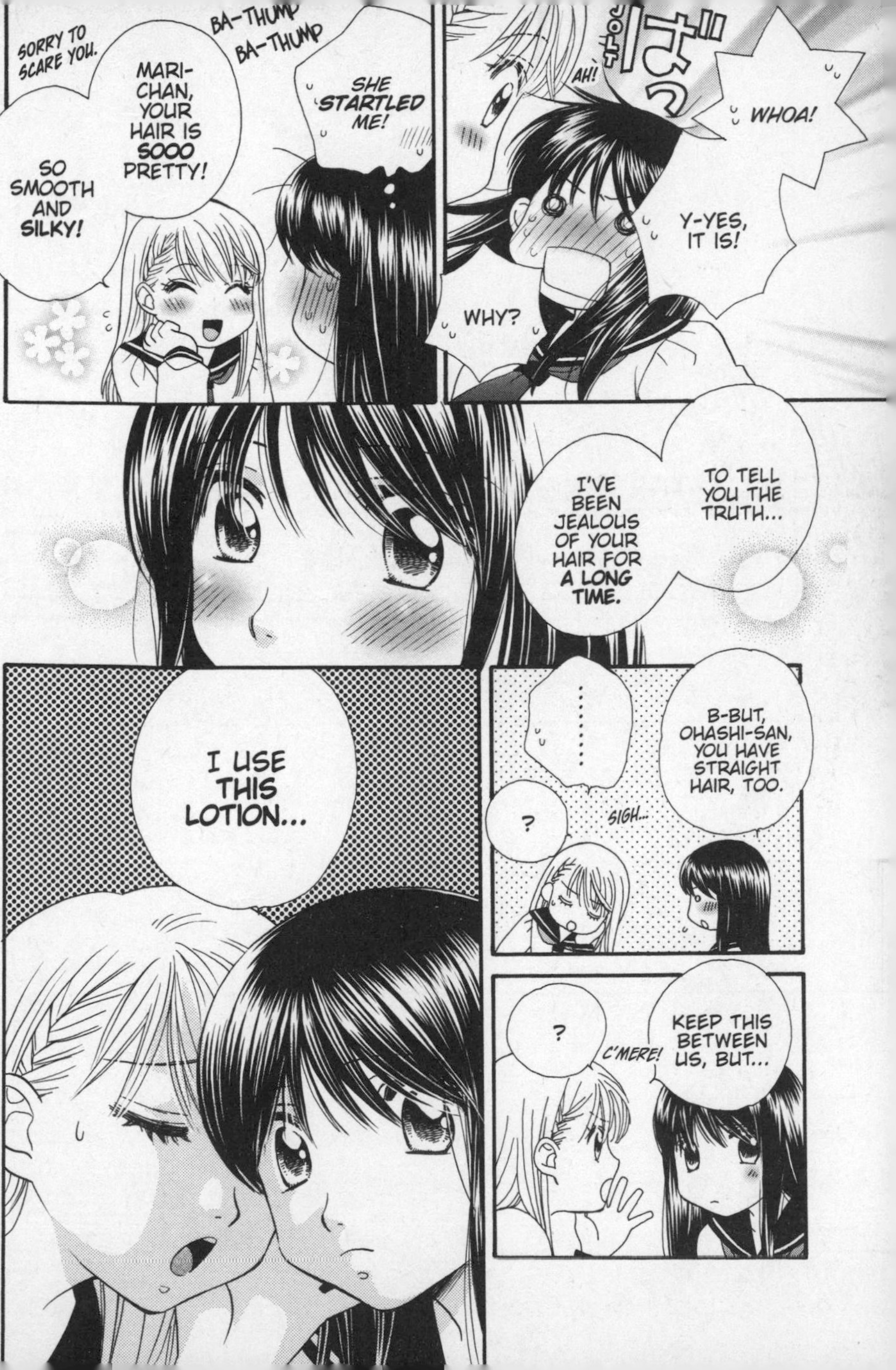
WHOA!
ばっ
AH!
Y-YES, IT IS!
WHY?
SHE STARTLED ME!
BA-THUMP BA-THUMP
MARI-CHAN, YOUR HAIR IS SOOO PRETTY!
SORRY TO SCARE YOU.
SO SMOOTH AND SILKY!
TO TELL YOU THE TRUTH...
I'VE BEEN JEALOUS OF YOUR HAIR FOR A LONG TIME.
B-BUT, OHASHI-SAN, YOU HAVE STRAIGHT HAIR, TOO.
......
SIGH...
?
KEEP THIS BETWEEN US, BUT...
C'MERE!
?
I USE THIS LOTION...

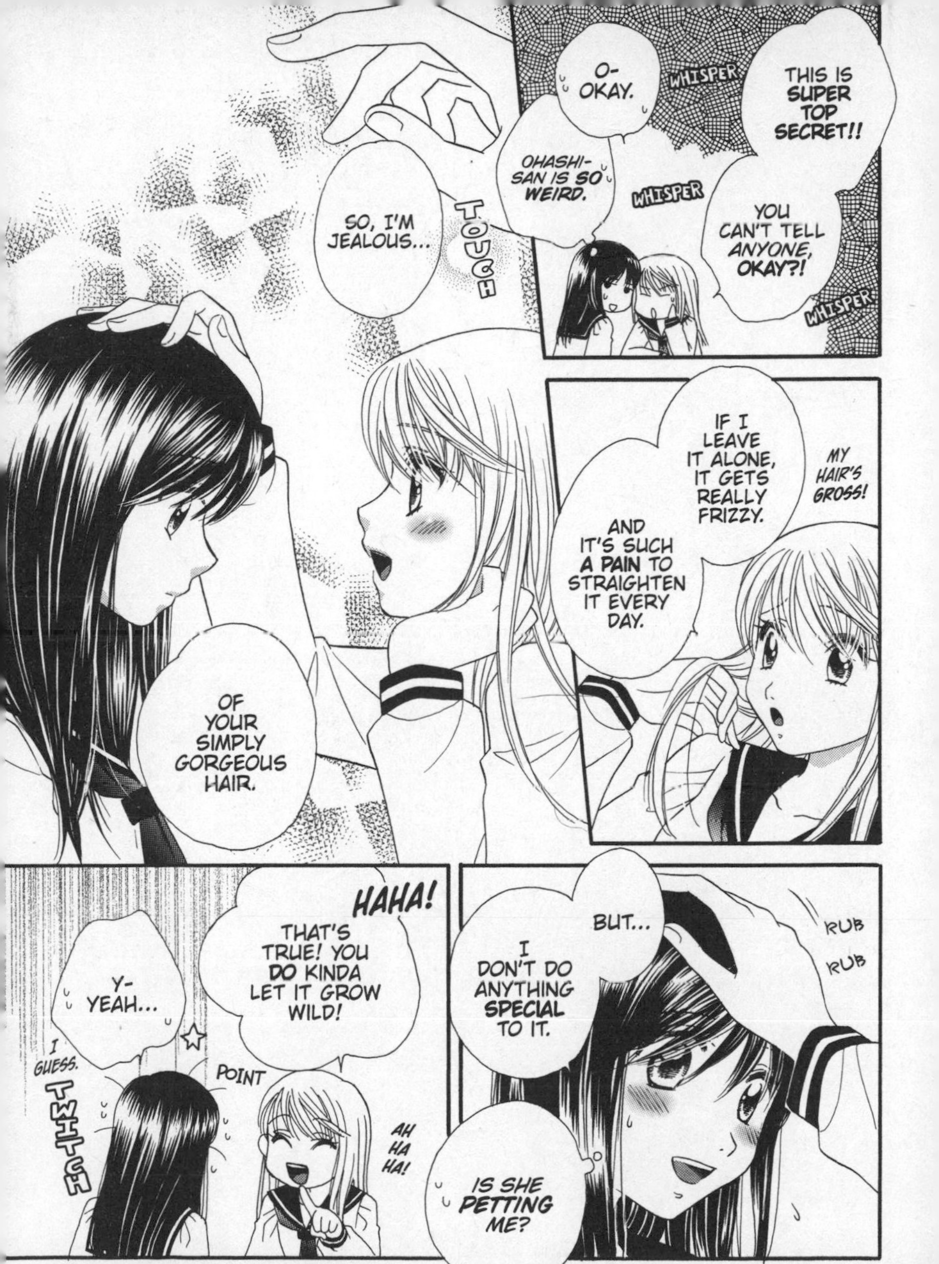
THIS IS SUPER TOP SECRET!!
WHISPER
O-OKAY.
YOU CAN'T TELL ANYONE, OKAY?!
WHISPER
OHASHI-SAN IS SO WEIRD.
WHISPER
MY HAIR'S GROSS!
IF I LEAVE IT ALONE, IT GETS REALLY FRIZZY.
AND IT'S SUCH A PAIN TO STRAIGHTEN IT EVERY DAY.
SO, I'M JEALOUS...
TOUCH
OF YOUR SIMPLY GORGEOUS HAIR.
RUB
RUB
BUT...
I DON'T DO ANYTHING SPECIAL TO IT.
IS SHE PETTING ME?
HAHA!
THAT'S TRUE! YOU DO KINDA LET IT GROW WILD!
Y-YEAH...
I GUESS.
POINT
TWITCH
AH HA HA!

Continued in *Girl Friends: The Complete Collection 1*!

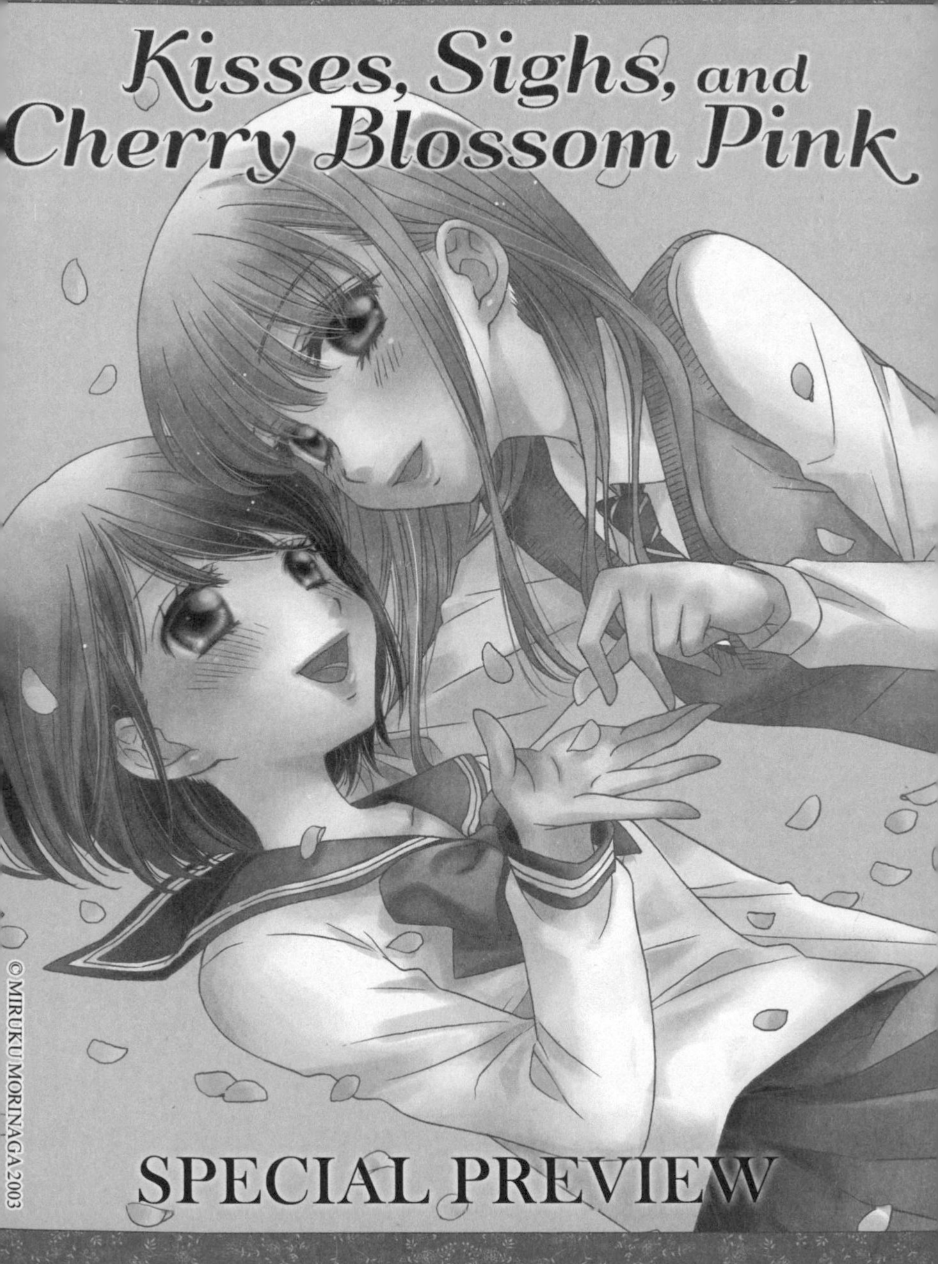
Kisses, Sighs, and Cherry Blossom Pink
SPECIAL PREVIEW
© MIRUKU MORINAGA 2003

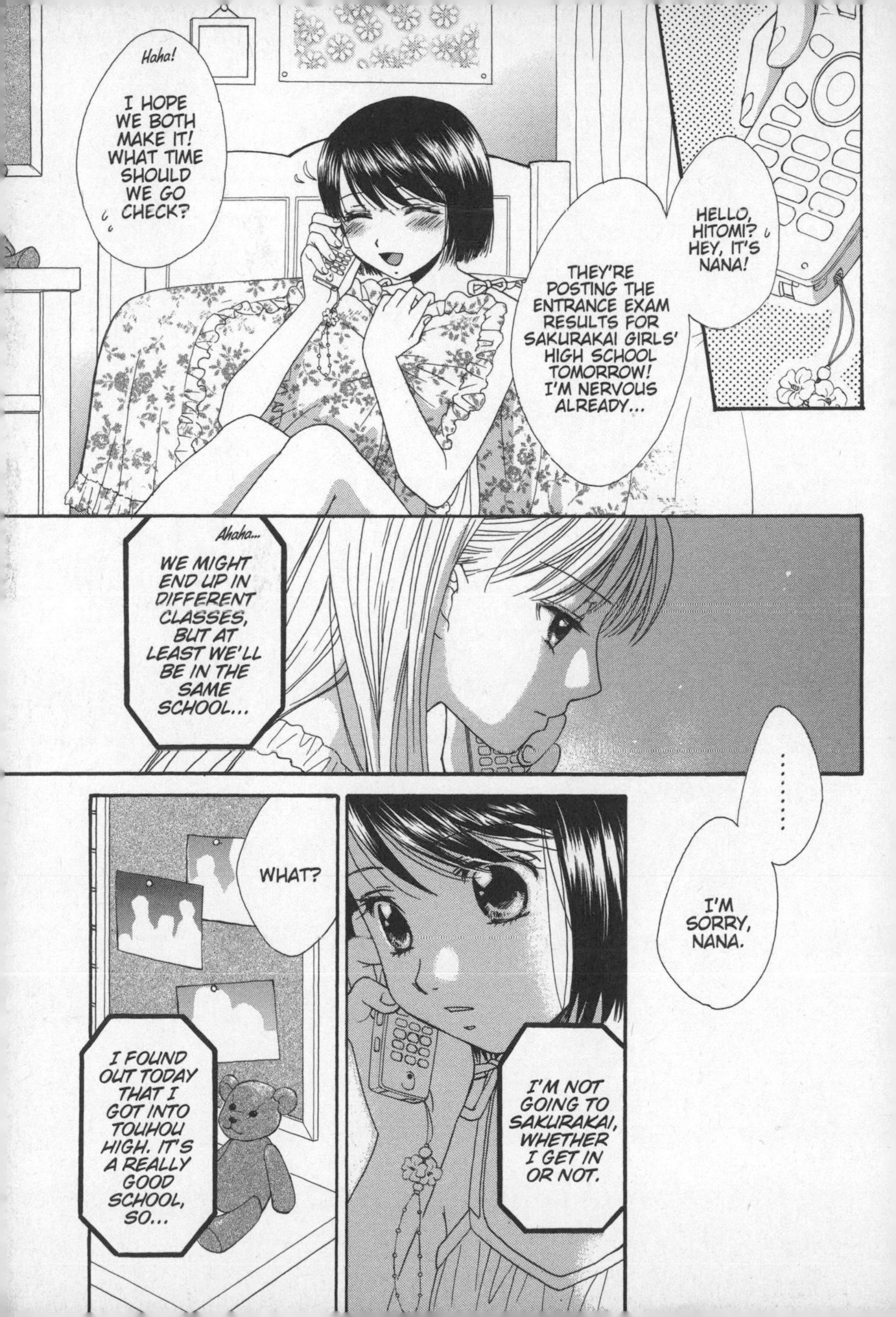
HELLO, HITOMI? HEY, IT'S NANA!
THEY'RE POSTING THE ENTRANCE EXAM RESULTS FOR SAKURAKAI GIRLS' HIGH SCHOOL TOMORROW! I'M NERVOUS ALREADY...
Haha!
I HOPE WE BOTH MAKE IT! WHAT TIME SHOULD WE GO CHECK?
Ahaha...
WE MIGHT END UP IN DIFFERENT CLASSES, BUT AT LEAST WE'LL BE IN THE SAME SCHOOL...
......
I'M SORRY, NANA.
WHAT?
I'M NOT GOING TO SAKURAKAI, WHETHER I GET IN OR NOT.
I FOUND OUT TODAY THAT I GOT INTO TOUHOU HIGH. IT'S A REALLY GOOD SCHOOL, SO...

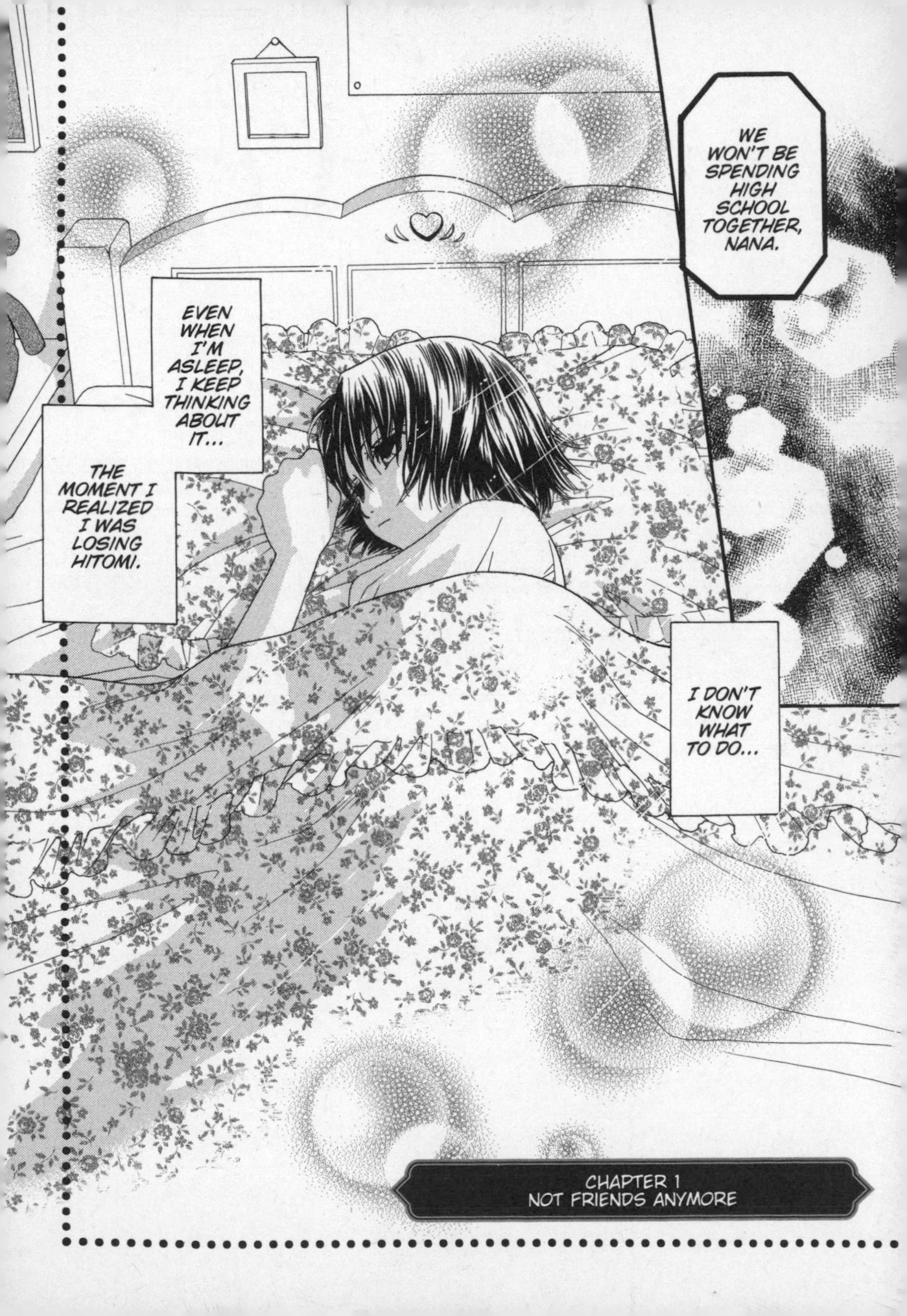

WE WON'T BE SPENDING HIGH SCHOOL TOGETHER, NANA.
EVEN WHEN I'M ASLEEP, I KEEP THINKING ABOUT IT...
THE MOMENT I REALIZED I WAS LOSING HITOMI.
I DON'T KNOW WHAT TO DO...
CHAPTER 1
NOT FRIENDS ANYMORE

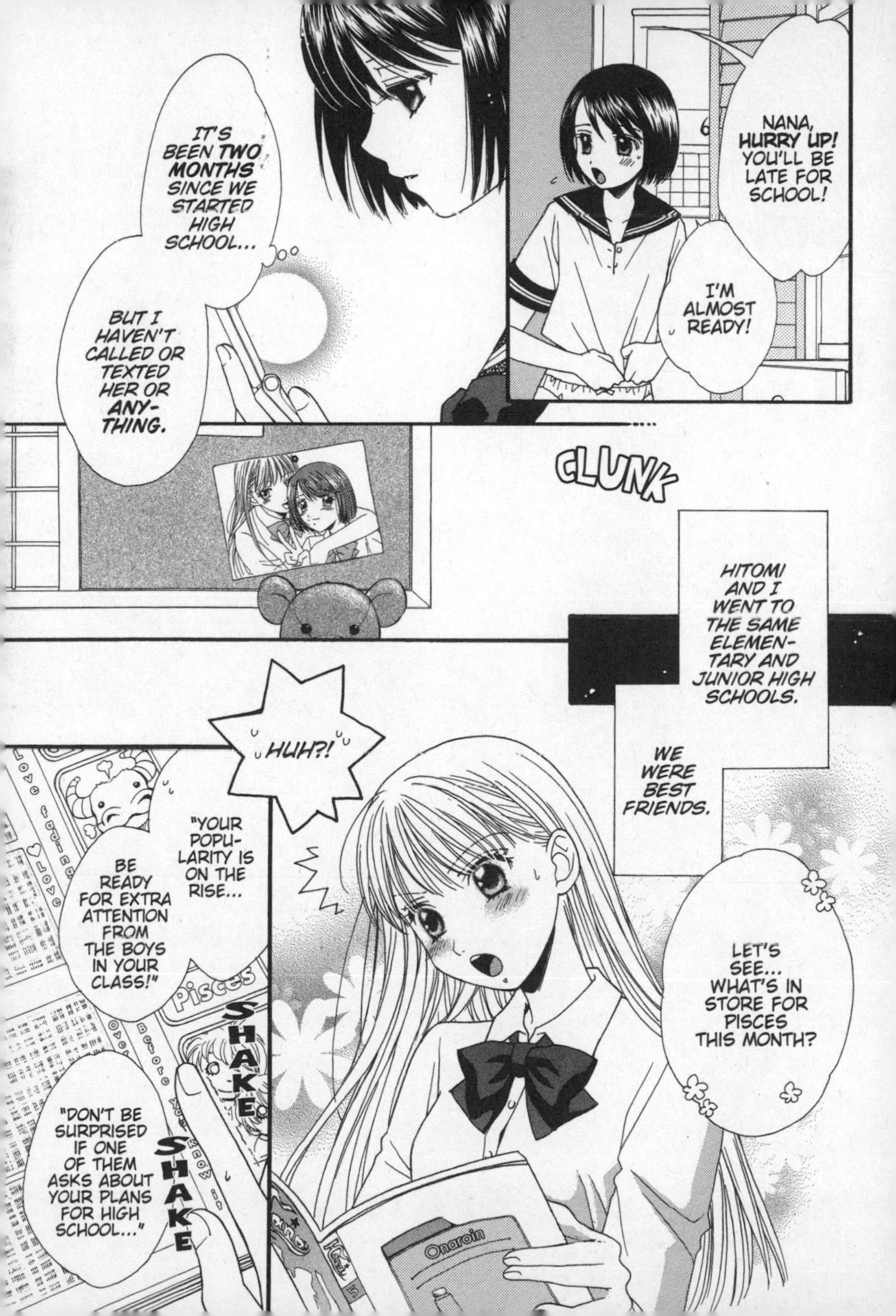
NANA, HURRY UP! YOU'LL BE LATE FOR SCHOOL!
I'M ALMOST READY!
IT'S BEEN TWO MONTHS SINCE WE STARTED HIGH SCHOOL...
BUT I HAVEN'T CALLED OR TEXTED HER OR ANY-THING.
CLUNK
HITOMI AND I WENT TO THE SAME ELEMENTARY AND JUNIOR HIGH SCHOOLS.
WE WERE BEST FRIENDS.
LET'S SEE... WHAT'S IN STORE FOR PISCES THIS MONTH?
HUH?!
"YOUR POPULARITY IS ON THE RISE...
BE READY FOR EXTRA ATTENTION FROM THE BOYS IN YOUR CLASS!"
Pisces
SHAKE
SHAKE
"DON'T BE SURPRISED IF ONE OF THEM ASKS ABOUT YOUR PLANS FOR HIGH SCHOOL..."
Onaroin

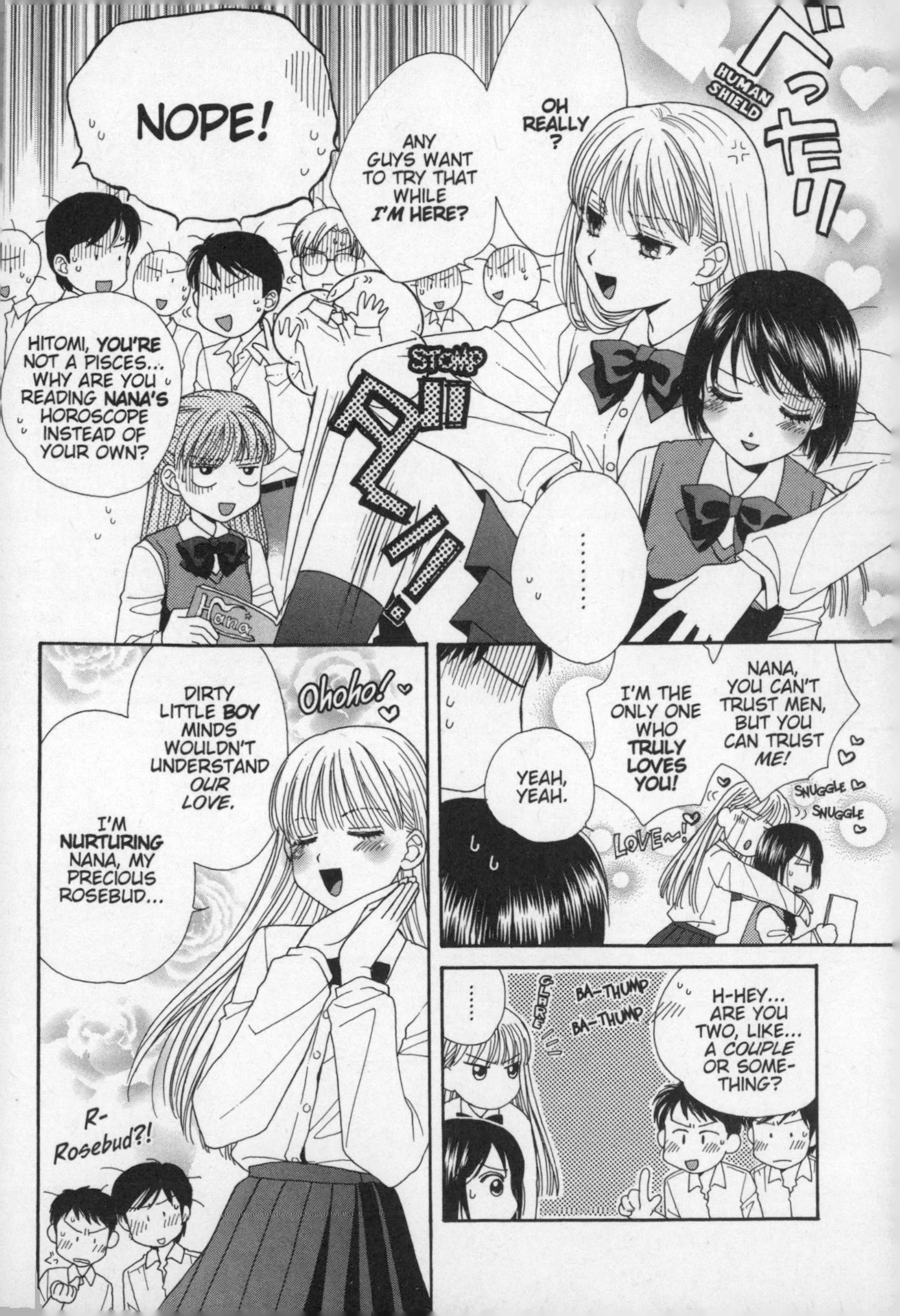
HUMAN SHIELD
OH REALLY?
ANY GUYS WANT TO TRY THAT WHILE I'M HERE?
NOPE!
STOMP
......
HITOMI, YOU'RE NOT A PISCES... WHY ARE YOU READING NANA'S HOROSCOPE INSTEAD OF YOUR OWN?
Hana
NANA, YOU CAN'T TRUST MEN, BUT YOU CAN TRUST ME!
I'M THE ONLY ONE WHO TRULY LOVES YOU!
SNUGGLE SNUGGLE
LOVE~!
YEAH, YEAH.
H-HEY... ARE YOU TWO, LIKE... A COUPLE OR SOMETHING?
BA-THUMP BA-THUMP
GLARE
......
Ohoho!
DIRTY LITTLE BOY MINDS WOULDN'T UNDERSTAND OUR LOVE.
I'M NURTURING NANA, MY PRECIOUS ROSEBUD...
R-Rosebud?!

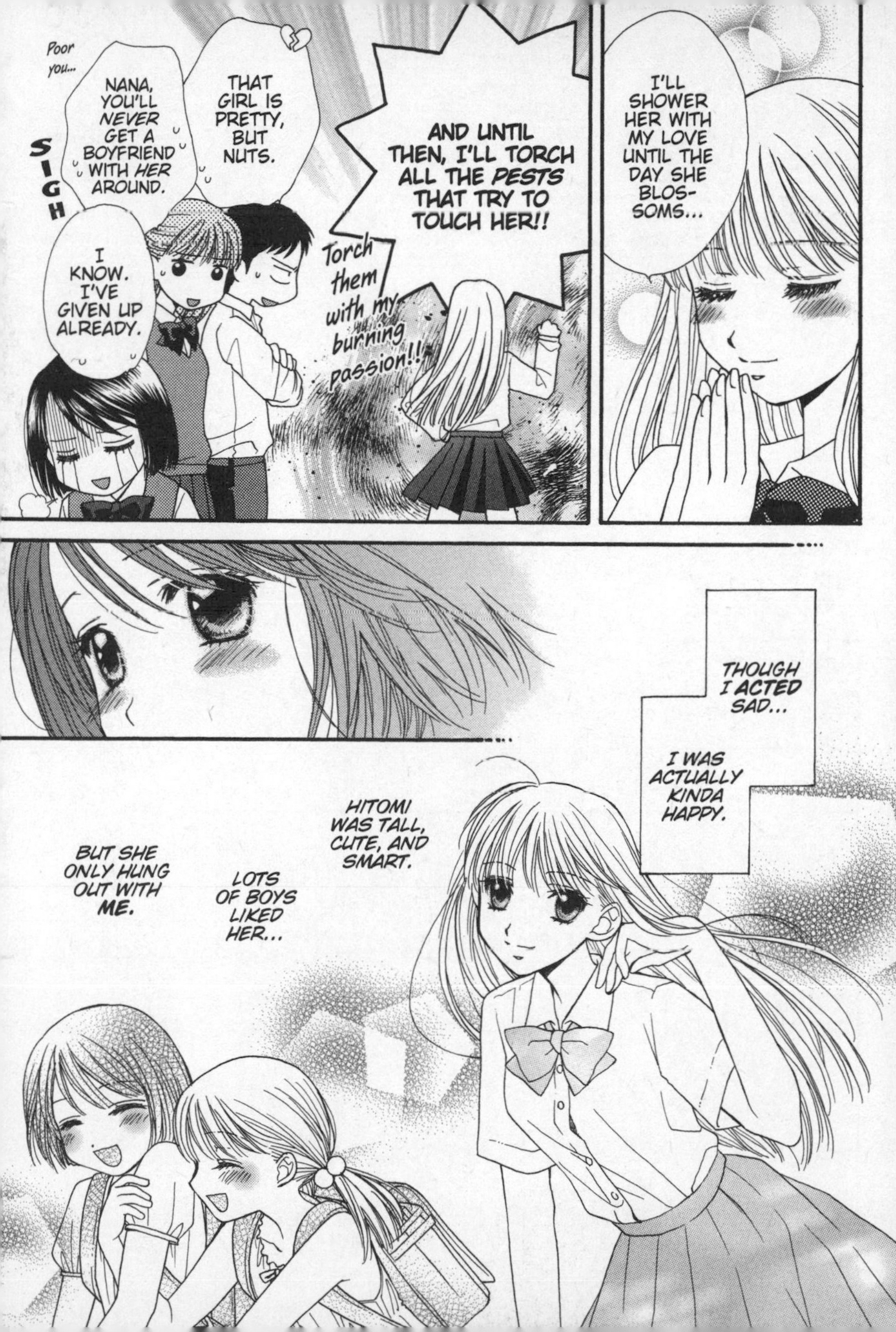
I'LL SHOWER HER WITH MY LOVE UNTIL THE DAY SHE BLOSSOMS...
AND UNTIL THEN, I'LL TORCH ALL THE *PESTS* THAT TRY TO TOUCH HER!!
Torch them with my burning passion!!
THAT GIRL IS PRETTY, BUT NUTS.
NANA, YOU'LL *NEVER* GET A BOYFRIEND WITH *HER* AROUND.
Poor you...
SIGH
I KNOW. I'VE GIVEN UP ALREADY.
THOUGH I ACTED SAD...
I WAS ACTUALLY KINDA HAPPY.
HITOMI WAS TALL, CUTE, AND SMART.
LOTS OF BOYS LIKED HER...
BUT SHE ONLY HUNG OUT WITH **ME.**

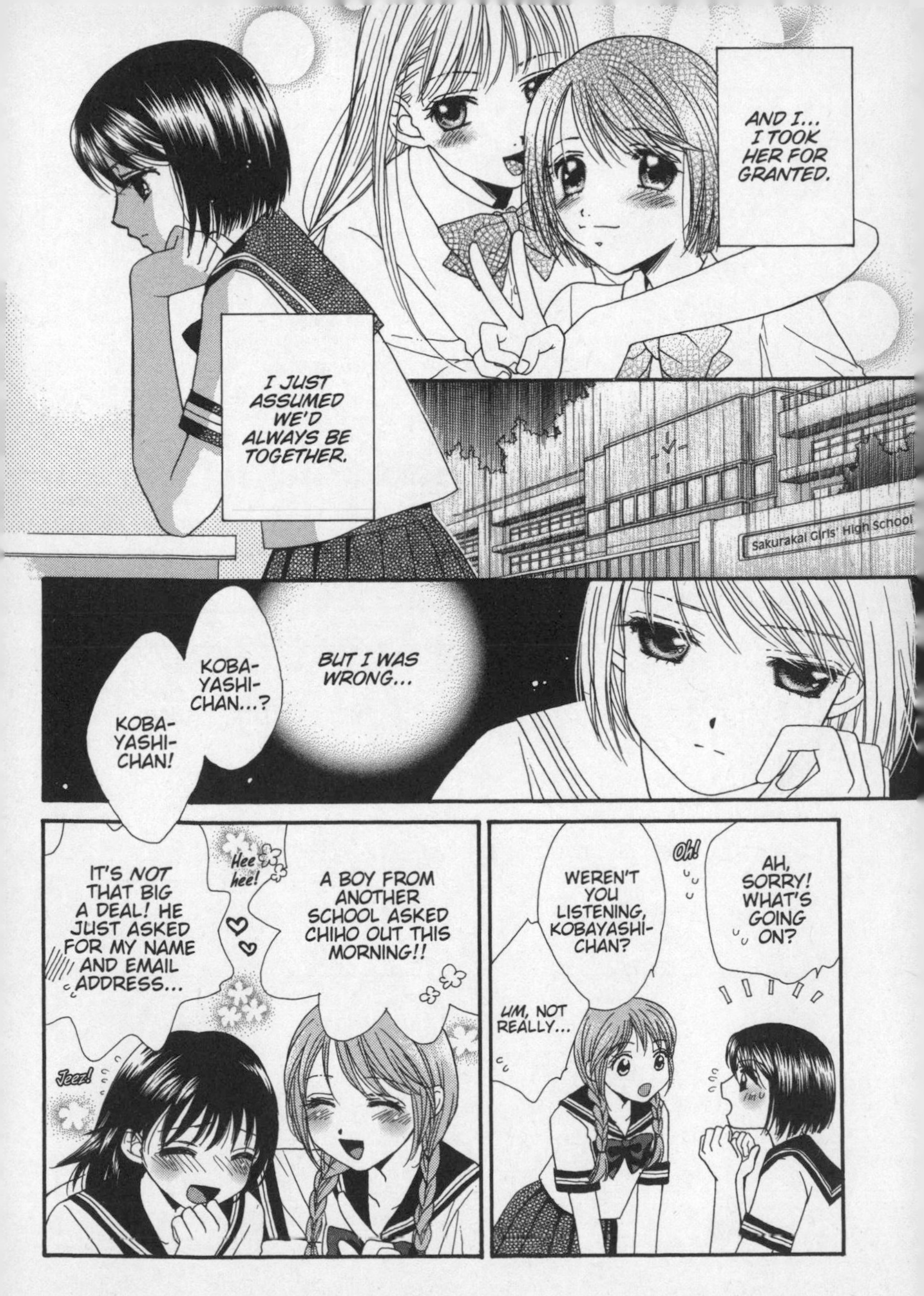
AND I... I TOOK HER FOR GRANTED.
I JUST ASSUMED WE'D ALWAYS BE TOGETHER.
Sakurakai Girls' High School
BUT I WAS WRONG...
KOBA-YASHI-CHAN...?
KOBA-YASHI-CHAN!
Oh!
AH, SORRY! WHAT'S GOING ON?
WEREN'T YOU LISTENING, KOBAYASHI-CHAN?
UM, NOT REALLY...
A BOY FROM ANOTHER SCHOOL ASKED CHIHO OUT THIS MORNING!!
Hee hee!
IT'S *NOT* THAT BIG A DEAL! HE JUST ASKED FOR MY NAME AND EMAIL ADDRESS...
Jeez!

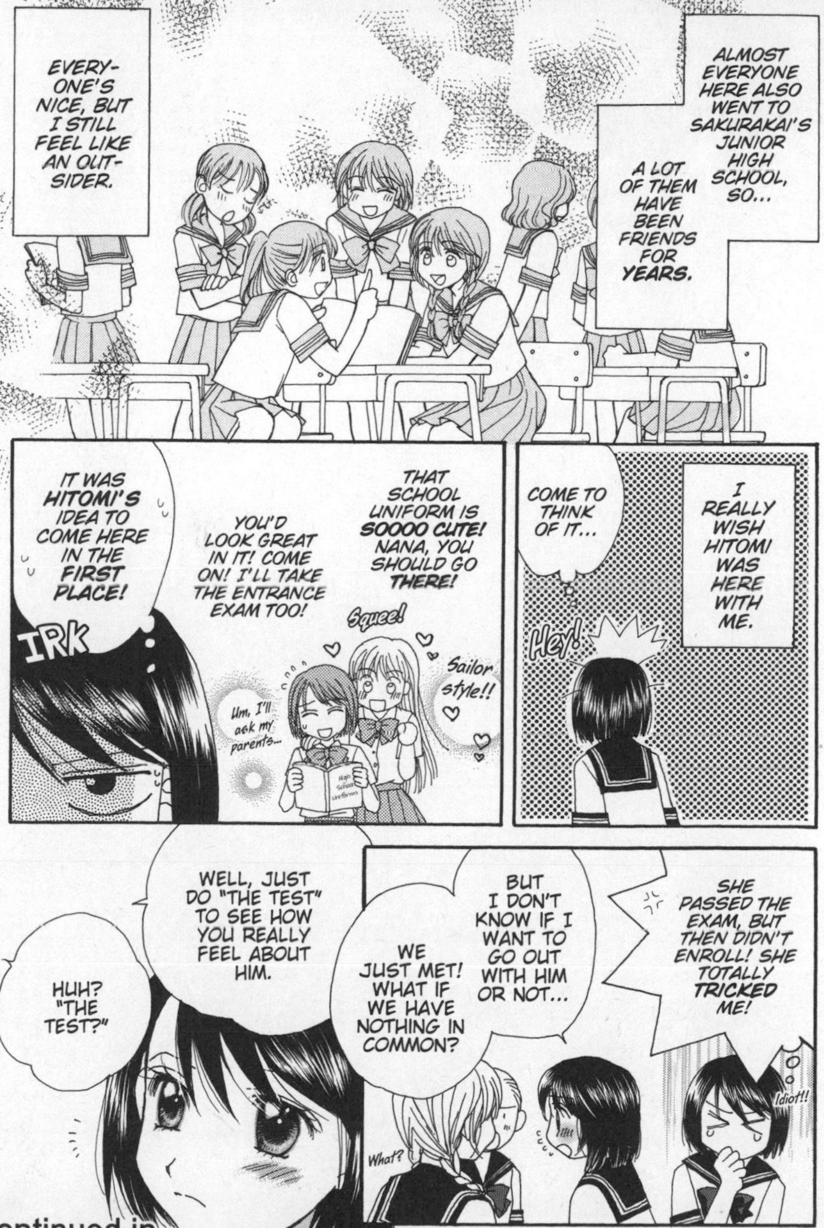
ALMOST EVERYONE HERE ALSO WENT TO SAKURAKAI'S JUNIOR HIGH SCHOOL, SO...
A LOT OF THEM HAVE BEEN FRIENDS FOR YEARS.
EVERYONE'S NICE, BUT I STILL FEEL LIKE AN OUTSIDER.
COME TO THINK OF IT...
I REALLY WISH HITOMI WAS HERE WITH ME.
Hey!
THAT SCHOOL UNIFORM IS SOOOO CUTE! NANA, YOU SHOULD GO THERE!
YOU'D LOOK GREAT IN IT! COME ON! I'LL TAKE THE ENTRANCE EXAM TOO!
Squee!
Sailor style!!
Um, I'll ask my parents...
High School Uniform
IT WAS HITOMI'S IDEA TO COME HERE IN THE FIRST PLACE!
IRK
SHE PASSED THE EXAM, BUT THEN DIDN'T ENROLL! SHE TOTALLY TRICKED ME!
Idiot!!
BUT I DON'T KNOW IF I WANT TO GO OUT WITH HIM OR NOT...
WE JUST MET! WHAT IF WE HAVE NOTHING IN COMMON?
What?
WELL, JUST DO "THE TEST" TO SEE HOW YOU REALLY FEEL ABOUT HIM.
HUH? "THE TEST?"

Continued in...
Kisses, Sighs, and Cherry Blossom Pink!